"This book addresses many unanswered questions concerning the nature of NER inside firms and both how these systems work 'on paper' and how they evolve and influence companies and employees over time. The quality of the authorship assembled here is second to none. This is a volume that will be used by students and talked about by employment researchers for many years to come."

—*Rafael Gomez, Associate Professor in Employment Relations and Human Resources, University of Toronto, Canada*

Voice and Involvement at Work

In the last decade, non-union employee representation (NER) has become a much-discussed topic in the fields of human resource management, employment relations, and employment/labour law. This book examines the purpose, structure, and performance of various types of employee representation bodies created by companies in non-union settings to promote collective forums for voice and involvement at the workplace.

This unique volume presents the first longitudinal evidence on the performance, success, and failure of NER plans over an extended time period. Consisting of twelve detailed, in-depth case studies of actual NER plans in operation across four countries, this volume provides unparalleled evidence on such matters as the motives behind the initial establishment of NER, different organizational forms of NER in industry, key success and failure factors over the long term, pro and con evaluations for employers and employees, and more. *Voice and Involvement at Work* captures an unequalled international and comparative perspective through a wide cross-section of different NER forms.

Paul J. Gollan is a Professor of Management and Associate Dean (Research) in the Faculty of Business and Economics at Macquarie University, Australia. Paul has authored, coauthored and co-edited 14 books in the fields of human resources and industrial relations. He has also written over 34 book chapters and 52 refereed journal articles.

Bruce E. Kaufman is a professor of economics at Georgia State University, Atlanta, United States, and a research fellow with the Department of Employment Relations and Human Resources and Centre for Work, Organisation and Wellbeing at Griffith University, Brisbane, Australia. He is a labour economist with broad research interests spanning economics, management, law, history, and industrial relations. He has written or edited 16 books and has published more than 100 articles and chapters.

Daphne Taras is Dean of the Edwards School of Business at the University of Saskatchewan, Canada, and she is a professor in labour and employment relations. Her academic work is at the intersection of labour relations, public policy, and law. She was named in the top 100 Women of Distinction in Canada in 2012.

Adrian Wilkinson is Professor and Director of the Centre for Work, Organisation and Wellbeing at Griffith University, Australia. He holds Visiting Professorships at Loughborough University, Sheffield University and the University of Durham, and is an Academic Fellow at the Centre for International Human Resource Management at the Judge Institute, University of Cambridge. Adrian has written/edited twenty books and more than 100 articles in academic journals.

Routledge Research in Employment Relations

For a full list of titles in this series, please visit www.routledge.com

Series editors: Rick Delbridge and Edmund Heery

Cardiff Business School, UK

Aspects of the employment relationship are central to numerous courses at both undergraduate and postgraduate level.

Drawing from insights from industrial relations, human resource management, and industrial sociology, this series provides an alternative source of research-based materials and texts, reviewing key developments in employment research.

Books published in this series are works of high academic merit, drawn from a wide range of academic studies in the social sciences.

Voice and Involvement at Work

Experience with Non-Union Representation

Edited by Paul J. Gollan, Bruce E. Kaufman, Daphne Taras, and Adrian Wilkinson

Routledge
Taylor & Francis Group

NEW YORK AND LONDON

First published 2015
by Routledge
711 Third Avenue, New York, NY 10017

and by Routledge
2 Park Square, Milton Park, Abingdon, Oxon OX14 4RN

First issued in paperback 2018

Routledge is an imprint of the Taylor & Francis Group,
an informa business

Library of Congress Cataloging-in-Publication Data
Voice and involvement at work : experience with non-union representation /
   edited by Paul J. Gollan, Bruce E. Kaufman, Daphne Taras, and Adrian
   Wilkinson.
      pages cm. — (Routledge research in employment relations ; 33)
   Includes bibliographical references and index.
   1. Industrial relations.   2. Works councils.   3. Labor-management
committees.   4. Management—Employee participation.   I. Gollan, Paul.
   HD6971.V63 2014
   331—dc23
   2014005982

ISBN 13: 978-1-13-834094-7 (pbk)
ISBN 13: 978-0-415-53721-6 (hbk)

Typeset in Sabon
by Apex CoVantage, LLC

Contents

    Representation   166
    PAUL J. GOLLAN AND SENIA KALFA

PART III
Canada

8   A Century of Employee Representation at Imperial Oil   197
    DAPHNE G. TARAS

9   Non-Union Employee Representation in the Royal Canadian
    Mounted Police: Resistance and Revitalization   227
    SARA SLINN

10 From Non-Union Consultation to Bargaining in the
    Canadian Federal Public Service: Expanding the Bounds
    of Employee Representation through the NJC   264
    RICHARD P. CHAYKOWSKI

PART IV
United States

11 Employee Involvement and Voice at Delta Air Lines:
    The Leading Edge of American Practice   295
    BRUCE E. KAUFMAN

12 The Intersection of NER and ADR: A Conceptual Analysis
    and Federal Express Case   341
    DAVID LEWIN

13 What Do NLRB Cases Reveal about Non-Union Employee
    Representation Groups? A Typology from Post–*Electromation*
    Cases   366
    MICHAEL H. LEROY

    Contributors   395
    Index   397

Tables

Figures

1 Voice and Involvement at Work
Introduction

*Paul J. Gollan, Bruce E. Kaufman,
Daphne Taras, and Adrian Wilkinson*

Competitive pressure on companies to boost productivity and performance
has intensified in the last two or three decades due to a confluence of events,
such as global integration of markets, a more finance-driven business environment, and industry deregulation and privatization. The ripple effects
spread across all functional areas of business, affect all stakeholders, and
can have positive or negative social consequences. Certainly employees and
the human resource function are a case in point. Companies may react to
greater competitive pressure by taking the low road through labour commodification, cost cutting, and worker disempowerment or the high road
through investment in human capital, high-involvement work practices, and
mutual-gain compensation.

This volume focuses on one particular component of human resource
management and industrial relations practices—voice and involvement
forums, committees and councils that represent employees in joint dealings
with management outside of a union context. As a shorthand, we refer to
these groups as non-union employee representation (NER). NER is a vivid
case study of the two alternative paths companies can take in reaction to
greater market competition. Proponents of NER, for example, advocate it
as an important component of the high-road approach that builds more
profitable organizations on employee empowerment and mutual gain. Critics, on the other hand, maintain that NER at best is ineffective in raising
organizational performance and at worst is a component of the low-road
approach, which increases profit by extending management control over
labour and ridding the workplace of unions.

The idea and practice of giving employees opportunity for voice and
involvement at the workplace has a long history, as does debate over its
most appropriate form. Traditionally, the major institution for employee
voice and involvement has been the independent labour union, often promoted as a way to achieve industrial democracy (Webb and Webb 1897) and
constitutional government in industry (Commons 1905). However, the proportion of the workforce covered by unions has greatly diminished in most
countries over the last three decades, opening or worsening what Freeman

and Rogers (1999) call an employee participation–representation gap. For this reason, and also from concern about boosting workplace productivity and national economic performance, interest in business, academic, and policy-making circles in non-union voice options has expanded greatly over the last two decades.

Government labour departments have for many years measured union coverage, and the data provide a reasonably reliable picture of the extent of decline in union density and its variation across firms and industries. No similar data exist on NER density, however, so our knowledge of the extent of non-union voice options—including not only indirect forms of representational voice but also direct face-to-face types of voice—and their variation among firms and industries is much less certain (for suggestive evidence, see Lipset and Meltz 2000; Freeman, Boxall, and Haynes 2007; Willman, Gomez, and Bryson 2009; Godard and Frege 2013; and Dobbins and Dundon 2014). We do know, however, that relative to independent unions, NER gives considerably more emphasis to a collaborative and integrative "grow the pie" philosophy and set of Human Resources Management (HRM) practices rather than an adversarial and distributive "split the pie" approach (Kaufman and Taras 2000; Gollan 2007; Wilkinson, Donaghey, Dundon, and Freeman 2014). Hence, key terms used in the context of NER are not *bargaining, contracts, shop stewards,* and *strikes* but, instead, *involvement, voice, participation, communication, team members,* and *mutual gain*. Whether these terms describe a functioning reality or a rhetorical facade remains a much-contested issue, as does the issue of whether the *union-avoidance* term should also be included in this list.

The available evidence from various countries (reviewed in what follows) does suggest that NER has expanded, albeit unevenly due to differences in national legal regimes, business practices, and cultural attitudes. Also, survey evidence and case studies indicate that NER comes in a wide diversity of forms with different agendas, functions, and influence resources (Dundon and Gollan 2007; Taras and Kaufman 2006; Kaufman and Taras 2010). Academic research finds that NER does have two faces, one positive and one potentially negative. In some companies, with the right kind of NER and in favourable business circumstances, it has a positive effect on both organizational performance and employee welfare; other studies, however, find that NER is largely a marginal and mostly ineffective practice and, sometimes, is employed mainly to keep workers from organizing independent unions (Dobbins and Dundon 2014; Pyman 2014).

This volume sheds additional light on these matters through in-depth case studies of non-union representation councils and committees in twelve organizations across four countries. Statistical studies using national survey data are very useful for identifying general NER patterns and effects (e.g., Bryson, Charlwood, and Forth 2006). They are, however, relatively blunt instruments for investigating the *process* of NER, the *strategies* and *motives* of the parties, organizational factors that lead to NER *success or failure*, *qualitative and subjective* considerations and outcomes, and *actionable implications* for business and government decision makers. Believing these considerations are under-explored and also crucial to informed evaluation and successful practice of NER, we have opted for the case-study method. Of course, these case studies also reflect many features and influences to some degree unique to each organization, so generalizations have to be duly tempered.

We have selected case studies and authors with several innovative criteria in mind. First, we have sought to introduce a *comparative cross-national element* by selecting examples of NER from four Anglo-American countries. The countries are Australia, Canada, Great Britain, and the United States. These countries exhibit interesting variations in legal regimes, union density, collective bargaining arrangements, company HRM practices, and individualist/neoliberal versus collectivist/social democratic cultural-political orientations—all of which may have discernible effects on the form, function, and success of NER. However, we have restricted our set of countries to English heritage nations in order to maintain similarity in basic framework characteristics related to business, political, and social-cultural institutions and practices. One consequence is that we do not include European-style works councils in our ambit (see Gumbrell-McCormick and Hyman 2010; Nieuhauser 2014).

A second innovative feature of the case studies is that they provide a *longitudinal* analysis of NER, sometimes extending over several decades. A criticism of NER is that the programs can have a short half-life, sometimes taking off with much management push and enthusiasm but then, after a few years, fading as the crisis goes away or a new management team takes over. Other NER plans, however, have lived and prospered for several decades and even nearly a century. So our chapter authors, as much as possible, go beyond the point-in-time snapshot in order to discover more about the life-cycle pattern of NER and the factors that lead to longevity versus fade-out.

A third feature of the case studies is that they span both *for-profit and not-for-profit organizations*. Nine of the case studies are private-sector companies, varying in size from a few hundred employees to more than 70,000 and across a range of industries and lines of business (e.g., banking, low-tech and hi-tech manufacturing, airline and rail transportation, and oil production and refining). Three of the case studies are public-sector organizations, including a national police force, a university, and a federal government.

Finally, we have chosen our authors to bring a mix of *human resource management (HRM) and industrial relations (IR) perspectives* to the case-study analyses. This combination gives adequate representation to the diverse purposes and perspectives surrounding NER, including organizations' interests in higher productivity and profit and workers' interests in improved terms and conditions of employment and a meaningful say at

work. We also bring together HRM and IR in this volume in order to promote more cross-field collaboration and melding of viewpoints among our
research colleagues. IR researchers have taken the lead in researching NER
but do so more from a perspective of workforce governance and interest
representation for workers (Ackers 2010). Many HRM researchers instead
look at employee voice structures as a management communication-
involvement tool evaluated primarily by their effect on organizational
performance (Klaas, Olson-Buchanan, and Ward 2012). They also often
gloss over the substantive difference between direct and indirect forms of
participation, including the sometimes complicated legal status of NER
(Morrison 2011). We seek to achieve a better melding of these diverse
perspectives.

NER: AN OVERVIEW OF FORMS AND FUNCTIONS

NER is an umbrella term for an unusually diverse set of forms and practices.
Further, the nomenclature varies from country to country. In Canada, for
example, a large-scale NER group may be called a Joint Industrial Council (JIC) or Employee-Management Advisory Committee (EMAC), while
in the UK and Australia a popular term is Joint Consultative Committee
(JCC). In the United States, labour law heavily restricts enterprise-level NER
forms (discussed in what follows), and so it typically appears in small-scale
form, such as an employee-involvement group, joint safety committee, or
gain-sharing committee.

NER is one form of providing voice to employees, but there are also
many others. Voice is defined in different ways in the academic literature.
Wilkinson, Dundon, Marchington, and Ackers (2004) conclude from field
interviews that managers associate workplace voice with "consultation,"
"communication," and "say." They also find that managers tend to define
workplace voice along two dimensions. The first is voice *form* (direct vs.
indirect) and the second is voice *agenda* (shared vs. contested). In a follow-up
article (Dundon, Wilkinson, Marchington, and Ackers 2004), they suggest
these two dimensions need to be rounded out with a third. This dimension
is voice *influence* and its close synonym, *power*.

Accordingly, the three principal dimensions of workplace voice can be
specified as *form, agenda, and influence*. Each, in turn, varies along a continuum with endpoints defined by polarities. For example, the three voice
dimensions may be represented as (with correlates):

- Direct versus indirect (individual, face-to-face vs. collective, representative)
- Shared versus contested (integrative, win-win vs. distributive, win-lose)
- Communication versus influence (suggestion, complaint vs. cost or
  benefit action)

These dimensions of voice yield a 2 x 2 x 2 matrix and eight permutations, which may be ordered from low to high in terms of organizational impact and employee influence. This idea is given parallel representation in a chapter by Wilkinson, Gollan, Marchington, and Lewin (2010) on conceptualizing employee participation. They show in diagrammatic form an "Escalator of Participation" (p. 11). It is a forward-sloped line with five steps going from low to high participation, based on degree, form, level, and range of subject matter.

Figure 1.1 repackages their diagram into an "Escalator of Voice" or, alternatively, "Menu of Voice Options." The figure shows that voice options in an organization vary along a continuum from low to high, as measured by an index of the three voice dimensions identified (form, agenda, and influence). For simplicity, the continuum of voice forms is presented along a straight line rather than an ascending eight-step function. At the low end are voice options where all three dimensions take a low value in terms of organizational impact. An example is the triplet Direct, Shared, and Communication, such as when an individual employee engages in cooperative discussion with a direct supervisor about a suggestion to improve customer service. At the high end are voice forms where the three dimensions collectively create the largest organizational impact. An example is Indirect, Contested, and Influence, such as a strong trade union that uses collective bargaining and strikes to gain higher wages for workers. Thus, at the left-hand side of the continuum are individual, informal, and communication types of voice, while moving rightward on the continuum leads to voice forms with increasingly collective, formal, and power attributes.

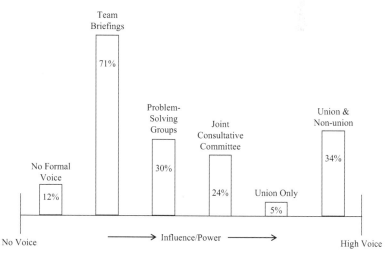

Figure 1.1 Voice Frequency Distribution, United Kingdom
Source: Willman, Gomez, and Bryson (2009): Tables 1 and 3.

Also shown in the diagram is a voice frequency distribution displayed above the continuum. It is a plot of data showing the percentage of British workplaces (twenty-five or more people) in 2004 with various voice forms. British data are used because they come from a nationally representative source (the 2004 Workplace Employment Relations Survey [WERS]), and the country's legal system is one of the least restrictive regarding employer–employee choice among voice options (Freeman, Boxall, and Haynes 2007; Willman, Gomez, and Bryson 2009).

In this survey, only a small minority (12 percent) of workplaces are reported as No Voice—meaning absence of at least one *formal* voice mechanism (informal voice may well still be present). Of the 88 percent that have a voice mechanism, they sort into three broad categories—with a fourth small residual category, "Nature not reported" (2 percent): Nonunion Only (48 percent), Union and Nonunion (34 percent, or dual channel), and Union Only (4 percent). In Figure 1.1, the No Voice option is placed at the left-hand endpoint (least influence), the combined Union/Nonunion Voice option is placed at the right-hand endpoint (having the most forms of voice and thus presumptively most influence), and Nonunion Only and Union Only occupy positions to the left and right of the middle. Rather than show just the Nonunion Only category, it is modestly disaggregated to show three particular types of voice arrangements. They are Team Briefings (71 percent), Problem-Solving Groups (30 percent), and Joint Consultative Committees (24 percent). These three voice forms are selected from a longer list provided by WERS for the Nonunion Only category because they help draw out the visual/descriptive notion of a voice frequency distribution and also illustrate the voice escalator idea in terms of ascending from direct and mostly communication forms to indirect and greater influence forms. Note that the bars in the figure do not sum to 100 percent because the percentages for these three items are non-commensurate (*within* frequency for Nonunion Only).

The key point to grasp from Figure 1.1 is that the central domain of NER is in the relative middle of the overall voice continuum. NER is by definition an indirect form of voice and, thus, typically involves groups of employees organized to represent others. This places NER to the right of the low end of the continuum occupied by organizations having only a direct form of voice. Examples are voice provided solely on an individual face-to-face basis, such the traditional "open door" policy (subsumed in the No Voice category in Figure 1.1). Going one step up the escalator, another form of direct voice is a morning meeting between team members and their supervisor (Team Briefings in the diagram). On the other hand, NER does not extend all the way to the high end of the voice continuum because it ranks lower than trade unions and other forms of independent representation (e.g., professional associations) on the dimension of influence/power. A NER form, for example, is the JCC in Figure 1.1 which is an indirect form of voice—like a trade union—but which does not use formal bargaining or strikes to gain more from the employer. As indicated earlier, sometimes organizations have both union and non-union voice forms (e.g., collective bargaining over wages and hours, joint employee–management consultation over process improvement), and this combination we treat as "most voice" and locate it at the high end of the continuum.

The fact that NER is in the relative middle of the voice continuum provides insight on why it is controversial and relatively fragile. As viewed by employers, NER is a significant delegation of authority, control, and influence to employees, and many shy away from it for this reason. Employees, on the other hand, often see NER as giving them too little authority, control and influence and find it disappointing viz. other more independent voice options. Hence, by being in the middle, NER can seem "too much" for employers but "too little" for employees.

Within the NER section of the voice frequency distribution are many different structures with different forms, agendas, and influence, creating a NER continuum within the larger voice continuum. A deeper look at the NER continuum is provided in Table 1.1. It depicts variation of NER in terms of six dimensions: form, function, topic, representation mode, extent of power, and degree of permanence. The elements in each column are arranged in a roughly ascending order from low to high in terms of organizational breadth, influence, and distributive agenda. Note that the elements going across in a row are not comparable.

In terms of organizational form, NER starts at the individual representative level, such as an ombud, and extends upward in steps, such as work group, plant department, plant-wide, company-wide, and occupation-wide. Regarding function and topic, NER has a multiplicity of objectives, starting with integrative items such as communication, safety, and employee involvement in production quality and extends upward to more distributive items, such as consultation on wages and benefits, grievance adjudication, and union avoidance. Similar variation occurs with respect to the other dimensions, such as whether representatives are elected or appointed, the NER group is consulted or has decision-making rights, and the temporary versus permanent nature of the group.

An insight of Table 1.1 is that NER is quite multi-faceted along numerous dimensions, thus making generalizations more difficult and stereotypes more inaccurate (also Dundon and Gollan 2007). Also, a significant portion of NER is relatively small scale and focused on one or several topics, such as safety committees and peer-review dispute-resolution panels, with evident pros and cons regarding effectiveness, impact, and employee influence. Finally, one also sees a continuum in NER groups with respect to whether they are complements or substitutes for what unions do and, also, a high-road or low-road form of union avoidance—often framed as union substitution (e.g., keeping unions out through superior wages and treatment) versus union suppression (e.g., heavy-handed methods, such as firing union supporters).

Table 1.1 Examples of Diversity of NER Plans

1. Forms
- Ombud
- Joint Safety Committee
- Dispute Resolution Panel
- Scanlon Plan & Gain-Sharing Committee
- Departmental Production & Coordination Committee
- Quality Improvement Committee
- Gender/Ethnic/Sex-Identity Groups
- Employee–Management Advisory Committees

2. Functions
- Communication & Information Flow
- Production and Organizational Coordination
- Employee Morale & Esprit de Corps
- Education and Training of Employees
- Employee Relations and Disposition of Irritants
- Employee Involvement
- Corporate Culture
- Cooperation & Common Purpose
- Management & Employee Development

3. Topics
- Benefits, Including Pensions and Health Insurance
- Safety/Health
- Working Conditions
- Grievances/Dispute Resolution
- Management Problems
- Employee Relations Climate
- Production Issues
- Equipment/Capital Issues
- Customer Service

4. Representation Modes
- Internal to the Firm (e.g., Elected Representative from among Workers in the Group)
- External to the Firm (e.g., Players' Agents in Sports)
- Representatives Appointed by Management
- Representatives Elected by Workers (Secret Ballot)
- Degree of Independence Given to Representatives

5. Extent of Power
- Completely Co-Opted by Management
- Scope of Power (e.g., Single Topic or Broad Authority)
- Informal Consultation
- Advisory Groups
- Decisions Made by Consensus Only
- "Dealing with" Management through Preparation of Formal Positions
- Chairing or Cochairing meetings

6. Degree of Permanence
- Short-Term, Ad Hoc Committee
- Time-Limited, until a Problem is Solved
- Disbandable Structure upon Notice by One or the Other Party
- Permanent Structure

Cross-Divisional Council for Employment Issues	"Trojan Horse" for Union Organizing	Quality of Products and Production	Ability to Seek Professional Expertise Outside Firm	Developing the Agenda
Plant Council	Union Substitution	Business Strategy		Negotiating
Employee Committee on Board of Directors	Union Avoidance	Wages and other Terms and Conditions of Employment		Distribution of Minutes and Positions
Company-Wide Representation Systems (JIC, JCC)	Lobbying Government	Status of the Occupation		Ability to Take Action to Promote Positions
Staff Associations				Vote-Taking in NER; Majority Wins
Professional Advocacy Groups				Worker Veto Power over Change

CONTROVERSY OVER NER: A FOUR FRAMES PERSPECTIVE

Until twenty years ago, researchers in management and labour economics mostly ignored NER, while researchers in industrial relations, labour history, and labour law were either dismissive (NER = shams) or critical (NER = union busting). For example, in their well-known book *What Do Unions Do?*, Freeman and Medoff (1984: 108) refer to NER plans as "window dressing," while a union leader (Basken 2000) derisively refers to NER groups as "donkey councils." As a third example, Gumbrell-McCormick and Hyman (2010) observe that German-style works councils—a definite upward step in employee influence and interest representation relative to Anglo-American forms of NER—were nonetheless until recent years regarded by a number of IR researchers as "marginal phenomena" because they lacked the right to strike and were intended to promote cross-class collaboration.

In the last two decades, however, the climate of opinion toward NER has shifted and broadened, partly because of union decline but also because of the rise of a unitarist-inspired high-performance work model (Dundon and Gollan 2007; Kim, MacDuffie, and Pil 2010; Harley 2014) . Looking back, the ice was broken by two books. The first, *What Workers Want* (1999) by Freeman and Rogers, found from a national survey of American workers that only a minority of employees want union representation and a larger proportion desire a more cooperative and less bargaining-oriented type of representation. They also found evidence of a large participation–representation gap (for Britain, see Towers 1997). These findings, coupled with the marked erosion of union density in most countries, stimulated IR researchers to think about voice alternatives to traditional unions. The second ice breaker was *Nonunion Employee Representation* (2000) by Kaufman and Taras. It dared to touch the "third rail" in North American industrial relations, the company union, and in thirty-one chapters gave a more balanced and open-minded investigation of all forms of non-union employee councils and committees from several different countries. Since then, numerous other books and articles have followed, containing to be sure continued skepticism/criticism but also counterbalanced by greater positive evaluation (e.g., Dundon 2004; Gollan 2007).

Illustrative of the shift in opinion, Freeman has recently much liberalized his position on NER. In the book *What Workers Say: Employee Voice in the Anglo-American Workplace* (2007), Freeman, Boxall, and Haynes end with this statement (p. 220):

> For their part, governments should encourage workers and firms to experiment with alternatives that best fit their circumstances rather than trying to box both sides into a single institutional frame. To enable workers to obtain the voice they want, the state must guarantee the right to union representation, which many workers want, and also give workers and management the right to establish nonunion forms of representative voice, where they seek that mode of voice regime.

The traditional animus toward NER, its continued controversy, and reasons for a broader and more nuanced view in recent years can be better appreciated with the help of the well-known IR *frames of reference* schema. Budd and Bhave (2008) explain that the frames-of-reference concept originates with Alan Fox, an industrial sociologist affiliated with the British Oxford School of industrial relations, in a report prepared for the Donovan Commission (Fox 1966). Fox originally divided industrial relations into two frames, unitarist and pluralist, but later broadened the typology to include a radical frame (Fox 1974). Budd and Bhave add a fourth frame, egoist (explained in what follows). They give a heuristic definition of a frame of reference as "how ones sees the world" and then, more formally, as "a theory used to guide and evaluate behaviors, outcomes, and institutions" (p. 92).

The frames-of-reference idea is used in industrial relations to represent alternative conceptions of the employment relationship. The exact number of frames varies somewhat from author to author, but Budd and Bhave (2008) specify four: egoist, unitarist, pluralist, and critical. They display the four frames in a table and list each frame's key characteristics. We have modestly reworked their table so it gives more highlight to employee voice and the different assumptions and implications each frame has for voice. See Table 1.2. We first describe each of the four frames of reference and then apply them more specifically to NER.

The four-frames-of-reference typology is a useful construct for understanding the long-standing controversy and shifting opinion about NER (also Dundon and Gollan, 2007; Kaufman and Taras 2010). Recall from Figure 1.1 that NER is one particular form of voice, situated in the middle between the informal individual voice option (No Voice in the diagram) and the collective bargaining option on the other end through independent labour unions—with the possibility of a complementary role between unions and NER at the far end of the voice continuum. An insight of the frames-of-reference model is that people's evaluation of NER depends on which frame of reference—that is, positive and normative lens—they adopt to analyse and evaluate NER.

Evidently, the verdict on NER varies along another continuum, starting at one end with the individualist frame and extending to the other end with the critical frame. If the employment relationship fits the individualist frame, the verdict on NER is "unnecessary" and "inefficient" because the combination of external labour markets and the exit option serves as an effective communication and adjustment device and does not require expensive management and organizational resources to implement. If workers feel exploited or unfairly treated, they can "voice with their feet" by leaving one company for another (Boeri and Van Ours 2008; Budd 2004).

If the employment relationship fits the unitarist frame, however, a much different verdict emerges. Viewed through a unitarist lens, NER is an essential component of a cooperative/mutual-gains workplace. The exemplar is

Table 1.2 Employment Relationships in Four Frames of Reference

Frame	Organizational Vision	Behavior Principle	Policy Stance	Voice Form
Individualist	Free Market	Competition	Laissez Faire	Open Door/Exit
Unitarist	Harmonious Team	Cooperation	Business Friendly	Bilateral Communication/ Employee Involvement
Pluralist	Competing Interest Groups	Negotiation and Compromise	Institutional Power Balancing and Democratization	Collective Representation: Councils and Unions
Radical	Capitalist Monopoly	Conflict and Struggle	Replace Capitalism	Workers' Control

today's High Performance Work System (HPWS) model (Appelbaum, Bailey, Berg, and Kallberg 2000; Boxall and Purcell 2011). With well-developed internal labour markets and considerable specific human capital, the exit option no longer works well and firms need an organized in-house method for bilateral communication, coordination, and problem solving. Given the mutual-gain orientation of unitarism, NER is an effective form of voice for workers because it promotes high organizational performance, which is shared with workers in the form of pay for performance, enhanced employment security, and fair treatment (Avgar and Owens 2014). Typically employees in unitarist firms are not represented by unions, but this result is not anti-social because the workers perceive no need for one. Hence, in the unitarist frame, the NER verdict shifts to "effective" and "mutually beneficial."

Next is the pluralist frame (Kochan 1998; Heery, Bacon, Blyton, and Fiorito 2008). External labour markets are imperfect and tip bargaining power in favour of companies, resulting in below-competitive wages and conditions. Workers need a countervailing form of interest representation, therefore, which NER cannot provide but independent trade unions can. Also, employees' impeded exit and employers' property right to run the business as they please means internal labour markets and workforce governance procedures are dominated by employers and often operated in a unilateral and perhaps coercive manner. Here again NER is inadequate; in fact, it is worse than inadequate because companies often use NER to preserve and strengthen their monopoly position by keeping workers from successfully getting outside representation (Hiatt and Gold 2000). Thus, in the pluralist frame, the verdict again shifts, this time to NER as "tool of employer domination" and "union avoidance."

The pluralist verdict is rendered with an even more negative pronouncement in the critical frame. NER is part of a larger strategy used by capitalist firms to exploit the labour force, preserve capitalist hegemony inside the firm, and prevent formation of independent trade unions to lead the class struggle (Hyman 1975; Lucio 2010). Employers in the unitarist or pluralist frames may simply be naively optimistic or short-sightedly opportunistic when they use NER; in the critical frame, NER is a more explicit and long-run element of capitalist domination used to extract surplus value and quell working-class resistance. The critical frame's NER verdict, therefore, is "exploitative" and "suppressive."

This framework yields a number of useful insights with regard to explanation of NER's controversial history and shifts over time in academic and public opinion on NER's workplace efficacy and appropriate legal regulation. NER, for example, originated in Europe and the United States in the late 1800s to early 1900s when the first companies pioneered in-house shop committees and works councils (Kaufman 2000). Here first appeared NER's positive unitarist face, billed as an innovative attempt by progressive employee welfare-oriented companies to solve the labour problem by fostering greater mutual trust, confidence, and cooperation. At the same time, here also first emerged a pluralist and critical assessment of NER for, in the eyes of critics, these early shop committees were irredeemably shot through with paternalism and union avoidance.

In the era of welfare capitalism after World War I, NER prospered—particularly in North America where several hundred companies, including many among the "corporate liberal" wing associated with the Rockefeller family and Special Conference Committee (e.g., the Standard Oil company and corporate spin-offs), introduced formal plans of employee representation (Kaufman 2000; Rees 2010). Evaluations of NER were guardedly positive, except among the trade unions, who hated them. A movement for plant-level joint committees also blossomed in the UK after World War I (known as Whitley committees), but they were expressly envisioned as including trade unions and thus were not NER (Fox 1985; Gospel 1992). Australia, because of its small industrial base at this time and centralized system of arbitration and extensive union density, had little NER presence. A person viewing NER in North America in the 1920s, therefore, would be more inclined to use a unitarist frame—or perhaps "liberal/progressive pluralist" frame—while a person in the UK would tend toward a pluralist or, in the case of leading labour intellectuals such as the Webbs and GDH Cole, a critical frame.

The entire tenor of thought about NER shifted dramatically in the Depression era of the 1930s and war years of the early to mid-1940s. The Great Depression greatly discredited the corporate liberal employers, and to save themselves from bankruptcy, these companies abandoned mutual gain and joint consultation and instituted several waves of deep wage cuts, massive layoffs, and work speed-ups (Kaufman 2000; Moriguchi 2005). The unitarist model lay in shreds in North America by 1933. Then in the United States, the New Deal arrived and ushered in industry-wide collective bargaining as a way to promote economic recovery (through higher wages and more consumption spending) and social justice (through union-led industrial democracy). Criticism of NER as a worthless sham and union avoidance scheme reached such a pitch in the United States that such organizations were largely banned under the National Labour Relations Act (NLRA, 1935). Although Canada adopted a version of the NLRA in 1944 (PC 1003), it did not ban NER, in part because Prime Minister Mackenzie King had three decades earlier helped Rockefeller design and install employee representation plans at his companies and remained favourable to them (MacDowell 2000; Taras 2000). Nonetheless, like in the United States, union density shot up in Canada into the 1950s, and NER seemed to be caught somewhere between an historical anachronism and marginal player at a few remaining progressive non-union companies. For all the same reasons cited earlier, NER continued to be an at-best shadow presence in Britain and Australia, particularly after World War II when union density was 80 to 100 percent among major companies in a number of manufacturing, transportation, utility, and natural resource industries (Gollan 2000).

The half century after World War II represented something of a consensus on the merits of the pluralist frame, including a skeptical to hostile stance on NER and favourable and encouraging stance on independent unionism (e.g., Bernstein 1970; Brody 1994; Hyman 1997). Union movements were given policy support in all four countries, and union densities rose to high points in the twentieth century. In the United States, NER had largely been ripped out root and branch, in Canada it largely survived in a few mostly ignored niches, and in the other two countries it was largely smothered and made irrelevant by a combination of industry-wide associations of employers and unions and underdeveloped personnel/human resource functions (Gospel 2014; Wright 2014).

Starting in the 1980s and continuing forward to the world financial crisis of 2008 to 2010, the individualist frame in the form of neoliberalism and the Washington Consensus made a comeback, most strongly in the United States but also with substantial effect in Australia, Britain, and Canada. Free-market solutions were emphasized while pluralist institutions, such as trade unions, protective labour laws, and social welfare programs, were singled out for criticism and dismantling. Union density in all four countries retreated and union power and influence diminished, opening up and worsening the participation–representation gap in the labour market (earlier described). Although the individualist frame gives little attention or place *per se* to management-led HRM, proponents of the unitarist frame saw that neoliberalism had created a strategic opening and receptive public opinion for HRM and took advantage of it. Traditional personnel management was repackaged as HRM with much greater emphasis on a strategic form of unitarism anchored on employee commitment and involvement in a high-performance work system (Boxall and Purcell 2011). Thus, the pluralist and critical frames retreated, as did trade unionism, while the individualist and unitarist frames advanced, bringing with them a renewed opportunity for NER to become an important and accepted player in the high-performance workplace.

The financial crisis of 2008 to 2010 considerably tarnished the neoliberal/individualist frame but so far has not seemed to noticeably hurt the unitarist frame or advance the pluralist and critical frames. As we write, therefore, the opportunity space for NER seems to remain open and growing, partly because unions show little sign of rejuvenation and non-union HRM continues to grow. The large overhang of surplus labour in all countries, however, is a threat to the continued expansion and legitimacy of both unitarism and NER because it incents firms to shift toward the low road.

We have given this review partly to put NER in a larger historical context. But another purpose has been to emphasize that controversy over NER arises in part because observers analyze and evaluate it through quite different positive and normative lenses. The verdict on NER comes out quite differently depending on whether it is observed through an individualist, unitarist, pluralist, or critical frame. Over time, the relative popularity of these alternative frames moves up and down, and so does the popularity and evaluation of NER.

INDIVIDUAL COUNTRY CONTEXTS

Because this volume features NER case studies from four countries—Australia, Canada, United Kingdom, and United States—some overview of national contextual factors is also helpful. As indicated earlier, all four countries share a common English language/heritage tradition, yet, to a surprising degree, they differ with respect to the NER experience and treatment. Provided next is a brief summary.

Australia

Viewed historically, the dominating feature of the Australian employment system is the centralized conciliation and arbitration system (i.e., awards system; Isaac and Macintyre 2004). Established at the federal level in 1904 and enacted by individual states at about the same time and in a largely similar form, the system mandated that in order to prevent damaging strikes and lockouts, the parties to an unresolved industrial dispute should submit their case for review and resolution before a federal or state court of conciliation and arbitration. Although not originally intended to be a wage-fixing institution, the court system soon took on this role as it settled bargaining disagreements by issuing what in effect were arbitration awards that set wages, hours, and most of the other terms and conditions of employment. This system fostered a high union density level (above 50 percent in the post–World War II period) because unions represented cases before the court and monitored employer compliance with the awards. Awards were typically extended to cover an entire occupation or industry, including employees not belonging to a union.

The combination of the centralized arbitration system, high union density, industry-wide coverage, and relatively small industrial base in Australia limited the space and scope for management-led HRM programs and innovations, particularly of the NER type, at the enterprise level (Wright 2014). For example, joint committees in other countries were often created in the first third of the twentieth century to help manage various employee welfare programs, such as cafeterias, savings and benefit associations, and recreational programs. Such activities were sparse in Australian industry, however, per one estimate that in the mid-1920s there were only six full-time welfare administrators in the entire country (Kaufman 2007: 24). Later, and particularly in conjunction with World War II, more companies created enterprise-level committees and councils, but they were typically limited to joint productivity or safety committees. As a general statement, neither employers, unions, or government were much interested in workplace committees, whether billed as employee participation or industrial democracy.

Since the mid-1980s, the economic, legal, and business environment in Australia has shifted—perhaps transformed is not an overstatement—in ways that have encouraged development and spread of NER (Gollan 2000). First, several Labour-led federal governments, followed more dramatically by a Conservative-led government, pared back, decentralized, and depowered the arbitration/awards system until today only a shadow remains. A particular emphasis, starting with the Keating government's Industrial Relations Reform Act (1993), was to spur productivity in firms and flexibility in labour markets by reorienting decision making to managers and employees at the enterprise level. Toward this end, the act allowed non-union companies to establish with their workforces a collective "Enterprise Flexibility Agreement." Here was an encouragement to NER because the law required that employers take reasonable steps to consult and inform employees—although it did not specify an institutional form for this process. In 1996, enactment of the Workplace Relations Act provided additional stimulus to joint workplace consultation. It enabled employers to enter into collective or individual contracts with non-union employees, known as Australian Workplace Agreements, but allowed that the employee(s) had the right to be represented by a representative agent in the negotiation process.

In a highly controversial move, the Howard-led Conservative government enacted in 2005 legislation popularly known as Work Choices. This law abolished most of the century-long central wage-fixing system and in a number of ways encouraged individual bargaining and enterprise bargaining and undercut union reach and power. Although again favorable to NER, the effect was indirect because no provision specifically mandated NER or specified a preferred institutional mechanism.

The unpopularity of Work Choices contributed to the defeat of the Howard government and election of a Labour Government under Kevin Rudd and Julia Gillard, respectively (Wailes 2010). New legislation, the Fair Work Act (2009), was enacted that substantially revised Work Choices. The act was a plus and minus for NER. On one hand, the legislation broadened and strengthened union representation and bargaining coverage and rights and, typically, unions see NER as a threat and try to squash it. However, the act also encourages extension of employee representation and consultation through a pluralism of devices, including complementary NER channels in which collective bargaining is in place (a dual-channel system), an articulated vehicle for consultation in negotiation of enterprise agreements, and consultation with employees (with or without a committee structure) in cases of substantial organizational change.

Empirical evidence on the density and performance of NER in Australia is growing but remains limited and somewhat fragmented. Starting from near zero in the early 1980s, forms of representative consultation and participation outside the formal structure of collective bargaining have significantly expanded, although they are still definitely a minority phenomenon. Findings from the Australian Worker and Representation and Participation Survey (2003–04), reported in Teicher, Holland, Pyman, and Cooper (2007), paint this picture of voice, participation, and representation in the Australian workplace (p. 138):

> A majority of respondents report access to one or more forms of nonunion and direct-voice arrangements, with 83 percent of respondents being in a workplace with an open door policy. . . . A smaller yet substantial number of workers report the occurrence of regular staff meetings (60.1 percent), and the presence of a personnel or human resources department or person (48.1 percent). Committees of employees (38.9 percent) and employee involvement programs such as quality circles (35.8 percent) are the least common nonunion voice arrangements. . . . Union presence is positively associated with the presence of several nonunion voice arrangements in Australia. This finding suggests that, contrary to intuition, nonunion arrangements complement rather than compete with union voice. . . . Overall, 50.3 percent report the presence of joint consultative committee in their workplace. . . . A majority of respondents rate their nonunion joint consultative committees as effective (79.9 percent).

Canada

One of the perplexing features of the Canadian industrial relations system is that it simultaneously protects collective action and unionization and is almost entirely permissive about the ability of enterprises to run non-union systems. This openness to various types of collective action on the part of workers is little known and greatly underappreciated.

Throughout the 1910s and by the end of World War I, Canadian public policy became cautiously interested in endorsing developments of "joint industrial councils as a means of furthering greater co-operations between employer and employees." This was the resolution of the 1919 Royal Commission on Industrial Relations. Experiments in cooperation were featured in the government's nascent Department of Labour's publication *Labour Gazette*.

The interest in non-union representation was not by happenstance. Rather, it was due to the influence of William Lyon Mackenzie King, who founded the department and was Labour Minister, a powerful elected politician and then prime minister for decades (Taras, 1997). As author of the Rockefeller Joint Industrial Council Plan, he was more intimately involved in non-union systems than any other policy maker of his time, or indeed, in the whole of the previous century. He strongly believed in encouraging collective bargaining—particularly in the absence of unions. He adroitly sidestepped the issue of whether joint councils should include or bypass unions. Mackenzie King was a keen researcher and urged the systematic collection of data in industrial relations. For example, the 1921 Department of Labour study on "Joint Councils in Industry" provided a detailed portrait of the range of issues, forms, and functions of non-union systems. Non-union plans were widely diffused throughout Canada (MacDowell, 2000; Taras, 2000).

Importantly, as there were bans against the unionization of public-sector employees, non-union plans also were developed for the civil service and the iconic paramilitary Royal Canadian Mounted Police, two chapters in this book. So not only did the non-union systems proliferate in industries that could be targets for unions as avoidance vehicles, but they also grew into robust union substitution systems.

In 1925, a major legal case known as *Snider* resulted in the surprise decentralization of Canadian labour relations and the finding that each province would have exclusive control of labour law within its provincial borders, except for federal enterprises. The Canadian policy scene is tremendously complex as a result of the decentralization, but there is a common model that prevails in the country, with comparatively small differences from one jurisdiction to another.

Instead of following the American National Labor Relations Act (NLRA, or Wagner Act) 1935 ban on company unions, the Canadians did not create a comprehensive Wagner Act equivalent until 1944, when the political and economic environment had changed profoundly. Whereas the American approach had been shaped by the Great Depression, Canadians wrote their labour law while Canada was fighting in Europe and Canadian employers feared Congress of Industrial Organizations (CIO) unionizing at home. Company unions were an attractive alternative to the type of radical industrial organizing favoured by the CIO. The war gave the federal government under Prime Minister Mackenzie King the authority to pass a labour law for the entire country. The Canadian law, PC 1003, contained many features of the Wagner Act, but it also emphasized Mackenzie King's traditional emphasis on conciliation and dispute resolution. PC 1003 was entirely silent on the matter of company unions. Indeed, during World War II, any form of worker–manager participation plan was encouraged as supporting essential war industries and the effort to save the world from fascism. After the war, the provinces tended to adopt the federal PC 1003 approach, and no province has banned company unions or created a proactive policy approach to them. Instead, the non-union model is almost entirely unregulated.

Given the constant presence of non-union plans, it is somewhat surprising that the dominant interest from scholars, practitioners, and policy makers involves unions and the regime of laws and protections that have been built to regulate relations in the unionized sector. The country has about 30 percent unionization, with growth of union density in the public sector and decline in the private sector.

Data on the non-union representation rates are difficult to come by. In 2000, Lipset and Meltz reported that about one fifth of non-union employees have formal representation other than unions (p. 225). This estimate was confirmed by Campolieti, Gomez, and Gunderson (2013). They found that "Canada with its more permissive legal framework may in fact be creating non-union institutions that are (at present) acting as substitutes to traditional unionization . . . NER appears to occupy spaces that are not covered by union workplaces" (p. 389).

A recent study (Timur et al., 2012) of six unionizations in Canada documents that the process of unionization differs between workplaces that have no form of collective representation at all—individual dealing systems— and those that start with a non-union plan. Workers who have their own non-union system are more reluctant to unionize, more likely to offer management another chance to rectify conditions, and when truly frustrated, worker representative in non-union systems lead the drive to unionize and become union officials. This recently happened even in the rarefied case of a 2012 faculty organizing drive at Osgoode Hall Law School at York University.

Now we come to a dramatic turn of events in Canada and a possible challenge to the non-union arena. To the astonishment of most experts, in 2007 the Supreme Court of Canada issued a decision known as *B.C. Health* that declared that Canada's Charter of Rights and Freedoms (the country's modern constitution) Section 2(d) guarantee of freedom of association protects the right to bargain collectively. Heralded as a remarkable victory for unions, the decision has ushered in a new era of litigation over the rights of unions. The Supreme Court has held that legislatures (and employers) must not "substantially interfere" with the ability of workers "to exert meaningful influence over working conditions through a process of collective bargaining conducted in accordance with the duty to bargain in good faith" (*B.C. Health* at para 90). There have been a series of cases (e.g., *Fraser v. Ontario*, *Mounted Police Association of Ontario*, and others) that seek clarity around the meaning of collective bargaining.

Here we arrive at the crux of the issues that might arise in the courts in the next decade. Might a non-union plan be construed to be a form of collective bargaining? Alternatively, would it be considered a form of "substantial interference" by employers? Is a non-union system with a duty to bargain in good faith permissible as a constitutionally protected entity? Should the courts privilege the Wagner model over other nascent forms of collective rights? These questions are entirely unresolved. Given Canada's protection of unions but silence on non-union systems, we anticipate interesting mental contortions as the highest court struggles with questions that would never have arisen prior to constitutionalizing the right to collective bargaining.

In conclusion, for Canadians interested in the interplay between unions and non-union systems, the riveting action will be in the highest courts rather than on the shop floors.

United Kingdom

Shop committees and joint consultative committees have a long history in Britain. A leading progressive employer, Cadburys, established an employee welfare department in 1902 and also installed an employee suggestion system (Nivens 1967: 4). Three years later it installed shop committees, in part to provide joint management of certain welfare programs (e.g., the plant cafeteria) and help coordinate and implement the suggestion system. The latter is a very early example of using NER to promote employee participation and higher organizational performance.

Although English newspapers and business periodicals carried many stories before World War I about the development of works councils and shop committees in advanced German companies and their purpose of fostering greater collaboration and cooperation between management and workers, the movement did not gain much foothold in Britain. Fox (1985) provides this portrait (p. 255):

> The British scene constituted unfavourable soil for joint works councils. Here and there employers had set-up worker-elected committees, having no connection with the unions and usually excluded from industrial questions, to deal with provident, welfare, canteen, and recreative facilities. Others might give employee spokesmen a voice in co-partnership or profit-sharing arrangements . . . Most, however, . . . were ineffective [and] isolated experiments.

He then gives this explanation for NER's lack of traction in British industry (p. 255):

> There was little in Britain's history, traditions and culture to lead many employers to suppose there was much to be gained from works councils. A social context of laissez-faire, individualism, and self-help, market forces, and emphasis on arms-length contractual relations . . . gave little encouragement to either employees or employers to think in terms of a "works community" [i.e., unitarist organization] which could command the participative loyalty of the rank and file. And there was certainly no prospect of Britain's trade unions following the lead of many German unions . . . [and supporting] a dual channel system of worker representation. Neither did the state find any reason to encourage them. The state's interest lay in industrial peace and effective joint regulation, and for those the best bet seemed to be a strong and uncluttered structure of union control. . . . Already, therefore, circumstances were favouring the single channel of employee representation.

Similar to other countries, an intense debate occurred in Britain during and immediately after World War I about how best to restore peace and stability to industrial relations. The option endorsed by the government was a two-track system with collective bargaining at the industry-occupation level and joint labour–management councils at the firm and regional levels. These new joint groups were popularly called Whitley councils (Gospel 1992). The Whitley councils were not NER because the trade unions would have vetoed creating a rival in the shops. Rather, the Whitley system extended a new tier of formal union representation to the workplace level, where to that point it had been very informal and spotty. The system did not catch on and soon atrophied. As before the war, a few British progressive employers continued with NER programs, and some others set up new ones. A famous example from this period is the John Lewis Partnership, Ltd.—a retail goods company that reorganized so that employees ("partners") received the bulk of profit and elected representatives to co-manage the company through store-level and company-level councils.

During World War II, the British government promoted establishment of joint production committees in war-related industries. They became widespread but soon died out after peace returned. Up to the 1980s, as in Australia, collective bargaining dominated British employment relations and NER was not really on the industrial radar.

After the election of Thatcher in 1979 and in conjunction with the rise of neoliberalism and its attendant free-market policies, union density started to drop in Britain and has continued on a gradual but cumulatively significant downward course to the present time (in 2012, 26 percent overall, 14 percent private sector). Collective bargaining also became more decentralized (Simms and Charlwood 2010). As unions lost membership and clout, the imperative of organizational survival made them more receptive (or acquiescent) to employer initiatives that created complementary NER bodies in a form of dual channel voice. Recall, for example, that Figure 1.1 shows that only 5 percent of British workplaces in 2004 had union-only voice.

Union decline in Britain was also matched by the rise of modern HRM and participative work practices (Gospel 2014). British companies in the postwar period had, as a general rule, lagged behind in globally competitive management practices. After the 1980s, they began a major effort to upgrade and innovate. A major area of transformation was in the practice of employee management, including adoption of high-performance/high-involvement practices imported from America and Japan. Evidence from the Workplace Employment Relations Surveys (WERS) in Britain indicates a mixed picture on this front (Brown, Bryson, Forth, and Whitfield 2009). On one hand, over a twenty-year period, British companies have upgraded their personnel/HRM functions, introduced a variety of HPWS-associated work practices (broader jobs, cross-functional training, pay for performance), and reduced the level of discontent and conflict at work. On the other, change in all these areas is modest and often piecemeal, and relatively few British workplaces match the stereotypical HPWS.

Another factor that influences NER adoption is change in the legal environment regulating employee representation. Since the 1980s, the British IR system has transitioned from "collective laissez-faire" in which workplace regulation was largely done through a voluntaristic system of collective bargaining to a more regulated and juridified system in which an expanded web of labour law establishes a variety of minimum standards and mandated procedures. Compared to other European nations, however, the British employment system still fits what Hall and Soskice (2001) call a liberal market economy. Interestingly, the one legislative change that most affects NER came from continental Europe. In 2004, Britain adopted a modified version of the European Union's Information and Consultation Directive. The directive mandates periodic information sharing and consultation with employees (if a minimum number of employees so request) in firms having fifty or more employees.

Data from WERS, as earlier depicted in Figure 1.1, reveal a heterogeneous range of voice options in British workplaces. The overall trend is a significant decline in union-only voice, a marked increase in forms of direct participation (team briefings town hall meetings), and modest increase in non-union representative voice. Based on the latest data from the 2011 WERS, Dobbins and Dundon (2014) report that 75 percent of British workplaces have no form of employee representation (union or non-union), NER density has increased among larger private-sector workplaces from 6 percent in 2004 to 13 percent in 2011, but nonetheless overall NER remains a small presence—7 percent of all workplaces in 2011. The most common issues these NER groups dealt with (ranked in descending order of frequency) are discipline and grievance, health and safety, rates of pay, pension entitlements, and staffing levels. Dobbins and Dundon conclude from a survey of the literature that NER in the British context has not been a major contributor to union decline. They also conclude that NER has failed to spread more widely in Britain because many companies take a short-run perspective on labour that precludes the long-term employee investment and mutual gain commitment necessary for JCCs and other higher-level forms of NER to payoff.

United States

As far as can be determined, a short pamphlet by Bayles (1886) is the first written discussion in the United States of the structure and advantages of a non-union shop committee arrangement. Perhaps a dozen shop committees, also sometimes referred to as works councils, were established by the 1910s. Due to proselytizing of John Leitch, a self-billed evangelizer for industrial democracy, several "plans of industrial democracy," modelled on the bicameral structure of the U.S. Congress, were adopted prior to World War I (Leitch 1919). The best-known NER plan of that era, however, was the Rockefeller employee representation plan at the strife-torn Colorado Fuel and Iron Company (Rees 2010).

NER has experienced a distinctly up-and-down life in the United States. During World War I and its immediate aftermath, more than 200 works councils and employee representation plans (ERPs) were established (Kaufman 2000). After becoming disillusioned that these non-union bodies would serve as a springboard for outside organization, the trade unions became bitter critics of NER. NER reached its peak of density and influence in the 1920s, when ERPs and consultative committees—centred in progressive but avowedly non-union welfare capitalist companies—spread to as many as 800 plants and covered more than one million workers. The welfare capitalism movement then went bust in the Great Depression of the 1930s and NER plans were widely discredited as employers abandoned consultation and mutual gain and shifted to the low road of wage cuts, mass layoffs, and work intensification. The pro-labour policies of Roosevelt's New Deal spurred union organizing and led to a strike wave and growing radicalization of employer–employee relations. To stabilize the system and promote unions for purposes of both economic recovery and industrial democracy, the National Labor Relations Act (NLRA) was enacted in 1935. It not only protected and encouraged collective bargaining but, at the insistence of the trade union movement and allies, the NLRA also placed a near-complete ban on all forms of NER that in any way involve joint dealing between managers and one or more employee representatives over a term or condition of employment (LeRoy 2000). Almost all ERPs and similar structures were forced to disband, transform into independent enterprise unions, or go underground.

The ban on "company unions" remains in place to the present day, thus severely limiting NER in the United States. Exceptions include NER when it deals with subjects unrelated to terms and conditions of employment, such as production, quality, or customer service, or when an employee committee or group completely assumes managerial decision making, thus obviating "joint dealing," such as when a self-managed work team makes a redundancy decision and reports it to management. The other significant exception is for the narrow range of companies outside the coverage of the NLRA. Principally included here are transportation companies, such as airlines and railroads, covered under the Railway Labour Act (RLA, 1926). The RLA follows more closely Canadian labour law and bars NER only when it interferes with workers' organizing rights or shifts into a vehicle for collective bargaining (Kaufman 2013).

As in other countries, union density in the United States has greatly declined since the early 1980s and, in 2013, was only 7 percent in the private sector. Given the bar on many forms of NER, the American employment relations system evidently has a growing and potentially quite large participation–representation gap (Freeman 2007). Of course, American employers are unconstrained when it comes to direct forms of voice and participation, and evidence indicates a thirty-year growth in various forms of employee involvement programs. The benefits of participative workplace structures have, indeed, been given considerable emphasis in a burgeoning literature in strategic HRM and industrial relations on the high-performance work system (Wood and Wall 2007; Frost 2008), although, as earlier noted, this literature—particularly in HRM—is surprisingly opaque in differentiating between legal forms of direct involvement and illegal forms of representational involvement.

A lively debate has taken place in the American industrial relations and labour law fields over the last two to three decades regarding whether the NLRA's restriction on non-union forms of representation has harmed the country's economic performance by impeding productivity-enhancing workplace practices, such as employee involvement initiatives (LeRoy 2000; Richardson 2010). The evidence of statistical studies is that involvement and participation practices in most cases have a positive effect on firm performance. Evidence that the NLRA's restrictive bar on representational groups has had a corresponding negative effect on productivity and performance is, however, largely anecdotal and circumstantial. Part of the reason is that statistical investigation of this relationship is made difficult by the paucity of formalized types of NER in the United States, such as JCCs and JICs in other countries.

Concern has also arisen regarding whether the NLRA has harmed companies' ability to adopt other cost-effective and mutual-gain workplace practices, such as alternative dispute resolution (ADR) programs. Traditional forms of dispute resolution are the open door in non-union companies and a multi-step grievance process in union companies. The former is often ineffective in fairly representing employees' interests and resolving disputes; the latter can be quite costly, time consuming, and adversarial. ADR is a middle way between these two poles, with a formal process for resolving disputes but within a management-created system with more emphasis on mediation, joint problem solving, and non-adversarial relations (Colvin 2013). NER can be a component of an ADR system, such as when employee representatives sit on an in-house peer review or arbitration panel.

The most recent evidence on NER in the United States comes from survey evidence reported by Godard and Frege (2013). They found that 28 percent of the American workforce, or 34 percent of the non-union workforce, reports they work in an organization with a company-created system in which worker representatives meet with management; 14 percent of respondents outside unions also reported that they were represented by another type of association, such as based on occupation, race, or gender. Interestingly, when asked whether their representatives "can be counted on to stand up for workers," the proportion of respondents (51 percent) in NER structures who answered strongly yes is similar to respondents in traditional unions (54 percent); with respect to the question "representatives actively consult with workers," NER significantly outperforms unions (54 percent vs. 41 percent). A surprising result in their survey is that when respondents with NER in the workplace were asked whether the representatives discussed wage and benefits with management (proscribed subjects under the NLRA), 42 percent said "to some extent" and 37 percent" said "to a great extent." Apparently the NLRA is less restrictive in practice than it is on paper.

OVERVIEW OF THE TWELVE CHAPTERS

Provided next is a brief overview of each of the upcoming twelve chapters. They are presented in the order given in the book with three chapters, respectively, for each country: Australia, Canada, United Kingdom, and United States.

Suncorp

Paul J. Gollan and Ying Xu present a case study of NER at one of Australia's largest financial service companies, Suncorp Group. The company has extensive operations in banking, insurance, and pension funds and has more than 16,000 employees. NER at Suncorp has evolved and grown over a twenty-five-year period as the company has gone through numerous acquisitions and mergers. Today, the NER is called the Suncorp Group Employee Council (SGEC). Unions, although active over the years in trying to organize the employees, have only a small presence among the workforce. The company has an explicit union-free policy and has adopted a high-road HRM strategy to create and maintain satisfied and loyal employees, so far relatively successfully according to survey results reported by the authors. A central component of the high-road strategy is the SGEC, in order to foster effective communication, give employees voice and influence over company policy and management decisions and surface and resolve areas of friction or discontent. Gollan and Xu report that the SGEC is one of the most advanced and formalized NERs in Australia, falling in the middle between a European works council and Anglo-American JCC. The SGEC gets a large annual budget from the company, has an executive director, administrative staff, and technical and consultant support, and provides a wide range of services to employees, thus making it more expansive than a JCC. But, unlike a statutorily created works council, the SGEC can be curtailed or eliminated at the company's discretion, is restricted from certain areas of operational and HRM decision making, such as job classifications and promotions, and lacks power beyond dialogue and lobbying to block a management initiative. The authors find that most Suncorp employees have a favourable opinion of the company and SGEC, prefer a cooperative form of voice over an adversarial style, and have disinterest in unions, partly from doubt they could make a difference.

Cochlear

Paul J. Gollan and Senia Kalfa examine the experience of NER at Australian medical manufacturer Cochlear, a world leader in electronic ear implants for people with impaired hearing. Its sales and employment have expanded considerably in the last decade, with the bulk of its 2,300 workforce located in several facilities in Sydney and Brisbane. At the beginning of the study in the mid-2000s, the terms and conditions for the Australian employees were set in an Enterprise Partnership Agreement, bargained with an independent union. In 2005, the company's management attempted to take advantage of the greater freedom provided by newly introduced workplace legislation to phase out the union and deal directly with the employees instead. Within that context, Cochlear management requested termination of the collective enterprise agreement and a shift to individual employment contracts. At the same time, the company's focus was on boosting productivity and quality by shifting to a lean manufacturing model, for which it thought successful implementation needed employee participation and buy-in. Therefore, in 2005—with consent of the union—the company created an employee consultative committee (ECC). It currently has nine employee representatives, including several people who are union members as well as shift supervisors, and meets once a month with management. During the conversion to lean manufacturing, the ECC was relatively active and given significant issues to work on; in recent years, however, the council has cut back meeting time and become more a conduit for communication and improving social conditions. Part of the reason is that both managers and employees express more comfort and sense of efficacy with personal face-to-face interaction (direct participation) for communication and problem solving than working through the council (indirect participation). The ECC continues to function, therefore, but in a relatively low-level role. In 2012, Cochlear lost a legal appeal challenging the union's right to represent the employees and, hence, it had to return to the bargaining table.

UNICO

Alison Barnes and Craig MacMillan study NER in an Australian university called UNICO. NER at this university was a direct outgrowth of new legislation introduced in 2005 by the Conservative government aimed at curtailing the power and position of unions in higher education. The legislation stated that to be eligible for government funding, universities had to allow employees to opt for individual contracts and that they had to establish an NER form for direct communication and consultation with the workforce. To comply with the NER requirement, the university and union agreed to the formation of a Consultative Employee Committee (CEC). It had elected representatives from both faculty and administrative staff ranks and met quarterly; an unusual feature was that no management person was an official member of the CEC but the head and assistant head of university HR attended meetings on an advisement and liaison basis. Most employees expressed support in principle for the CEC and collaborative voice idea; however, in practice the CEC proved disappointing to many because it lacked power to change management decisions or influence policy. Management did, however, use the CEC as a sounding board before it rolled out several new programs or policy changes and made revisions based on feedback. A dynamic that introduced divisiveness into the NER was that some representatives favoured collaboration and took a more positive view toward management, while others were union members and used the CEC to attack management and promote the union's organizational interests and bargaining agenda. The situation was further complicated when a Labour-led government came into power and replaced the earlier legislation. The CEC ceased operation while a new collective contract was negotiated; although the union wanted to drop the CEC and restore single-channel voice, it compromised and agreed to maintain NER and dual-channel voice. The new council, CEC2, was restructured, however, so it met more often, had management members, and had a degree more influence by mandating that management actively consider the views or proposals from the CEC2. At the time of Barnes and MacMillans's study, the CEC2 had only met twice, precluding conclusions on its efficacy and performance.

Manufacture Co.

Jimmy Donaghey, Niall Cullinane, and Tony Dundon examine a single-plant NER council in Belfast, Northern Ireland, created, in part, as a response to British adoption of the European Union's Information and Consultation Directive. The plant is engaged in manufacture and employs about 300 people. The NER was formed in 2005, called the Employee Forum, and organized with seven representatives who meet with managers in quarterly meetings. A number of themes and insights about NER are contained in this case study. For example, one sees a combination of managerial motives at work, including the articulated desire to foster closer and more collaborative relations with employees but also a largely unstated but evident desire to keep out unions. Also instructive, the Employee Forum lapsed into inactive status after only a year and—after an unsuccessful union organizing campaign—was resuscitated and reconfigured. The authors find managers voice support for the forum and view it as a positive vehicle for better plant operations and employee relations but express frustration that employees want to use the NER for "gripe" and "me" issues rather than more business-related subjects. The employee representatives, and even more so the shop floor employees, take a different view. The representatives have a moderately positive attitude toward the forum but feel it underperforms for a variety of reasons, such as a tilted company-oriented agenda and lack of time and training for representatives to do an effective job. The employees interviewed for the study expressed a mix of apathy, cynicism, and distrust, fuelled in part by certain management decisions regarded as inequitable (e.g., terminating a bonus program) and perception that NER is ineffective and remote to important employee interests.

WebBank

Stewart Johnstone and Adrian Wilkinson look at NER in a high-growth British financial services firm specializing in online banking. The firm, called WebBank, began as a small entrepreneurial startup in 1997 and quickly grew to be a major player in the retail banking market, having at its peak 2,500 employees. In an interesting example of corporate flame-out, the company just as quickly declined and ceased to operate in 2011. Two years after its founding, top management decided to establish an NER organization called the Employee Forum. The motives were diverse, including more effective employee communication in a rapidly growing company, using employee input to gain better organizational decisions, getting ahead of government legislation (the EU directive), and keeping the company non-union in a highly organized industry. Starting out, the forum had only three part-time representatives, management set the agenda and kept it low level, and the main function was for managers to pass on to representatives information on decisions already made. Two years later, the chief executive officer, feeling disappointed in the results of the forum, decided to strengthen and expand its structure and function. It now had three full-time representatives and a series of part-time area representatives and an expanded budget for training and initiatives and was more involved in working through and improving management proposals than simply distributing finalized decisions. While the relaunch of the forum seemed successful, WebBank's business position deteriorated and losses mounted. In 2007, it was acquired by an American financial services company that brought in a new top management team. The organizational climate turned defensive and distrustful because of lack of confidence in the new outside management and fear their agenda was large layoffs and cutbacks. This climate also undercut the effectiveness of the forum, particularly because the new management did not embrace it. The forum became inactive and, despite substantial retrenchment and new business initiatives, WebBank continued downhill and was closed in 2011.

Eurotunnel

Paul J. Gollan and Senia Kalfa examine the performance of the NER-type Company Council (CC) in the British-operated portion of Eurotunnel, a British-French joint enterprise that operates the rail tunnel connecting the two countries under the English Channel. The CC was established in 1992 at the company's inception. Originally, the workforce was not affiliated with an outside union, and the CC was the single channel of voice between management and workers. The council was composed of eight elected representatives from the different parts of the company's operations; it met monthly and could consider all matters of operational and employment practice except individual concerns and grievances. Gollan has followed developments at Eurotunnel for almost two decades and conducted periodic surveys and interviews. The authors conclude the CC proved largely ineffective in its mission of fostering cooperation, higher organizational efficiency, and mutual trust/gain. Portions of the blame lie with poor communication with the workforce and management of employee relations, the company's severe financial losses with substantial cost cutting and employee discontent, and employees' perceptions that the CC largely promoted the company's agenda and gave workers little influence. Although workers initially expressed ambivalence about union representation, frustration with the company and CC brought unionism to Eurotunnel in 2000. The CC was maintained but restructured, thus establishing a dual-channel voice and representation system. Gollan and Kalfa find that over the next ten years, employees remained dissatisfied both with company management and with the union and NER, with the former because they believed it was untrustworthy and with the latter because they believed neither effectively represented their interests or concerns. The union and CC also engaged in turf battles, power plays, and contests for worker loyalty. Gollan and Kalfa conclude that part of the failure of NER at Eurotunnel lies with ineffective management, although chances for failure were high because of built-in conflict generated by lack of profit and consequent "us-against-them" cost cutting.

Imperial Oil

Daphne G. Taras examines the oldest continuously operating NER in North America—the JIC system at Calgary-based Imperial Oil. Imperial Oil was acquired early in the twentieth century by the Rockefeller family's Standard Oil company. After Rockefeller and his Canadian labour consultant Mackenzie King established in 1914 the famous (some would say infamous) employee representation plan at the Colorado Fuel and Iron Co., it was soon launched at other Rockefeller-connected companies, including Imperial Oil in 1919. The company has numerous operating divisions and individual production facilities scattered across a wide and often remote geographical area. The JIC is a two-tier organization with plant-level NER councils that meet once a month, composed of local management and elected employee representatives, and higher-level district councils that periodically meet each year with corporate executives, HR managers, and select representatives from the local councils. The JIC system is highly formalized, including lengthy and detailed written agreements for each local facility. Taras notes that Imperial Oil is open about its desire to avoid unions and that it operates the JIC partly with this purpose in mind, albeit as part of comprehensive HRM strategy that makes unions unnecessary to the workers. She also notes, however, that Imperial has remained committed to NER over many decades because it bestows numerous other important benefits, such as a committed and loyal workforce, a partnership method for working out terms and conditions of employment, and a formal process for problem solving and dispute resolution. An insight of her study is that this type of high-level NER is neither cheap nor easy, for it requires considerable investment in management time and talent, significant operating costs, and above-industry-average wages and benefits in order to take conflict-generating distributive issues off the table. Despite considerable turbulence in the oil industry, a number of mergers and nonoil expansions, and continual pressure for cost cutting and headcount reduction, the JIC at Imperial has not only survived but remains successful and a deeply embedded part of the company's HRM program and corporate culture.

Royal Canadian Mounted Police

Sara Slinn examines the Staff Relations Representation Program (SRRP) in the Royal Canadian Mounted Police (RCMP). Her case study is an interesting example of NER for a specialized public-sector workforce group (police) in which doubts have long been expressed about the applicability and appropriateness of traditional unionism and collective bargaining. The case of the SRRP provides a particularly detailed and insightful example of NER's up-and-down fortunes over many decades and its somewhat contentious and dialectical evolution in response to changing economic currents, legislative enactments and court rulings, member dissatisfaction, and managerial opposition to unionization. Echoing a theme described earlier in this chapter, NER in this case has a somewhat "caught in the middle" character whereby a significant part of RCMP management prefers to run the organization using traditional command and control with no formal employee representative, while a significant portion of the officers prefer a stronger and more independent form of trade union representation. NER has thus endured and—to some substantial but shifting degree—performed successfully because it is a "better than the alternative" compromise for both sides to the employment relationship. A stressor on employer–employee relations in the RCMP and source of employee support for replacing the SRRP with an outside union has been widespread perception among the officers that management suffers from a number of defects from which it needs protection. Examples are flawed policies and administration, authoritarian and unilateral decision making, and discrimination and retribution against people who for some reason fall out of favour.

Canadian Federal Public Service

Richard P. Chaykowski's chapter on the Canadian Federal Public Service provides an illuminating case study of NER as part of a dual-channel voice system. Also illuminated is the evolution of representation in the public sector from individual dealing to voluntary but not required bilateral dealing with staff associations to legally required consultation and joint dealing through a formally organized NER to collective bargaining with independent unions. The NER in this case is the National Joint Council (NJC), established in 1944. Until 1967, the NJC was the single-channel voice system for federal public-service workers in Canada; in that year, legislation was enacted permitting the workers to collective bargain through independent unions. As Chaykowski describes, many observers thought the NJC would disappear and collective bargaining would become the new single-channel voice system. Instead, the NJC has not only survived but has also carved out a relatively secure and successful place as an institutional complement to collective bargaining. Chaykowski offers a number of reasons for the NJC's longevity and relative success but identifies the root cause as its ability to advance the mutual interests of all the parties—employees, management, and unions—through an alternative forum for problem solving on issues of a more integrative, nontraditional, or strategic nature.

Delta Air Lines

Bruce E. Kaufman examines the NER system at Delta Air Lines. Delta is the world's second-largest airline and has more than 70,000 employees. The company also has what is probably the most highly developed and extensive system of representation for non-union employees in the United States. Delta is able to operate its NER system because as a transportation company, it is covered by the Railway Labour Act and not the NLRA. The RLA allows companies to form and operate non-union employee committees and councils as long as they do not engage in bargaining or negotiation with the company over terms and conditions of employment and do not interfere with employees' rights to non-interference in choosing outside representation. Delta had a reputation in earlier years as a very pro-employee company and had an intensely loyal and committed workforce. With industry deregulation in 1978 and entrance of numerous low-cost competitors, Delta's high cost structure became non-competitive, and starting in the early 1990s, it went through a series of retrenchments, including unprecedented layoffs, wage cuts, and benefit reductions. This downward escalator quickened with the steep industry downturn after 9/11 and, in 2005, the company declared bankruptcy. Before the mid-1990s, Delta did not use NER and instead gained employee commitment and non-union status (except for pilots) through a generous paternalism. When profits disappeared, the company had to dramatically reengineer its business model and HRM system with the challenging objective of paring billions of dollars from its cost structure while still preserving its partnership and non-union relationship with employees. Starting in 1996, Delta created a cascading set of employee councils and forums from the board of directors level to the hangar and cabin level. These NER groups involved employees in finding cost reductions and operational improvements and, with the implementation of profit sharing and other forms of performance pay, gave them a sense of influence and shared reward in the cost-reduction program. Delta has returned to profitability, the NER councils are an embedded part of the company, and despite bankruptcy and merger with highly unionized Northwest Airlines, its employees voted against union representation in a series of elections held among mechanics, flight attendants, and other groups.

FedEx

David Lewin's case study is on the intersection of NER and ADR at the Federal Express (FedEx) company. Founded in 1973 as an overnight package delivery company centred in Memphis, Tennessee, FedEx has expanded into a worldwide operation with 160,000 employees. From the beginning, FedEx had an explicit policy of remaining non-union and adopted a high-road HRM strategy for this purpose. Believing that employee dissatisfaction, particularly with regard to disputes and grievances either ignored or unfairly handled by managers, was a major impetus to union organizing, the company early on established a formal alternative dispute resolution system. It has two main components. The first is the Guaranteed Fair Treatment Procedure (GFTP). An employee files a written complaint and it is resolved at one of several ascending levels of management, ending at an Appeals Review Board. The GFTP is different from a union grievance process because it includes all ranks of employees below the executive level, a broader range of issues subject to appeal (e.g., a promotion decision), and greater use of consultation and mediation. The second is the Survey-Feedback-Action (SFA) program, a twice-annual employee survey. It is also distinctive because the company promises that responses are sent to the relevant group of managers, who will take appropriate action and communicate the outcome to the employees.

NLRA

Michael H. LeRoy presents hard-to-acquire evidence on the structure and function of NER groups in the Unites States through examination of Section 8(a)(2) "company union" cases adjudicated by the National Labour Relations Board (NLRB). As described earlier in the chapter, most companies in the United States fall under the National Labour Relations Act and its ban—contained in Section 8(a)(2) and companion Section 2(5)—of all forms of bilateral dealing ("dealing" being a wider net than bargaining or negotiation) between management and one or more representatives of the employees over a term or condition of employment. Shortly after enactment of the NLRA in 1935, hundreds of NERs were challenged as 8(a)(2) violations and were voluntarily disbanded or ordered disestablished. By the early

1990s, the number of 8(a)(2) cases had dwindled to only a handful a year, partly because most prohibited forms of NER were gone, companies had learned how to structure and operate NER committees in ways that would pass legal review, and most NER challenges come from unions during organizing campaigns, which have markedly declined. LeRoy found evidentiary records for twenty-three 8(a)(2) cases since the NLRB's famous *Electromation* (1992) decision. We learn from these cases that NER continues to be highly variegated in terms of structure, function, and motive. Some NERs are clearly part of a HPWS high-involvement system, others are clearly animated by union avoidance, and yet others are a hasty management response to a crisis situation or collaborative attempt to improve productivity and morale in an otherwise traditionally run firm. Likewise, some NERs are small groups with a narrow focus on one or two subjects, such as grievances or safety, while others are company wide with a broad focus on all aspects of company operations and policy.

IMPLICATIONS FOR NER

We encourage the reader to go through all twelve chapters, because each has a unique and interesting story to tell about NER and its ups and downs and pros and cons. For those who do not have time or would appreciate an up-front summary of key findings before diving in, presented next are what the four editors believe are some of particularly salient implications and lessons learned. Certainly the case studies contain numerous others we cannot list and, in keeping with the alternative-frames-of-reference idea, some readers may come to different conclusions than we do.

1. **Recent Renewal but Long History.** The concept of employee voice and practice of a non-union form of employee representation has experienced a renewal—even perhaps renaissance—in the last thirty years due to a confluence of factors such as union decline, rise of high-performance work practices, and desire of employers and employees for a more cooperative and less strife-prone relationship. The case studies in this volume reveal, however, that these ideas and practices go back a century and more and were not only articulated by pioneer HRM/IR writers but also implemented by pioneer companies led by visionary and progressive leaders. Present-day NER is certainly practiced in a more managerially sophisticated and organizationally advanced form than a century ago; the animating ideas and distinctive challenges have long roots, however.
2. **Multiplicity of Forms, Shapes, and Sizes.** The stereotypical example of NER is some kind of company union. Actually, NER comes in an amazing welter of forms, shapes, and sizes. NER can be as small as an individual ombud or as large as a company council representing tens

of thousands of employees from many different countries. Frequently companies structure NER around a well-defined workplace issue, such as a joint committee for safety-health, compensation review, or ADR. Other times the NER group has a wider compass, such as a plant or company council, but the size can vary from a few hundred employees with part-time representatives to many thousands of employees with full-time representatives and salaried director and staff. There is definitely "no one size fits all" in NER.

3. **Multiplicity of Employer Motives.** It is fair to say that most employers/managers prefer not to deal with an outside labour union. The desire to avoid unions is, therefore, certainly a common motive behind companies' adoption of NER. However, the matter of employer motives and evaluation of their positive and negative sides are considerably more complex than simply "union busting." Many employers (and employees) feel unions bring their own problems and shortcomings to the workplace, such as adversarialism, non-competitive costs, and inflexible and restrictive practices, and these beliefs cannot simply be written off as a façade for greed and control. Further, many employers adopt NER for other reasons quite separate from union avoidance. Considerations include more effective communication with employees, improved coordination of production, higher morale and esprit de corps, a spur to organizational change and learning, stronger partnership and unity of interest, more effective formulation and delivery of HRM, fewer disputes and their more effective resolution, and leadership development for both managers and employees. Employer motives with NER also have a dark side, such as preserving control and power, easing the way for employee give-backs, low-cost damage control for managerial mistakes and shortcomings, and placating employees long enough to squelch a union drive. In practice, employers typically get into NER for a multiplicity of overlapping motives that fall along a continuum from low road to high road and negative sum to positive sum. A corollary is that HRM researchers tend to overemphasize the high-performance HPWS side of NER, while IR researchers tend to overemphasize its union-avoidance side.

4. **Checkered Performance Record.** The performance record of NER has to be evaluated in terms of serving both employer and employee interests. These case studies, as well as the broader research literature, indicate a considerably checkered experience with a significant minority of NERs centred on failure to ineffective, a somewhat larger and perhaps median group centred on marginal to modest, and a small-sized but impressive minority that qualify as high performance. The absolute value of these performance effects is also reduced by the often narrow-to-modest size and scope of NER in organizations (say as compared to a union that covers all hourly employees). NER tends to generate returns in rough proportion to the investment of

material, time, and emotional resources both sides put into it, with a
high return coming from a process captured by the HPWS paradigm
(i.e., a high-involvement employer with high-commitment employees). The problem is that relatively few companies have the incentives,
resources, and managerial capability to implement an HPWS. As one
moves downstream from the HPWS model, the return to NER for
both company and workers diminishes and can soon approach marginal to zero. On the company side, getting and keeping high employee
morale and productivity through NER requires considerable up-front
cost through above-market wages, employment security, and training;
the returns, on the other hand, are relatively fragile, intangible, and
long run. Many firms, therefore, decide to limit their NER investment
to a small-scale and perhaps token effort, realizing few benefits in
return. On the employee side, the further one goes from an HPWS, the
less reason workers have to get excited and actively contribute, partly
because without assured job security and gain sharing, they may not
benefit and, partly, because a lower-level NER provides few opportunities to make a difference. Here again is small investment and marginal return. In academic terminology, the employment relationship
has an inherent prisoner's dilemma problem, and for NER to be a
successful performer, both management and workers must commit to
the long-term mutual-gain option. Unfortunately, in many situations,
either the company or the workers or both feel they cannot trust the
other side to make and sustain this commitment, thus undercutting
the basis for a high-performance NER.

5. **Conditions Helpful to Success.** A variety of factors and conditions
help NER to be adopted more widely and practiced more successfully. One that comes through in nearly all the case studies is a significant union threat. The stronger is this threat, the more likely
companies will respond with their own voice and representation program, although depending on the situation, it may take the form of a
high-road union-substitution NER or a low-road union-suppression
NER. Another important factor is a stable and full-employment
economic environment. With a stable or growing business environment, companies are more likely to make long-term investments in
employees, including internal labour markets and NER voice programs. Similarly, a full-employment labour market forecloses using
the inexpensive "fear of being fired" stick to motivate employees and
induces companies to instead adopt high-road practices, including
NER, to get valued employees to stay and contribute through the
carrot of voice and involvement. A killer for many NER programs
is economic deterioration, whether due to a macroeconomic recession or a firm-specific slump, because companies find it very difficult to sustain partnership while wielding the axe to cost. Another
critical success factor for NER is top management commitment to

the process and their willingness to drive this commitment down to the bottom foreman-supervisor level. An advanced HPWS type of NER also requires a high-calibre management team adept at managing in a team-based/collaborative environment and willing to say "I screwed up." Just as a skilled and collaborative management team helps make for successful NER, so does a skilled and collaborative set of employee representatives. NER functions better when companies invest resources in training representatives in business, negotiation, and interpersonal skills; likewise, NER also performs better with representatives who approach their jobs not as militant union shop stewards but as junior partners on a team looking to make the company successful with knowledge that the employees also become more successful.

6. **Contributions from Public Policy.** The United States appears to have the most misaligned policy on voice and employee representation, leading to small union representation and small non-union representation and therefore a large participation–representation gap. We are not in a position to make specific recommendations on American labour law, but it surely seems too blunt and draconian to *per se* ban most types of NER in order to eliminate only the anti-social bottom part. On the other hand, the experience in Britain with the EU Information and Consultation Directive also offers a cautionary lesson; in particular, it appears that simply mandating information sharing and consultation may cause many companies who do not have their heart in it to simply go through the motions with some expense but little gain. The several cases in this volume from Australia, Britain, and Canada with dual-channel voice systems also offer food for policy thought. On one hand, the combination of union and NER voice offer the promise of a win-win to the degree they are complements and work effectively together in their respective domains. However, the evidence suggests that a dual-channel system can also become dysfunctional if the union and NER cross over into the other's territory or become rivals for the loyalty of the employees. Some clear lines of demarcation, therefore, seen desirable. The cases from Britain also suggest that a positive contribution government can make to successful NER is to provide a model "best practice" guidebook for companies and consultants who can go to the company and help set up the NER. Finally, we put out just for thought and discussion a "what if" inspired by the Delta Air Lines case. That is, what if corporate governance law were revised to require corporations to include one or more employee representatives as members? This requirement might well bring more balance, a longer-term perspective, and greater accountability to corporate conduct; also, it would give NER a potentially strategic role to play and provide employees a voice at the top where it really counts.

REFERENCES

Ackers, P. 2010. "An Industrial Relations Perspective on Employee Participation." In A. Wilkinson, P. Gollan, M. Marchington, and D. Lewin (eds.), *The Oxford Handbook of Participation in Organizations*, pp. 52–75. Oxford: Oxford University Press.

Appelbaum, E., Bailey, T., Berg, P., and A. Kalleberg. 2000. *Manufacturing Advantage: Why High Performance Systems Pay Off*. Ithaca, NY: Cornell University Press.

Avgar, A., and S. Owens. 2014. "Voice in the Mutual Gains Workplace." In A. Wilkinson, J. Donaghey, T. Dundon, and R. Freeman (eds.), *The Handbook of Research on Employee Voice*, pp. 327–41. Northampton: Elgar.

Basken, R. 2000. "My Experience with Unionization of Nonunion Employee Representation Plans in Canada." In B. Kaufman and D. Taras (eds.), *Nonunion Employee Representation: History, Contemporary Practice, and Policy*, pp. 487–97. Armonk, NY: M. E. Sharpe.

Bayles, J. 1886. *The Shop Council*. New York: Shirley.

Bernstein, I. 1970. *The Turbulent Years: A History of the American Worker, 1933–1941*. Boston: Houghton-Mifflin.

Boeri, T., and J. Van Ours. 2008. *The Economics of Imperfect Labour Markets*. Princeton, NJ: Princeton University Press.

Boxall, P., and J. Purcell. 2011. *Strategy and Human Resource Management*, 3rd ed. London: Palgrave MacMillan.

Brody, D. 1994. "Section 8(a)(2) and the Origins of the Wagner Act." In R. Sieber, S. Friedman, and J. Uehlein (eds.), *Restoring the Promise of American Labour Law*, pp. 29–44. Ithaca, NY: ILR Press.

Brown, W., A. Bryson, J. Forth, and K. Whitfield. 2009. *The Evolution of the Modern Workplace*. Cambridge: Cambridge University Press.

Bryson, A., A. Charlwood, and J. Forth. 2006. "Worker Voice, Managerial Responsiveness, and Labour Productivity." *Industrial Relations Journal*, 37(5): 438–56.

Budd, J. 2004. *Employment with a Human Face*. Ithaca, NY: Cornell University Press.

———, and D. Bhave. 2008. "Values, Ideologies, and Frames of Reference in Industrial Relations." In P. Blyton, N. Bacon, J. Fiorito, and E. Heery (eds.), *The Sage Handbook of Industrial Relations*, pp. 92–112. London: Sage.

Campolieti, M., R. Gomez, and M. Gunderson. 2013. "Does Non-Union Employee Representation Act as a Complement or Substitute to Union Voice? Evidence from Canada and the United States." *Industrial Relations*, 52(S1): 378–96.

Colvin, A. 2013. "Participation Versus Procedures in Non-Union Dispute Resolution." *Industrial Relations*, 52(S1): 259–83.

Commons, J. 1905. *Trade Unionism and Labour Problems*. New York: Kelly.

Dobbins, T., and T. Dundon. 2014. "Non-Union Employee Representation." In A. Wilkinson, J. Donaghey, T. Dundon, and R. Freeman (eds.), *The Handbook of Research on Employee Voice*, forthcoming. Northampton: Elgar.

Dundon, T. 2004. *Employee Relations in Non-Union Firms*. London: Routledge.

———, and P. Gollan 2007. "Re-Conceptualizing Voice in the Non-Union Workplace." *International Journal of Human Resource Management*, 18(7): 1182–1198.

———, A. Wilkinson, M. Marchington, and P. Ackers. 2004. "The Meanings and Purpose of Employee Voice." *International Journal of Human Resource Management*, 15(6): 1149–70.

Fox, A. 1966. *Industrial Sociology and Industrial Relations*, Royal Commission on Trade Unions and Employers' Associations Research Paper 3. London: HMSO.

―――. 1974. *Beyond Contract: Work, Power, and Trust Relations.* London: Faber and Faber.

―――. 1985. *History and Heritage: The Social Origins of the British Industrial Relations System.* London: Allen & Unwin.

Freeman, R. 2007. "Can the United States Clear the Market for Representation and Participation? In R. Freeman, P. Boxall, and P. Haynes (eds.), *What Workers Say: Employee Voice in the Anglo-American Workplace*, pp. 25–48. Ithaca, NY: Cornell University Press.

―――, P. Boxall, and P. Haynes. 2007. *What Workers Say: Employee Voice in the Anglo-American Workplace.* Ithaca, NY: Cornell University Press.

―――, and J. Medoff. 1984. *What Do Unions Do?* New York: Basic Books.

―――, and J. Rogers. 1999. *What Workers Want.* Ithaca, NY: ILR Press.

Frost, A. 2008. "The High Performance Work Systems Literature in Industrial Relations." In P. Blyton, N. Bacon, J. Fiorito, and E. Heery (eds.), *The Sage Handbook of Industrial Relations*, pp. 420–33. London: Sage.

Godard, J., and C. Frege. 2013. "Labour Unions, Alternative Forms of Representation, and the Exercise of Authority Relations in U.S. Workplaces." *Industrial and Labour Relations Review*, 66(1): 142–68.

Gollan, P. 2000. "Nonunion Forms of Employee Representation in the United Kingdom and Australia." In B. Kaufman and D. Taras (eds.), *Nonunion Employee Representation: History, Contemporary Practice, and Policy*, pp. 410–49. Armonk, NY: M. E. Sharpe.

―――. 2007. *Employee Representation in Non-Union Firms.* London: Sage.

Gospel, H. 1992. *Markets, Firms, and the Management of Labour in Modern Britain.* Cambridge: Cambridge University Press.

―――. 2014. "The Evolution of Human Resources Management in the UK." In B. Kaufman (ed.), *The Development of Human Resource Management Across Nations*, pp. 186–210. Northampton: Elgar.

Gumbrell-McCormick, Rebecca, and Richard Hyman. 2010. "Works Councils: The European Model of Industrial Democracy?" In Adrian Wilkinson, Paul Gollan, Mick Marchington, and David Lewin (eds.), *The Oxford Handbook of Participation in Organizations*, pp. 286–314. Oxford: Oxford University Press.

Hall, Peter, and David Soskice. 2001. *Varieties of Capitalism: The Institutional Foundations of Comparative Advantage.* Oxford: Oxford University Press.

Harley, B. 2014. "High Performance Work Schemes and Employee Voice." In A. Wilkinson, J. Donaghey, T. Dundon, and R. Freeman (eds.), *The Handbook of Research on Employee Voice*, forthcoming. Northampton: Elgar.

Heery, E., N. Bacon, P. Blyton, and J. Fiorito. 2008. "Introduction: The Field of Industrial Relations." In P. Blyton, N. Bacon, J. Fiorito, and E. Heery (eds.), *The Sage Handbook of Industrial Relations*, pp. 1–32. London: Sage.

Hiatt, J., and L. Gold. 2000. "Employer–Employee Committees: A Union Perspective." In B. Kaufman and D. Taras (eds.), *Nonunion Employee Representation: History, Contemporary Practice, and Policy*, pp. 498–510. Armonk, NY: M. E. Sharpe.

Hyman, R. 1975, *Industrial Relations: A Marxist Introduction.* London: Macmillan.

―――. 1997. "The Future of Employee Representation." *British Journal of Industrial Relations,* 35(3): 309–36.

Isaac, J., and S. Macintyre. 2004. *The New Province for Law and Order: 100 Years of Australian Industrial Conciliation and Arbitration.* Cambridge: Cambridge University Press.

Kaufman, B. 2000. "Accomplishments and Shortcomings of Nonunion Employee Representation in the Pre-Wagner Act Years: A Reassessment." In B. Kaufman and D. Taras (eds.), *Nonunion Employee Representation: History, Contemporary Practice, and Policy*, pp. 21–60. Armonk, NY: M. E. Sharpe.

———. 2007. "The Development of HRM in Historical and International Perspective." In P. Boxall, J. Purcell, and P. Wright (eds.), *Oxford Handbook of Human Resource Management*, pp. 19–47. Oxford: Oxford University Press.

———. 2013. "Keeping the Commitment Model Up in the Air During Turbulent Times: Employee Involvement at Delta Air Lines." *Industrial Relations*, 52(S1): 343–77.

Kaufman, B., and D. Taras. 2000. *Nonunion Employee Representation: History, Contemporary Practice, and Policy*. Armonk, NY: M. E. Sharpe.

———. 2010. "Employee Participation through Non-Union Forms of Employee Representation." In A. Wilkinson, P. Gollan, M. Marchington, and D. Lewin (eds.), *The Oxford Handbook of Participation in Organizations*, pp. 258–85. Oxford: Oxford University Press.

Kim, J., J. MacDuffie, and F. Pil. 2010. "Employee Voice and Organizational Performance: Team versus Representative Influence." *Human Relations*, 63(3): 371–94.

Klaas, B., J. Olson-Buchanan, and A. Ward. 2012. "The Determinants of Alternative Forms of Workplace Voice: An Integrative Perspective." *Journal of Management*, 38(1): 314–45.

Kochan, T. 1998. "What Is Distinctive about Industrial Relations Research?" In K. Whitfield and G. Strauss (eds.), *Researching the World of Work*, pp. 31–50. Ithaca, NY: Cornell University Press.

Leitch, J. 1919. *Man-to-Man: The Story of Industrial Democracy*. New York: Forbes.

LeRoy, M. 2000. "Do Employee Participation Groups Violate Section 8(a)(2) of the National Labor Relations Act? An Empirical Analysis." In B. Kaufman and D. Taras (eds.), *Nonunion Employee Representation: History, Contemporary Practice, and Policy*, pp. 287–306. Armonk, NY: M. E. Sharpe.

Lipset, S., and N. Meltz. 2000. "Estimates of Nonunion Employee Representation in the United States and Canada: How Different Are the Two Countries?" In B. Kaufman and D. Taras (eds.), *Nonunion Employee Representation: History, Contemporary Practice, and Policy*, pp. 287–306. Armonk, NY: M. E. Sharpe.

Lucio, M. 2010. "Labour Process and Marxist Perspectives on Employee Participation." In A. Wilkinson, P. Gollan, M. Marchington, and D. Lewin (eds.), *Oxford Handbook of Participation in Organizations*, pp. 131–63. New York: Oxford University Press.

MacDowell, L. 2000. "Company Unionism in Canada." In B. Kaufman and D. Taras (eds.), *Nonunion Employee Representation: History, Contemporary Practice, and Policy*, pp. 96–120. Armonk, NY: M. E. Sharpe.

Moriguchi, C. 2005. "Did American Welfare Capitalist Employers Breach Their Implicit Contracts During the Great Depression? Preliminary Findings from Company-Level Data." *Industrial and Labour Relations Review*, 59(1): 51–81.

Morrison, E. 2011. "Employee Voice Behavior: Integration and Directions for Future Research." *Academy of Management Annals*, 4: 373–412.

Nieuhauser, W. 2014. "Works Councils." In A. Wilkinson, J. Donaghey, T. Dundon, and R. Freeman (eds.), *The Handbook of Research on Employee Voice*, pp. 247–63. Northampton: Elgar.

Nivens, M. M. 1967. *Personnel Management 1913–1963*. London: Institute of Personnel Management.

Pyman, A. 2014. "Joint Consultative Councils." In A. Wilkinson, J. Donaghey, T. Dundon, and R. Freeman (eds.), *The Handbook of Research on Employee Voice*, pp. 264–80. Northampton: Elgar.

Rees, J. 2010. *Representation and Rebellion: The Rockefeller Plan at the Colorado Fuel and Iron Company 1914–1942*. Boulder: University of Colorado Press.

Richardson, J. 2010. "In Name Only: Employee Participation Programs and Delegated Managerial Authority after *Crown, Cork & Seal*." *Administrative Law Review*, 62(3): 871–905.

Simms, M., and A. Charlwood. 2010. "Trade Unions: Power and Influence in a Changed Context." In T. Colling and M. Terry (eds.), *Industrial Relations: Theory and Practice*, pp. 125–48.Chichester, UK: Wiley & Sons.

Taras, D. 1997. "Why NonUnion Representation Is Legal in Canada." *Relations Industrielles/Industrial Relations*, 52(4): 761–80.

———. 2000. "Portrait of Nonunion Employee Representation in Canada: History, Law, and Contemporary Plans." In B. Kaufman and D. Taras (eds.), *Nonunion Employee Representation: History, Contemporary Practice, and Policy*, pp. 121–46. Armonk, NY: M. E. Sharpe.

———, and B. Kaufman. 2006. "Nonunion Employee Representation in North America: Diversity, Controversy and Uncertain Future." *Industrial Relations Journal*, 37(5): 513–42.

Teicher, J., P. Holland, A. Pyman, and B. Cooper. 2007. "Australian Workers: Finding Their Voices?" In R. Freeman, P. Boxall, and P. Haynes (eds.), *What Workers Say: Employee Voice in the Anglo-American Workplace*, pp. 125–44. Ithaca, NY: Cornell University Press.

Timur, A., D. Taras, and A. Ponak. 2012. 'Shopping for Voice': Do Pre-Existing Non-Union Representation Plans Matter When Employees Unionize? *British Journal of Industrial Relations*, 50: 214–38.

Towers, B. 1997. *The Representation Gap: Change and Reform in the British and American Workplace*. Oxford: Oxford University Press.

Wailes, N. 2010. "Employment Relations in Australia and New Zealand." In M. Barry and A. Wilkinson (eds.), *Research Handbook of Comparative Employment Relations*, pp. 286–302. Northampton: Elgar.

Webb, S., and B. Webb. 1897. *Industrial Democracy*. London: Longmans, Green.

Wilkinson, A., J. Donaghey, T. Dundon, and R. Freeman. 2014. *The Handbook of Research on Employee Voice*. Northampton: Elgar.

———, T. Dundon, Mick Marchington, and Peter Ackers. 2004. "Changing Patterns of Employee Voice: Case Studies from the UK and Republic of Ireland." *Journal of Industrial Relations*, 46(3): 298–322.

———, P. Gollan, M. Marchington, and D. Lewin. 2010. "Conceptualizing Employee Participation in Organizations." In A. Wilkinson, P. Gollan, M. Marchington, and D. Lewin (eds.), *Oxford Handbook of Participation in Organizations*, pp. 3–25. Oxford: Oxford University Press.

Willman, P., R. Gomez, and A. Bryson. 2009. "Voice at the Workplace: Where Do We Find It, Why Is It There, and Where Is It Going?" In W. Brown, A. Bryson, J. Forth, and K. Whitfield (eds.), *The Evolution of the Modern Workplace*, pp. 97–119. Cambridge: Cambridge University Press.

Wood, S., and T. Wall. 2007. "Work Enrichment and Employee Voice in Human Resource Management-Performance Studies." *International Journal of Human Resource Management*, 18: 1335–72.

Wright, C. 2014. "Human Resource Management in Australia: Historical Development and Contemporary Tensions." In B. Kaufman (ed.), *The Historical Development of Human Resource Management Across Nations*, pp. 46–65. Northampton: Elgar.

Part I
Australia

2 NER at Suncorp Group
The Suncorp Group Employee Council

Paul J. Gollan and Ying Xu

INTRODUCTION

Non-union employee representation (NER) can be generally defined as 'one or more employees who act in an agency function for other employees in dealings with management over issues of mutual concern, including the terms and conditions under which people work' (Kaufman and Taras 2000: 7). More specifically, Kaufman and Taras (2010) describe the way NER works as

> Selected workers' representatives meet with managers, usually in committee-type structures in which communication and exchange of thoughts is fostered. Representatives usually are internal to the company and serve in leadership roles for limited terms. NER is based on a quid pro quo between managers and workers. In setting up such plans, management expects that the plans will encourage cooperative, advisory, and consultative modes of interaction so that problems can be creatively resolved and frictions amicably reduced. In taking on a representational function, workers expect that NER will provide a meaningful forum for employee voice, a capacity to influence managerial decision making and recognition by managers that workers have a right to fair and respectful treatment.
>
> (p. 259)

NER as an indirect form of employee voice has attracted growing academic, managerial, and policy interest. This renewed interest has been largely attributed to two factors: first, the desire and the practices of management to improve organisational efficiency through high-involvement/ high-performance working systems and second, the reality of declining trade union membership and the resulting 'representation gap' (Dundon and Gollan 2007; Gollan 2007; Kaufman and Taras 2010; Markey 2007). In Australia in 2010, union membership had dropped to 18 per cent, with approximately 41 per cent of the workforce in the public sector unionised and only 14 per cent in the private sector (Australian Bureau of Statistics [ABS] 2011). Various mechanisms for employee voice enjoyed a period of concerted interest and some legislative support in Australia between the late 1980s to the mid-1990s, but these have since been eroded. With continuous processes of mergers, takeovers, reorganisation, and internationalisation of companies and the growing global character of business, it is important for Australia to develop countervailing power at the corporate level (Knudsen and Markey 2002). This is particularly relevant in private-sector firms, where organisational change is now being perceived by employees more as the norm than the exception and where recent corporate collapses have highlighted the vulnerability of employee stakeholder interests in comparison to the interests of other corporate stakeholders, particularly shareholders (Muir 2003).

Despite the renewed interest in NER, case studies undertaken in Australia remain limited, especially within the services sector (Gollan 2006; Markey 2007), the sector that accounts for about 80 per cent of industry contribution to GDP (Australian Trade Commission 2013). Furthermore, although there is a long history of non-union forms of employee participation in Australia, 'little is really known about their long-term successes and failures' (Markey 2007: 193). Building on initial studies by Gollan (2006) and Markey (2007) on the Suncorp Metway Employee Council (SMEC), which has been recently renamed Suncorp Group Employee Council (SGEC), this study begins to fill the research gap through exploring the changes and development of the SMEC/SGEC over the last decade (2002–2012). This longitudinal case study will enhance the knowledge base on the detailed operations, processes, and evolution of existing NER arrangements in Australia.

Suncorp Group is unique given its extensive customer base and its high profile in the finance industry as a largely non-union organisation. It is one of the few large firms in Australia with a relatively formal and established non-union representative framework. The Employee Council at Suncorp Group is an unusual NER arrangement, representing Suncorp employees since 1988 through an entity that is different from both the works council and Joint Consultative Committee (JCC) models.

The remainder of this chapter outlines the research methodology and introduces the external and organisational contexts. We then examine the SGEC's development in structure, functions, and outcomes within a changing external and organisational context, with a focus on evaluating the legitimacy and effectiveness over time of the SGEC as a form of non-union employee representation. Given that sufficient literature reviews on NER have been covered elsewhere in this book (such as Chapter 1), this chapter will not devote a separate section to reviewing the literature on NER; however, we will draw on relevant literature for analysis and discussion of implications.

METHODOLOGY

This study adopts a mixed-methods case study approach, involving both qualitative and quantitative methodologies. A case study approach is particularly appropriate for observing and understanding events within the context in which they take place and for examining how events unfold, exploring causal relationships, and 'researching motives, power relations, or processes that involve understanding complex social interactions' (Kitay and Callus 1998: 104). A case study can be conducted using qualitative or quantitative methods or a combination of both (Yin 2003). The mixed-method approach assists theoretical advancement and provides a more convincing explanation of how processes relate to outcomes, enhancing the robustness of the research (Davis et al. 2011; Ivankova et al. 2006).

This three-stage case study was initially conducted between 2002 and 2004 (Study 1), with data collected through an employee survey, focus groups, and semistructured in-depth interviews with Suncorp Group staff members at all levels, SGEC representatives, and members at the SGEC executive office. The survey (conducted in March 2004) was designed to reveal company-wide representation of employees' attitudes towards the SGEC and their views on the role of trade unions at Suncorp Group. Potentially, the case study could also highlight attitudes towards management–employee relations at Suncorp. The main objectives of the survey were to capture SGEC members' and non–SGEC members' views on the information they receive in Suncorp Group, the extent to which they are consulted on workplace matters, and the avenues for representation available to Suncorp employees (Gollan 2006). This was the first survey of its kind for Suncorp employees, and while the survey provides empirical evidence in relation to employee awareness, perceptions of, and attitudes towards the SGEC as their representative entity, the focus groups and interviews also enable an understanding of processes and mechanisms and why certain policies and procedures had been adopted. Additionally, a range of documentation from Suncorp Group and the SGEC was consulted for information triangulation.

Two subsequent studies were conducted in 2009 (Study 2) and 2011 to 2012 (Study 3), employing similar data collection methods (in-depth interviews, employee survey, and examination of documentation). These two studies were conducted following two major external events: the 2008 global financial crisis (GFC) and the enactment of the Fair Work Act 2009 (*Cth*). Table 2.1 provides an overview of the data collection components and respondents involved. The primary focus of these two studies was to identify major changes in and development of the SGEC and to gain more insight into the Suncorp NER over time and within changing contexts. To best achieve this research aim, selected key informants who had been interviewed in earlier stages were revisited wherever available. Otherwise, people

Table 2.1   Overview of Major Data Collection Components and Number of Participants

Data Collection Components	Focus Groups and/or Semistructured In-depth Interview	Employee Survey
Study 1 (2002–2004)	Twenty-six interviews involving staff at all levels, SGEC representatives, and members at the SGEC executive office, and one focus group involving twelve employees	$n = 1,449$ (Response rate: 28%)
Study 2 (2009)	Twenty-four interviews involving staff at all levels, SGEC representatives, and members at the SGEC executive office	$n = 1,486$ (Response rate: 30%)
Study 3 (2011–2012)	Three interviews with key informants at the SGEC executive office	$n = 2,951$ (Response rate: 46%)
Total	Fifty-three interviews	$N = 5,886$

employed in the same positions in the organisation as the original respondents were interviewed instead. In total, this case study involved fifty-three in-depth interviews, one focus group with employees, and three waves of annual employee surveys.

THE EXTERNAL AND ORGANISATIONAL CONTEXTS

Dundon and Gollan (2007) have suggested that in the non-union setting, employee voice has to be contextualised against a broader set of managerial strategies, worker responses, and internal and external environmental influences. Marchington and colleagues (2001) point out the issues in a simple model of managerial choice for employee consultation and representation and call attention to several factors that impinge on employers' choice of voice arrangements, including the regulatory environment and the organisational culture and history (see also Ackers et al. 2005; Johnstone et al. 2010). Therefore our research will examine the SGEC's changes and its development within the major external and organisational contexts so as to assist future development of contingency theories in relation to NER formation and effectiveness. In the following section, we discuss the context for this study at three levels: regulatory, industry/sector, and organisational.

The Regulatory Environment in Australia

Australian industrial relations (IR) systems dating back to the 1900s have been predominantly centralised systems of conciliation and arbitration. However, IR systems have undergone some transformation over the past two decades. From the early 1990s, the focus of the system shifted away from regulation towards 'enterprise-level bargaining'. Through this process, improvements in wages and working conditions were linked to business productivity and efficiency measures (Campling 1998; Forsyth 2009). The Australian Labor government under Paul Keating introduced nationwide reforms to extend enterprise bargaining to the non-union sector. These reforms were introduced under the Industrial Relations Reform Act 1993, making NER structures a topic of serious discussion and debate. The collective agreements made through enterprise bargaining were regulated and enforceable under statute. However, these provisions did not prescribe the means (structure or mechanisms) through which such consultation was to occur (Mitchell et al. 1997: 203).

In 1996, John Howard's Coalition (conservative) Government took office after thirteen years of Labor rule. The Coalition swiftly implemented deregulatory labour law reforms by way of the Workplace Relations Act (WRA) 1996, aimed mainly at speeding up the shift to enterprise bargaining and allowing (for the first time under federal law) the making of individual statutory agreements (known as Australian Workplace Agreements or AWAs). However, it was not until the Coalition gained control of the Australian Senate in the 2004 federal election that it was able to fully implement its agenda for labour market deregulation. This was in the form of the 'Work Choices' legislation—widely considered 'the most far-reaching reforms of Australian IR system since 1904' (Forsyth 2009: 2). The changes (which commenced operation on 27 March 2006) included allowing AWAs to totally override awards and collective agreements (so that, for example, award conditions such as overtime or penalty rates could be removed without compensation to employees); limiting the functions and powers of the Australian Industrial Relations Commission (AIRC); and placing significant constraints on trade union activity and industrial action. The policy rationale for these reforms was to avoid the influence of 'external third parties' from workplace relations, enabling employers and employees to deal directly with each other for the benefit of the organisation and (subsequently) the national economy (Forsyth 2009: 3).

Work Choices proved to be deeply unpopular in the Australian community, and this contributed to the defeat of the Howard Government in the November 2007 election. The new Labor Government subsequently implemented the Fair Work Act 2009 (*Cth*) (FWA). The FWA encourages collective bargaining and employee representation through a pluralistic approach encompassing both union and non-union forms. Enterprise agreements under Parts 2–4 of the FWA can be negotiated between various bargaining representatives of employers and employees, for which unions have automatic bargaining representative status if any of their members employed in the organisation are covered by the agreement, except where employees appoint someone else to act as their bargaining representative (Forsyth 2012). This provision has opened up opportunities for NER in collective bargaining. Meanwhile, the FWA requires enterprise agreements to include a provision requiring consultation of representatives about major workplace change (FWA s 205). In September 2011, 43.4 per cent of the workforce in Australia was covered by enterprise agreements, among which 67 per cent of agreements were union and 33 per cent were non-union (ABS 2012; Fair Work Review Panel 2012: 142–43). It is expected that the mandatory nature of consultation will lead to a correlative increase in numbers of representative consultation arrangements over major workplace change, although currently the mandated scope for consultation is limited and there is still a lack of prescribed structure when compared with the EU Directive (Gollan and Patmore 2012, 2013).

The Australian Financial Sector

The financial sector (which includes banking, insurance, and building societies, etc.) has been the third–fourth largest sector and among the fastest growing in the Australian economy over the past ten years. In fact, the sector has most recently become the largest contributor to the Australian economy, eclipsing mining, manufacturing, and construction (Innovation and Business Skills Australia [IBSA] 2013). The finance sector generates approximately $400bn in revenue each year, with almost half of this coming from superannuation funds that are largely nonemploying establishment. The strength of the Australian financial services industry was evident in the resilience of the Australian economy during the financial downturn. Australian banks are among the strongest in the world, and there is a sophisticated system of regulation in place. The strength of the financial services industry is underpinned by mandated retirement savings, a highly skilled and multilingual workforce, and advanced business infrastructure. This sector employs around 432,000 people (approximately 349,000 in the 2006 census), with half of them working in the banking sector (IBSA 2013). Employment in a number of occupations in the industry was contracted in the last five years due to the ongoing efficiencies created by technology and the impact of the financial downturn. However, all sectors are expected to increase employment levels over the next five years (IBSA 2013).

Employee participation practices have been extremely diverse within the sector and similar to events in the UK (see, for example, Upchurch et al.

2006); the financial service sector has been especially affected by mergers, acquisitions, and takeovers in conjunction with deregulation and then reregulation of financial markets. After the 2008 GFC, the Australian government, through the Australian Prudential Regulation Authority (APRA), introduced a range of measures for stronger financial prudency while maintaining appropriate levels of market competition (Australian Government 2013). This process has meant further competition pressure for financial institutions to maintain profit margins and/or gain increased market share within current market conditions.

The Suncorp Group

Suncorp Group (2013a) includes leading general insurance, banking, life insurance, and superannuation brands in Australia and New Zealand. The Group has around 16,000 employees and relationships with nine million customers. It is a Top 20 ASX–listed company with more than $93bn in assets and a market capitalisation of $14.4bn (Suncorp Group 2013a). It has five core businesses: Personal Insurance, Commercial Insurance, Vero New Zealand, Suncorp Bank, and Suncorp Life (Suncorp Group 2013a). The company was originally created in December 1996 from a merger of three entities: Suncorp, QIDC, and Metway Bank of Queensland. The first two of these organisations were previously owned by the State of Queensland: Suncorp was originally the State Government Insurance Office (SGIO), which commenced operations in 1916 and eventually extended its operations into superannuation, building society, and finance activities. QIDC evolved from the Queensland Agricultural Bank that was established in 1902. The Metway Bank had been the Metropolitan Permanent Building Society before converting to bank status and listing on the Australian Stock Exchange in 1988. In 1990, the new Metway Bank also had acquired Prudential Finance Limited and, in 1992, the Household Building Society. The 1996 merger was proposed by the Queensland government, which originally held 68 per cent of shares but over the next two years sold all its shareholding in two special public issues. The group then further expanded through a series of large-scale mergers and acquisitions. In 2001, Suncorp Metway acquired AMP's Australian general insurance interests, which included GIO Australia, and obtained controlling shareholdings in the insurance operations of RACQ in Queensland, RAA in South Australia, and RACT in Tasmania (Suncorp Group 2013b). In 2007, Suncorp Metway merged with Promina (which owned brands including AAMI, APIA, Shannons, and Vero), forming the Suncorp Group.

This constant organisational change, especially the large-scale mergers, acquisitions, and restructuring, has provided a complex employment relations environment (see also Gollan 2006; Markey 2007). Many employees have experienced redundancies, redeployment, relocation, and changed working conditions. The company has also significantly altered its status of enterprise agreement with employees: its 2001 merger with GIO and the major defeat suffered by the Finance Sector Union (FSU) during this process has in effect reduced the FSU power structure and role in the negotiation process—the FSU was suddenly no longer a party to agreements. Suncorp's non-union certified agreement was negotiated with Agreement Development Teams (ADTs) comprising volunteers who receive 60 per cent time off from their normal work duties for ADT activities. The agreement covers around half of all staff, with the remainder on individual contracts. The SMEC then became formally recognised as the main advisory body to the ADTs (Markey 2007). These agreements were renegotiated after the implementation of the FWA in 2009. By 2012, Suncorp employees were mostly covered by an enterprise agreement with only a few (less than 1 per cent) senior managers covered by individual contracts (2012 interviews). Interestingly, upon enactment of the FWA, the FSU was again able to represent Suncorp Group employees as one major bargaining party negotiating for the enterprise agreement. This was made possible under the 2009 FWA (FWA s. 2–4) due to its effect of strengthening union power (see explanation in the Australian regulatory environment). Although there are also approximately twenty other negotiation participants, they are largely individual employees who decided to negotiate for themselves. The union membership level at Suncorp Group has remained at about 4 per cent since 2009, whereas this level was much higher (13 per cent) back in 2002 (2004 survey and 2009 and 2012 interviews with SGEC).

From 2009 to 2012, no significant merger took place at Suncorp Group, although there are still ongoing restructuring and redundancies as a result of organisational partnering and outsourcing/offshoring. In these processes, the SGEC supported employees through the processes of being redeployed— some of them found other roles in the organisation and some were retrenched. During such processes, the situations that staff members face can be quite difficult. For example, people who were retrenched were given the responsibility of training the people who were coming in to do the role from the outsourced or partnering companies (2012 interviews with SGEC).

SUNCORP GROUP EMPLOYEE COUNCIL (SGEC)—AN EVOLUTION OVER TWENTY-FIVE YEARS

SGEC (the Council) has evolved over a period of some twenty-five years. It originated as the Metway Group Industrial Organisation of Employees (MGIOE) in a small Queensland regional bank (Metway Bank) of around 600 employees in 1988 (Gollan 2006; Markey 2007; Muir 2003). While most other large banking/financial institutions in Australia have a history of dealing with collective employee representation via unions, the rapid merger and acquisition process that has occurred in Suncorp since 1996 has shaped a number of smaller organisations into a national group of some 16,000 employees in which only a minority (approx. 4 per cent) of employees are members of trade unions. It is useful here to provide a brief snapshot of the journey taken by the Council in its promotion of employee voice before moving on to consider the characteristics of the Council and its comparisons to works councils.

1988–1996

In Australia, industrial relations legislation is enacted at both the federal/ national level and at the state level and can vary considerably. The Queensland industrial relations legislation in 1988 supported the negotiation of wages and conditions (traditionally the right of trade unions only) via voluntary employment agreements directly between employer and employee representatives (Muir 2003). After a failed attempt by the Finance Sector Union to try to negotiate terms and conditions with Metway management, a group of employees approached management, established a cooperative relationship, and successfully negotiated a number of favourable benefits and conditions for employees via two voluntary agreements registered in the Queensland Industrial Relations Commission in 1992 and 1994. This group of employees became the pioneers of the current-day Council. Also established at that time was an employee advisory, advocacy, and representation role for the Council in the grievance-resolution process, including representing employees in workplace disputes before the state's industrial tribunal.

1996–2002

In 1996, when Suncorp Metway was created by merger, the MGIOE became the Suncorp Metway QIDC Staff Association (SMQSA). This body was active in representing staff during an eighteen-month period of restructuring involving retrenchments and extensive workplace change. In addition to dealing with numerous individual cases, the SMQSA negotiated a superannuation increase for permanent staff, altered pay and staff banking arrangements, and a refined Retrenchment Agreement (Gaffney and Gollan 2004; Markey 2007). In late 2000, the SMQSA began a review that led to the adoption of the Strategic Plan for 2001 to 2004, which involved a move away from the enterprise union model towards an employee council. This move is also due to the rejection by the AIRC of the Council's application for setting up an enterprise union under the WRA 1996. It is argued that although the intent of the legislation's 'enterprise union' provisions under the WRA 1996 was to encourage an alternative form of enterprise-based employee representation, the rigours of meeting the registration criteria and combating the resistance of trade unions have meant only a handful of successful registration applications (Muir 2003). This change towards the employee council model also meant that while the Council still offered a 'collective' enterprise voice for all employees in the organisation and could continue to assist employees with dispute resolution, its powers no longer extended to negotiating with management on wages and conditions. At a special conference in June 2001, a change of name to SMEC was adopted together with a new constitution (Markey 2007). SMEC was incorporated on October 9, 2001, with its goal 'to improve the lives of employees through promotion of the principles of continuing employability, equity, recognition and reward' (Markey 2007: 197).

In terms of role and function, the SGEC aims to provide employees with 'an independent avenue to voice their ideas, opinions and concerns about issues that concern their working lives' (Markey 2007: 197). SMEC (2003: 1) also states that it 'exists to lobby management on group issues, provide individuals with an independent avenue to voice grievances and to offer assistance to all staff in times of dispute'. Essentially, the SMEC provides free advocacy and advisory services, representation on major issues of concern such as dispute resolution, HR information sessions, and grievance resolution to all employees. Other services offered by the SMEC exclusively to members include discount schemes, accounting and taxation services, legal services, fitness and sport activities, and special information sessions concerning policy and legislative requirements.

2002–2012

Both the function and structure of the Employee Committee remained largely unchanged over the past decade. However, its executive office underwent a major change in 2006: the member services and support functions that were previously outsourced to a consultancy company were internalised, and the new executive officer recruited a team consisting of Suncorp employees to provide these services. The rationale for the move was to provide better access to the senior management in the organisation and to achieve a far greater acceptance by the employees (2009 and 2012 interviews). The new executive office uses Suncorp facilities and meeting rooms. The case volume has recorded a significant increase since 2006 as a result of the internalisation of the executive office functions. Also contributing to this growth in cases is the merger with Promina in 2007, which saw the raw number of employees almost doubled from about 8,000 to 16,000 employees organisation-wide. The Council also changed its name from SMEC to SGEC following this most recent merger and the name change of the organisation.

The SGEC (2013) now sets its mission as being 'to provide Suncorp Group employees and other stakeholders with individual and group services that focus on: credible and timely information, professional and balanced mediation, independent and passionate advocacy, credible and focussed representation'. To achieve this goal, the SGEC has recently started to strengthen the employee voice mechanisms within the organisation and describes its role as being twofold:

- It is first a safety valve, providing an effective internal mechanism to assist all Suncorp Group employees manage and resolve workplace issues; and
- Second, it is a voice mechanism within the Suncorp Group, providing a means through which all Suncorp Group employees can have input into decisions which affect their working lives.

Noticeably, although the SGEC will continue to perform its core function of assisting employees at work, especially with dispute resolution, it now has a dual focus on employee voice; the SGEC describes it as a 360-degree feedback loop which intends to enable two-way communication between employees and the management. Voice mechanism will be the new strategic focus for the next two years. A Voice Strategy Manager has been specifically employed for this goal in 2012.

MANAGEMENT MOTIVES FOR NER

Managerial attitudes and strategies to avoid or substitute unionisation have been identified as the most significant influence on organisational choice and outcomes of NER within the integrated framework proposed by Dundon and Gollan (2007: 1194). The union-avoidance motive is evident in the case of the SGEC: the Finance Sector Union (FSU) had enjoyed a strong presence in a previous company before it was merged into Suncorp. However, despite a vigorous campaign, the FSU suffered a major defeat in 2002 when a large majority of the previous company's employees voted in favour of the non-union agreement, Suncorp/GIO General Insurance Business Integration Agreement under the Workplace Relations Act 1996. The FSU had campaigned strongly among staff to reject the Agreement. According to the FSU, the Agreement facilitated Suncorp's objective of developing uniform conditions between GIO and Suncorp staff by providing for GIO staff conditions to be contained in individual employment contracts, thus allowing more advantageous conditions to be 'whittled away' (Finance Sector Union 2003; Markey 2007). SMEC and FSU officers believe that GIO staff voted for the 170LK non-union agreement because of fear that if they rejected it, they would be left without access to any agreement to protect their conditions. At that stage, Suncorp has successfully pursued a unitarist policy of dealing directly with its employees without the intervention of the FSU. The FSU has an estimated membership density of about 10 to 12 per cent in Suncorp as a whole (Clifford and Hannan, 2005). Suncorp was refusing to consult with the FSU, which experienced difficulty in communicating with staff because Suncorp blocked its email access and physically prevented entry of union officials to workplaces (Clifford and Hannan, 2005).

Meanwhile, many SGEC and non-represented respondents were not convinced that unions alone would solve these issues. The challenge for unions at Suncorp is the lack of confidence, among SGEC members and those with no representation, regarding core trade union activities. Moreover, the 2004 survey results also suggest that most respondents believe that the SGEC should play a very important role regarding increases in pay and benefits and changes to work practices (with 90 per cent and 86 per cent consider very/fairly important, respectively).

Adding to these issues is the marginalisation strategy used by the FSU in excluding the SGEC from its industrial campaigns during 2002 to 2004 in response to management's union-substitution and union-avoidance strategies. Such an approach contrasts with union strategies of colonisation as a response to union avoidance as seen in the UK (Gollan, 2002). Union membership at Suncorp dropped from approximately 13 per cent in 2004 to about 4 per cent in 2009 and essentially remained at this lower level until 2012.

Apart from union avoidance, another major reason for Suncorp management to establish NER arrangements was a desire to have a more direct relationship with employees without the mediating forces of a third party through union representation. On a positive note, it seems that employees in general are satisfied with their relationship with management, with our longitudinal findings consistently indicating positive views of management from lower-level employees on a range of issues (see also Table 2.2 for positive results from the three annual employee surveys on perceived relations between employees and managers at Suncorp). This lack of dissatisfaction could also indicate that any campaign by the trade union movement (or, for that matter, the SGEC) to target and capture the hearts and minds of this non-represented group of employees at Suncorp may present a number of challenges.

LEGITIMACY OF THE SGEC

Gaffney (2002: 150–1) has identified five points of reference for examining the legitimacy of non-union forms of employee participation: composition, independence, representivity, expertise, and accountability. Applying these to the case of the SGEC and drawing on Muir (2003) and Markey (2007), we assess the legitimacy of its structure and process.

Composition

The Employee Committee is made up of twenty-five 'councillors' representing different business units. The councillors meet quarterly and canvas and promote employee views and opinions and lobby management on behalf of employees. As discussed earlier, this committee structure has remained unchanged over the past decade. It administers the Council between Annual General Meetings and is elected every three years by a secret ballot of members. These councillors also elect an Employee Committee Executive of five members, comprising the president, two vice presidents, secretary and treasurer. The five committee executive members meet every month. In addition to the Annual General Meeting, a special general meeting may be called upon by the Employee Committee or by a written request of at least 10 per cent of members (Markey 2007).

Alongside the employee committee, there is an executive office of the SGEC, which provides employee consultation and membership services on a daily basis. The main SGEC executive office is located in Brisbane and has had an executive officer employed full time since 2006. Under the leadership of this executive officer, there are currently four full-time and one part-time industrial relations advisors (located at Brisbane, Sydney, and Melbourne), one full-time Voice Strategy Manager, and two administrators, an increase from a total of five people in 2004.

Independence

The SGEC is a separate legal entity and is governed by its Constitution. Based on its 2001 Memorandum of Understanding, a guaranteed level of funding is provided to the Council by Suncorp Group: initially up to 0.5 per cent of yearly gross profit, which was later changed to an amount directly given per staff member (2002, 2009, and 2012 interviews). This is similar to the statutory provisions for funding provided for works councils (Muir 2003). While councillors do not enjoy statutory backing for their duties and functions under the agreement mentioned, they are allowed some time off from normal duties to undertake SGEC work and receive an allowance for training and development. The councillors are also provided protection against detrimental action by the employer, financial and technical resources, and access to external service providers, such as legal advice, when required. Councillors follow a Code of Conduct in performance of their Council duties and are assessed annually by the Executive Committee against set objectives based on the promotion of employee interests.

The Council considers that it has demonstrated its independence from the influences of external unions and management and that it provides membership services, autonomously sets its own budget, and engages staff to assist in the administration of its operations and that it offers support and advocates for employees in the grievance-resolution process. In reality, a cautionary note is needed regarding this independence, as the funds for the SGEC are provided from the HR line budget and are subject to certain strict conditions. The 'guarantee' in fact has no legal status and can be withdrawn at any time with thirty days' notice or when more than half of the Employee Committee are or become union members (Gaffney and Gollan, 2004). It could be argued that this not only undermines the independent voice at the SGEC but also can be used as a union-avoidance strategy to suppress union recognition (Gollan 2006).

Representivity

Suncorp Group currently has about 16,000 employees, with half of them being SGEC members. The membership rate is up from 35 per cent in 2004 on a smaller employee base (Markey 2007), with the SGEC aiming to eventually represent all staff at the Suncorp Group. Employee representation though the SGEC is facilitated through twenty-five elected employee Councillors and a team of around twenty delegated regional/interstate committee members who canvas the views of employees in their work areas across the nation. A major responsibility of the Councillor's role is to regularly communicate with his/her constituents on issues that affect employees in the organisation and report those issues for attention at Council meetings. This is achieved through a variety of means including staff surveys or individual or group meetings when approached by employees. The Council then makes a decision on which of those issues should be brought to the attention of management. The core representative services of the SGEC are available to all employees, whereas some extra membership benefits were developed exclusively for members, including a discount buyer scheme, taxation accounting and legal services, and a health club. Membership is free and simply requires completion of an application form. SGEC members enjoy exclusive right of committee election compared with non-members.

Expertise

The Council provides a development program to educate and maintain the skills of Councillors. The program involves training on topics such as employee relations, conflict resolution, public speaking, meeting procedures, and so forth. The Council has the ability to engage the services of external consultants such as industrial advocates and occupational health and safety specialists to assist on particular issues. Council meetings are conducted quarterly and a formal agenda is circulated prior to all meetings. Individual councillors are delegated to conduct research on employee-related issues for reporting to and consideration by the Council. All councillors make a formal report to the meeting on topical matters in their work area and communicate outcomes back to employee constituents.

Prior to the internalisation of the SGEC in 2006, it largely relied upon the expertise of an external consultant as its executive office. Now, through its internal employee relations advisors, the council offers all employees advice, advocacy, and representation services and brokers independent mediation on workplace disputes. It also offers information sessions for employees on 'hot spots' in policy interpretation identified from employee feedback and on employee rights and obligations along with training programs tailored for line managers and supervisors (2002, 2009, and 2012 interviews). The Council performs an advisory role to employees during the renewal of certified agreements by offering a benchmarking and information service on employment terms and conditions.

Accountability

Accountability infers that management cannot provide employee representatives with the necessary mandate—this must be obtained directly through the decision of colleagues and thus the electing of representatives is considered the appropriate mechanism (Gaffney 2002). Employees in the organisation are eligible to nominate themselves for election to the Council every three years. The election process is conducted by an external independent scrutineer, and the Council Constitution provides a mechanism to temporarily fill casual vacancies between elections to maintain interim representativity. As a corporate entity, the Council is also required to produce audited annual financial statements on its accounting operations at its Annual General Meeting and submit these to the Queensland and federal statutory bodies with which it is registered. Under all these dimensions, the SGEC can substantiate its legitimacy as a non-union representative of employee voice.

SGEC COMPARED WITH WORKS COUNCIL AND JCC MODELS

To fully understand the nature and operation of the SGEC, a brief comparison with two dominant NER models, the European Works Council model and the Australian Joint Consultative Committee (JCC) model, is provided.

SGEC versus the Works Council Model

The NER at Suncorp Group, the SGEC, is consistent with the European Works Council model in the following ways: it is company based and consists entirely of and is managed by elected employees (see also Gollan 2006; Markey 2007). Despite being a legally independent entity, the Council is fully funded by Suncorp management, which also resembles the works council model. The major area in which the works council model is more influential than the Suncorp NER model is in the scope of employee participation. Works councils have mandated co-determination rights on important matters such as company organisation, working hours, holidays, technical monitoring of employee conduct or performance, accident-prevention rules, occupational diseases and health-protection regulations, allocation of company-owned housing or termination of tenancy as well as company pay structures, remuneration principles, and bonus and incentive schemes (Muir 2003). The SGEC aims to represent all employees. However, it has no power of co–decision making like the kind enjoyed by works councils, and it has no statutory basis. Its representation scope is yet to be extended to cover wages and conditions, although the SGEC has played an important advisory role to Suncorp employees during renegotiation of their collective agreement. On the other hand, the SGEC focuses on a non-adversarial relationship with management, which is typical of a works council approach, while it differs from many European works councils in not being able to draw on wider resources by linking informally with a union (Markey 2007).

Additionally, works councils have considerable say in job descriptions, work processes, and so on. In certain circumstances, the employer must obtain approval from works councils on matters concerning personnel, such as hiring, job classification, departmental restructuring, and transfers, while works councils can refuse under governing law to give approval. The employer must also consult the works council before any dismissal; otherwise the dismissal has no effect and any dispute over the matter van be referred to the Labour Court for a decision (Muir 2003).

SGEC versus the JCC Model

The incidence of JCCs had more than doubled since 1990 in workplaces with more than twenty employees, increasing from 14 per cent to 33 per cent by 1995, and these increases were found across all industries over the last two decades (Forsyth et al. 2006; Morehead et al. 1997). Morehead and colleagues (1997) found that the development of enterprise bargaining, which had been formalised in the Industrial Relations Act 1993 (*Cth*), was a significant encouragement for the development of alternative voice mechanisms such as JCCs. The new labour law, the Fair Work Act (FWA), requires that consultation with representatives about major workplace change be a provision in an enterprise agreement (FWA s. 205). If an enterprise agreement does not contain such a provision, the model term is taken to be part of the agreement. The model term is provided in the regulations: it requires that information be provided to employees and consultation with relevant employees or appointment of an employee representative to be undertaken (FW Regs. Schedule 2.3). The representative can be a union or non-union member.

The JCC is a more common form of NER in Australia compared with Works Council and company association (Holland et al. 2009; Markey 2007). Unlike the statutory works councils, JCCs are usually initiated unilaterally by management or joint management–union agreement. They are commonly composed of up to 50 per cent managers and 50 per cent employee representatives. The employee representatives can be appointed by management or unions or, less commonly, elected directly by employees. Obviously, the SGEC differs from the typical Australian JCC in some important respects, such as composition, independence, and representivity; however, it shares similar limitations with JCCs within the context of Australia (Markey 2007). For example, JCCs usually only play an advisory role to management, representation scope is often restricted to a narrow range of issues, such as occupational health and safety, and they often have specific missions for only a limited period of time (Holland et al. 2009; Markey 2007). The inclusion of management representatives on JCCs also potentially affects their independence.

EFFECTIVENESS OF THE SGEC

The effectiveness of NER arrangements is influenced by the expectations that employers and employees bring to such arrangements. For employees, the effectiveness of NER arrangements is mainly determined by their perceptions of its influence on decision making and the extent to which these arrangements satisfy and advance employee interests. For employers, perception of NER effectiveness is related to the extent to which NER arrangements increase employee understanding of company policy, enhance employee attitudes and productivity, and secure employee consent to organisational change. The longevity of the SGEC and the continuous management and employee support have, in a way, demonstrated the value that the SGEC brings to both parties. Table 2.2 provides some longitudinal evidence from the perspectives of employees.

Given the centrality of influences on decision making to the study of employee voice in general, we turn now to an examination of the effectiveness of the SGEC in terms of its influence on organisational decision making and then assess its effectiveness on other dimensions from the perspective of employees.

Influence on Decision Making

Empirical studies of workplace relations indicate that the level of joint decision making in Australia is poor (Holland et al. 2009). Consultative committees, which are the more common form of collective employee voice generally, have an advisory capacity, with management retaining the discretion to act. In comparison to trade unions, alternative forms of employee representation in Australia have been much slower in taking root, mainly as a result of management reluctance to voluntarily cede their prerogative (Markey 2001).

Our interviews with Suncorp employees from 2002 to 2012 found that employees and the SGEC generally do not have influence on the business decision-making processes. Information sharing and consultation between the organisation and the SGEC at a level other than grievances and negotiations is mainly achieved through a consultation mechanism called the National Consultative Forum (NCF). The NCF was established in November 2003, consisting of representatives from Suncorp management and the SGEC committee members. The forum was initially only focused on occupational health and safety issues but then expanded to deal with broader policy issues (Markey 2007). The SMEC seeks an impact upon corporate policy through the NCF.

This body bears some similarities to a Works Council Special Negotiating Body, which comprises both employer and employee representatives. The written Terms of Reference agreed between the Council and management require that the forum meet quarterly to discuss a range of significant issues that affect employees at a group or national level. All participants agree that confidentiality be observed on sensitive information or discussions at forum meetings. Management nominees, including senior management HR, inform the NCF on current organisational topics, including major restructuring or programs put in place for the renewal of industrial agreements or for health and safety systems. However, the scope of the issues addressed by the NCF is yet to extend to organisational financial and business investment matters addressed by Works Councils (Muir 2003). Meanwhile, the SGEC informs management on a range of significant issues identified from employee feedback and surveys and submits proposals for consideration by the forum.

Apart from the NCF, the SGEC's new strategic focus on employee voice represents its effort on influencing management decision making on a collective basis. However, the Council does not seem to have intent to confront management about decisions in relation to restructuring or retrenchment because, first, they believe the business acumen of Suncorp management should be trusted, and, second, the SGEC wants to differentiate itself from unions' sometimes adversarial approach in dealing with management. Additionally, the SGEC's influences on the terms and conditions of the enterprise agreement are limited to an advisory and supporting role. This limitation is in part due to the lack of statutory support from the current labour law, despite its provision of consultation as mentioned.

Impact beyond Influences on Business Decision Making

Although the influence of the SGEC on business decision making is limited, its value to the organisation and employees is evident. Drawing on longitudinal data collected through the three waves of employee surveys and interviews, we assessed its impact on the following dimensions: meeting employee needs, employee awareness of and satisfaction with the SGEC, enabling of employee voice, and contribution to the cooperative and harmonious work environment. Table 2.2 provides related survey results from the three data collections of this research.

Meeting Employee Needs
In 2000, the SGEC handled some 60 cases entrusted by Suncorp employees, which grew to 330 a year by mid-2004, reflecting a dynamic change environment and restructuring in Suncorp during this period (Markey 2007). This figure has almost doubled from approximately 500 cases in 2006, to roughly 1,000 cases in 2009, during which period a merger between

Suncorp and Promina was taking place. The SGEC case load has doubled again to more than 2,000 cases annually in the three-year period between 2009 and 2012. From 2009 to 2012, the top three functions the SGEC performed included (a) dispute resolution and consultation, especially those related to retrenchment and redeployment; (b) performance management; and (c) policy interpretation. Moreover, against a background of low trade union involvement at Suncorp, overwhelmingly more respondents remain convinced that the SGEC, as opposed to a trade union, should continue to represent the workforce for a range of issues, especially when it comes to issues in relation to discipline, complaints, and pay and basic conditions (Table 2.2). Interestingly however, there is a slight increase in expecting trade union representation for employees' pay and benefits from 2009 (9%) to 2012 (11%), which may correspond to the enactment of FWA and the resultant increased trade union power since 2009 as discussed earlier.

Employee Awareness of and Satisfaction with the SGEC

There was a sharp increase in employees' awareness of the SGEC presence from 43 per cent in 2004 to 99 per cent in 2012. The level of satisfaction with services provided by the SGEC has also improved over the past few years.

Workplace IR Climate, Perceived Justice, and More

As the survey results indicate (Table 2.2), perceived relations between management and employees are generally good, especially with staff and their immediate managers (2009 and 2011 surveys). This good relationship has been maintained over time, with majority respondents (no less than 70% in all three surveys) considering the overall relations between employees and the management good (Table 2.2). The drop from 2004 to 2009 is largely attributed to the significant change of employee base as a result of the large-scale merger with Promina in 2007 (2009 interviews with SGEC). This is consistent with previous studies that show NER contribute to a more cooperative workplace culture as compared with its union counterpart (see, for example, Gollan 2007; Holland et al. 2009; Kaufman and Taras 2010; Markey 2007). Meanwhile, a majority of employees (77–79% in all three surveys) think their line managers treat them and their co-workers fairly and Suncorp Group is a desirable place to work due to the way it treats employees (69–71% from 2004 to 2011). Employees also demonstrate a high level of confidence and/or trust towards their leaders as reflected by employees' preference of having their leaders represent them for issues to do with workplace change and complaints (Table 2.2).

Because of the enterprise-specific focus of the Council and its service, it has become apparent that employees tend to approach the Council for assistance at an earlier stage of a problem or issue before it escalates to a formal dispute with management. This early intervention often results in the satisfactory resolution of matters within the enterprise that ultimately makes things easier for both management and staff to resume their work

Table 2.2 Digest of the Employee Survey Results (2004, 2009, and 2011)

	Study 1 (2004 Survey) n = 1,449	**Study 2 (2009 Survey) n = 1,486**	**Study 3 (2011 Survey) n = 2,951**
Total number of employees at Suncorp Group	8,000 employees	16,000 employees	16,000 employees
Approximate SGEC case load (additional info from SGEC)	330+ cases	1,000+ cases	2,000+ cases
What's important for employees	• Pay and basic conditions • Job security • Work/life balance	• Pay and basic conditions • Job security • Work/life balance	• Pay and basic conditions • Job security • Work/life balance
Awareness of SGEC	43%	89%	99%
Satisfaction with SGEC services	—*	67%	71%
Relations between managers and employees are good (% Agreed)	83%	70%	75%
Best representation of employees for—pay and benefits	SMEC—24% Union—12% HR—21% Myself—39% Other (Peer, coworker)—4%	SMEC—24% Union—9% HR Adviser—13% Leader**—23% Myself—26% Other (Peer, coworker, leader once removed**)—6%	SMEC—23% Union—11% HR Adviser—12% Leader**—27% Myself—22% Other (Peer, coworker, leader once removed**)—5%
Best representation of employees for—complaint about working in Suncorp	SMEC—33% Union—12% HR Adviser—16% Myself—32% Other (Peer, coworker)—7%	SMEC—30% Union—5% HR Adviser—10% Leader**—39% Myself—9% Other (Peer, coworker, leader once removed**)—7%	SMEC—29% Union—6% HR Adviser—10% Leader**—41% Myself—8% Other (Peer, coworker, leader once removed**)—5%

Best representation of employees for—discipline by manager	SMEC—29% Union—13% HR Adviser—19% Myself—33% Other (Peer, coworker)—5%	SMEC—41% Union—10% HR Adviser—10% Leader*—23% Myself—9% Other (Peer, coworker, leader once removed**)—7%	SMEC—39% Union—11% HR Adviser—10% Leader*—27% Myself—7% Other (Peer, coworker, leader once removed**)—6%
Best representation of employees for—change to workplace (immediate workplace in 2009/2011 surveys)	SMEC—26% Union—9% HR Adviser—13% Myself—37% Other (Peer, coworker)—15%	SMEC—14% Union—3% HR Adviser—4% Leader*—54% Myself—9% Other (Peer, coworker, leader once removed**)—14%	SMEC—14% Union—3% HR Adviser—5% Leader*—60% Myself—8% Other (Peer, coworker, leader once removed**)—9%
Line managers—treating employees fairly (% Agreed)	79%	77%	79%
Suncorp's treatment of employees makes it desirable to work here (% Agreed)	71%	69%	69%
I would recommend others to work at Suncorp (% Agreed)	60%	61%	62%

*Note 1: Equivalent question is not included available in the 2004 survey. Instead, *effectiveness of trade union representation* was measured with 23 per cent of respondents considering it somewhat effective to very effective;

**Note 2: These two codes, *Leader* and *Leader once removed*, are not provided in the answer list for this question in the 2004 survey.

relationship. On a number of occasions, the SGEC has lobbied management on major issues of concern that have been brought up by large numbers or groups of employees. On each of these occasions, management and SGEC representatives have engaged in extensive consultation that ultimately led to change in the decision outcome.

Encouraged by these results, the SGEC has made employee voice its strategic focus for now and over the next a couple of years. The aim of this initiative is to enable two-way or 360-degree communication between employees and management and hence increase employees' impact on organisational decision making.

CONCLUSION

NER at Suncorp Group is a unique case. It resembles the European Works Council model and is organisation-based NER with its committee members elected by employees. Union avoidance by management could be seen as a motive for its establishment. Although the SGEC is a legally separate entity, it is entirely funded by the company, which may potentially jeopardise its independence and representing power.

The SGEC so far has limited influence on organisational decision making. However, as a NER of twenty-five years' standing, it has been effective in increasing employee voice and maintaining a more cooperative labour–management relationship. This is consistent with the literature in terms of a major function of non-union forms of employee representation being to channel dissatisfaction, facilitate communication, and encourage cooperation in the absence of a strong union that could otherwise perform these functions (Gollan 2007; Kaufman and Taras 2010; Markey 2007). Terry (1999) and Watling and Snook (2003) have indicated that for a large majority of non-union firms, the main aim of NER is to enhance information sharing and communication rather than negotiation. Most of these organisations see non-union representation and consultation as providing a more effective channel of communication than that facilitated by unions, stressing more 'harmonious' and less conflicting relations with the workforce and thus building and encouraging an atmosphere of mutual cooperation. The SGEC also appears to be an effective avenue for greater workplace justice and more effective dispute resolution, which is another function of NER identified by previous research (Kaufman and Taras 2010).

Compared with the Works Council model in Europe, the SGEC model demonstrates similar limitations to those of other JCCs in Australia (see also Markey 2007). For instance, as a form of employee voice, JCCs are typically constrained to an advisory role to management and are often limited in their jurisdiction to a narrower range of issues. To the extent that JCCs rely on management discretion in their formation, structure, and powers, their limitations are clear.

Freeman and Medoff (1984) argue that where unions have been weak or entirely absent from the workplace, which is becoming increasingly the case, employers may be motivated to instigate alternative voice mechanisms through NER. However, as Taras and Kaufman (1999: 14) argue, 'It [NER] is no easy substitute for unions, and employers who believe they can use NER for this purpose are seriously deluding themselves'. This is because the interests of the employer may moderate the interests of the employees, thus not fully satisfying employees' desired outcomes. Not surprisingly, unions are usually perceived to be more effective in providing employees with representation on pay, benefits, work rules, and other 'distributive justice' issues, whereas NER arrangements are perceived to be more effective in providing employees with consultation and sometimes representation on workplace productivity, personal development, and other 'mutual gains' aspects of the employment relationship. Therefore, union representation and NER arrangements can be used to satisfy different employee and management needs and expectations within the contemporary workplace.

The current labour law allowed the FSU to resume its status of being a negotiation party for the enterprise agreement with Suncorp employees, which suggests the possibility of a more balanced employee voice solution. On the one hand, this possible solution permits the union to represent employees in collective bargaining for pay and basic conditions, a scope beyond the power of the SGEC, while on the other hand allows NER to play a complementary role in representing employees' interests and provides a channel of consultation and dispute resolution without necessarily developing an adversarial relationship with management. A harmonious and cooperative workplace environment is important to employees and employer as well as to the economy. A collaborative IR climate is associated with positive organisational outcomes and provides a supportive and healthy working environment for employees (Deery et al. 1994; Deery and Iverson 2005; Gollan and Patmore 2006; Hatch 1987). Policy makers, however, still need to consider the statutory status of NER in their influence and involvement with organisational decision making with reference to, for instance, the EU model, as some commentators have suggested (Gollan and Patmore 2006; McCallum and Patmore 2002).

Kaufman and Taras (2010) argue that NER enjoys its greatest success when used as part of a long-run, high-involvement, and high-performance work system emphasizing competitive advantage through participation. Given the devolution of decision making in many organisations and the greater focus on employee commitment and effective organisational change, these findings will be of particular interest to policy makers and practitioners looking for ways of improving workplace productivity and efficiency as well as employee well-being. Kaufman and Taras (2010) and some other commentators (see, for example, Acker et al. 2005; Dundon and Gollan 2007) suggest that the success of NER does not only rely on investment and commitment but is also contingent on a series of complex and not always controllable factors, such as the economic and legal environment. Also to be considered are internal employment contexts, including trust, managerial responsiveness, and emphasis on integrative problem solving rather than distributive bargaining; a supportive economic environment in which a win-win outcome is achieved—the company is profitable and workers enjoy job security and satisfaction; and, more importantly, a 'human asset' HRM strategy is adopted, making employees partners in a longer-term business relationship. These could also be fruitful directions for future research.

REFERENCES

Ackers, P., M. Marchington, A. Wilkinson, and T. Dundon. 2005. "Partnership and Voice with or Without Trade Unions: Changing UK Management Approaches to Organisational Participation." In M. Stuart and M. Martinez-Lucio (eds.), *Partnership and Modernisation in Employment Relations*, pp. 23–45. London: Routledge.

Australian Bureau of Statistics (ABS). 2011. *Employee Earnings, Benefits and Trade Union Membership, Australia, August 2009* (6310.0). Canberra: Australian Bureau of Statistics.

———. 2012. *Employee Earnings, Benefits and Trade Union Membership, Australia, August 2010* (6310.0). Canberra: Australian Bureau of Statistics.

Australian Government. 2013. "Australian Banking Reforms: Why Is the Government Reforming the Banking System?" Available on www.bankingreforms.gov.au/content/Content.aspx?doc=whyreform.htm, accessed July 2, 2013.

Australian Trade Commission. 2013. "Financial Services: A Sophisticated Hub for the Asia-Pacific." Available on www.austrade.gov.au/Buy/Australian-Industry-Capability/Financial-Services/default.aspx, accessed July 2, 2013.

Campling, J. T. 1998. "Workplace Bargaining in Non-Unionised Australian Firms." *International Journal of Employment Studies*, 6(1): 59–82.

Clifford, M., and D. Hannan. 2005. Queensland State Secretary and NSW Branch Organiser respectively, teleconference interview, 2 March.

Davis, D. F., S. L. Golicic, and C. N. Boerstler. 2011. "Benefits and Challenges of Conducting Multiple Methods Research in Marketing." *Journal of the Academy of Marketing Science*, 39: 467–79.

Deery, S. J., and R. D. Iverson. 2005. "Labor–Management Cooperation: Antecedents and Impact on Organizational Performance." *Industrial & Labor Relations Review*, 58(4): 588–609.

———, and P. J. Erwin. 1994. "Predicting Organizational and Union Commitment: The Effect of Industrial Relations Climate." *British Journal of Industrial Relations*, 32(4): 581–97.

Dundon, T., and P. J. Gollan. 2007. "Re-conceptualising Voice in the Non-Union Workplace." *International Journal of Human Resource Management*, 18(7): 1182–98.

Fair Work Review Panel. 2012. *Towards More Productive and Equitable Workplaces: An Evaluation of the Fair Work Legislation*. Canberra: Australian Government.

Finance Sector Union. 2003. Various Documents Relating to GIO Working Conditions in Suncorp Takeover. Article nos. 5191, 5295, 5308, 5365, 5757. Available at www.fsunion.org.au, accessed June 6, 2004.

Forsyth, A. 2009. "Good Faith Bargaining: Australian, United States and Canadian Comparisons." Paper presented at Chairman's Lunch Seminar, U.S. National Labor Relations Board, Washington DC, November 4, 2009. Available at http://papers.ssrn.com/sol3/papers.cfm?abstract_id=1509825&download=yes, accessed July 3, 2013.

———. 2012. "An American Transplant on Australian Soil: Comparing Purposes and Concepts in United States and Australian Collective Bargaining Law." In B. Creighton and A. Forsyth (eds.), *Rediscovering Collective Bargaining: Australia's Fair Work Act in International Perspectives*, pp. 203–24. New York: Routledge.

———, S. Korman, and S. Marshall. 2006. "Joint Consultative Committees in Australia: An Empirical Update." Paper presented to the Third Australian Labour Law Association National Conference, Brisbane, September 22–23.

Freeman, R., and R. Medoff. 1984. *What Do Unions Do?* New York: Basic Books.

Gaffney, F. 2002. "Reconstituting the Collective? Non-Union Employee Representative Structures in the United Kingdom and Australia." In P. J. Gollan, R. Markey, and I. Ross (eds.), *Works Councils in Australia. Future Prospects and Possibilities*, pp. 149–79. Sydney: Federation Press.

———, and P. J. Gollan. 2004. "Enterprise Unions—a False Hope or the New Frontier?" Paper presented to Employment Regulation for the Changing Workplace, 2nd Biennial Conference of the Australian Labour Law Association, University of Sydney, September 24–25.

Gollan, P. J. 2002. "So What's the News? Management Strategies towards Non-Union Representation at News International." *Industrial Relations Journal*, 33(4): 316–31.

———. 2006. "Representation at Suncorp: What Do the Employees Want?" *Human Resource Management Journal*, 16(3): 268–86.

———. 2007. *Employee Representation in Non-Union Firms*. London: Sage Publications.

——— and G. Patmore. 2006. "Transporting the European Social Partnership to Australia." *Journal of International Relations*, 48(2): 217–56.

——— and G. Patmore. 2012. Submission to the Fair Work Act 2009 (*Cth*), review panel. Available at www.deewr.gov.au/WorkplaceRelations/Policies/FairWorkAct Review/Submissions/Pages/default.aspx, accessed June 20, 2012.

——— and G. Patmore. 2013. "Perspectives of Legal Regulation and Employment Relations at the Workplace: Limits and Challenges for Employee Voice." *Journal of Industrial Relations*, 55(4): 488–506.

Hatch, O. 1987. "U.S. Labor Law and the Future of Labor–Management Cooperation." *Labor Law Journal*, 38(1): 3–10.

Holland, P., A. Pyman, B. K. Cooper, and J. Teicher. 2009. "The Development of Alternative Voice Mechanisms in Australia: The Case of Joint Consultation." *Economic & Industrial Democracy*, 30(1): 67–92.

Innovation and Business Skills Australia (IBSA). 2013. *Environment Scan— 2013: Financial Services Industry*. Available at www.ibsa.org.au/sites/default/files/media/Escan%202013%20Financial%20Services%20Industry.pdf, accessed July 3, 2013.

Ivankova, N. V., J. W. Creswell, and S. L. Stick. 2006. "Using Mixed Methods Sequential Explanatory Design: From Theory to Practice." *Field Methods*, 18(1): 3–20.

Johnstone, S., P. Ackers, and A. Wilkinson. 2010. "Better than Nothing? Is Non-Union Partnership a Contradiction in Terms?" *Journal of Industrial Relations*, 52(2): 151–68.

———, and Taras, D. G. (eds.). 2000. *Nonunion Employee Representation: History, Contemporary Practice, and Policy*. Armonk, NY: M. E. Sharpe.

———, and Taras, D. G. 2010. "Employee Participation through Non-Union Forms of Employee Representation." In A. Wilkinson, P. J. Gollan, M. Marchington, and D. Lewin (eds.), *The Oxford Handbook of Participation in Organizations*, pp. 258–85. Oxford: Oxford University Press.

Kitay, J., and R. Callus. 1998. "The Role and Challenge of Case Study Design in Industrial Relations Research." In K. Whitfield and G. Strauss (eds.), *Researching* the World of Work: Strategies and Methods in Studying Industrial Relations, pp. 101–13. Ithaca, NY: Cornell University Press.

Knudsen, H., and R. Markey. 2002. "Works Councils: Lessons from Europe for Australia." In I. Ross, R. Markey, and P. J. Gollan (eds.), *Works Councils in Australia—Future Prospects and Possibilities*, p. 104. Annandale, New South Wales: Federal Press.

Marchington, M., A. Wilkinson, P. Ackers, and T. Dundon. 2001. *Management Choice and Employee Voice*. Research Report. London: Chartered Institute of Personnel and Development.

Markey, R. 2001. "Introduction: Global Patterns of Participation." In R. Markey, P. Gollan, A. Hodgkinson, A. Chouraqui, and U. Weersma (eds.), *Models of Employee Participation in a Changing Global Environment. Diversity and Interaction*, p. 8. Burlington, UK: Ashgate Publishing Co.

———. 2007. "A Case Study of Non-Union Employee Representation in Australia: The Suncorp Metway Employee Council Inc. (SMEC)." *Journal of Industrial Relations*, 49: 187–209.

McCallum, R., and G. Patmore. 2002. "Works Council and Labour Law." In P. Gollan, R. Markey, and I. Ross, I. (eds.), *Works Councils in Australia—Future Prospects and Possibilities*, pp. 74–100. Annandale, New South Wales: Federation Press.

Mitchell, R., R. Naughton, and R. Sorensen. 1997. "The Law and Employee Participation: Evidence from the Federal Enterprise Agreements Process." *Journal of Industrial Relations*, 39(2): 196–217.

Morehead, A., M. Steele, M. Alexander, K. Stephen, and L. Duffin. 1997. *Changes at Work: The 1995 Australian Workplace Industrial Relations Survey*. Melbourne: Longman.

Muir, S. 2003. *Being Heard—Employee Voice "Making a Difference."* SUN Employee Council, an Australian case study. Working paper for the precongress of the 13th World Congress of the International Industrial Relations Association (IIRA), the Free University, September 8–12, Berlin.

SGEC. 2013. "SGEC Mission Statement." Internal document provided by the Suncorp Group Employee Council in 2013. Also available to Suncorp Group employees on intranet.

SMEC. 2003. "Your Questions Answered." Internal document provided by the Suncorp Employee Council in the 2003 interview.

Suncorp Group. 2013a. "Who We Are." Available from www.suncorpgroup.com.au/about-us/who-we-are, accessed July 2, 2013.

———. 2013b. "Our History." Available from www.suncorpgroup.com.au/about-us/our-history#, accessed July 2, 2013.

Taras, D. G., and Kaufman, B. E. 1999. *What Do Non-Unions Do? What Should We Do about Them?* Working Paper No. WP14, Task Force, Symposium on Changing Employment Relations and New Institutions of Representation, Washington, D.C.

Terry, M. 1999. "Systems of Collective Representation in Non-Union Firms in the UK." *Industrial Relations Journal*, 30(1): 16–30.

Upchurch, M., M. Richardson, S. Tailby, A. Danford, and P. Stewart. 2006. "Employee Representation and Partnership in the Non-Union Sector: A Paradox Of Intention?" *Human Resource Management Journal*, 16(4): 393–410.

Watling, D., and J. Snook. 2003. "Works Council and Trade Unions: Complementary or Competitive? The Case of SAGCo." *Industrial Relations Journal*, 34(3): 260–70.

Yin, R. K. 2003. *Case Study Research: Design and Methods.* Thousand Oaks, CA: Sage Publications.

3 NER in a Leading Australian Medical Manufacturer

Paul J. Gollan and Senia Kalfa

INTRODUCTION

This chapter examines the case of Cochlear, a medical manufacturer in Sydney, Australia, and its non-union voice arrangements. It draws on interviews conducted in 2009 and 2012 with management and employees to argue the following points. First, representative non-union employee representation (NER) arrangements can be used in periods of organisational change in a problem-solving capacity (Butler 2009) and as means to address short-term communication needs. However, when the change at hand is embedded in the organisation and the circumstances that gave rise to representative NER dissipate, the centrality and role of a collective non-union representation body wanes. In other words, we concur with much literature that finds that NER arrangements diminish in importance in the long term. Second, direct-voice arrangements can substitute for collective NER and in fact be more effective in capturing employee concerns over production and/or other matters. Third, embedding employee voice mechanisms within a broader human resources (HR) framework is crucial and preferred to a "narrow, one-dimensional employee participation initiatives" (Wilkinson et al. 2010: 9). In other words, the existence of voice mechanisms per se is not enough; what is needed is a high-involvement strategy that emphasises competitive advantage through people (Kaufman and Taras 2010).

This chapter explores only the functions and effectiveness of the non-union voice arrangements in Cochlear, although we do briefly touch upon the issue of union representation so as to provide a better context and enrich our understanding of the case study organisation. The chapter is structured as follows: first, we briefly present some literature on employee voice and its role during organisational change initiatives. We continue with the methodology we followed and the company and participant profile. Third, we provide the context that led to the adoption of non-union voice arrangements. Fourth, we describe and evaluate the Employee Consultative Committee and its functions and continue to present direct forms of employee voice. Finally, we conclude the chapter by highlighting what other organisations can learn about managing the employment relationship from a relatively small Australian organisation that is the leader in its field.

LITERATURE REVIEW

Employee Voice

Research on employee voice is experiencing a renewed interest among academics, practitioners, and policy makers, primarily due to the "representation gap" (Taras and Kaufman 2006) noted in the Anglo-Saxon world, resulting from continuous declines in union membership. In Australia, the proportion of employees who are union members currently stands at 18 per cent (Australian Bureau of Statistics 2012), with the highest union membership in education, nursing, and public service (Sloan 2012).

Overall, employee voice encompasses mechanisms for employees to have "a say" in organisational decision making (Freeman et al. 2007; Marchington and Wilkinson 2005). The scholarship examining employee voice generally falls into two research paradigms: industrial relations (IR) and human resource management (HRM). Both literatures focus primarily on the definitions, structures, processes and effectiveness of employee participation (Gollan and Patmore 2013). Fundamental to this research is the examination of the power inequality inherent in the employment relationship, what specific voice arrangements and practices actually mean for relevant stakeholders, and whether such schemes can improve organisational effectiveness and employee well-being (Gollan and Patmore 2013).

Scholars in the area use terms such as *voice, participation, involvement*, and *industrial* or *organisational democracy* almost interchangeably, leading to contested definitions of the concept (Lewis et al. 2006). As Heller and colleagues (1998: 15; emphases in original) noted:

> In general the term refers to how employees are able to have a say over work activities and organizational decision-making issues within the organization in which they work. Some authors insist that participation must be a group process, involving groups of employees and their boss; others stress delegation, the process by which the *individual* employee is given greater freedom to make decisions on his or her own. Some restrict the term "participation" to formal institutions, such as works councils; other definitions embrace "informal participation," the day-to-day relations between supervisors and subordinates in which subordinates are allowed substantial input into work decisions. Finally, there are those who stress participation as a *process* and those who are concerned with participation as a *result*.

In examining the transformation of British industrial relations over a period of approximately thirty years, Gomez, Bryson, and Willman (2010) highlighted the wide variety of voice "regimes" available. The authors argue that an employer has four broad choices: to provide no voice mechanisms to their employees; to buy voice, or in other words use a trade union; to make voice, or adopt a "sophisticated HRM approach" (87) and execute it through joint consultative committees, problem-solving groups, team briefings, and so on; and finally to hedge, which includes a combination of making and buying voice. Furthermore, within these categories, Gomez and colleagues (2010: 387) add further subcategories of direct and representative voice mechanisms, resulting in a six-fold typology.

While a well-established literature exists which examines union representation, the effectiveness of non-union arrangements is still a relatively new topic (Gollan 2007). In part, this chapter contributes to this literature by examining the non-union voice arrangements present in Cochlear. Our case study organisation adopted the last of the four options identified by Gomez and colleagues (2010) and has both union and non-union voice, the latter taking both direct and representative forms. It is important to note here that Cochlear's senior management has not hedged its voice options out of choice: as is explained later in the chapter, after a long dispute with one of the recognised unions, it is being forced to cooperate.

Communication and Employee Voice during Periods of Organisational Change

Literature has established that during periods of change, communication with employees is of paramount importance. For example, Kotter (1996), in his seminal albeit highly normative eight-step model of leading change, argued that step four is "communicating the vision" and maintained that "without credible communication, and lots of it, the hearts and minds of the troops are never captured" (Kotter 1995: 63). Similarly, Lewis, Schmisseur, Stephens, and Weir (2006: 118) highlighted that the principal role of change agents is to "promote communication and participation." While the authors recognise that in the majority of cases, management leads and controls organisational change efforts, they argued that "participation gives members a sense of control and reduces uncertainty about changing circumstances, such that if people can feel part of the implementation process, they will be more committed to the change" (120). Lines (2004: 198) maintains that the success of change initiatives is determined by perceptions of procedural fairness in an organisation and, drawing on Folger (1977), argues that

> perceived fairness in the context of strategic change is likely to depend on whether those affected by the change are invited to voice their opinions . . . the opportunity to merely voice an opinion however, does not seem to lead directly to the perception of procedural fairness. The impact of voice seems to depend on whether people believe that decision makers consider their input.

Furthermore, drawing on the expectancy theory, Lines (2004) argues that participation can lower employee resistance because it provides management with opportunities to explain the rationale underpinning the change initiative and employees with forums to voice their concerns and become directly involved in the substantive content of change.

A recent area of research has looked at employee silence, which is defined as an employee's "motivation to withhold or express ideas, information and opinions about work-related improvements" (Van Dyne, Ang, and Botero 2003: 1361). This body of research investigates the circumstances under which employees will choose silence over expressing their concerns, as well as the topics that lend themselves to such an approach. In an examination of process failures at hospitals, Tucker and Edmondson (2003: 69) highlighted that employees will choose to be silent when they feel that "managers are not present and receptive enough." Wolfe-Morrison and Milliken (2000: 707) suggest that a lack consideration of multiple and even conflicting viewpoints is detrimental to organizational change efforts, because it restricts the level of critical analysis decision makers can engage in. They further suggest that organizational silence compromises change by blocking negative feedback and "hence an organization's ability to detect and correct errors" (719). Similarly, Donaghey, Cullinane, Dundon, and Wilkinson (2011: 53) have argued that employee silence prevents management from "receiving information that might allow for improvements or circumvent problems before the effects become seriously damaging." The importance of discovering errors quickly and rectifying and learning from them is also a point emphasised by Weick and Sutcliffe (2007), who claim that only establishing a culture in which individuals are not afraid to speak up will make recovering from inevitable errors possible.

Management literature thus emphasises the importance of consultation with employees during periods of change. However, research has highlighted that in some cases, the collaboration imperative remains in the sphere of rhetoric. For example, Beer, Eisenstat, and Spector (1990: 159) pointed to "the fallacy of programmatic change" in arguing that change initiatives often fail because top management does not successfully engage the periphery, hence missing out on crucial implementation details. Doyle, Claydon, and Buchanan (2000), in a survey of ninety-two managers, found that communication and employee involvement were issues that all survey participants agreed were missing from change implementation processes.

In fact, this is an argument also supported in the lean manufacturing literature, especially when lean is brought to replace an older system of production. Briefly, lean manufacturing practices were born in Japan in the 1940s and are underpinned by three principles: value identification, waste elimination, and the generation of flow of value to the customer (Melton 2005). Seventy years later, the term *lean manufacturing practices* is almost synonymous with *good manufacturing practices*. For example, in the largest study of manufacturing practices in the world, Bloom and van Reenen (2007) define good practices in operations management as those practices that revolve around the implementation of modern and lean manufacturing techniques, such as Just-in-Time (JIT), Kanban (scheduling system for replenishment), 5S (method of organising and driving workplace efficiency), Enterprise Resource Planning (ERP), and others, that help improve efficiency, quality, and flexibility in manufacturing firms. Lean manufacturing practices have been shown to improve inventory turnover and efficiency (Demeter and Matsuyz 2011), thus enhancing operational and supply chain performance (Flynn and Flynn 2005; White, Ojha, and Kuo 2010) and financial performance (Hofer, Eroglu, and Hofer 2012; Hsu et al. 2009). Implementation of lean practices helps standardize operations (Linderman 2008; Naveh et al. 2004) and results in significant strategic benefits (Gonzalez-Benito and Gonzalez-Benito 2008; Wadell and Bodek 2005).

Manufacturing literature has highlighted that when implementing lean, other management practices need to be modified accordingly (Hancock and Zaycko 1998), and particular emphasis should be placed on communication. Utley, Westbrook, and Turner (1997, cited in Bhasin and Burcher, 2006: 65) recommend a change of focus "from controlling to helping; from evaluating to empowering; from directing to coaching; and from planning to listening." Forrester (1995: 22) thus argues, "the whole process becomes a more people-centred one, with employees becoming more involved and flexible. In its simplest terms, lean production has to be a people-driven process, because only the employees can identify ways of improving the existing process or product."

It appears, therefore, that like any other change initiative, successful implementation of lean manufacturing is premised significantly on consultation and communication with employees. As with any other change program, however, the theory can differ significantly from practice. For example, Morley and Doolen (2006) found that lack of employee participation in an electronics manufacturing company that was implementing lean led to resistance and dissatisfaction. Similarly, Bhasin and Burcher (2006: 65) see people and culture as "predominant reasons for lean failures" and Chung (1996: 283) even argued that 50 to 75 per cent of failures in the United States are due to "improper attention to human aspects of implementing technology."

Given the transformational change that began in Cochlear in 2006, we argue that our case study organisation lends itself to a unique analysis of the role of NER arrangements during periods of significant organisational change. As will be shown through the qualitative data, in our case study, collective NER arrangements in the form of an employee consultative committee (ECC) in addition to direct voice mechanisms were useful as a means to address communication needs that arose during the transition to the lean manufacturing system.

METHODOLOGY AND COMPANY PROFILE

Cochlear is an Australian medical manufacturer, headquartered in Sydney, engaged in the production of devices for the hearing impaired. Their primary products are cochlear implants, which are a system of electronic components and software that are surgically inserted in the patient's mastoid bone. The patient wears an external speech processor which converts speech into a code of electrical impulses. This code is then transmitted to the implant via radio waves which also power the implant. The implant is connected to an array of electrodes that stimulate the cochlear nerve within the ear, and the brain perceives these electrical impulses as sound.

Cochlear's manufacturing facilities are in Sydney and Brisbane, but there is also a smaller production plant in Sweden. In 2009, Cochlear had 1,888 employees and contractors worldwide, with 320 people employed in manufacturing in Sydney. In 2012, the company had grown to 2,390 people worldwide with 450 employed in manufacturing in Sydney. By all accounts, Cochlear is a world leader in their field. The company retains approximately 65 to 70 per cent of the worldwide market share, and historically it has been growing at a rate of approximately 15 per cent per annum (Cochlear 2009).

The data collected can be considered to examine a juncture in Cochlear's life: "a series of images, impressions and experiences which act to give the appearance of a coherent whole and which influence how [an] organisation is understood" (Mills, Durepos, and Wiebe 2010: 509). Helms-Mills and Mills (2000) argue that to understand a particular time frame in an organisation's history, numerous factors have to be combined in order to fully portray the worldview of organisational members at the time. To comply with this imperative and to overcome the problems associated with a single case-study approach, we relied upon data triangulation, "explicitly searching for as many different data sources as possible, which bear upon the events under analysis" (Denzin 2009: 301). The primary sources of data included four semistructured interviews and seven focus groups, which were conducted with Cochlear's staff members ($N = 24$) in the second half of 2009. The employees interviewed were all engaged in the production of electrode units, which is one of the three components of the Cochlear implant (see Table 3.2). Table 3.1 presents the profile of the research participants. Furthermore, in August 2012, we went back and interviewed the senior vice president of human resources (VPHR) for a second time to get an update about employee voice arrangements in Cochlear.

In addition, supplementary material was reviewed, which was either publicly available or provided to us by the company's management. The main strength of broadening the data beyond a more constricted single source is that it results in a thick description of the phenomenon under investigation that would not have otherwise been possible (Johnstone 2004; Mathison 1988; Thurmond 2001). Such an approach creates innovative ways of understanding non-union representation, reveals unique findings (Jick 1979), and, as a result, provides a more nuanced understanding of the debate.

Table 3.1 Participant Profile

Participant's Role	Tenure at the Time of Interview/Focus group
Senior VPHR	1–5 years
HR Manager (Manufacturing)	1–5 years
HR Professional (Manufacturing)	Unassigned
CEO	5–10 years
Senior VP Manufacturing	5–10 years
Head of Manufacturing and Logistics (Head of M&L)	1–5 years
ECC Member 1	1–5 years
ECC Member 2	Unassigned
ECC Member 3	> 15 years
ECC Member 4	Unassigned
Female Team Leader	5–10 years
Female Team Leader 2	Unassigned
Male Team Leader	5–10 years
Female Team Member 3	10–15 years
Female Team Member 4	1–5 years
Female Team Member 1	5–10 years
Maintenance Engineer (S)	5–10 years
Business Support Manager (J)	> 15 years
Production Engineer (NPI)	5–10 years
Production Manager (M1)	Unassigned
Production Manager (M2)	Unassigned
Production Manager (M3)	Unassigned
Production Manager (F1)	Unassigned
Production Manager (F2)	Unassigned

The importance of Cochlear as a case study organisation rests on two factors. First, it is one of the leading medical manufacturers in the world. Studying it allows us to make useful suggestions to academics and public policy makers as well as business and trade union representatives engaged in the debate on non-union representation and its long-term effectiveness. Second, the value of the case study is pronounced due to the significant organisational change that was happening in Cochlear simultaneously with the establishment of non-union voice.

CONTEXT

To understand NER arrangements and their outcomes at Cochlear, it is pertinent that we first view the broader context. The importance of the context has been highlighted by Ackers (2012), who, in his critique of radical pluralism, vehemently advocated the importance of the institutional environment in understanding the employment relationship. To present the context, we draw on Dundon and Gollan's (2007) framework of factors influencing non-union employee voice. The authors identify macro- as well as micro-environmental factors that can shape NER arrangements. We present these contextual factors historically, beginning with the shift to lean manufacturing, continuing with the dispute with one of the recognised unions, and finishing with the voluntary recall of Cochlear devices in 2011.

The Shift to Lean Manufacturing

In January 2006, Cochlear embarked on a significant change of their production system to be redesigned under lean manufacturing principles. The primary reason that led to the adoption of lean was the fact that Cochlear could not keep up with the growth in their business (Head of Manufacturing and Logistics [M&L]) under the previous batch production system, which saw each individual operator being responsible for an implant from start to finish. On that topic, the Head of M&L argued that the previous work mode fostered an individualistic work culture. As such, the first change that preceded lean practices in Cochlear was a re-organization from silo-based operations to "businesses within the business" (internal presentation). Operators were reorganized in smaller teams of eight instead of larger groups of forty and were cross-trained to perform all tasks within the team (team member; Head of M&L).

To produce a cochlear implant, six processes are followed: welding, moulding, helix, sorting, cleaning, and inspection (senior VPHR). The manufacturing process is summarised in Table 3.2.

As part of the lean implementation and to allow the management of operators' training needs as well as the management of their performance, the HR team in Cochlear, under the leadership of the Senior VPHR, put together a classification matrix which "lists all operations and all members in a team and plots each member's competency against each operation" (HR professional, M&L). The classification matrix enables team members to apply for promotion by progressing through assessment steps and allows team leaders to know "where skills are in their team and where the risk areas are" (HR professional, M&L). Organisationally, the purpose of the matrix was to "build flexibility within the team and remove business risk" (HR professional, M&L).

Table 3.2 Production Process of the Cochlear Implant

The Cochlear implant is made up of three main functional components:

1. the stimulator
2. the antenna coil and
3. the electrode unit.

The heart of the stimulator is the Cochlear implant chip, an integrated circuit. The stimulator also contains a ceramic disk, or feedthrough, with twenty-four platinum pins to which each of the twenty-two electrode wires and two coil wires are attached in the final assembly. The stimulator is responsible for picking up the signals from the antenna and sending out the appropriate electrical energy to the electrodes. The stimulator is encased in titanium shells, which are laser welded together.

The antenna coil, which forms the loop of the implant, is welded to the stimulator to form a functional antenna. It is then wound into the shape that you see in the final implant. An extracochlear electrode is assembled using fine platinum wire and is also attached to the stimulator. Stimulator components are prepared and cleaned prior to entering the clean room. All antenna coil assembly is conducted in the clean room.

The clean room is a totally controlled environment with set temperature and humidity levels in which electrode assembly and final implant assembly takes place. Strict controls are required during the final assembly of implants to ensure that the final product is clean and, after sterilisation, ready for implantation. Full-body garments are worn in the clean room: boots, overalls, hood, mask, and gloves.

The electrode unit can be made up of either a straight electrode array or a contoured array.

1. Each platinum electrode wire is welded to a platinum ring. The wires are fed through the rings and, one at a time, each wire is attached to one ring. A lead wire is attached, and the whole thing is encased in silicone.

2. This electrode unit is attached to the stimulator, and the individual wires are attached to the corresponding pins on the stimulator.

3. The assembly is electrically tested and then silicone is injected to insulate the stimulator.

4. The outside titanium shell is laser welded to the stimulator, and the unit is tested again.

5. The implant assembly is baked overnight in a vacuum oven and then undergoes final hermetisation, which means that the small hole in the stimulator shell is fused, resulting in a gas-tight seal around the stimulator.

6. A small magnet is then inserted in the outer moulding, and the entire implant assembly is placed in a moulding die into which silicone is injected to completely encase the implant.

7. The implant is bent so that the coil is at an angle to the stimulator and the magnet is removed.

(*Continued*)

Table 3.2 (Continued)

8. The implant is washed, the magnet reinserted, and the assembly is electrically tested.
9. Finally the product is packed in a sterile pouch, this complete assembly is sterilised, and the implant is packed.
This is a basic overview of the manufacturing processes involved in producing the components necessary for a functional Cochlear implant system, which transmits signals from outside the body to the electrode inside the cochlea, allowing the recipient of the implant to hear.

(www.powerhousemuseum.com/hsc/cochlear/commercial.htm)

The implementation of lean at Cochlear was initially treated with scepticism from employees, as it was believed that "they were going to ask us for more [output]" (Team leader). However, this perception had largely changed by the time of our interviews in 2009, and the employees we talked to preferred the lean manufacturing system, as it allowed them to be more efficient in the production line. In fact, lean practices enabled the firm to almost quadruple its productivity from a daily production of 35 electrodes to 120 electrodes within three years of implementation.

The Dispute with the Australian Manufacturing Workers' Union (AMWU)

From 1998 to 2007, the terms and conditions for Cochlear employees were governed by Enterprise Partnership Agreements (EPAs), which were collective agreements negotiated in accordance with the Industrial Relations Act 1996 (NSW). The last EPA was formed in 2005 and had a two-year expiration date, although the law gave life to the agreement after its expiry date unless a party sought its termination. In 2007, Cochlear applied to the Australian Industrial Relations Commission (AIRC) for the termination of its EPA with the intention of moving to individual agreements under the new labour law (Work Choices) that had come into effect. Work Choices gave employers the option to refuse to engage in bargaining with recognised unions, even when the majority of workers wished to have a collective agreement.

The AMWU began a community campaign to try to get Cochlear to change its mind about individual agreements, which continued into and through the 2007 Australian federal elections, which saw the conservative government lose primarily due to the highly unpopular Work Choices. In August 2008, Cochlear lost its application to have the by-then-expired EPA terminated with the AIRC, arguing that it was not "in the public interest to do so" despite accepting that the individual contracts Cochlear offered its workforce were "generally superior" to the certified deal (Australian Human Resources Institute and Holding Redlich Lawyers 2009).

Cochlear appealed the decision but lost in January 2009. The federal government, under Australia's Labour Party, had, by that stage, replaced Work Choices with the Fair Work Act (Cth), which requires parties to bargain in good faith. Good Faith Bargaining (GFB) requires parties to be timely in meetings and share information, give genuine consideration to proposals, justify responses, and refrain from capricious or unfair conduct (Fair Work Australia 2009).

In July 2009, the AMWU applied to Fair Work Australia to have Cochlear return to the bargaining table. The union argued the company failed to start negotiations for a new agreement despite repeated requests from the union and clear support among a majority of workers for bargaining to commence (Australian Human Resources Institute and Holding Redlich Lawyers 2009). In August 2009, Fair Work Australia ordered a ballot to resolve whether the AMWU has majority support among workers at Cochlear. They ruled in favour of the AMWU after a majority of production employees voted "yes" to collective bargaining ($N = 185$, about 57 per cent of direct M&L employees; Fair Work Australia 2009).

However, this decision did not see the finalisation of the dispute. In December 2011, negotiations broke down after the AMWU backed away from the bargaining table, arguing that Cochlear was not serious about reaching an agreement (Gollan 2011). The AMWU sought a "bargaining order" from Fair Work Australia to oblige Cochlear to consider requests for an across-the-board 5 per cent pay rise and greater access for union officials to workers. In August 2012, Fair Work Australia ordered Cochlear to allow the union to meet with workers to discuss collective bargaining and give them access to the lunchroom, although it did not find the company in breach of GFB rules. On behalf of Cochlear, the Australian Industry Group said that the company was not prepared to enter an agreement that it did not support, and at this stage employees were still covered under individual common law contracts (Skulley 2012).

The (Voluntary) Product Recall

In September 2011, Cochlear management decided to initiate a voluntary recall of their latest implant—the CI 500 range—alarmed by increasing number of reported failures. The device made up more than 50 per cent of Cochlear's sales, amounting to more than $800 million. The recall was deemed voluntary because the devices had not caused injury to any patients but had simply failed (Ahmed 2011). As such, patients were advised to only consult with their doctors regarding the explanting process if their device stopped working.

In a rather dramatic fashion, the recall was decided on Saturday, September 10, with hospitals and medical practitioners being informed on Sunday (Ahmed 2011). The Senior VPHR explained that management initiated the recall because they did not want to risk the company's reputation with more device failures, lose market share, and eventually make job cuts. The Head of M&L (personal communication 2011) recalls:

> On the Friday we all went home, on the Monday we had to move people from making one product to making something completely different . . . so we had a meeting with manufacturing employees and explained to them what the impact of the recall was going to be . . . and the way they responded was superb. . . . It's actually been a lesson for me . . . helped me realise how flexible we've actually become.

The Senior VPHR attributes this flexibility to "the work that we'd done since 2007 on the skills matrix to build multiskilling and ensure that . . . people could work in all areas." However, both she and the Head of M&L highlighted that it is people's commitment to Cochlear that enabled them to shift to the production of a different device within twenty-four hours: "people were willing to support and go the extra effort in terms of overtime, work in new areas, do different things, and really leverage their skills." In fact, the company was able to move from producing 150 implants weekly before the recall to 150 implants daily after the recall (Senior VPHR).

Financially, Cochlear was hit hard by the recall: in July 2012, the company reported a significant reduction in profits by 68 per cent (Janda 2012). However, the impressive growth in productivity after the recall allowed the company to grow its workforce by approximately 40 per cent.[1]

REPRESENTATIVE NON-UNION VOICE IN COCHLEAR

Within this context, we can now begin to analyse representative voice in Cochlear. The Senior VPHR argued that one of the reasons that led to the establishment of the ECC was an "employee voice" survey conducted in 2004 which showed that there was a need for more communication channels as well as a concern that management was not attentive to employees' issues (HR Manager, M&L).

The consultative committee was constituted in 2005 in order to:

1. Assist in the correct application of [the 2005 Enterprise Partnership] Agreement, particularly in the light of the provisions of the relevant Awards
2. Review and recommend further measures to be considered for implementation consistent with the commitment of the parties to bring about further structural efficiency, or with a view to modernising this Agreement
3. Apply Manufacturing and Logistic values to work practices (Industrial Relations Commission of New South Wales 2005).

According to the EPA document, the consultative committee was to be composed of "an equal number of employees and management representatives" and to be used as a means to discuss matters of importance with employees, such as the adoption of flexible working arrangements, production targets, and training opportunities. The consultative committee was also expected to coordinate the newly established production teams within Cochlear and "feed to those teams data and information which may be relevant to the undertakings and performance of the teams" (Industrial Relations Commission of New South Wales 2005). Finally, the committee was expected to contribute to dispute resolution and "any issue of relevance to the operations of Cochlear, or of the employees . . . with no reasonable limit placed on the agenda for such consideration" (Industrial Relations Commission of New South Wales 2005).

In examining the reasons that led to the establishment of the ECC, the first issue to examine is managerial choice, a factor that Wilkinson and Dundon (2010) claim has received little scholarly attention. Wilkinson and Dundon (2010) note that the choice of model of voice in an organisation is influenced by the ideologies of senior managers, who will be positively predisposed to either union or non-union arrangements. In the interviews we conducted in 2009, the stance of upper and middle management towards the AMWU was made quite clear. For the HR Manager (M&L), the AMWU does "not understand our system . . . they don't understand what our people are really doing, what they build, why we change cycle times . . . they have not given any indication that they understand in the last couple of years." The interviewee kept referring to the fact that the AMWU viewed lean as a "carrot and stick" mechanism designed to exploit and mistreat workers. Similarly, the Senior VPHR mentioned that the assumption under which the union operated was that the classification system was put in place in order to "make employees work harder . . . which couldn't be further from the truth." Finally, an HR professional working at the Manufacturing division highlighted that the AMWU did not really understand the classification structure and the broader lean system, which is "quite complex and intimate to the product." In our follow-up interview in 2012, the Senior VPHR reiterated the rift between Cochlear and the AMWU, explaining how union representatives "come and sit in the training room," as one of the concessions made after the latest order from Fair Work Australia, "just so they can continue to get access to the lunch room . . . which they use as a membership drive."[2] Thus we could argue that, in general, Cochlear management is largely opposed to union involvement and in particular viewed the AMWU as removed from the reality of the workplace.

Given this rather difficult relationship, it could be argued that the ECC was established in Cochlear as a means of union avoidance. The significance of the union threat effect has been widely documented in the literature, with scholars arguing that employers are particularly keen to invest in non-union forms of voice when unions are strong (Butler 2009; Donaghey et al. 2012; Taras and Kaufman 2006) but usually allow them to fall into disuse once the threat has subsided. Taras and Kaufman (2006) argue that in their effort to keep the unions out, employers are inclined to offer workers above and beyond what unions could gain, such as superior wages, an approach which focuses on the carrot as opposed to the stick. This is true for Cochlear employees, who are paid 45 per cent above award wages (Hannan and Warne-Smith 2009).

However, as noted by Gollan (2007), assuming NER arrangements are used only as a means to substitute for the union is oversimplifying a complex issue. This case demonstrates said complexity: because the establishment of an ECC was agreed between Cochlear and the AMWU, before the bitter dispute between them erupted, can it really be considered a means of union substitution? Given the ambiguity, we believe it is pertinent to adopt more than one conceptual lens to avoid a simplistic analysis. As Morgan (2006: 5) notes, while any metaphor or lens "is capable of creating valuable insights, it is also incomplete, biased and potentially misleading."

Looking at the ECC through the unity-of-interest face of NER (Kaufman and Taras 2010) and taking into consideration the importance of people engagement in the success of a lean manufacturing program, we could argue that Cochlear and the AMWU established the ECC as a means to create a high-performance workplace and improve organisational performance by fostering greater cooperation. The implementation of the ECC could also be interpreted as a means for the company to increase employee morale and commitment (Kaufman and Taras 2010), because both are traditionally low during periods of change (Armenakis and Bedeian 1999). In fact, the HR manager (M&L) noted that the ECC was about "how can we work together to make [Cochlear] a more positive working environment." Thus, it could be that Cochlear adopted indirect voice arrangements for "defensive" reasons (Kaufman and Taras 2010) and with a paternalistic philosophy that assumes what is good for the business is good for the workers (Dundon et al. 2006). The pervasiveness of this philosophy in Cochlear is made quite clear with this example: in a 2009 interview, a production manager recalled that she received a number of complaints about union reps trying to recruit in the lunchroom. As a result, union representatives were not allowed in the lunchroom but were given an allocated area where employees could meet with them. She continued to argue that this move was taken in order to protect Cochlear employees: "we're not trying to say anything bad about them [the union officials], because we don't want to be seen as saying bad things. But then also, we've got to protect our employees. *They are our employees*" (our emphasis). However, as explained previously, this decision has now been overturned by Fair Work Australia.

ECC–Function and Topics

In our discussion of the ECC in Cochlear, we use Taras and Kaufman's (2006) framework that breaks down the diversity of NER arrangements according to six dimensions: form, function, topic, representation mode, extent of power, and degree of permanence. In order to avoid repetition, a distinction between 2009 and 2012 will only be made when there are actual differences in any of those dimensions describing the ECC.

As explained in Cochlear, the ECC was a condition of the 2005 Enterprise Partnership Agreement. Prior to the establishment of the ECC, a charter was drafted regarding "how the ECC would run, its actual outcomes, what kind of issues we were going to raise and its benefits " (HR Manager, M&L). For example, the HR Manager (M&L) was adamant that the ECC is not the appropriate context to discuss problems with specific individuals in a shift and/or area.

In 2009, the ECC had twelve members: it was chaired by the four production managers and attended by the occupational health and safety manager and the Head of M&L (HR Manager, M&L). There were six employee representatives who were nominated by their peers but had to accept their nomination (ECC member). As it currently stands (August 2012), the ECC has nine employee representatives for a three-year term and includes shift supervisors, a new hierarchical level introduced to cope with the increasing demand for the product. The selection process remains the same, and given its form, it is unlikely that the ECC is filled with "hand-picked management cronies" (Gollan 2007: 214). In fact, union members can be members of the ECC, and the Senior VPHR and an HR representative (M&L) named two individuals who fulfilled both roles. While one of them has resigned from Cochlear, the second continues to remain an active member of the ECC and has on many occasions discussed the benefits of union membership in ECC meetings (HR rep, M&L). The HR rep (M&L) maintained that it is possible that there is more than one AMWU member in the ECC, but as the company "doesn't keep member records," it would be difficult to confirm. This is inconsistent with Gollan's (2010) findings that a representative body will have no or limited connection to trade unions.

Cochlear provides training to the employee representatives, which includes an understanding of the topics appropriate to be raised in the ECC context, although the Senior VPHR admitted that no investment had been made in the ECC since September 2011 due to the product recall. Overall, however, this is consistent with Gollan's (2010) assertion that the employing organisation will provide resources for the representative body. In 2009, the committee was meeting once a month for two hours; however, in 2012, due to the product recall, this meeting was shortened to one hour a month. Employee representatives are paid overtime to attend if the forthcoming scheduled meeting is not in their shift.

According to the HR Manager (M&L), the agenda is driven by the employee representatives, although manager representatives can also include any issues they want to raise. The role of the ECC representatives is to "keep their ear to the ground" (HR Manager M&L), and ECC members interviewed claimed to be very much in tune with what their peers were concerned about through talking to them "basically all the time."

As previously mentioned, one of the elements in Taras and Kaufman's (2006) framework is power, which is the most controversial in the NER literature. The argument is the following: NER arrangements are inherently flawed because they are initiated by management and, as such, controlled by them. What is particularly problematic is that whilst NER arrangements can function as a forum to express dissatisfaction, they lack the power to push any adversarial topics. Upchurch and colleagues (2006) termed this phenomenon the "paradox of intention": while attractive language might be used to present an image of cooperation and trust between employer and employees, NER arrangements in effect consolidate existing power discrepancies. Similarly, Wilkinson and colleagues (2007) highlight that efforts for employee involvement do not assume the sharing of managerial power but are established as a means to ensure that employees will engage in organisational citizenship behaviours which will, in turn, enhance organisational performance. Thus Johnstone and colleagues (2010: 163) argue that it is a balancing act for the representative body: if it appears to have no "independence, legitimacy or credibility," it will not serve its purpose, whereas if it develops a strong identity and voice, it might be perceived as a threat from management.

The content of the ECC meetings can help us understand the level of power the ECC in Cochlear has. Our 2009 interviews show that some substantive issues were discussed, such as progress on the Enterprise Partnership Agreement, new chairs for the operators in the clean room, split shifts, and changes to the classification matrix. The last one is the single most substantive example of influence we found the ECC in Cochlear to have: in 2009, the HR Manager (M&L) recalled that concerns were brought to management via the ECC about Time to Proficiency (TTP), the point system used for staff accreditation, not matching the actual requirements of the job and resulting in dissatisfaction among manufacturing staff. As a result, the classification matrix was changed to recognise those processes that are more complex. The HR Manager (M&L) highlighted that this was a particularly successful outcome, and as a result, the issue of accreditation was being further explored with other production areas—*not through the ECC but through focus groups*. This seems to suggest that the ECC was not regarded by management as the appropriate forum for substantive topics even if they are integrative.

In fact, the majority of the topics discussed in the ECC meetings focused on the social aspect of work (Taras and Kaufman 2006), such as the annual and very popular Ping-Pong competition, lunchroom cleanliness and provisions, and parking. The impact of the 2008 Global Financial Crisis (GFC) on Cochlear profitability was, at the first round of interviews, an issue raised at the ECC, in addition to the possibility of offshoring manufacturing operations (HR Manager, M&L). However, employees were reassured by the Senior VP manufacturing and the Senior VPHR that their jobs were safe. In the words of a production manager, "we're a world leader . . . there's a security in what we're doing. If you look at our share price you look at how we've weathered the financial storm that's going on, we are doing extremely well." In 2012, topics were largely the same, with the addition of employee shares[3] and the employee bonus scheme (in terms of its timing).

Thus, our evidence suggests that early in its life, the ECC could exert some limited pressure on management on *integrative* issues, as the accreditation example illustrated. However, this was not the case when we revisited the company in 2012: the Senior VPHR in her 2012 interview mentioned that issues regarding the flexibility matrix had not been the focus of the ECC in the last two years, as the system had been "ironed out." In addition, the ECC had no input into the resolution of the recall crisis. Finally, as the ECC did not ever deal with any distributive issues, such as pay or bonuses, it is legitimate to question the extent to which they could really challenge management prerogative if the need arose.

Looking at the issues discussed, therefore, we can confidently argue that the primary function of the ECC in Cochlear was the improvement of communication flow between managers and workers and not negotiation (Gollan 2007). This is in line with arguments made by several scholars who highlight that the majority of NER arrangements are focused on communication and consultation as opposed to negotiation and/or bargaining (e.g., Gollan 2010; Kaufman and Taras 2010; Markey 2007). Furthermore, the ECC had limited input in the decisions that guided that change of the production process, a change which was tightly controlled by management. Thus, the role of ECC in Cochlear is similar to what Markey (2007) argues is the case with most Australian workplaces where consultative committees are almost exclusively advisory. As Charlwood and Terry (2007) found, in dual-channel workplaces, non-union representatives are consulted on integrative issues, and we found this to be the case with Cochlear. As such, the level of power the ECC possesses is highly questionable.

To ensure that the remaining Cochlear's employees were aware of the issues discussed in the ECC, copies of the minutes are provided in the lunchroom. Moreover, each employee rep personally informs his/her team/area in the weekly team meeting that follow the ECC meeting. The ECC members we interviewed took a lot of pride in their role and saw themselves as the voice of workers:

> We are the voice [of workers]. We are the messengers. So I am really proud to be in the ECC because it's good for us . . . It's also good for the company. Otherwise, if we don't have a committee, then we don't know what's really going on.
>
> (ECC member)

On the other hand, in our 2009 interview, the Head of M&L was critical of the ECC, arguing that the focus on "parties and barbeques" did not capture substantive issues regarding everyday work on the line, including concerns about team leaders showing favouritism to some operators, thus disadvantaging others. However, he claimed that the reason behind the emphasis given on such "silly" issues was that "our employees are generally happy."

Interestingly enough, an ECC representative highlighted that being a member of the committee was "good for [his] career," which is an issue Butler (2009) as well as Donaghey and colleagues (2012) presented as a double-edged sword. Although there is no harm in being career minded, these authors underline that it could lead to the reps not pursuing issues of a conflictual nature with the management so as not to jeopardise their own progression in the company.

Evaluation of the ECC

According to Kaufman and Taras (2010), the effectiveness of an NER arrangement depends on the premise upon which the arrangement was initially put together. In this particular case study, it appears that NER arose as a response to a temporary challenging situation. This situation was the confluence of two factors: first, the transition to lean manufacturing and second, the company's desire to move away from collective bargaining to individual contracts through Work Choices and the subsequent dispute with the AMWU. In combination with the 2004 Voice Survey mentioned earlier, evidence suggests that management came to the realisation that they needed to provide employees with more communication channels and they chose an ECC to do so. It could further be argued that the ECC was used as a means to ensure employee cooperation to the (then) upcoming workplace change (Butler 2009).

Kaufman and Taras (2010: 278) further identify several mediating variables that significantly impact] the effectiveness of NER arrangements: emphasis on integrative problem solving; managerial responsiveness to employee concerns; company profitability, which guarantees some level of job security; and trust between management and workers. While we did not examine the trust between Cochlear management and workers, we can confidently comment on the remaining mediating variables identified. We begin with company profitability, which is historically high: before the product recall, Cochlear was growing at approximately 15 per cent per annum. Even with the recall crisis, the company did not initiate redundancies, a fact the Senior VPHR attributed to the proactive response of the company to failing devices.

Furthermore, evidence from our first round of interviews suggests that the ECC in Cochlear was limited to the discussion of integrative issues as per Kaufman and Taras's (2010) suggestion. In addition, managerial responsiveness to employee demands was high, *as long as these demands were related to productivity enhancement,* as the incident with the accreditation point illustrated, *and were not challenging managerial prerogative.*

Thus, although the ECC in Cochlear was positioned to be a consultative body with input into decision making, our evidence demonstrates that it was in fact limited to a forum that allows management and employees to come together and express concerns that are not a threat to the managerial agenda. Even more concerning is the fact that the single most substantive contribution of the ECC, the accreditation (TTP) example, was eventually taken off their role and was to be explored through focus groups.

Finally, if we were to look at NER in Cochlear through a longitudinal lens, we would see that the role of ECC diminished even more after the transition to lean manufacturing was complete. When we visited the company in 2012 when the change to lean was well established, the ECC had become a social function organiser and had even more limited input into the decision-making processes. Similarly, we are not aware of any input the ECC had on the resolution of the recall crisis, and as such, we are questioning whether it has any significant input into organisational decision making. Overall, our case study suggests that companies adopt collective NER when specific management and employee relations problems arise, such as union disputes and production changes. However, at least in our case, collective NER appears to have a relatively short life span with a diminished role when the problems that led to its establishment gets resolved or, alternatively, when better solutions are found. These better solutions that Cochlear adopted are explored next.

DIRECT VOICE MECHANISMS

In this section, we explore direct voice mechanisms that were utilised in Cochlear in addition to the indirect voice mechanisms explored thus far. To analyse direct employee participation, we use Wilkinson and Dundon's (2010) framework. It is important first to note that direct voice in Cochlear was underpinned by an "economic efficiency" philosophy, which sees employees involved in decision making because they can enhance decision making as opposed to an "industrial democracy" philosophy, which views employee participation as an inherent democratic right of workers. It is also important to note here that direct participation has not changed form between 2009 and 2012 and therefore, to avoid repetition, we will only be distinguishing among years when significant differences exist.

Wilkinson and Dundon (2010: 173) argue that there are four dimensions in which to view direct employee participation. First, depth explores the extent to which employees can have a say in organisational decisions. This range from influence in decisions that are considered traditionally part of managerial prerogative to simply information. Second is the level of participation, such as work group, department, or corporate level. Third is the scope of participation, which covers the topics employees can have a say on. These range from minor matters such as parking to important matters such as strategy. Finally, the fourth element is the form that participation takes; in direct arrangements, popular forms are quality circles and problem-solving groups, where employees can directly contribute to their jobs.

In our interviews, Cochlear managers argued that they valued the input of employees especially on the line, where operators were encouraged to give their suggestions to their team leaders, who could then escalate to their supervisors if the idea was good and could help the line. Interestingly enough, consultation regarding problem solving and line improvement happened in both directions: bottom up, as argued before, but also top to bottom: production managers consulted with team leaders when issues arose. A production manager argued this approach empowered team leaders but also helped production managers form a stronger relationship with them: "[team leaders] like the attention. They like that you're coming to them for information, that you don't presume to know more than them, that you're actually going to some of them saying: I need your experience to help us."

More formally, and in their effort to enhance the production process, Cochlear utilises daily meetings between team leaders and team members, as well as daily meetings between the production managers and the team leaders. Utilising Wilkinson and Dundon's (2010) framework, these daily meetings can be characterised as "shallow" as they are primarily informational. The former serve to communicate to the team members "how many and what types of rejects we have from the previous day" (team member), and the latter sought to keep production managers abreast of any "constraints that might stop us from achieving our targets for the day" (production manager). Furthermore, on a departmental level, there is a weekly plant meeting with team members, team leaders, and production managers. In either case, we were not made aware that employees (whether team leader or team member) were given any scope for decision making, although they could share any ideas they have to improve the production process.

In 2009 and in their effort to give voice to staff who "are not comfortable going to the rep or for people who are shy, don't feel comfortable with their level of English" (senior VPHR), Cochlear utilised a suggestions box. However, three years later, the suggestions box is not used as much because of its location:

> When asking people about the box they advised me that they felt it was too open and if people saw them putting suggestions in there they were challenged about what was put in there. Most people I have spoken to are comfortable speaking with their ECC representatives directly though so we don't feel that topics are being missed despite the box not really being used.
>
> (HR rep M&L, personal communication)

In 2009, the Head of M&L took measures to ensure that complaints regarding the team leaders that were not captured by the ECC were heard: "I'm running these focus groups. So I sit down with 10 people at a time, 320 of them, so I have to do 32 sessions . . . I am trying to find out what is going on, because they won't necessarily bring it to the ECC." These focus groups were not continuing in 2012; however, Cochlear runs engagement surveys on a biennial basis, where employees are given the opportunity to voice any concerns they have, such as team leaders' skills, in the open-ended questions asked. Finally, the Senior VP Manufacturing runs monthly communication meetings, and ad hoc meetings have taken place in the lunchroom to update employees on the bargaining process and the ongoing dispute with the AMWU.

Evaluation

For Wilkinson and Dundon (2010), direct participation arrangements are particularly hard to assess for three reasons. First, it is difficult to isolate the cause-and-effect mechanisms and conclusively argue that participation leads to higher organisational performance. Second, it is difficult to attribute one particular date to the beginning of the participation scheme: "should this be the date at which the new participative mechanism . . . is actually introduced into the organisation, or should it be some earlier or later date?" (Wilkinson and Dundon 2010: 178). Third, on whose terms is impact evaluated? The managers', in which case the evaluation would focus on the outcomes of participation, or the workers', in which case the evaluation would focus on the process of participation?

While we cannot evaluate the extent to which direct participation had an immediate effect on Cochlear's performance, we cannot discount the fact that at least the concerns of direct manufacturing operators regarding team leaders' lack of (primarily people management) skills were heard by Cochlear's management and measures were taken to rectify the situation. Team leaders were expected to complete a development program to help them build on their skills. The initiative for the training program was taken by the HR Manager (Manufacturing), because after the implementation of lean, team leaders "were not required to do so much fire fighting in their teams . . . with the lean process having streamlined the business . . . they are now required to do more leadership work" (HR professional, M&L). The Competitive Manufacturing Program was delivered through the Technical and Further Education Commission (TAFE) and taught team leaders principles of "continuous improvement" (team leader) and "people management" (team leader). Therefore, in addition to covering a curriculum on lean manufacturing practices, an important part of the program was to ensure that team leaders have the skills to "lead change within [their] teams" (HR professional, M&L). It is important to note that the Competitive Manufacturing Program qualified team leaders with a Certificate IV;[4] thus it is "transferable anywhere else" (Senior VPHR).

Furthermore, it is pertinent to mention that although the daily meetings outlined earlier had primarily an informational character, as opposed to one that allowed employees to have a significant say in the organisation of the production process, we are of the opinion that in their implementation of lean manufacturing, Cochlear management exerted significant efforts to enlist the support of their employees. We interpret the daily team and weekly plant meetings as concerted efforts for communication with the employees *within the confines of the lean manufacturing philosophy*. As Wilkinson and Dundon (2010: 179) note, "the degree of participation offered is strictly within an agenda set by management . . . In terms of whether it leads to greater worker influence over business decisions, the answer appears to be yes, but within heavily constrained terms." In other words, employees in Cochlear are invited to contribute and voice their opinion, to the extent that the opinion is related to production issues and does not challenge managerial prerogative. While the strategic decision to move to lean was not subject to negotiation with employees, the implementation details were.

We could argue that possibly Cochlear has no other choice but to collaborate with employees, as their production process is still highly manual. As such, any change in the production process that failed to capture employees' feedback would be significantly hindered in its implementation. Interestingly enough, in 2009, the Head of M&L highlighted that the Australian national culture necessitated a highly consultative approach to change due to a disdain for authority (Ashkanasy and Trevor Roberts 2001):

> For example, in Japan . . . you still have the luxury as a manager to tell your team members what to do . . . and they'll go and do it. They won't necessarily challenge you. Whereas in Australia, if you say "you must do this," they will say "well how about you do it?" So it's leading by example.

Regardless of the motivation, however, the fact of a successful implementation with impressive results remains.

CONCLUSION AND IMPLICATIONS FOR RESEARCH, POLICY, AND PRACTICE

Having examined both direct and indirect voice mechanisms at Cochlear, we are obliged to question the effectiveness of the ECC in comparison to the direct voice mechanisms presented above. The ECC's major contribution to Cochlear during 2006 through 2009 was to facilitate communication during the change from batch to lean production and to help management iron out issues related to the classification matrix that was introduced at the time. However, as the 2012 interviews showed, since then their role has diminished to that of a social function organiser. As such, and in combination with the fact that the ECC does not have the scope to discuss bargaining issues, its actual role as a representative body is highly questionable. On the other hand, we find that for integrative problem solving, direct voice mechanisms are more effective compared to indirect ones like the ECC. Cochlear is a prime example of successfully utilising team and department meetings alongside targeted focus groups in order to gauge employees' views on production-related issues. Their targeted approach has in fact contributed largely to the impressive jumps in productivity.

Having said this, we do not in any way claim that Cochlear was paying lip service to the importance of people management for organisational success. In fact, through our case study, we wish to underline the importance of an integrated HR agenda which includes NER arrangements alongside "training, induction, culture change or more open management styles" (Dundon, Wilkinson, Marchington, and Ackers 2004: 1163) for periods of organisational change. We argue this despite the fact that the contribution of the official NER mechanism in the form of the ECC was and remains rather limited to social functions.

For us, the most striking example of this integrated HR strategy was the Well Placed English Language Speakers (WELL) English language training program that unintentionally gave voice to Cochlear workers, although it was probably not initiated for this particular purpose, by enabling them to speak better English and communicate both with leaders and peers. A voice survey conducted in 2006 showed that employees spoke languages other than English in the workplace, which was problematic for management as "operators were unable to understand technical work instructions and terminology" (Senior VPHR). Given the strict regulatory framework Cochlear operates under, "the main driver was to make sure there's open communication and a common standard that everyone follows within the team" (Senior VPHR). The WELL program was thus initiated and "in the first year we had about 200 people participate" (HR professional, M&L). Cochlear continued to fund the program even after the government grant that initially paid for it was exhausted; even more importantly, staff were paid overtime to participate in the program (team leader). The primary benefit reported from this program was increased confidence: "most people who have gone through the program have come back and said we feel more confident now standing up and talking to our teams and our team leaders compared to before" (HR professional, M&L). A production manager highlighted:

> The intangible aspect was appreciated much more than the actual ability to speak English. There was difference in the overall confidence levels and the ability to speak in a team and be comfortable talking to people from different cultures. It was more that . . . and the appreciation that Cochlear made an investment and gave people an opportunity to learn.

The HR Manager (M&L) gave an example of an individual who at the time of the interviews was being considered for a team leader role as a result of enhanced English language competency: "and it's looking quite likely that that person may be getting [the role] whereas a couple of years ago because of his language skills . . . we would not be able to consider him." The ability to improve their English competency levels was very much appreciated by employees: "Where are you going to find a company that's going to take you to English class? Plus, we're paid overtime to do these classes . . . We're spoiled already!" (team leader). In our follow-up interview, we asked if the WELL program was still continuing, and indeed it was in the Brisbane operations, as the Sydney contingent had already gone through it: "in the selection process we're hiring people with much more [sic] English competence. So that particular program isn't necessarily what we have to invest in anymore" (Senior VPHR).

In combination with the training program for team leaders and the highly thought-out classification matrix and performance management practice, this example illustrates that workers were indeed valued in Cochlear and that management made substantial investments in money and time to ensure that they had a voice.

In our mind, Cochlear's success was partly due to a strong HR department, and it is here that we wish to draw practitioners' attention. In our interviews, we found that the HR department at Cochlear was not a support unit but that it was viewed as a value-adding function in the organisation. In fact, the significance of the HR department for Cochlear's success was emphasised by the majority of our participants and was even a point of interest in our interview with the CEO, who found it "surprising but quite pleasing" that people actually used HR. A development that facilitated the overwhelmingly positive view of HR was the establishment of an HR division in manufacturing. A maintenance engineer with more than five years' tenure in Cochlear recalls:

> HR's role has certainly changed over the last few years. When I started here, HR . . . I knew all of their names and I could go in and say hello but really I didn't have any kind of real interaction with them other than dropping forms off. [It used to be that] manufacturing was way down the back and HR was right at the front, upstairs near the CEO. When we actually moved a couple of HR reps down here, I saw that as a massive turning point. That's where we had our own dedicated manufacturing people. Really, maybe 40 per cent of [Cochlear] people worked here but no one from HR ever went near them. To have that now, this regular interaction—we'd be talking to [HR rep name] and [HR rep name] at least a couple times a week, maybe more often than that. To have people here constantly offering you support, advice, assistance, I think is a huge difference . . . Distinctly I think the quality of the advice and the willingness to be involved is certainly there now. That wasn't

there in the past . . . I think the implementation and the delivery have changed hugely in the last few years.

We view the move of HR reps to manufacturing as a shift that signified that manufacturing operators were indeed significant for Cochlear, and in our mind that was an important step in making employees feel valuable and improving trust levels between manufacturing operators and senior management. This is a move, we believe, that many manufacturers, whether in Australia or overseas, can emulate.

Further, in our recommendations to practitioners, we wish to emphasise the need for them to adopt good people management practices. Recent research examining the management practices of Australian manufacturers (see Green et al. 2009) has found, that although in operational practices Australian organisations are amongst the best the world, they lag behind in their adoption of "best practice" in HR. While we are cognizant of the costs, both monetary and in time, associated with the design and implementation of good HR practices, our case study shows that, in the long term, the benefits significantly outweigh these costs. It is important here to note that adopting lean practices can only be a long-term commitment if a company expects to see positive results from its efforts (Emiliani 2003; Gregory 2002; Liker 2004).

Our findings also have implications for policy makers. We believe that there is a big need to recognise that regulatory frameworks on industrial relations should move away from the adversarial mentality that was appropriate in the beginning of the twentieth century but is now outdated, to say the least. Gollan (in Roberts 2012) has drawn particular attention to regulated works councils systems prevalent in continental European countries such as France and Germany, where external unions are involved in bargaining over wages and working conditions, whereas internal employee committees focus on how to improve the workplace and enhance productivity.

It is not our intention through these suggestions to discount the importance of trade unions or the impact they have on the employment relationship. Indeed, arguing that unions are only detrimental to the workplace is parochial. We are also cognisant that by adopting a combative stance towards the AMWU, Cochlear management has, for a long time, not been listening to the voice of a minority of employees who wish to be represented by the union. However, we do believe it is time that the role of unions changed from a narrow focus on collective bargaining to a true agency of employee voice—in other words, from the "us and them" approach, which is admittedly facilitated by Australia's conflictual industrial relations framework, to true partners in the business focusing on enlarging the cake rather the narrow view of increasing the share of the cake.

Finally, in terms of academic research, we wish to emphasise that traditional views on the employment relationship are "very much a product of twentieth century mass production industrial society" (Ackers 2012: 13).

However, as we now live in a service economy—or, according to Drucker (1954), in a knowledge society—the expectations of employers and employees are markedly different. It is this difference we academics must capture through our research. This can happen in numerous ways, not least of which involves moving beyond the traditional radical framework to one that can recognise both the differences and, as importantly, the commonalities of interests between employers and employees. While we recognise the power imbalance that exists in the relationship of employers and employees, we seek to address it by providing realistic examples of workplace cooperation as opposed to continuing to promote a social science paradigm that assumes conflict will predominate over a true partnership.

NOTES

1. From 320 direct operators in Sydney in 2009 to 450 in 2012.
2. The senior VPHR maintained that union membership has declined since the 2009 surveys to approximately twenty seven per cent.
3. Cochlear employees receive $1,000 worth of shares on an annual basis.
4. The Certificate IV qualifies individuals who apply a broad range of specialised knowledge and skills in varied contexts to undertake skilled work and as a pathway for further learning (Australian Qualifications Framework Council 2011, p. 15).

REFERENCES

Ackers, Peter. 2012. "Rethinking the Employment Relationship: A Neo-Pluralist Critique of British Industrial Relations Orthodoxy." *International Journal of Human Resource Management* DOI: 10.1080/09585192.2012.667429.

Ahmed, Nabila. 2011. "Big Risk in Cochlear's Precautionary Recall." *The Australian*, 13 September. Available from www.theaustralian.com.au/archive/business/big-risk-in-cochlears-precautionary-recall/story-fn7rgef9-1226135201443.

Armenakis, Achilles A., and Arthur G. Bedeian. 1999. "Organizational Change: A Review of Theory and Research in the 1990s." *Journal of Management,* 25(3): 293–315.

Ashkanasy, N. M., and E. Trevor Roberts. 2001. "Leadership Attributes and Cultural Values in Australia and New Zealand Compared: An Initial Report Based on GLOBE Data." *International Journal of Organisational Behaviour*, 2: 37–44.

Australian Bureau of Statistics. 2012. *6310.0—Employee Earnings, Benefits and Trade Union Membership, Australia, August 2011*. Canberra: Australian Bureau of Statistics 2012 [cited 5 September 2012].

Australian Human Resources Institute and Holding Redlich Lawyers. 2009. "The Cochlear Dispute—Unions Back at the Table under the Fair Work Act 2009 (Cth)." *HR Monthly*, September.

Australian Qualifications Framework Council. 2011. *Australian Qualifications Framework*. edited by Department of Education Employment and Workplace Relations. Canberra, Australia: Australian Qualifications Framework Council.

Beer, Michael, Russell A. Eisenstat, and Bert Spector. 1990. "Why Change Programs Don't Produce Change." *Harvard Business Review,* 68(6): 158–66.

Bhasin, S., and P. Burcher. 2006. "Lean Viewed as a Philosophy." *Journal of Manufacturing Technology Management*, 17(1): 56–72.

Bloom, N., and J. Van Reenen. 2007. "Measuring and Explaining Management Practices across Firms and Countries." *Quarterly Journal of Economics*, CXXII: 1351–1408.

Butler, Peter. 2009. "Non-Union Employee Representation: Exploring the Riddle of Managerial Strategy." *Industrial Relations Journal*, 40(3): 198–214.

Charlwood, Andy, and Mike Terry. 2007. "21st-Century Models of Employee Representation: Structures, Processes and Outcomes." *Industrial Relations Journal*, 38(4): 320–37.

Chung, C. A. 1996. "Human Issues Influencing the Successful Implementation of Advanced Manufacturing Technology." *Journal of Engineering and Technology Management*, 13(3–4): 283–99.

Cochlear. 2009. *Annual Report*. Sydney, Australia.

Demeter, K., and Z. Matsuyz. 2011. "The Impact of Lean Practices on Inventory Turnover." *International Journal of Production Economics*, 133: 154–63.

Denzin, N. 2009. *The Research Act: A Theoretical Introduction to Sociological Methods*. New Brunswick, NJ: Transaction Publishers, Rutgers.

Donaghey, Jimmy, Niall Cullinane, Tony Dundon, and Tony Dobbins. 2012. "Non-Union Employee Representation, Union Avoidance and the Managerial Agenda." *Economic and Industrial Democracy*, 33(2): 163–83.

Donaghey, Jimmy, Niall Cullinane, Tony Dundon, and Adrian Wilkinson. 2011. "Reconceptualising Employee Silence: Problems and Prognosis." *Work, Employment and Society*, 25(1): 51–67.

Doyle, Mike, Tim Claydon, and Dave Buchanan. 2000. "Mixed Results, Lousy Process: The Management Experience of Organizational Change." *British Journal of Management*, 11 (Special Issue): S59-S-80.

Drucker, P. F. 1954. *The Practice of Management*. Oxford, UK: Butterworth-Heinemann.

Dundon, Tony, Deirdre Curran, Paul Ryan, and Maureen Maloney. 2006. "Conceptualising the Dynamics of Employee Information and Consultation: Evidence from the Republic of Ireland." *Industrial Relations Journal*, 37(5): 492–512.

Dundon, Tony, and Paul J. Gollan. 2007. "Re-Conceptualising Voice in the Non-Union Workplace." *International Journal of Human Resource Management*, 18(7): 1182–98.

Dundon, Tony, Adrian Wilkinson, Mick Marchington, and Peter Ackers. 2004. "The Meanings and Purpose of Employee Voice." *International Journal of Human Resource Management*, 15(6): 1150–71.

Dyne, L. Van, S. Ang, and I. C. Botero. 2003. "Conceptualizing Employee Silence and Employee Voice as Multi-Dimensional Constructs." *Journal of Management Studies*, 40(6): 1359–92.

Emiliani, B. 2003. *Better Thinking, Better Results*. New York: CLBM.

Fair Work Australia. 2009. *Decision: Automotive Food, Metals, Engineering, Printing and Kindred Industries Union V Cochlear Limited*. Edited by Fair Work Australia. Canberra, Australia: Australian Industrial Relations Commissions.

Fair Work Commission. 2012. *Bargaining and Workplace Determinations*. [cited May 3rd 2012]. Available from www.fwc.gov.au/awards-and-agreements/agreements/about-agreements/enterprise-bargaining.

Flynn, B. B., and E. J. Flynn. 2005. "Synergies between Supply Chain Management and Quality Management: Emerging Implications." *International Journal of Production Research*, 43(16): 3421–36.

Folger, R. 1977. "Distributive and Procedural Justice: Combined Impact of 'Voice' and Improvement on Experienced Inequity." *Journal of Personality and Social Psychology*, 35: 108–19.

Forrester, R. 1995. "Implications of Lean Manufacturing for Human Resource Strategy." *Work Study,* 44(3): 20–4.

Freeman, R. B., P. Boxall, and P. Haynes (eds.). 2007. *What Workers Say: Employee Voice in the Anglo-American World.* Ithaca, NY: Cornell University Press.

Gollan, Paul. J. 2007. *Employee Representation in Non-Union Firms.* London: Sage.

———. 2010. "Employer Strategies towards Non-Union Collective Voice." In A. Wilkinson, P. J. Gollan, M. Marchington and D. Lewin (eds.), *The Oxford Handbook of Participation in Organizations*, pp. 212–36. Oxford, UK: Oxford University Press.

———. 2011. "Message from Cochlear Loud and Clear." *Australian Financial Review*, 19 December. Available from www.afr.com/p/opinion/message_from_cochlear_loud_and_clear_pkKaXsSKC8Sonj09fxnYFP.

———., and Glen Patmore. 2013. "Perspectives of Legal Regulation and Employment Relations at the Workplace : Limits and Challenges for Employee Voice." *Journal of Industrial Relations*, 55(4): 488–506.

Gomez, Rafael, Alex Bryson, and Paul Willman. 2010. "Voice in the Wilderness? The Shift from Union to Non-Union Voice in Britain." In A. Wilkinson, P. J. Gollan, M. Marchington and D. Lewin (eds.), *The Oxford Handbook of Participation in Organizations*, pp. 383–406. Oxford, UK: Oxford University Press.

Gonzalez-Benito, J., and O. Gonzalez-Benito. 2008. "Operations Management Practices Linked to the Adoption of ISO 14001: An Empirical Analysis of Spanish Manufacturers." *International Journal of Production Economics*, 113: 60–73.

Green, R., R. Agarwal, J. Van Reenen, N. Bloom, J. Mathews, C. Boedker, D. Sampson, P. Gollan, P. Toner, H. Tan, K Randhawa, and P. Brown. 2009. *Management Matters—Just How Productive Are We? Findings from the Australian Management Practices and Productivity Global Benchmarking Project.* Edited by Department of Innovation Industry Science and Research (DIISR). Canberra, ACT: DIISR.

Gregory, A. 2002. "Can Lean Save UK Manufacturing?" *Works Management,* 55(7): 1–6.

Hancock, W., and J. Zaycko. 1998. "Lean Production—Implementation Problems." *IIE Solutions,* 30: 1–9.

Hannan, Ewin, and Drew Warne-Smith. 2009. "ACTU Trumpets Cochlear Victory." *The Australian*, 21 August. Available from www.theaustralian.com.au/archive/politics/actu-trumpets-cochlear-victory/story-e6frgczf-1225764574918.

Heller, F., E. Pusić, G. Strauss, and B. Wilpert. 1998. *Organizational Participation: Myth and Reality.* New York: Oxford University Press.

Helms Mills, J. C., and A. J. Mills. 2000. "Rules, Sensemaking, Formative Contexts and Discourse in the Gendering of Organisational Culture." In N. Ashkanasy, C. Wilderom, and M. Peterson (eds.), *Handbook of Organisational Climate and Culture*, pp. 55–70. Thousand Oaks, CA, Sage.

Hofer, C., C. Eroglu, and A. R. Hofer. 2012. "The Effect of Lean Production on financial Performance: The Mediating Role of Inventory Leanness." *International Journal of Production Economics*, 138(2): 242–53.

Hsu, C. C., K. C. Tan, V. R. Kannan, and G. Keong Leong. 2009. "Supply Chain Management Practices as a Mediator of the Relationship between Operations Capability and Firm Performance." *International Journal of Production Research*, 47(3): 835–55.

Industrial Relations Commission of New South Wales. 2005. *Cochlear Limited Enterprise Agreement 2005 Between Cochlear Limited and the Employees of Cochlear Limited and Australian Manufacturing Workers Union (AMWU).* Sydney: Industrial Relations Commission of New South Wales.

Janda, Michael. 2012. *Cochlear Profit Hit by Recall Costs.* [cited 6 September 2012]. Available from www.abc.net.au/news/2012–08–07/cochlear-profit-hurt-by-write-downs/4182474.

Jick, T. D. 1979. "Mixing Qualitative and Quantitative Methods: Triangulation in Action." *Administrative Science Quarterly,* 24: 602–11.

Johnstone, P. L. 2004. "Mixed Methods, Mixed Methodology: Health Services Research in Practice." *Qualitative Health Research,* 14(2): 259–71.

Johnstone, S., P. Ackers, and A. Wilkinson. 2010. "Better than Nothing? Is Non-Union Partnership a Contradiction in Terms?" *Journal of Industrial Relations,* 52(2): 151–68.

Kaufman, B. E., and D. G. Taras. 2010. "Employee Participation through Non-Union Forms of Employee Representation." In A. Wilkinson, P. J. Gollan, M. Marchington and D. Lewin (eds.), *The Oxford Handbook of Participation in Organizations,* pp 258–85. Oxford, UK: Oxford University Press.

Kotter, John P. 1995. "Leading Change: Why Transformation Efforts Fail." *Harvard Business Review,* 73(2): 59–67.

———. 1996. *Leading Change.* Boston, MA: Harvard Business School Press.

Lewis, Laurie K., Amy M. Schmisseur, Keri K. Stephens, and Kathleen E. Weir. 2006. "Advice on Communicating during Organizational Change: The Content of Popular Press Books." *Journal of Business Communication,* 43(2): 113–37.

Liker, J. K. 2004. *The Toyota Way—14 Management Principles from the World's Greatest Manufacturer.* New York: McGraw-Hill.

Linderman, K. 2008. "Six Sigma: Definition and Underlying Theory." *Journal of Operations Management,* 26(4): 536–54.

Lines, Rune. 2004. "Influence of Participation in Strategic Change: Resistance, Organizational Commitment and Change Goal Achievement." *Journal of Change Management,* 4(3): 193–215.

Marchington, M., and A. Wilkinson. 2005. "Direct Participation." In: S. Bach (ed.), *Personnel Management: A Comprehensive Guide to Theory and Practice,* pp. 398–423. 4th ed. Oxford: Blackwell.

Markey, Raymond. 2007. "Non-Union Employee Representation in Australia: A Case Study of the Suncorp Metway Employee Council Inc. (SMEC)." *Journal of Industrial Relations,* 49(2): 187–209.

Mathison, S. 1988. "Why Triangulate?" *Educational Researcher,* 17: 13–17.

Melton, T. 2005. "The Benefits of Lean Manufacturing: What Lean Thinking Has to Offer the Process Industries." *Chemical Engineering Research and Design,* 83(A6): 662–73.

Mills, A. J., G. Durepos, and E. Wiebe. 2010. *Encyclopaedia of Case Study Research.* Thousand Oaks, CA: Sage Publications.

Mills, J., C. Helms, and A. J. Mills. 2000. "Rules, Sensemaking, Formative Contexts and Discourse in the Gendering of Organizational Culture." In N. Ashkanasy, C. Wilderom and M. Peterson (eds.), *Handbook of Organizational Climate and Culture,* pp. 55–70. Thousand Oaks, CA: Sage.

Morgan, Gareth. 2006. *Images of Organization.* Thousand Oaks, California: Sage.

Morley, J. M., and T. L. Doolen. 2006. "The Role of Communication and Management Support in a Lean Manufacturing Implementation." *Management Decision,* 44(2): 228–45.

Naveh, E., A. Marcus, and H-K. Moon. 2004. "Implementing ISO 9000: Performance Improvement by First or Second Movers." *International Journal of Production Research,* 42(9): 1843–63.

Roberts, Peter. 2012. "Study on Cochlear Puts Opposing IR Views in Perspective." *The Australian Financial Review,* 24 July. Available from www.afr.com/p/national/study_on_cochlear_puts_opposing_YQeTArfiM9X8TaWYscr6nO.

Skulley, Mark. 2012. "Cochlear Told to Help Union." *Australasian Business Intelligence*, 5 August. Available from www.highbeam.com/doc/1G1-298655737.html.

Sloan, Judith. 2012. "Membership Fall Crisis for Unions." *The Australian*, 1 May. Available from www.theaustralian.com.au/opinion/columnists/membership-fall-crisis-for-unions/story-fnbkvnk7-1226343081983#.

Taras, Daphne G., and Bruce E. Kaufman. 2006. "Non-Union Employee Representation in North America: Diversity, Controversy and Uncertain Future." *Industrial Relations Journal*, 37(5): 513–42.

Thurmond, V. A. 2001. "The Point of Triangulation." *Journal of Nursing Scholarship*, 33(3): 253–8.

Tucker, Anita L., and Amy C. Edmondson. 2003. "Why Hospitals Don't Learn from Failures: Organizational and Psychological Dynamics That Inhibit System Change." *California Management Review*, 45(2): 56–72.

Upchurch, Martin, Mike Richardson, Stephanie Tailby, Andy Danford, and Paul Stewart. 2006. "Employee Representation and Partnership in the Non-Union Sector: A Paradox of Intention?" *Human Resource Management Journal*, 16(4): 393–410.

Wadell, W., and N. Bodek. 2005. *The Rebirth of American Industry*. New York: PCS Press.

Weick, Karl E., and Kathleen M. Sutcliffe. 2007. *Managing the Unexpected: Resilient Performance in an Age of Uncertainty*. San Francisco: John Wiley & Sons, Inc.

White, R. E., D. Ojha, and C. C. Kuo. 2010. "A Competitive Progression Perspective of JIT Systems: Evidence from Early US Implementations." *International Journal of Production Research*, 48(20): 6103–24.

Wilkinson, Adrian, and Tony Dundon. 2010. "Direct Employee Participation." In A. Wilkinson, P. Gollan, M. Marchington, and D. Lewin (eds.), *The Oxford Handbook of Employee Participation*, pp. 167–185. Oxford, UK: Oxford University Press.

Wilkinson, Adrian, Tony Dundon, and Irena Grugulis. 2007. "Information but Not Consultation: Exploring Employee Involvement in SMEs." *International Journal of Human Resource Management*, 18(7): 1279–97.

Wilkinson, Adrian, Paul J. Gollan, Mick Marchington, and David Lewin. 2010. "Conceptualizing Employee Participation in Organizations. In A. Wilkinson, P. J. Gollan, M. Marchington, and D. Lewin (eds.), *The Oxford Handbook of Participation in Organizations*, pp. 1–25. Oxford, UK: Oxford University Press.

Wolfe-Morrison, Elizabeth, and Frances J. Milliken. 2000. "Organizational Silence: A Barrier to Change and Development in a Pluralistic World." *The Academy of Management Review*, 25(4): 706–25.

4 The Difficult Challenge Faced by Hybrid Employee Voice in the Australian University Sector

Alison Barnes and Craig MacMillan

INTRODUCTION

Employee voice has attracted much academic attention and interest over the last thirty years. While traditionally the research has focussed on union voice (Freeman and Medoff 1984), more recently a steady stream of studies has begun to emerge examining non-union employee representation (Gollan 2000, 2007; Kaufman and Taras 2000). This research has tended to examine the relative merits of non-union versus union forms of employee voice and has left relatively underexplored hybrid forms of voice (for example, see Kim and Kim 2004). Hybrid voice refers to a mechanism that combines both union and non-union representation (Hall, Hutchinson, Purcell, Terry, and Parker 2010). This chapter draws on a case study of an Australian university, UNICO, to examine the emergence, operation, and effectiveness of hybrid voice mechanisms. More specifically, the chapter explores, from the point of view of union and non-union members of staff, university management and union officials, the functioning of a university committee, the Consultative Employee Committee (CEC). The committee was established in response to the Australian federal government's Higher Education Workplace Relations Requirements (HEWRRs). The aim of the committee, as stated in the collective agreement at UNICO, was to provide employees with the opportunity to monitor the implementation of the university's collective agreement and to comment on and alter policies that govern working conditions.[1]

The findings suggest that although in principle employee voice expressed through the CEC had wide support from both union and non-union committee members, due to the context in which the CEC operated, there were many difficulties that undermined its effectiveness. These difficulties included the gap between the rhetoric of managerial support and the actual resources provided for the committee. In particular, members of CEC pointed to the lack of induction training, inadequate workload release for committee members, the failure to establish effective mechanisms for non-unionised members to communicate with their constituents, and the limited time frames provided for discussion of policy. These limitations ensured that the CEC was unable to function in as consensual and effective manner as members may have wished. The chapter begins by providing an overview of the relevant literature on employee voice. This is followed by an examination of the political climate that gave rise to the establishment of hybrid voice mechanisms in the university sector. The case study and method of inquiry are then explained. The findings from the interviews regarding the operation of the CEC are reported, as is an update on the latest developments in employee voice at UNICO since the CEC ceased operation. The chapter closes with a discussion of the findings in the light of recent research.

RELEVANT LITERATURE ON EMPLOYEE VOICE

Following the landmark contribution of Freeman and Medoff (1984), employee voice and participation have attracted considerable interest across a range of fields of academic inquiry (See, for example, Gollan 2000, 2007; Kaufman and Taras 2000; Wilkinson et al. 2010). Employee voice broadly refers to efforts by employees to communicate their preferences and views to their employer with the aim of furthering their interests regarding the terms and conditions of work, as well as the organisation and performance of work. Scholars differentiate employee voice into two categories: direct and indirect voice (Dundon, Wilkinson, Marchington, and Ackers 2004). Direct voice refers to communication between employees and employers that is not mediated by a representative. Examples include the operation of an open-door policy between an employee and his or her manager and regular staff meetings between workers and management. By contrast, indirect employee voice involves the communication of employee preferences and views through a representative. Indirect voice is typically divided into two types: union and non-union voice. Union voice occurs when unions represent the interests of their members to management, while non-union voice operates when workers elect representatives to communicate their views to management. Hybrid voice is also a form of indirect voice that combines in one mechanism both union and non-union voice (Hall et al. 2010).

Traditionally, in the Anglo-American countries of the United States, Canada, the United Kingdom, Ireland, Australia, and New Zealand, union representation has been the most significant form of employee voice (Freeman, Boxall, and Hayes 2007). However, over recent years, the decline in union density has been associated with an increasingly prominent role for direct and non-union representative forms of employee voice in workplaces in these countries (Freeman 2007; Gollan 2007; Kaufman and Taras 2000; Teicher, Holland, Pyman, and Cooper 2007; Willman, Bryson, and Gomez 2007). Associated with this has been a surge of academic interest in non-union voice in general (Dundon and Gollan 2007; Dundon, Wilkinson, Marchington, and Ackers 2005; Gollan 2007; Haynes 2005; Kaufman and Taras 2000; Markey 2001) and in particular comparing the relative benefits of union and non-union voice (Bryson 2004; Charlwood and Terry 2007; Pyman, Cooper, Teicher, and Holland 2006). A common finding from this research is that workplaces with multiple forms of voice outperform those with single voice. For example, Bryson (2004) examined British workplaces and found that effectiveness, as measured by employee perceptions of managerial responsiveness, was greatest in workplaces that had both direct and non-union representative voice mechanisms operating. Charlwood and Terry (2007) also investigated British workplaces and reported that workplaces with both union and non-union representation outperformed single-voice workplaces on measures that included wage dispersion, procedural fairness, and managerial perceptions of worker productivity. In addition, Hall and colleagues (2010) reported that among the UK workplaces they studied when examining the impact of the Information and Consultation of Employees (ICE) regulations, those with hybrid forms of voice elicited higher levels of employee satisfaction than did those with solely non-union voice. For Australian workplaces, Pyman and colleagues (2006) found that the combination of direct and non-union representative voice outperformed all other forms of voice and voice combinations on three measures of voice effectiveness: worker perceptions of managerial responsiveness, job control, and influence over rewards. Furthermore, the second most effective form of voice was a combination of direct and union and non-union representative mechanisms. Indeed, both Bryson (2004) and Pyman and colleagues (2006) found that union voice was more effective when combined with other forms of voice than when it was the sole form of voice. Results such as these have been interpreted as indicating that direct and indirect non-union representation are complementary to union representation rather than a substitute for it, as suggested by the union-substitution thesis (Fiorito 2001).

Kaufman and Taras (2010), following Taras and Kaufman (2006), put forward a taxonomy of perspectives on non-union employee representation. One of the perspectives, complementary voice, views union and non-union representative voice as operating in distinct domains, creating a dual-channel voice system. They noted that such systems are popular in Britain and Canada where core employment conditions are negotiated by the union while company policies relating to staff are dealt with using non-union employee representation in a more cooperative less adversarial forum. This perspective would seem to be a useful one through which to view the CEC at UNICO in that the unions exclusively negotiated the collective agreement with management, while the CEC, composed mainly of elected staff representatives, was concerned primarily with reviewing employment relations policies and monitoring the implementation of the collective agreement.

Another area of research relevant to the current study has looked at the role of the state in shaping the forms of employee voice that emerge in an economy. For example, it has been noted that the 1935 National Labor Relations Act (NLRA) in the United States essentially mandated against non-union forms of employee representation (Freeman 2007; Kaufman

1999). In Europe, in many countries including Germany, the Netherlands, and Belgium, worker representation through works councils has been instituted through legislation that determines both the form and range of powers enjoyed by them (Gumbrell-McCormick and Hyman 2010). In the United Kingdom, the EU Directive on informing and consulting with employees has been enacted through the 2005 Information and Consultation of Employees (ICE) Regulations. These regulations give employees in establishments employing fifty or more workers the right to request that their employers inform and consult with them (Gollan and Wilkinson 2007; Hall 2010). In Australia in 2005, the federal government imposed requirements on the university sector that tied access to funding to implementing various measures, one of which was a strengthening of direct employee consultation, which in this context meant non-union consultation (Barnes, MacMillan, and Markey 2013).

In the light of this research, a reasonable expectation is that the introduction of hybrid voice at UNICO would be perceived as good thing by employees and lead to improvements in the effectiveness of employee voice. However, as we will see in the next section, the political context in which the CEC was established undermined the possibility of such a positive outcome.

THE POLITICAL CLIMATE AND THE HEWRRS

In the 1996 federal election, a conservative Liberal-National Party Coalition led by John Howard was swept to power and immediately began a process of reregulating the labour market through legislative change. Ostensibly the rationale of these reforms, which began with the 1996 Workplace Relations Act and concluded with the Workplace Relations Amendment (WorkChoices) Act of 2005, was to increase the choice available to both employers and employees when contracting with each other. However, as has been well documented, the underlying intent of this program of legislative change was to increase the bargaining power of employers at the expense of workers and in particular unions (Barnes 2006; Cooney 2006; Forsyth and Sutherland 2006; Hall 2006).

Universities were at the forefront of Howard's antiunion agenda, and the introduction of the HEWRRs in 2005 foreshadowed the controversial WorkChoices legislation that was to follow. The federal government is a key source of funding for Australian universities, and in order to get access to funds linked to the Higher Education Support Act (2003), universities had to comply with the HEWRRs. The HEWRRs covered a number of areas of employment relations, including (i) offering all existing and new staff employment on an individual contract known as an Australian Workplace Agreement; (ii) the establishment of direct forms of employee consultation; (iii) the removal of unnecessary detail from collective agreements; (iv) transparent and fair systems for managing and rewarding staff performance; and

(v) freedom of association with particular reference to the use of university facilities by unions (Department of Education, Science and Training [DEST] 2005). This chapter focuses primarily on the HEWRRs requirements that universities establish direct forms of employee consultation and that unnecessary detail such as limits on the use of fixed-term contracts be removed from collective agreements. These requirements were viewed to constitute a significant challenge to union voice in the university sector.

The requirement concerning direct forms of employee consultation specified that union representation of staff was permitted only if non-union forms of representation had been established. It is important to note that there is a mismatch in the meaning of direct employee consultation between the academic literature and the HEWRRS. As discussed, in the academic literature direct consultation refers to a situation in which employees represent themselves to the employer and do not use a representative, either union or non-union, to do so. However, the HEWRRs requirement (ii) concerning direct consultation was deemed to be satisfied when (a) employees could only be represented by their union if they explicitly request it and (b) at least some positions on consultative committees were filled by staff representatives through elections in which all staff could vote (DEST 2005). In practical terms, (a) clearly reduced the prospect of unions raising issues with management on behalf of members because management was free to ignore the matter until the union had provided the names of the individual members raising the issue, and many union members were uncomfortable with this, and (b) meant that in universities across the sector, consultative committees which previously had been composed of management and union representatives now had to be constituted so that it was possible for some positions to be filled by staff representatives through competitive elections. Consequently, the consultative committees, in principle at least, went from being a form of union voice to hybrid voice.

The situation at UNICO was complicated by the HEWRRs requirement (iii) that universities remove unnecessary detail from collective agreements. In Australia, collective bargaining occurs at the enterprise level rather than at the industry level. More specifically, in the university sector, bargaining between management and the unions occurs separately at each university. The outcome of the collective bargaining process is an enterprise agreement (EA) that sets down the terms and conditions of employment for employees of the university. The HEWRRs requirement (iii) afforded management the opportunity to move detail that had been part of the pre–HEWRRs EAs into policy that increased managerial control of workplace relations, because policy could be varied without consultation with staff or unions. For example, at UNICO, the pre–HEWRRs EA that covered the period 2003 through 2006 had forty-five subclauses within the clause dealing with the crucial issue of academic staff access to sabbaticals (study leave). By contrast, the EA negotiated to satisfy the HEWRRs had only two subclauses dealing with this issue, with all other details now in policy that management was free to vary. Again, the underlying aim of this requirement was to diminish the strength of union voice by reducing the range of matters over which unions could take formal disputes on behalf of members. Consequently, the CEC became a highly contested forum in which the union sought to ensure that staff policies were consistent with the intent of the EA. However, their power to do this through the CEC was truncated because the HEWRRs requirement on direct consultation made clear that consultative committees could in no way supplant managerial prerogative.

UNICO: THE CASE STUDY

UNICO is a large university located in Sydney with more than 35,000 students enrolled. Two thirds of the student population are enrolled full time, and close to one third are from overseas. As of 2009, UNICO had a full-time equivalent workforce of 2,365, of which 1,120 were academic staff and 1,245 were nonacademic staff. Two unions represented workers, the Community and Public Sector Union (CPSU) representing nonacademic or general staff and the National Tertiary Education Union (NTEU) representing both academic and general staff, which was by far the larger of the two unions in terms of membership at UNICO.

Prior to the implementation of the HEWRRs, the forms of indirect employee representation operating at UNICO were determined by the EA covering the period 2003 through 2006. According to the agreement, virtually all consultative committees were union–management committees, with both parties generally appointing an equal number of representatives. These consultative committees covered the most important areas of working life, including work design teams, work practices review teams, and grievance review panels. In other words, at UNICO there was an absence of non-union employee voice on these committees. One of the few exceptions was the Occupational Health and Safety committee at UNICO, which not only had management and union appointees as members but also included a large number of elected staff representatives.

Contiguous with the implementation of the HEWRRs was the expiry of the 2003 through 2006 EA at UNICO. Across the sector, the unions adopted a compliance strategy for the new round of bargaining in that they cooperated where possible with management to ensure that the new EAs satisfied the HEWRRs. They did this because they were concerned that if a new EA was deemed to be noncompliant with the HEWRRs, job losses would follow as a result of not having access to the government funding linked to the HEWRRs (Barnes, MacMillan, and Markey 2013). Consequently, the unions did not strongly resist the movement of employment matters out of collective agreements and into policy unless they related directly to an employee entitlement. For example, as pointed out earlier, the pre–HEWRRs EA at UNICO had forty-five subclauses dealing with sabbaticals, and the HEWRRs–compliant EA that followed only had two, which primarily dealt with establishing who was entitled to apply; all other detail was moved to policy. As mentioned, at UNICO under the pre–HEWRRs EA, consultative committees were composed of only management and union representatives. However, in order to satisfy the HEWRRs, the new EA that covered the period 2006 through 2009 included an undertaking to form a committee titled the Consultative Employee Committee (CEC) within three months of the agreement coming into operation. According to the new EA, the CEC would provide a mechanism for direct consultation on employment relations such as the implementation of the EA, university policy, and procedure (whether included in the EA or not) staff development, and policy and programs concerned with workplace diversity and occupational health and safety.

The new EA stipulated that the CEC would be composed of nine elected academic and ten elected nonacademic members of staff, as well as four staff nominees from each of the two unions. Academics participated in faculty-based elections to determine two academic representatives for each of the four faculties, and one representative was elected to represent academics not aligned to a particular faculty. A similar process was followed to elect the nonacademic members. Committee members were elected for a two-year term and were scheduled to meet on a quarterly basis. The CEC had a Chair elected by committee members who would communicate with university management through the Director of Human Resources (DHR).

Importantly, management representatives were not formal members of the CEC; however, the DHR and an assistant attended and participated in meetings and gave feedback to the CEC from university management. This relationship between the CEC and management was also made manifest in the physical organisation of meetings, with the formal members of the CEC sitting around a large table and the DHR and assistant sitting to the side, at a separate table. The university signalled its support for the CEC in the EA by committing to provide members with adequate preparation time for meetings and for releasing resources to ensure the proper functioning of the committee. The CEC came into existence at the end of 2006 and operated for four years. Every two years, new union nominees were appointed and new elections were held for staff representative positions.

This case study was based on seventeen semistructured interviews. The interviews were conducted with the DHR, the only representative of management that attended CEC meetings on a regular basis; the union nominated members of CEC from the NTEU and the CPSU; both union and non-union elected staff representatives, and senior officials and organisers of both unions (five NTEU and one CPSU). A greater proportion of interviews was conducted with participants in the second incarnation of the CEC, largely because of the relocation or retirement of members from the first. Interviews covered such themes as the role of the CEC, the role of participants on the CEC, the relationship of management to the CEC, the attitude of the unions to the CEC, the relationship between union and non-union members of the CEC, the perceived effectiveness of the CEC, and developments in employee voice post–CEC. Interviews were transcribed and coded in order to identify common themes and points of difference among the groups. Interviews were lengthy and ranged in duration from forty-five minutes to two hours.

RESULTS

Understanding of Members' Role on the CEC and Understanding of the Role of the CEC

All participants interviewed had a clear understanding that their role on the CEC was to reflect the views of their constituencies. More specifically, elected staff representatives understood that they represented the faculties that had elected them. A non-union elected general staff member stated, "Well I think it (the CEC) was a voice for our faculty . . . I suppose I was the voice" (non-union elected general staff 1). Another non-union elected general staff member responded, "So I thought my role was to contribute obviously, representing the members I was elected to represent" (non-union elected general staff 2). In addition, union nominees saw themselves representing their respective unions, although some union nominees drew no distinction in practice between representing their union and representing staff generally. For example, a union nominee stated, "I always saw the role as one in which I would be speaking to management as a member of staff and a member of the union, I don't make a distinction to be honest" (union nominee 1).

While all committee members understood that their function was to voice their constituencies' views, only some representatives knew that the committee existed to satisfy a government requirement, and these tended to be union members. While the committee's primary function was to provide a forum for discussion of university policy relating to the employment relationship, this purpose was not widely understood by non-union elected representatives. A number of both non-union academic and general staff participants had a particularly broad view of what would be discussed and believed it should primarily function as a highly cooperative committee that would find more efficient ways of running the university.

A non-union elected general staff member reported:

> I thought the role of the CEC was a place where staff came together and they discussed all sorts of issues to do with the university, the direction, the key priority areas and where you think improvements should be made, anything to do with the university and what it was about.
>
> (Non-union elected general staff 2)

A non-union elected academic member expressed a similar view:

> Before I got there my interpretation of the role of the CEC was to give voice to staff and to work collaboratively with management within the university to effect improvements in the university, at every level . . . so that's the way I thought, very much a team based approach was the way I perceived it before I got there.
>
> (Non-union elected academic 1)

A consequence of holding this more expansive view concerning the purpose of the CEC was that these non-union elected staff representatives were more likely to become frustrated and disillusioned by the operation of the committee and its focus on the employment relationship, resulting in a number informally withdrawing from the committee. This in effect rendered their constituents "voiceless":

> I'd gone in with the expectation of the role that we could or should play and I was very excited about it, but when that wasn't realised and I just felt like we were concentrating on policy and procedure very ineffectively or union led issues, I just didn't see the point in me going.
>
> (Non-union elected general staff 2)

As this quote suggests, some non-union members perceived the committee's focus on employment-related matters as being union driven when this focus actually resulted from the formal terms of reference as laid out in the EA. This highlights management's failure to provide induction and proper support for elected staff members that would have enhanced their understanding of the purpose of the committee. Indeed, one non-union elected staff member lamented:

> It was never really clear [the purpose of the committee] it's in the EA what it is supposed to do, but no one ever sits you down and says right, your role within this group is to do this and what we want to achieve from this group is this, this and this, you're not actually given any induction of any sort whatsoever.
>
> (Non-union elected general staff 2)

The Relationship between Management and the CEC

What Was Management's View of the CEC?
The DHR reported that the CEC was useful because it provided both an important forum for communication and consultation and a level of security for staff. The DHR maintained that the committee functioned as a form of "first voice" and, on occasion, the "only voice" on policy matters.

The DHR stated, "we put a policy to the CEC, we test it with them, and if it didn't seem to be too contentious we wouldn't send it out to staff more generally . . . if anything the CEC might have been a harder test than the general population."

For both management and unions, the CEC provided information and insights into each other's position on employment issues. The DHR stated, "so I think they [unions] got a better understanding of why we were taking certain decisions." In a similar vein, management believed that the CEC provided them with an opportunity "to get a measure of the heat around issues" before proceeding with a policy, and it was their view that, ultimately, this reduced the likelihood of formal disputes and grievances later emerging.

The HEWRRs required that many employment issues typically covered in the pre–HEWRRs EA be moved into policy, and this afforded management the opportunity to change policy on key employment issues without staff consultation. Previously, when such matters were part of the enterprise agreement, staff could initiate a formal dispute if management attempted to act unilaterally. The DHR believed that the CEC allowed management to reassure staff that they would be consulted in the formulation of policy. Specifically, the DHR reported,

> As you know when the HEWRRs came in we had to take all the policies out of the enterprise agreement . . . a lot of our policies were embedded in the agreement, so staff were quite concerned and the unions were quite concerned . . . that all the policies would be developed without any input from staff and so part of developing the CEC was to provide a conduit for them [staff and unions] to feel like we wouldn't put draconian policies in place.
>
> (DHR)

University management were not formally members of the committee. However, the DHR, supported by an assistant who kept the minutes, attended meetings to answer questions and provide responses from the university management to the policy recommendations of the committee. The DHR believed that on balance, it would have been better if management representatives were formal members of the committee. She maintained that nonmembership diminished her capacity to contribute to discussion. This led to committee members believing they should debate an issue and come to a decision that she would formally convey to the university's executive, whose response she would also communicate back to the CEC. She believed this inadvertently led to the development of an adversarial relationship between the committee and the university management rather than one that was more cooperative and consultative. The DHR believed that a more favourable relationship could have developed if she had been freer to contribute to discussion in the CEC. This view was shared by a number of committee members, including one of the Chairs of the CEC who was also a union nominee.

> Well it's just a different dynamic, it means that motions of decisions that come out of the CEC are the voice of the staff. Management can take that and do what they like with it really, they're not part of those decisions so they just take it as feedback and it's more formal, whereas when you have management as part of the committee I think the emphasis is less on motions and decisions, it's more on the exchange of information.
>
> (Union nominee 1)

Perceptions of Management by Members of the CEC

Management's lack of formal membership of the committee was symbolised in the seating arrangements at meetings. Specifically, as noted earlier, they did not sit at the committee table but rather were seated to the side of it:

> I wouldn't sit at the table, I'd physically sit a little back from the table, it felt a bit weird, but we did it to symbolise that [management were not formally members], and at times I'd be biting my lip because they'd be . . . debating something, where I had a piece of knowledge to throw in that I wouldn't throw in because I wasn't allowed.
>
> (DHR)

Committee members expressed a considerable diversity of views concerning the relationship of management to the committee. Some members did not think that the functioning or the legitimacy of the CEC was diminished by management not being formally represented on the committee, while others thought it was counterproductive. For example, an elected general staff member stated, "We kind of sat at this table and the DHR was kind of there with his people . . . it felt like he was just sitting in but that we were all addressing him and talking to him, it was funny" (union elected general staff 1). More stridently, an elected academic member declared, "I thought it was terrible, embarrassing, bizarre, couldn't actually believe that they were sitting away from the committee, not even physically on the table, it was like you had to look over someone to get an opinion" (non-union elected academic 1).

A number of other members felt management's informal presence at meetings was indicative of the little value placed on the committee. An elected general staff member argued:

> Well that indicated what they thought of it. We will only spare one person because that's all we can afford time wise, I would look around the table and think wow, this is costing the university ten thousand dollars an hour, you know realistically, why don't they actually do something

with it, if we had to bill them for it, it's like because they got it for free it wasn't worth anything to them.

(union elected general staff 2)

Notwithstanding this wide range of views about management's presence at committee meetings, virtually all members reported not being intimidated or constrained in their contributions by the presence of management.

The Unions and the CEC

The CEC represented an opportunity for non-union employee representation to gain a strong foothold at UNICO. In addition, as previously discussed, the unions were concerned by the HEWRRs–driven movement of a number of key employment issues out of the enterprise agreement and into policy. Once in policy, the only forum in which these issues could be discussed was the CEC. Both unions formed the view that the intent of the HEWRRs was to significantly weaken union voice:

> One of the objectives of the HEWRRs was to remove the unions from the consultative framework . . . (and) introducing the concept of (non-union) employee representatives was at its heart an attempt to circumvent the union process. [CPSU Union Official 1]
>
> The employer could always communicate directly with employees, the union never stopped that, but we certainly insisted on our role as the legitimate employee representative and the HEWRRs were set up to undermine that role.

(NTEU Union Official 2)

Consequently, across the university sector, the unions sought to ensure they were strongly represented on staff consultative committees that were established to satisfy the HEWRRs. Either jointly or individually, the unions put members forward to contest the staff representative elections. Indeed, the NTEU formed the view that it was crucial that they convincingly win the elections in order to provide convincing support for their position that they were the legitimate voice of staff:

> We had to win those elections, we had to win because our argument to the government and to the universities was that this is a waste of time, the HEWRRs is a waste of time, we're actually doing what you want to do, we're actually providing the universities with the opportunity to hear what their staff have to say so consequently we had to win those elections and win them handsomely . . . and this is what we did.

(NTEU Union Official 3)

At UNICO, the unions adopted this strategy for the CEC elections and were successful, with the majority of elected positions—more than 85 per cent—filled by union members. This highlights a very important point that while nominally a hybrid form of voice, the CEC actually functioned primarily as a vehicle for union voice. Moreover, it was a conscious union strategy to get members to stand for the elected positions and for union members to be encouraged by their union to vote for union candidates.

The unions were also quite critical of the notion of non-union representation on the CEC, and some senior union officials questioned whether such representation was even meaningful:

> The elected staff representatives don't represent anybody because there's no structure articulating to their representation, there's no constituency for them to consult with, there are no structures to direct them, they can't be employee representatives because there's no representative structure sitting underneath them to ensure some sort of authentic voice, whereas the union has elective committees, general meetings, etc. There's no process and in that sense, non-union is not a category.
>
> (NTEU Union Official 1)

A by-product of the strong union presence on the CEC was that while management clearly valued it as a vehicle for consultation with staff, they also questioned whether the views put forward at the CEC were truly representative of all staff. This led to the DHR utilising other forms of voice as a check on the deliberations of the CEC. For example, the DHR stated:

> I had to check whether or not the view being raised [in the committee] was the general view of the university [staff] or only of union members and for example sometimes we'd find that other staff survey results seemed to be quite counter to what the unions were saying [on the committee].

There were a variety of attitudes expressed by non-union members of the CEC about the strong union presence on the committee. Some reported being frustrated because they believed this led to the union dominating the agenda of meetings. For example, a non-union elected general staff representative stated:

> I probably felt more frustrated than constrained because I did feel as though it was union dominated, and I have nothing against unions . . . I just felt it was a very biased representation because it was union heavy and discussion was quite union focussed.
>
> (Non-union elected general staff 2)

In addition, a non-union elected academic member believed that CEC meetings were "always confrontational" and that the "union has moved into this confrontational [way of relating] and it's embarrassing" (non-union elected academic 1). Despite this, the same representative did not believe that the presence of the union on the CEC inhibited their contribution at meetings. A somewhat different view was expressed by a non-union elected staff representative who did not see anything negative or confrontational in the union presence on the CEC; in fact, they "just enjoyed listening to them, they got so excited" (non-union elected general staff 1).

The unions clearly enjoyed the benefits of voice on the CEC through their staff nominees and the many elected staff representatives who were also union members. Despite this, some union officials expressed frustration that they now only heard about important issues regarding changes to university policy second hand, if at all. This point was made strongly by an NTEU industrial officer, who stated,

> While I was doing the bargaining I came across policy changes . . . I did a whole audit of the university of the policies, and there were changes. [When] I raised it, when was this changed, "Oh we did this through the committee," I wasn't aware of it. As the industrial person who's supposed to provide the support and the advice on this sort of stuff, I don't think that's good enough. If there is a policy being discussed in a forum like the committee and it changes, then we need the state office [of the NTEU] represented . . . because we have that wider interest and perspective.
>
> (NTEU Union Official 2)

The Effectiveness of the CEC

While there were some ideological differences about the merits of hybrid forms of employee voice, interviewees all agreed on the importance of employee voice in the workplace. Despite this general support, both union and non-union members believed that the committee was not an effective form of voice. The interviews suggested there were two main reasons the CEC was perceived to be ineffective. These were (i) the lack of resources provided to support its effective functioning—workload release and IT support—and (ii) the restraints placed on the CEC's capacity to exert real influence on management's decision making.

Workload Release

The overwhelming majority of both academic and general staff members believed that the university had not adequately resourced the functioning of the committee. They believed there had not been any resources allocated to induct staff to the committee, that while staff were given time release to attend meetings, they were not given time release to prepare for meetings.

In addition, and most importantly for many general staff committee members, they were not given any workload reduction to offset their participation on the CEC.

The EA stipulated that the university would provide reasonable time release during normal working hours for members of the committee to attend and prepare for meetings. Management believed they were supportive of the functioning of the committee. The DHR reported writing to the relevant managers informing them that one of their team was a member of the committee and required time release to attend meetings. Moreover, the DHR also reported offering to write further letters if they were needed. Interestingly, however, the DHR only reported writing to managers to let them know they should release workers to attend meetings. While none of the participants revealed that they had been discouraged from participating by their line managers, a number of participants believed that inadequate workload release was given, and consequently they could not properly prepare for and attend meetings of either the main committee or subcommittees that deliberated on particular university policies. These concerns were particularly expressed by general staff representatives, who were essentially permitted to attend meetings but then had to later complete work that they were not able to undertake while attending. In addition, many documents needed to be read prior to meetings, and general staff reported doing this in their own time. So for general staff participants, membership of the committee was simply an addition to their duties. The following exchange with one of the elected general staff members was particularly revealing of these issues:

> *INTERVIEWER*: Did you find it difficult to ask for time off to participate in the committee?
>
> *CEC MEMBER*: No my manager is fine, but it is more in the back of your mind that you've got to catch up after being missing for two hours.
>
> *INTERVIEWER*: So that was a problem?
>
> *CEC MEMBER*: It always is, you've got to catch up.
>
> (Non-union elected general staff 1)

The situation was different for academic staff because they have a service component built into their workload. This component was not well specified and hence it could always be argued that participation in the committee was part of their workload and did not require any offsets. Despite this, a number of academic representatives believed they were not given adequate workload recognition for their participation on the CEC, especially with regard to meeting preparation, for example:

> Well I never did this (preparation) in office hours, no it was always a night time activity, and there was often a fair lot of documents that need

a fair amount of thought. . . . There was no work release . . . it was just kind of shuffled into some other period of time.

(Union elected academic 1)

Overall, it would appear that management released staff to attend meetings but did not provide release for preparation. Moreover, general staff members especially did not have their workload reduced but rather were still expected to complete all their work. Therefore, participation on the committee was ultimately at the staff member's expense. Some staff members resented this and others did not, and it should be noted that the latter were more senior general staff who had greater discretion over their workload. Some also believed that this underresourcing was a significant constraint on the effectiveness of the committee and especially the lack of preparation, which diminished the willingness of some members to voice their views.

Interaction with Constituents and IT Support

For the CEC to have functioned effectively as a form of employee voice, representatives needed the capability to interact with their constituents. Given the limitations placed on workload release, virtually all the elected staff representatives reported severe constraints on their ability to engage with their constituents. Elected academic members were typically restricted to only being able to consult with their immediate departments and found it virtually impossible to interact with staff in other departments within the faculty they were elected to represent. This difficulty was exacerbated by management's failure to provide contact details for staff that would have facilitated this interaction. For example, an elected general staff representative could not email only general staff within the faculty they had been elected to represent, nor could an elected academic member email only academic staff in their faculty. Ultimately, this was an IT problem, and it was neither resolved nor adequately explained why management could not provide contact details.

An elected academic member stated,

> We asked for that sort of stuff (an email list) that was a constant call, there was a constant call for the ability to email our constituents, and even with guys from IT on the committee, it still proved to be difficult . . . you would try to say stuff at department meetings but you can't go to every department meeting.

(Union elected academic 1)

This view was echoed by an elected general staff member:

> One of the things I did ask for immediately after being elected, was an email list of who all the members in my elected area were, so I could

contact them, because I thought that was pretty important, but they didn't have that and they couldn't get that information so I had no way to communicate with the area I was supposed to be representing and I thought that was a major downfall.

(Non-union elected general staff 2)

By contrast, union nominees on the CEC had no difficulty in communicating with the union members that they were representing. Union nominees had ready-made forums for interacting with their constituencies through union meetings, the delegate structure, emails to members, and union publications:

Obviously it was easy to feedback to the union people because you can just send an email out to members . . . one of the problems non-union reps had was communicating with constituencies the management faffed around and faffed around for years, despite all requests "can we have email lists for our constituencies" and they reckoned they couldn't do it and couldn't update it . . . and I'd say well you managed to send out the notices for the election to all the constituencies so how about you just give us those lists, "oh they're not up to date," well we'll take out of date lists then, you know it's better than nothing, and we never satisfactorily resolved that, ever . . . and it really did worry the people who'd been elected as representatives of an electorate because they could not get an email list of their electorate, so they said how are we supposed to consult and represent, and it was a fair question.

(Union nominee 1)

This quote demonstrates how the effectiveness of hybrid forms of voice is dependent upon management's preparedness to provide adequate resourcing, particularly for non-union employees.

The Lack of Power Invested in the CEC

According to the EA, the CEC was a mechanism for consultation only between staff and management. The CEC could deliberate on matters before it and could make recommendations to management. However, management was not obliged to act on any of these recommendations, and the committee had no power to enforce its views irrespective of how strongly they were held. Indeed, the federal government made clear that for a consultative committee to be compliant with the HEWRRs, it could in no way supplant managerial prerogative (DEST 2005).

A number of committee members believed the lack of power vested in the CEC led to management largely ignoring the deliberations of the committee. Indeed, some participants believed that for management, the committee was a tokenistic expression of employer interest in employee perspectives: "Oh well, [the committee], it had no mandated authority, it had no powers, no nothing, so that allowed it to be mere window dressing" (union elected academic 1). Interviewees gave specific examples of policies that the CEC had reviewed and provided extensive feedback on, which was then ignored: "It seemed to be a lot of banging its head against a wall . . . well we couldn't make decisions we could only recommend, and then when you recommend they get knocked back" (non-union elected general staff 1).

These quotes appear quite damning of the university's attitude towards the committee. However, another participant suggested that such outcomes were mainly due to the committee not meeting frequently enough, which led to policies being put up by the university before the consultation process with the CEC could be concluded:

> Well I think the processes around it were very slow . . . turn-around time was completely inefficient in trying to move different things forward I found, and because it would only meet quarterly or something, I just didn't see how it could be very effective, because you'd meet at the quarterly meeting and they'd decide yes, they would review a policy or procedure and then they'd meet again the next quarter to discuss what their findings were so that was an 8 month process.
>
> [Non-union elected general staff 2]

Despite this general view that management was not listening to the committee, there were a couple of prominent instances in which university management took seriously the committee's recommendations and concerns. An example was the development of policy governing staff appraisal and performance. The DHR described the impact of the CEC's concerns with this policy in the following manner:

> Firstly, we delayed the process, we were going to roll it out and we ended up stopping that and doing some pilots instead and that was pretty much because we tested it with the CEC and it didn't fly, and secondly we changed the design of the process quite significantly, we had a kind of two factor approach which was both performance and behaviours and after strong feedback from the CEC we dropped the behaviour stuff, similarly we dropped ratings for academic staff except in those areas we needed them for salary loadings . . . so some of the essential elements of the appraisal and performance process were changed as a result of the feedback from the CEC.
>
> (DHR)

In conclusion, committee members made a number of suggestions about how the operation of the CEC could be improved, including that the frequency of meetings be increased, proper time and workload release be provided to members to both prepare for and attend meetings, management representatives be formal members of the committee, and appropriate IT support be provided so that members could interact with their constituents. In addition, the unions argued that the functioning of the committee could be enhanced if union officials were granted formal membership on the committee or at least were permitted to attend meetings in an informal capacity.

Developments Since the CEC

The election of a Labour Federal Government in 2007 meant that when bargaining recommenced at UNICO for a new EA in mid-2009, there were no HEWRRs requirements to be satisfied. This round of bargaining was highly conflicted, as the unions sought to strengthen their influence in areas where it had been diminished due to the HEWRRs. In addition, the NTEU and the CPSU, which had previously been united in their efforts to combat the effects of the HEWRRS, were divided on the issue of whether academic staff and general staff should have separate agreements or come under a single agreement, as had been the case in recent times. Consequently, bargaining was a drawn-out process and concluded with separate agreements for general and academic staff at the end of 2010 and the end of 2011, respectively.

The CEC continued to operate until the end of 2010, when the two-year appointments of the committee members ended. New elections were not held because the future of the CEC had been a key area of bargaining. The unions clearly preferred a return to a situation in which management consulted only with unions, while management desired to preserve a model of consultation that allowed for non-union representation. Importantly, management now argued for this, not because it was a government requirement but because more than half of UNICO staff were not union members and deserved to have the option of non-union representation in the workplace. The outcome of bargaining on this issue was that UNICO management was able to maintain a modified form of hybrid employee representation.

The new EA replaced the CEC with a new committee, CEC2. The terms of reference of the CEC2 were the same as that of the CEC in that it would be a mechanism for consultation on matters relating to the implementation of the EA; any university policy or procedure; staff development; and policy and programs concerned with workplace diversity and occupational health and safety. The new committee continued to have four nominees from each union but now only had four academic and four nonacademic representatives elected from across the university, in effect reducing by more than 50 per cent the potential number of non-union committee members. Overall, the new committee had twenty members compared to twenty-seven on the old one, and this reduction was a response to the generally held view that the CEC was too big and unwieldy. In addition, a number of important differences between the old and new committees should be noted. Firstly, there were four management representatives on the CEC2, whereas previously there had been none. Secondly, each union could now invite a paid union official to attend meetings, although they would not be formally regarded as members of the committee. Both these changes meant that the CEC2 was structurally more like a joint consultative committee. Thirdly, the EA committed management to actively consider the views or submissions of the CEC2, although it did not extend any formal decision-making power to the committee. Finally, the new committee would meet more frequently than the old committee had, five times annually compared to quarterly, but importantly, it had been given the formal option of calling for additional meetings if required. As can be seen, a number of ways in which the new committee was constituted was consistent with improvements recommended by CEC members.

The CEC2 did not formally commence operation until early 2011 and had only met twice when interviews for this study started, so it was not possible to assess its operation in this chapter. However, it can be reported that six of the eight positions determined by staff elections were won by union candidates. This gave the unions a dominant voice on the new committee, with unionists occupying fourteen of the available twenty seats. In addition, when the members of the CEC were interviewed, the structure of the CEC2 was known, and a number of the participants compared the two committees. One union nominee believed the structure of the CEC2 could have a negative effect on the strength of the committee's recommendations due to a likely lack of unanimity on resolutions due to the four management representatives being likely to vote against resolutions critical of management and/or existing policy. By contrast, the DHR believed that the presence of management representatives on the CEC2 was an advantage over the CEC because it was likely to create a less adversarial atmosphere at committee meetings:

> The CEC is a kind of a less collegiate model in some ways, it's more adversarial . . . I think it is probably more effective [for management] to be part of the committee rather than sitting outside and receiving recommendations from the committee. Yes it's an advantage of the CEC2.
> (DHR)

DISCUSSION

It is interesting to think about the findings of this study in the light of recent research investigating the ICE Regulations in the UK referred to earlier. Hall and colleagues (2010) examined how twenty-five organizations in the UK responded to the 2005 ICE Regulations that gave workers the right to request information and consultation with their employer through representative bodies. Hall and colleagues (2010) classified organizations into two distinct categories: communicators and active consulters. Communicators were organizations that used staff representative bodies primarily to convey information to employees with only a limited role for consultation. By contrast, active consulters were organizations that used staff representative bodies as forums for consultation around strategic issues and showed evidence of staff influence on final decisions. The current study examined a situation in which a government requirement around employee consultation led to the formation of a staff representative committee. The evidence from the interviews indicated that UNICO was an active consulter. As the interview with the DHR revealed, the CEC was used by management as a sounding board for some very important staff policies, and there were also a few instances, most notably the staff performance and appraisal policy, in which management changed policies in the light of feedback from the CEC.

At UNICO, only one managerial representative was present at CEC meetings. By contrast, Hall and colleagues (2010) found that with the exception of two organizations, and irrespective of whether an organization was classified as a communicator or active consulter, a number of senior managers attended meetings of the staff consultative committees they studied. According to Hall and colleagues, the attendance of senior managers at meetings is an important indicator of management support for the consultative process, and certainly some of the members of the CEC inferred from the presence of only one manager at CEC meetings that UNICO placed a low value on the committee. A potential drawback, however, of a strong managerial presence at committee meetings is that members feel frightened of adverse managerial reactions to what they contribute. Bull, Pyman, and Gilman (2012) also investigated the impact of the ICE Regulations and found that this was an important issue in one of the two organizations they studied, while at UNICO the overwhelming majority of members interviewed did not express any such concerns.

In contrast to the Hall and colleagues (2010) study, in which unions were not always active in ensuring strong membership on consultative bodies, at UNICO, the strategy of the unions was to ensure that they dominated as much as possible membership of the CEC. However, similar to the Hall and colleagues (2010) findings in organizations with a union presence, management at UNICO did not seek to use the CEC to destabilize or undermine unions.

A common theme from the interviews was that management did not commit enough resources to the operation of the CEC, especially in the form of induction training, workload release, and the IT support for elected staff representative. While at UNICO, induction training was entirely absent, Hall and colleagues (2010) reported that virtually all organizations, whether communicators or active consulters, provided induction training to staff representatives. Bull and colleagues (2012) also found that non-union representatives in particular gained considerable benefit from induction training regarding their role and participation on consultative committees. At UNICO and at almost all the organizations studied by Hall and colleagues (2010), committee members were given time release to attend meetings. Unlike the situation at UNICO, Hall and colleagues (2010) also found that nearly all organizations classified as active consulters provided time release for representatives to attend premeetings. However, as with UNICO, it would appear that the overwhelming majority of representatives in organizations studied by both Hall and colleagues and Bull and colleagues did not receive workload reduction to offset their participation on consultative committees. It is interesting to speculate whether the lack of managerial commitment to the CEC may have been due to the consultation requirement being forced on UNICO by the federal government. The situation may be different with the CEC2 because in the absence of a government requirement, UNICO management actively pushed for a consultative committee with elected staff representatives within the new enterprise agreement, presumably indicating that management would have a greater sense of commitment to its success. It remains a task for future research to examine whether CEC2 is better resourced by management and also if this results in greater perceived effectiveness of operation.

CONCLUSION

The chapter has examined a hybrid form of voice, the CEC at UNICO, which emerged as a result of a government requirement that linked access to government funding to the strengthening of non-union employee representation. These same requirements also resulted in the removal from UNICO's collective agreement and put into separate policy matters that were key aspects of the employment relationship. This created a strong incentive for the unions at UNICO to maximise their presence on the CEC, which the unions were successful in achieving. This meant that while the CEC, in terms of its formal structure, was a hybrid form of voice, it actually functioned more as a form of union voice. The chapter also explored the operation of the CEC through a series of interviews. The interviews revealed that all committee members expressed a high level of support for this form of employee voice, although they also all believed that the committee was largely ineffective. Ineffectiveness was seen as resulting from inadequate resourcing of the committee by the university and the lack of committee influence over managerial decision making. In terms of lack of influence, most committee members were not aware that the HEWRRs prevented the CEC being invested with powers to enforce its recommendations. Notably, management at UNICO believed that in a few important instances, policies were significantly modified to reflect the views of the CEC. The rather negative assessment of the CEC by its members was due to the perception that management did not seem adequately engaged with the CEC. This perception was enhanced because management did not have any formal representation on the committee, a fact also lamented by management. Interestingly, the CEC has recently been replaced by a new committee that does include management representatives as formal members. It is a task for future research to examine whether the new committee, which exists not because of a government requirement but because of managerial preference, is a more effective hybrid form of employee representation.

NOTE

1. In order to protect the anonymity of UNICO, it is not possible to provide explicit details of UNICO documents.

REFERENCES

Barnes, A. 2006. "Trade Unionism in 2005." *Journal of Industrial Relations*, 48(3): 369–83.
Barnes, A., C. MacMillan, and R. Markey. 2013. "Maintaining Union Voice in the Australian University Sector: Union Strategy and Non-Union Forms of Employee Participation." *Journal of Industrial Relations*, 55(4): 565–82.
Bryson, A. 2004. "Managerial Responsiveness to Union and Non-Union Worker Voice in Britain." *Industrial Relations*, 43(1): 213–41.
Bull, E., A. Pyman, and M. Gilman. 2012. "A Re-Assessment of Non-Union Employee Representation in the UK: Developments Since the 'ICE' Age." *Journal of Industrial Relations*, 55(4): 546–64.
Charlwood, A., and M. Terry. 2007. "21st-Century Models of Employee Representation: Structures, Processes and Outcomes." *Industrial Relations Journal*, 38(4): 320–37.
Cooney, S. 2006. "Command and Control in the Workplace: Agreement-Making Under WorkChoices." *Economic and Labour Relations Review*, 16(2): 147–64.
Department of Education, Science and Training (DEST). 2005. *Questions and Answers on the HEWRRs—14 September, 2005*. Memo to NTEU.
Dundon, T., and P. J. Gollan. 2007. "Re-Conceptualizing Voice in the Non-Union Workplace." *International Journal of Human Resource Management*, 18(7): 1182–98.
Dundon, T., A. Wilkinson, M. Marchington, and P. Ackers. 2004. "The Meanings and Purpose of Employee Voice." *International Journal of Human Resource Management*, 15(6): 1149–70.
Fiorito, J. 2001. "Human Resource Management Practices and Worker Desires for Union Representation." *Journal of Labor Research*, 22(2): 335–54.
Forsyth, A., and C. Sutherland. 2006. "From 'Uncharted Seas' to 'Stormy Waters': How Will Trade Unions Fare Under the WorkChoices Legislation?" *Economic and Labour Relations Review*, 16(2): 215–35.
Freeman, R. 2007. "Can the United States Clear the Market for Representation and Participation?" In R. Freeman, P. Boxall, and P. Haynes (eds.), *What Workers Say: Employee Voice in the Anglo-American Workplace*, pp. 25–48. Cornell, NY: Cornell University Press.
Freeman, R., P. Boxall, and P. Haynes. (eds.). 2007. *What Workers Say: Employee Voice in the Anglo-American Workplace*. Cornell, NY: Cornell University Press.
Freeman, R., and J. Medoff. 1984. *What Do Unions Do?* New York: Basic Books.
Gollan, P. J. 2000. "Non-Union Forms of Employee Representation in the United Kingdom and Australia." In B. Kaufman and D. Taras (eds.), *Non-Union Employee Representation: History, Contemporary Practice and Policy*, pp. 410–52. Armonk, NY: M. E. Sharpe.

Gollan, P. J. 2007. *Employee Representation in Non-Union Firms.* London: Sage.

Gollan, P. J., and A. Wilkinson. 2007. "Implications of the EU Information and Consultation Directive and the Regulations in the UK—Prospects for the Future of Employee Representation." *International Journal of Human Resource Management,* 18(7): 1145–58.

Gumbrell-McCormick, R., and R. Hyman. 2010. "Works Councils: The European Model of Industrial Democracy." In A. Wilkinson, P. Gollan, M. Marchington, and D. Lewin (eds.), *The Oxford Handbook of Participation in Organizations,* pp. 286–314. Oxford: Oxford University Press.

Hall, M. 2010. "EU Regulation and the UK Employee Consultation Framework." *Economic and Industrial Democracy,* 31(4S): 55–69.

Hall, M., S. Hutchinson, J. Purcell, M. Terry, and J. Parker. 2010. *Information and Consultation Under the ICE Regulations: Evidence from Longitudinal Case Studies.* Employment Relations Research Series, 117. London: Department of Business, Innovation and Skills.

Hall, R. 2006. "Australian Industrial Relations 2005—The WorkChoices Revolution." *Journal of Industrial Relations,* 48(3): 291–303.

Haynes, P. 2005. "Filling the Vacuum? Non-Union Employee Voice in the Auckland Hotel Industry." *Employee Relations,* 27(3): 259–71.

Kaufman, B. 1999. "Does the NLRA Constrain Employee Involvement and Participation Programs in Non-Union Companies? A Reassessment." *Yale Law and Policy Review,* 17(Spring): 729–811.

Kaufman, B., and D. Taras. 2000. *Non-Union Employee Representation: History, Contemporary Practice and Policy.* Armonk, NY: M. E. Sharpe.

———. 2010. "Employee Participation Through Non-Union Forms of Employee Representation." In A. Wilkinson, P. Gollan, M. Marchington, and D. Lewin (eds.), *The Oxford Handbook of Participation in Organizations,* pp. 258–85. Oxford: Oxford University Press.

Kim, D., and H. Kim. 2004. "A Comparison of the Effectiveness of Unions and Non-Union Works Councils in Korea: Can Non-Union Employee Representation Substitute for Trade Unionism? *International Journal of Human Resource Management,* 15(6): 1069–93.

Markey, R. 2001. "Introduction: Global Patterns of Participation." In R. Markey, P. J. Gollan, A. Hodgkinson, A. Chouraqui, and U. Veersma (eds.), *Models of Employee Participation in a Changing Global Environment: Diversity and Interaction,* pp. 3–22. Aldershot, UK: Ashgate.

Pyman, A., B. Cooper, J. Teicher, and P. Holland. 2006. "A Comparison of the Effectiveness of Employee Voice Arrangements in Australia." *Industrial Relations Journal,* 37(5): 543–59.

Taras, D., and B. Kaufman. 2006. "Non-Union Employee Representation in North America: Diversity, Controversy and Uncertain Future." *Industrial Relations Journal,* 37(5): 513–42.

Teicher, J., P. Holland, A. Pyman, and B. Cooper. 2007. "Australian Workers: Finding Their Voice." In R. Freeman, P. Boxall, and P. Haynes (eds.), *What Workers Say: Employee Voice in the Anglo-American Workplace,* pp. 125–44. Cornell, NY: Cornell University Press.

Wilkinson, A., P. J. Gollan, M. Marchington, and D. Lewin. 2010. "Conceptualizing Employee Participation in Organizations." In A. Wilkinson, P. J. Gollan, M. Marchington, and D. Lewin (eds.), *The Oxford Handbook of Participation in Organizations,* pp. 3–25. Oxford: Oxford University Press.

Willman, P., A. Bryson, and R. Gomez. 2007. "The Long Goodbye: New Establishments and the Fall of Union Voice in Britain." *International Journal of Human Resource Management,* 18(7): 1318–34.

Part II
Britain

5 Legislating for NER?

NER and the ICE Regulations at Manufacture Co.

Jimmy Donaghey, Niall Cullinane, and Tony Dundon

INTRODUCTION

The transposition of the Information and Consultation (I&C) Directive, in the form of the Information and Consultation of Employees (ICE) Regulations 2004, placed for the first time on the UK statute books the possibility that UK–based companies could be legally required to establish an employee representation forum, albeit a non-union one (Storey, 2005; Hall et al. 2013). Such a body might be seen to have the characteristics of a non-union employee representation (NER) system. Indeed, as evident from other chapters, the ICE Regulations coincide with a period of growing interest in the NER phenomenon and concerns around the effectiveness of such mechanisms in securing employee voice. New waters for NERs have been effectively chartered by the introduction of a legislative component in the form of the ICE Regulations. This potentially offers fresh opportunities and a new context for establishing NER voice regimes.

This chapter thus presents a single, in-depth case study of an NER established to fulfil the requirements of the ICE Regulations in the UK. The findings suggest that the NER, despite being established under the auspices of the Regulations, was, for various reasons, problematic and failed to adequately plug the institutional voice gap. The first section of the chapter presents a very brief overview of the literature on NERs in the UK and the ICE Regulations. This is followed by a presentation of the case. Finally, the chapter considers the key issues arising from the case, including a consideration of whether legislatively inspired NERs, formed under the ICE Regulations, are a basis for developing meaningful forms of non-union voice.

REGULATING FOR VOICE IN THE UK: NERS AND THE ICE REGULATIONS

Scholarly interest in NER, historically, has been a largely North American phenomenon (Kaufman 2000; MacDowell, 2000). In recent years, however, interest in NER has steadily assumed international dimensions, most notably in countries like the UK, Ireland, Australia, and New Zealand (Gumbrell-McCormick and Hyman, 2006; Pyman et al. 2006; Dundon and Gollan, 2007). Yet for the most part, scholarship was initially unconvinced about the role of NER in labour relations (Hyman, 1997; Terry, 1999), although over time, this has shifted towards a somewhat more optimistic assessment (Ackers et al. 2006; Johnstone et al. 2010). From the 1990s, NER began to markedly increase in the UK, although the most recent empirical evidence suggests that just about one in five employers appear to have a non-union representative form as their exclusive mode of voice (Bryson et al. 2006; Gollan, 2007).

Rather, the evidence suggests that dual-channel voice arrangements have steadily increased in the last decade as employers seek to complement union-only voice with an amalgamation of union and NER voice. This arrangement is frequently observed more favourably in addressing integrative issues and circumventing workplace antagonisms (Gollan, 2007). Indeed, Bryson (2004) found that employees had a more favourable perception of managerial responsiveness in companies with NER plans than with trade unions. Yet no single characterisation of NER prevails; rather, variety is the mark of NER in relation to their structures, purpose, and influence (Willman et al. 2003; Marchington, 2005). As such, this makes generalisation on NER challenging. For example, NER can emerge in workplaces for a variety of reasons. Employers can adopt NER in the quest for higher organisational performance and competitive market advantage (Applebaum et al. 2000). In this context, NER is a fundamental element of a much larger "high-performance work system" package. Or, more simply, as Marchington (2005) observes, NER can be introduced by employers to improve the quality of communication between management and employees. NER can act to increase morale, acquire employee ideas for organisational problem solving, and act as an arena for resolving grievances or in presenting a progressive image to stakeholders as a responsible employer (Taras and Kaufman, 2006).

In other instances, NER operates to avoid trade unions or undermine union organising campaigns: once the union is conquered, however, employer interest in NER readily dwindles (Ramsay, 1980). Aside from the purpose and rationale of creating NER, conclusions on the outcomes and performance of NERs are also diverse: some studies point to relatively positive outcomes across a spectrum of criteria, with others coming to more negative assessments. NERs exhibit positive elements, like increasing morale and commitment, when used as part of an enduring high-performance work system package, emphasising competitive advantage through people (Wood and Wall, 2007; Kaufman and Taras, 2010). Employers of this calibre provide excellent terms and conditions which are conducive to removing distributive issues as a source of contention in the workplace. In turn, this frees up NER to focus on the more integrative, mutual-gains–type outcomes. Nonetheless, other studies find that NER is somewhat ineffectual as a medium for distributive bargaining and employee interest representation (Butler, 2005; Upchurch et al. 2008). In this context, NER is considered to lack the power and autonomy essential to wield substantial clout in securing certain interests of employees relating to the wage-effort bargain—therefore, as a representative agency of employees, it is defective. It seems that NER prove less successful in delivering positive outcomes for employees where utilised to evade unions (Taras and Copping, 1998) or where employers give the NER little power or autonomy for influence and opt for unilateral decision making on employment issues of importance to employees (Badigannavar and Kelly, 2005). NER also appear ineffectual where the employer fails to ensure that the NER is a responsive medium for employees or where the employer simply allows it to atrophy over time (Upchurch et al. 2008). Indeed, the latter scenario is particularly problematic: whilst some NER do endure through time, others seem to have a relatively short shelf life. This can occur where the employer sets up NER to address immediate problems or use them superficially in response to the most current of managerial fashions (Dundon et al. 2006). In these cases, the NER appears to lose whatever initial energy it had and/or in time disbands due to inactivity.

Significantly in the UK, the context in which NER function has the potential for reconfiguration in light of the ICE Regulations 2004. Formally, the Regulations implementation is of importance for traditionally voluntarist regimes like the UK where statutory voice regulation is weakly embedded. The provisions offered what Hall (2005) describes as a "legislatively prompted voluntarism" for worker information and consultation (the former referring to data transmitted by the employer, the latter meaning the exchange of views and establishment of a dialogue). Emphasis is placed on workers and management reaching a voluntary agreement, with standard legal provisions offering a "fallback" (providing for election of employee representatives on collective forums with accompanying rights to information and consultation) where there is a failure to agree. Prior to transposition, some scholars foresaw the potential for far-reaching consequences in the way UK employers informed and consulted employees over a wide range of workplace issues (Sisson, 2002). Yet the limited number of reviews to date suggests that the uptake of legally enacted rights does not appear transformative of the information and consultation terrain in the UK (Hall et al. 2013). However, some firms may have been influenced by the Regulations to either review arrangements or initiate new arrangements (Wilkinson and Gollan, 2007; Koukiadaki, 2010).

The ICE Regulations add a nuance to appreciating NER, as such arrangements are now supported by legislation and are, in theory, provided with some formal institutional distance from management. As such, an element of increased resources and independence is afforded to those NER schemes legislatively backed by the Regulations. In firms with fifty or more employees, I&C forums are formally no longer wholly managerially sponsored but, theoretically, have recourse to independent statutory backing where workers seek to pursue it. The UK legal instruments theoretically enable greater "scope" and "range" over issues influenced. Employees are provided with the right to information and consultation about issues impacting employment, work organisation, or contractual relationships should they wish to actively pursue it. Thus the scope is fixed at the intermediate level of consultation with the range of issues impacting more high-level substantive and procedural aspects of employment. The regulatory framework specifies that information must be given in such ways as to enable representatives to conduct an adequate study and prepare for consultation. Where in place, employers are obliged to give employee representatives an opportunity to meet with them and give their opinion on matters subject to consultation.

Notably, the regulations in the UK have been viewed as a minimalist transpositional interpretation of the EU Directive: it is highly significant that such rights are not automatic and must be triggered by employees. Employers may utilise "preexisting agreements," which can further dilute the regulations' potential, although the regulations state that these must be approved by employees, set out information and consultation provisions, and be capable of independent verification. Thus, as Wilkinson and Gollan (2007: 1138) argue, "the I&C regulations could easily result in 'weak' employer-dominated partnerships and non-union firms using direct communications and information while marginalizing collective consultation." However, it could be proposed that ICE–sponsored NERs—even in their preexisting agreement format—have shadow legislative backing, for if they do not meet sufficient criteria and workers remain dissatisfied with extant arrangements, the force of the law can be called upon to reconstitute information and consultation in the firm. As such, the Regulations might promise the potential for NERs to be of greater durability in process, as well as offer greater robustness in outcome. In light of this, the remainder of the chapter considers a case study of a company in which the ICE Regulations initiated and structured a newly created NER. We consider what impacts, if any, such legislative heritage had on the NER.

CASE STUDY COMPANY BACKGROUND

Manufacture Co. was a family-owned firm based in Belfast, trading across the UK, Ireland, and Europe. The company had been in operation since the 1970s. The data for the case were derived from interviews with the Chief Executive, the Human Resource Manager, and a member of the Human Resource Support team responsible for coordinating the NER, four out of seven of the employee representatives, and eight production employees and two supervisors. At the time of research (undertaken between June 2009 and February 2010), Manufacture Co. employed close to 300 employees in its single-site manufacturing and operations facility. Employee occupational grades were spread across a number of categories, although they were principally concentrated in the building, adjustment, and despatch of company products.

There appeared to be a considered effort towards developing an internal human resource management programme: a specialist human resource department existed within dedicated staff for operational human resource issues, learning and development, health and safety, and payroll and compensation. The company's performance, whilst negatively affected by the broader economic downturn in house building and construction, had remained reasonably robust. Throughout 2009 and 2010, company production had increased in order to meet market demand. However, buoyancy in production was qualified by increased cost of sales and exchange rate fluctuations, which had adverse financial effects. The downturn had also resulted in Manufacture Co. management seeking new ways of generating revenue streams. This was achieved via the introduction of new product lines at specific price points and new product lines targeted at a higher customer market less inclined to price sensitivity. Environmental pressures resulted in company products being inserted into a market where the average price generated was lower. In terms of company revenue streams, less money was being generated, whilst the underlying cost base had remained the same. In an attempt to lessen these pressures, management targeted supply lines to reduce material costs. Internally, a review of standard production times was also executed to get underlying costs down. In this context, shop-floor efficiency rates were increased. Allied to this were changes in internal quality standards and the introduction of barcode systems, which allowed for full quality control right across the production process.

EMPLOYMENT RELATIONS BACKGROUND

Evidence gathered during the research portrayed a mixed picture of the employee relations climate within the company. In general, members of senior management articulated a view that employee relations within the organisation were good. A number of reasons were advanced for this, including the relatively small company size and the family-owned origins. Senior management also identified the company's non-union status as a positive contributory factor. A member of the human resource management team noted how, in a previous role in a unionised organisation, much of the human resource function's work was with grievances and appeals. In contrast, this was noted to be less prevalent in Manufacture Co. However, management did not take a wholly benign view of the current climate, and pragmatic considerations on how shop-floor workers would evaluate employee relations were evident.

Notably, evidence from employees was much different. In most cases, employees expressed or alluded to a wider reservoir of workforce mistrust or cynicism. Chief amongst employee grievances appeared to be the suspension of a company bonus (discussed in what follows), but dissatisfaction also existed with the introduction of the aforementioned new efficiency rates. The latter were perceived by a selection of employees to be indicative of "unreasonable" work intensification. Senior management contested this evaluation, arguing that the increased efficiency rates were based on rigorous time study, the introduction of supporting new machinery and assistant production processes, and, furthermore, fundamental to the continued survival of the firm and employment. Also, it is worth noting that an attempt to secure trade union recognition had been made in 2006 and 2007. However, this campaign, described by management as "highly aggressive," appeared to have dissipated due to a lack of employee support. Management advanced that there was no appetite for a recognised trade union within the organisation and estimated that perhaps only 10 per cent of the workforce was supportive of trade union representation.

Despite this, management were particularly insistent to the research team that one condition of company access was that no issues pertaining to unionisation would be raised in the research instruments. Indeed, the researchers' data collection instruments were vetted by both a senior company director and a human resource manager to ensure that no mention of unionisation was evident. Consequently, the only evidence of employees' views regarding unions emerged where they voluntarily opted to articulate a view on the matter themselves: where this happened, attitudes evinced either a passive neutrality or positive support to the idea of unionisation.

THE MOTIVES AND PURPOSE OF THE NER

In 2005, Manufacture Co. established a company NER simply named the Employee Forum to be a formal means for providing employees with information and consultation (the Forum's constitution deployed ICE Regulation terminology insofar as it defined information as "data transmitted by the employer to employee representatives in order to enable them to examine and acquaint themselves with the subject matter of the data" and consultation as a "means the exchange of views and establishment of dialogue between the employer and the employee representatives"). There appeared to be an assemblage of factors, all of which came together in 2004, which spurred management to initiate the Forum. As the company had grown in organisational size, management became conscious of a need to formalise employment relations. In attempting this, the company had asked the Investors in People (a management standard promoted by the UK Commission for Employment and Skills Group) to conduct a company employment relations audit. One consequence of this was a recommendation by the Group to create an employee forum, which would also assist the company in securing the standard accreditation. The Group highlighted the possibilities contained in the then-forthcoming ICE Regulations to management and encouraged them to speak to the National Labour Relations Agency about designing a forum on those lines.

As a result, management attempted to implement a voice structure in accordance with the then-forthcoming Regulations. A consultant from the Northern Ireland Labour Relations Agency was brought into the company to assist in the design of the Forum's constitution and structure to ensure compliance. As noted, the forum's formal characteristics matched the requirements set down by the ICE Regulations. Furthermore, as the constitution of the forum explained:

> Manufacture Co. realises the importance of information and consultation and recognises that they provide the basis of good employment relations and are essential in creating an effective workplace. Employees are only able to perform at their best if they know their duties, obligations and rights and have opportunities to make their views known to management on issues that affect them. Manufacture Co. believes that this Forum and agreement provide the most appropriate structure and framework for effective and improved performance for all employees based upon concepts such as openness, effective communication, dialogue and mutual respect for different opinions.
>
> (Employee Forum Constitution)

Of note is that the human resource manager outlined that the Forum had "fallen by the wayside" in 2006, only a year after initiation, but was then "fully reinstated" in 2008. In its first year of operation, the initial focus of the Forum had been primarily dominated by health and safety and "housekeeping" issues: participants were said to have found such matters tedious, undermining any early enthusiasm for the project. However, in 2006 and 2007, there was the aforementioned union recognition campaign. Support for the union appears to have been at a low level: the union involved, despite lodging an application for statutory union recognition under the UK union recognition provisions, did not satisfy the Central Arbitration Committee (CAC) that 10 per cent of workers in the company were union members or that a majority of workers at the plant would be likely to favour recognition. Although support for the union was low, it seems to have encouraged management to promote the NER scheme at the firm. Health and safety issues were then moved to their own specific forum and the NER was re-oriented towards a focus on information and consultation in the areas of "core employee relations–type issues" as originally specified in the Constitution.

ORGANISATIONAL STRUCTURE OF THE NER

The arrangements for the NER were laid out in detail in the Forum constitution. According to the constitution, topics raised at the Forum were specified as needing to be "central to the needs of the business and relevant to the common interests of employees." Typically, the subject matter for information and consultation was formally specified to include communication methods, work-related social functions, launch of new products/ services, changes/discontinuation of products/services, increase or reduction in production or sales as a result of under- or overcapacity, fluctuations in consumer demand, moving into a new market, cost-saving measures, acquisitions and disposals, restructuring plans, new IT developments, production processes, reorganisation of ways of working, transfer of production location, changes to business aims/mission/objectives/strategy, changes in senior management, competitive environment, trading conditions, order book, and financial situation based on sales turnover. Information and consultation could also be provided regarding developments of business activities and the economic situation as well as probable developments with regard employment and decisions which may lead to substantial changes in work organisation or contractual relations (the latter here incorporating information and consultation on terms and conditions of employment).

Notably, the constitution specified that the information provided by management would offer a background and rationale for subsequent decisions, including recent past and probable future developments. Furthermore, the constitution specified that information would be presented in the form of "information papers" distributed to the employee representatives three weeks prior to the scheduled meeting, providing representatives with the opportunity to give their opinions, make suggestions, and obtain a reasoned response.

The NER consisted of seven employee representatives who were either elected and/or appointed, if unopposed, and five representatives for management who were appointed. The constitution specified that all employee representatives had a duty to act as genuine representatives of employees within the company and as such were expected to canvass the views of the employees from their respective constituencies. To assist employee representatives to carry out their role, the constitution provided them with a reasonable period of paid time off to perform relevant duties, to attend training, to conduct an adequate study of information (i.e. information papers), and to prepare for consultation and an appropriate amount of time to canvass the views of constituents and feedback information derived from Forum meetings. By way of a general principle, there were employee representatives from each business section to ensure that employee interests are being represented across the company.

Employee representatives were nominated and elected through a number of procedural steps. First, constituents proposed the name of the employee(s) they wish to represent them, subject to the nominee giving his/her permission. Potential representatives had to be permanent company employees. Each candidate had to be seconded by two members of the same constituency. Should the number of nominations match the number of representatives required for that constituency and the employee(s) was/were agreeable to accepting the role, they would automatically become that constituent's employee representative(s). However, were it to arise that there were more nominations than places, elections would occur. Elections were by secret ballot and overseen by the human resource department, with an independent ballot examiner to oversee events. Employee representatives normally resided in the post for two years. The Labour Relations Agency helped write up "job vacancies" for the role, which were then advertised internally, outlining the roles and responsibilities of the employee representative position. Management appointees carried out the "officer" roles of the Forum, which were the Chairperson (assumed by one of the general managers), a Vice Chair (assumed by one of the general managers), a Forum Secretary (assumed by a member of the human resource management team), and Clerical Support (assumed by a member of the human resource management team).

Formally, the Forum was designated to meet four times a year. However, a certain degree of flexibility was presupposed in this provision and generally, given that not all company-related developments were recognised to be unforeseen, special or emergency meetings to inform and consult on issues could be called at the discretion of the Chairperson. The constitution provided for this. In practice, at the time of research in 2009 and 2010, the Forum was meeting monthly (this was attributable to the climate of uncertainty in the wider economy and employee concerns over employment security). The Forum Secretary was designated to liaise with both management and employee representatives to agree on points to be included in the agenda. Furthermore, the Secretary was required to notify all representatives to remind them of the specific date and time of each meeting at least fourteen days prior to the meeting to ensure adequate preparation. A copy of the agreed-on agenda was specified to be issued at least one week prior to the Forum meeting. Items could be added to the agenda by employees, and there could also be premeetings between the coordinator and the representatives before the main Forum meetings wherein representatives outlined the main "points" they had collected from constituents. In order to canvass employee views and seek points for the agenda, employee representatives were formally allocated up to one hour prior to generation of the agenda for representatives to discuss with their constituency members what they wish to be included. The constitution also afforded representatives a degree of flexibility to meet as appropriate.

Minutes derived from the Forum meetings were approved by the Secretary and issued within fourteen days of the meeting or as so far as was reasonably practicable. Each member of the Forum was provided with a set of minutes, and copies are proposed to be distributed in the staff canteen, sent by email and/or posted on notice boards. Major issues/decisions are also proposed to be communicated via the information screens in the canteen. To ensure effective information and consultation arrangements, representatives were advised under the constitution to inform employees of deliberations as soon as possible. Notably, however, representatives were expected to liaise with relevant supervisors and managers to ensure that meetings caused minimum disruption to the running of the business. Finally, the arrangements were bound by confidentiality clauses. The constitution of the Forum provided that some items for consultation would be sensitive, and therefore management could be permitted to restrict access or indeed to withhold information and not consult where disclosure might be prejudicial to the functioning of the business. Management reserved the right to restrict the circulation of any information or document that was provided to representatives. A breach of this confidentiality clause by a representative may lead to a disciplinary sanction being imposed, up to and including dismissal.

OPERATION OF THE NER

Whilst the Employee Forum was ensconced with a detailed constitutional ambit, in practice, the operation of the NER was found to diverge often from its specifications.

With regard to employee representatives on the Forum, for example, while highly detailed electoral procedures were in place, in practice it appears that ballots had not regularly occurred given the limited numbers of employees expressing interest in the role. Management admitted that it could be difficult to get people to come forward. Only one of the four employee representatives interviewed in the company was actually elected, whilst only one of the remaining three not interviewed had also gone through electoral procedure. In some instances, the human resource management team had contacted supervisors to encourage an employee from the floor to sign up.

Usually, the Forum meetings followed a set structure. Prior to the formal meeting, premeetings occurred between the coordinator and employee representatives. These were regarded as important by management in distilling issues which were not considered "appropriate" for the Forum. Some points raised by representatives were regarded by management as often more appropriate for the Health and Safety Committee or were perhaps "too personal" or were held to be too focused on "minor operational-level issues." The Forum meetings themselves followed a set format: first, there were introductions and a report of business performance followed by a presentation on financial developments. The human resource manager typically spoke about policies which could potentially be introduced or changes to existing procedures. One example provided in this regard was the introduction of childcare vouchers. Employee representatives could then speak on specific points of concern or raise questions.

Notably, the final minutes were distributed to employee representatives to make sure that they were satisfied with what they contained before being circulated more widely through company notice boards. Minutes were not circulated until two or three days after the meeting to give employee representatives an opportunity to communicate back to constituents. In practice, employee representatives appeared to communicate back to constituents in a variety of ways: those who had access to email used that mechanism, whilst employee representatives on the shop floor used more face-to-face means. There had been some practice of representatives giving feedback through team briefings, at least in the early years of the Forum: the employee representative would ask the supervisor for ten minutes at the end of the briefing to report back to his/her constituents. However, in the latter instance, shop-floor employee representatives often appeared in practice to relay information on an individual-by-individual basis (an issue explored in more depth in what follows).

In terms of the kinds of issues raised at the Forum, there appeared to be considerable variation. Both management and employee representatives interviewed referred to a breadth of issues like employee bonuses, employee appraisals, and issues over annual pay rises as items being raised for discussion. Further to this were more operational issues, such as the need for water filters, the temperature within the shop floor, and shop-floor lighting, although management were extremely frustrated at employees' repeated attempts to raise these matters through what they hoped would be a more "strategic forum" focusing on the "central needs of the business." In practice, management described the Forum as leaning more towards communication than consultation; an interesting example of the latter was the use of the Forum by employee representatives to express concern over the bonus for efficiency and productivity. It appeared that shop-floor employees had articulated a grievance that there was a bonus for "productivity," but none for "quality." The bonus system appeared to be previously team based, with one resulting outcome being that poor individual performers could drag the overall team down and erode the bonus payout. These concerns were brought to management through the Forum. Management consequently reviewed existing procedures and, in light of this review and employee suggestions, implemented an amalgamated efficiency and quality bonus in September 2008. This same bonus was, however, short lived and later frozen at the end of 2008 in light of economic uncertainty in the organisation (an issue returned to in the following).

EVALUATIONS OF THE NER: MANAGEMENT

In aggregate, management appeared to view the existing Forum as an important arrangement. One senior manager noted how the Forum provided a space wherein employee representatives could talk freely, air collective shop-floor grievances, and provide a point of contact with directors. Furthermore, the process was seen to allow a consensus of opinion to occur within the decision-making process. In particular, management evaluated the Forum favourably from the point of view of dispelling myths and rumours within the company. For example, when the Manufacture Co. facility closed for Christmas in 2008, the site shut on Friday 19th, as this was felt to be more appropriate than re-opening on Monday 22nd and then closing once again on Tuesday 23rd. Yet for some unknown reason, this intention was interpreted by a section of employees that the company was shutting down the company's operations in its entirety and that Manufacture Co. would not open at all in the New Year. In that type of context, it was advanced by the human resource manager that the Forum was of significance in allowing management to clearly articulate their intentions and dispel unwarranted rumours.

Yet perhaps more robust evidence of how management positively viewed the Forum for countering potential employee misperceptions was in relation to the freezing of bonus payments. The continued suspension of the bonus appeared to have occurred within a context in which the organisation was subsequently increasing production and hiring new staff. Such actions seemed to have resulted in a certain dissonance in employees' perceptions and understandings of what was occurring. The Forum was used to outline to employee representatives that whilst the company was doing well in terms of increased production, it was experiencing increased cost of sales, and unfavourable exchange rate fluctuations, as well as being squeezed for discounts by customers. Explaining the financial context within which the company was operating through the medium of the Forum offered an opportunity to displace inaccurate employee perceptions (although it is not clear that this was successful, as will be detailed in what follows). Notably, one of the negative aspects of the Forum from management's perspective was in relation to a tendency for employee representatives to raise issues that were perceived to be "too departmentalised or narrow," such as grievances over unclean toilets.

Management were also uncertain as to how well some employee representatives were communicating with their constituents. In total, however, management were committed to the NER; indeed, access to the company had been granted to the researchers on the grounds that management were keen to find out how well the Forum was working for employees in the organisation.

EVALUATIONS OF THE NER: EMPLOYEES

In the case of employee representatives, the Forum was perceived favourably, though there was more scepticism evident than from management interviewees. Whilst employee representatives indicated positive attitudes to the Forum and indeed were positively disposed towards management, they appeared to face a number of hurdles in competently executing their responsibilities. As such, there appeared to be a combination of influences at work which may well have diminished the effectiveness of employee representatives at Manufacture Co. In some cases, for example, representatives reported difficulties in securing "points" from their constituents. In particular, all representatives reported that many employees tended to "hold back" on articulating grievances, opting instead to bring issues individually to their line supervisors. Indeed, this was confirmed by employees interviewed, who tended to articulate positive relations with their supervisors and their preference for raising individual concerns with them. Employee representatives felt that it was unlikely that some employees would want to share individual grievances with a fellow employee, even if that employee was their representative. Of course, it was difficult to ascertain whether this might necessarily be a problem for the workings of the Forum given that personal or idiosyncratic issues were not part of the Forum's agenda. Employee representatives appeared to be under the mistaken assumption that their role was to address individual as well as collective grievances. But in the case of the former, it could be expected that line supervisors (or the individual company grievance procedures) would have been the suitable point of contact. But even on collective issues, representatives claimed that many employees were disillusioned with the Forum because a perception existed that employees had to repeatedly advance the same points to representatives with little evidence of substantive progress.

An additional difficulty facing employee representatives also appeared to be a lack of training across a number of different areas of their role. A number of representatives interviewed suggested that they would have liked more "training," although they were less clear about which areas they would specifically like training in. One representative claimed to be surprised at the lack of training for the role and claimed to have expected more. It was noted by representatives themselves (often in reviewing their peers on the Forum) that some representatives were weak in articulating complex points, whilst others were viewed as being afraid to cause friction with management, refraining from raising issues that would have lead to an adversarial climate at the Forum meeting. From representatives and employees interviewed, there also appeared to be problems about the effectiveness of representatives in reporting back to constituents. In part, this appears to have been derived from a number of influences stemming from employee representatives themselves but also from shop-floor employees and line supervisors. For example, it appears that representatives reporting back to constituents as a group was relatively rare. Rather, representatives claimed that they reported back to an individual employee who had raised a particular issue. Two representatives reported pressures from line supervisors to resume their work duties on return from the Forum, thus limiting opportunities to adequately deliver feedback to constituents. However, interviews also indicated that individual representatives personally opted to return to work, as they themselves feel they have too much work to complete. One representative, for instance, reported difficulties in sparing time to complete

Forum duties due to personal workload. Further to this, representatives and supervisors noted that employees did not necessarily want to hold collective meetings, as this distracted them from their own work duties.

Despite the formal allocation of time for representatives to undertake their duties, as outlined in the constitution, it was reported that in most instances, this allocated time was not available or utilised. Representatives reported "rushing around" before meetings in attempts to gather points from employees. This was felt to have limited their overall capacity to prepare adequately for and contribute to Forum meetings. As already indicated, however, representatives may have been as much the source of this problem as line supervisors in opting to prioritise their own work requirements over and above their responsibilities under the Forum constitution.

Part of this trend must be understood in the context of the market downturn the company faced around the time of the research in 2000 through 2010. As a consequence of this downturn, management had resultantly sought new ways of generating revenue streams. Cost pressures had led to company products being inserted into a market where the average price generated was lower: less money was thus being generated, but at the same time, the underlying costs of production had remained constant. In an attempt to lessen these pressures, standard production times on the shop floor were reviewed to get underlying costs down. Workers' efficiency rates were subsequently increased. Changes also occurred in internal quality standards, particularly the introduction of barcode systems, which allow management to have full quality control right across the manufacturing process. The pressure to meet increased production and quality targets explains why the pressure of the production quotas stymied the work of representatives. Indeed, there was a widespread view on the shop floor by both line supervisors and employees that the achievement of rates was difficult and has been further exacerbated by the new quality controls, which significantly intensified the work effort, with its attendant performance pressures on both parties. Individually, each employee, including representatives, was responsible for his or her efficiency/quality standard, whilst line supervisors were responsible for their groups meeting their targets as a whole for each respective area.

One final issue emanating from employee representatives refers to the fact that shop-floor employees' views on the Forum, and indeed the representative function, tended towards apathy and cynicism. This was claimed to exist because little in the way of adequate progress had been made on particular substantive points raised at the Forum, such as the bonus or the cold temperature on the shop floor. Representatives felt that management should be seen to "compromise more" on certain issues raised at the Forum, if only to consequently portray an image to employees that the Forum and the representative function could deliver on shop-floor concerns. Although not clearly articulated, the underpinning assumption of this request by representatives appears to be that if management conceded on some major employee request through the Forum, this might have afforded more credibility to the representative role, undermined employee cynicism, and fostered some sense of enthusiasm for the Forum.

As one employee claimed, "most people have no interest in the Forum. Most things people ask for get turned down." In another instance, one employee claimed that whenever a representative was pushed for progress on a particular issue—like the frozen bonus—the representative's response was repeatedly that the issue was under review and would be addressed in the near future. Such indeterminacy, it was claimed by employees, led to widespread frustration. In some instances, employees did not actually know who their designated employee representative was. Alternatively, whilst minutes on the proceedings of the Forum were made available on company notice boards, as one employee claimed, "when we come in on tea-break we don't want to read a notice board." In many instances, however, when employees were interviewed about the Forum, they appeared to be less interested in its working and more concerned about existing grievances within the workplace. On the shop floor, there was a strong level of mistrust between workers and senior management (partly as a consequence of the intensification of work through rate increases and the frozen bonus) and widespread job dissatisfaction.

CONCLUSIONS, LESSONS, AND POLICY IMPLICATIONS

This chapter sought to consider the influence of the ICE Regulations on the workings of NER in a company in which the latter was introduced under the guidance of the former. Yet the construction of the NER under the shadow of the law really remained as far the ICE Regulations went in terms of shaping the dynamics of the Forum in the case study. In large measure, this derives from the fact that ICE Regulations constituted a highly flexible approach, both procedurally and substantively, to implementing the original directive (Koukiadaki 2009; Hall et al. 2013). Employers have ample scope to agree to voluntary I&C arrangements with employees—the preexisting agreements—that can remain outside the ambit of the regulations' procedures for legal enforceability. Against this background, specific, internal organisational dynamics and particularly the approach of management determined the trajectory of I&C. Yet whilst the legal framework was peripheral, it did help shape the constitutional format of the body in specifying the provision and the understanding of information and consultation as well as identifying a broad and meaningful range of topics for legitimate discussion, including developments in business activities, economic situation, employment, and decisions likely to lead to changes in work organisation or contractual relations.

Yet in light of the very background influence of the ICE Regulations, the NER (and its wider impact) in this case displays many themes consistent with extant knowledge, although it does perhaps highlight potential avenues for further consideration. Employees in the organisation demonstrated an apparent lack of interest in the NER, evidenced by the managerial difficulty in securing employee representatives but also in terms of the scarcity of employee interest about what was considered at the body. It is not implausible that many of the details of such forums are not of interest to shop-floor employees, particularly when, as evident in the case study, the same workers displayed an element of dissatisfaction with their immediate work conditions. As Fox (1974) observed, workers positioned in low-discretion, Taylorised roles are unlikely to respond with high-trust, high-commitment postures and may well lack interest in wider organisational events. Perhaps operating in a context of high-commitment Human Resource Management (HRM), where the NER features as part of a wider package of excellent terms and conditions of employment such as status harmonisation, semi-autonomous teams and the like, such a forum and its content might prove of greater interest to the employee body.

In any case, it appears that expressing employee grievances in the NER was not considered entirely appropriate by management, who favoured more "strategic" issues being raised at the Forum. Rather, management saw the Forum, in a fashion partly consistent with its constitutional definitions, as a mechanism for information and consultation on matters "central to the needs of the business." Yet the latter constitutional ambit of the forum as dealing with I&C on needs "relevant to the common interests of employees" appears to have been somewhat less certain, and this coincides with a problem of defining what precise function the NER was designed to fulfil: management-led I&C with employees to keep abreast of business developments or a forum for collective grievance resolution or, indeed, both. Defining the appropriate domain was thus problematic. One issue to be considered here is that effective NER would seem to require clear specification of function and certainty as to whether the forum acts to resolve contestable issues or not. A corollary of this might be the need, particularly evident amongst employees, to manage expectations so that the NER is understood not as a distributive mechanism relating to the wage-effort bargain but primarily of a more integrative calibre or an awareness- rather than grievance-raising forum. As Kim and Kim (2004) note, NER is a domain usually intended to align employees with management goals; it may not strictly be intended or indeed suitable to act on distributive or employee advocacy issues. Managing employee expectations pertains as much to employee representatives as to the wider body of employees: the former spoke about handling with individual grievances, when it was evident from the constitution that this was not their assigned task. This aligns with the issue of training, which the representatives seemed conscious they were lacking and which in turn resulted in unclear role specification and muddled expectation (c.f. Varman and Chakrabarti, 2004).

The lack of employee interest in the NER and the articulated preference for relations with line managers in securing favourable outcomes—particularly on individual matters—appears to give some support to the notion that workers may well prefer direct lines of contact and communication to more indirect mechanisms of a NER variety, particularly in the resolution of individual grievances (Townsend et al. 2012; Marchington and Suter, 2013). Indeed, using Workplace Employment Relations Survey (WERS) data, Bryson (2004) found that such mechanisms lead to better employee perceptions of managerial responsiveness than either non-union representative voice or union participation. However, as a form of voice, this is not unproblematic, as the effectiveness of direct communication may well be arbitrary, contingent on circumstance and indeed open to exploitation. Nonetheless, in spite of these limitations, direct forms of communication between line supervisor and employee appeared to be partially plugging the void in employee voice channels in the firm given the apparent irrelevance of NER and the lack of manifestly active support for a union voice channel.

In sum, the NER of the variety discerned in this case—and which would appear reasonably reflective of many others—would tend to suggest that NER should really be viewed as playing but a fairly partial rather than transformative role in terms of organisational voice dynamics. NER of the type seen here, with its modest role of information and consultation, will at best engender very modest impacts on the quality of employee voice within firms.

REFERENCES

Ackers, P., M. Marchington, A. Wilkinson, and T. Dundon. 2006. "Employee Participation in Britain: From Collective Bargaining and Industrial Democracy to Employee Involvement and Social Partnership—Two Decades of Manchester/Loughborough Research." *Decision*, 33(1): 75–87.

Applebaum, E., T. Bailey, P. Berg, and A. Kalleberg. 2000. *Manufacturing Advantage: Why High Performance Work Systems Pay Off.* Ithaca, NY: Cornell University/ILR Press.

Badigannavar, V., and J. Kelly. 2005. "Labour–Management Partnership in the Non-Union Retail Sector." *International Journal of Human Resource Management*, 16(8): 1529–44.

Bryson, A. 2004. "Managerial Responsiveness to Union and Non-Union Voice." *Industrial Relations*, 43(1): 213–41.

Bryson, A., A. Charlwood, and J. Forth. 2006. "Worker Voice, Managerial Responsiveness and Labour Productivity: An Empirical Investigation." *Industrial Relations Journal*, 37(5): 438–56.

Butler, P. 2005. "Non-Union Employee Representation: Exploring the Efficacy of the Voice Process." *Employee Relations*, 27(3): 272–88.

Dundon, T., D. Curran, M. Maloney, and P. Ryan. 2006. "Conceptualising the Dynamics of Employee Voice: Evidence from the Republic of Ireland." *Industrial Relations Journal*, 37(5): 492–512.

Dundon, T., and P. J. Gollan. 2007. "Reconceptualising Voice in the Non-Union Workplace." *International Journal of Human Resource Management*, 17(7): 1182–98.

Fox, A. 1974. *Beyond Contract: Work, Power and Trust Relations.* London: Faber.

Gollan, P. 2007. *Employee Representation in Non-Union Firms.* London: Sage.

Gumbrell-McCormick, R., and R. Hyman. 2006. "Embedded Collectivism? Workplace Representation in France and Germany." *Industrial Relations Journal,* 37(5): 473–91.

Hall, M. 2005. "Assessing the Information and Consultation of Employees Regulations." *Industrial Law Journal,* 34(2): 103–26.

Hall, M., S. Hutchinson, J. Purcell, M. Terry, and J. Parker. 2013. "Promoting Effective Consultation? Assessing the Impact of the I&C Regulations." *British Journal of Industrial Relations,* 51(2): 355–81.

Hyman, R. 1997. "The Future of Employee Representation." *British Journal of Industrial Relations,* 35(3): 309–36.

Johnstone, S., P. Ackers, and A. Wilkinson. 2010. "Better Than Nothing? Is Non-Union Partnership a Contradiction in Terms?" *Journal of Industrial Relations,* 52(2): 151–68.

Kim, D. O., and H. K. Kim. 2004. "A Comparison of the Effectiveness of Unions and Non-Union Works Councils in Korea: Can Non-Union Employee Representative Substitute for Trade Unionism?" *International Journal of Human Resource Management,* 15(6): 1063–93.

Kaufman, B. 2000. "The Case for the Company Union." *Labour History,* 41(3): 321–50.

Kaufman, B. E., and D. G. Taras. 2010. "Employee Participation through Non-Union Forms of Employee Representation." In A. Wilkinson, P. J. Gollan, M. Marchington, and D. Lewin (eds.), *The Oxford Handbook of Participation in Organizations,* pp. 258–85. Oxford: Oxford University Press.

Koukiadaki, A. 2010. "The Establishment and Operation of Information and Consultation of Employees' Arrangements in a Capability-Based Framework." *Economic and Industrial Democracy,* 31(3): 365–88.

MacDowell, K. 2000. "Company Unionism in Canada." In B. Kaufman and D. Taras (eds.), *Non-Union Employee Representation: History, Contemporary Practice and Policy,* pp. 96–120. Armonk, NY: M. E. Sharpe.

Marchington, M. 2005. "Employee Involvement: Patterns and Explanations." In B. Harley, J. Hyman, and P. Thompson (eds.), *Participation and Democracy at Work,* pp. 20–37. Basingstoke, UK: Palgrave Macmillan.

Marchington, M., and J. Suter. 2013. "Where Informality Really Matters: Patterns of Employee Involvement and Participation in a Non-Union Firm." *Industrial Relations,* 52(1): 284–313.

Pyman, A., B. Cooper, J. Teicher, and P. Holland. 2006. "A Comparison of the Effectiveness of Employee Voice Arrangements in Australia." *Industrial Relations Journal,* 37(6): 573–59.

Ramsay, H. 1980. "Phantom Participation: Patterns of Power and Conflict." *Industrial Relations Journal,* 11(3): 46–59.

Sisson, K. 2002. *The Information and Consultation Directive: Unnecessary "Regulation" or an Opportunity to Promote "Partnership"?,* Warwick Papers in Industrial Relations, no. 67. Coventry, UK: Industrial Relations Research Unit, University of Warwick.

Storey, J. 2005. "Employee Information and Consultation: An Overview of Theory and Practice." In J. Storey (ed.), *Adding Value through Information and Consultation,* pp. 2–20. Houndmills, Basingstoke, UK: Palgrave-Macmillan.

Taras, D. G., and J. Copping. 1998. "The Transition from Formal Non-Union Representation to Unionisation: A Contemporary Case." *Industrial and Labor Relations Review,* 52(1): 22–44.

Taras, D. G., and B. E. Kaufman. 2006. "Non-Union Employee Representation in North America: Diversity, Controversy and Uncertain Future." *Industrial Relations Journal,* 37(5): 513–42.

Terry, M. 1999. "Systems of Collective Employee Representation in Non-Union Firms in the UK." *Industrial Relations Journal*, 30(1): 16–30.

Townsend, K., A. Wilkinson, and J. Burgess. 2012. "Filling the Gaps: Patterns of Formal and Informal Voice." *Economic and Industrial Democracy*. Available at eid.sagepub.com/content/early/2012/06/07/0143831X12448442.

Upchurch, M., A. Danford, S. Tailby, and M. Richardson. 2008. *The Realities of Partnership at Work*. Basingstoke, UK: Palgrave Macmillan.

Varman, R., and M. Chakrabarti. 2004. "Contradictions of Democracy in a Workers' Cooperative." *Organization Studies*, 25(2): 183–208.

Willman, P., A. Bryson, and R. Gomez. 2003. *Why do voice regimes differ?*, CEPDP, no. 591. London: Centre for Economic Performance, London School of Economics and Political Science.

Wilkinson, A., and P. J. Gollan. 2007. "The EU Information and Consultation Directive and the Future of Employee Consultation in the UK." *International Journal of Human Resource Management*, 18(7): 1145–58.

Wood, S., and T. Wall. 2007. "Work Enrichment and Employee Voice in Human Resource Management-Performance Studies." *International Journal of Human Resource Management*, 18(7): 1335–72.

6 Employee Voice in a Dot Com

The Rise and Demise of the Employee Forum at WebBank

*Stewart Johnstone and
Adrian Wilkinson*

INTRODUCTION

This chapter examines the employee involvement and voice (EIV) system at a UK–based Internet bank, referred to by the pseudonym "WebBank," which was established in 1997 and ceased trading in 2011. The company quickly grew from a small city-centre startup operation to employing more than 2,500 in a large purpose-built operations centre at its peak. The context provides an interesting opportunity to explore the evolution and development of EIV in a greenfield context over its entire lifecycle. Given the importance of context and management choice in shaping EIV systems (Wilkinson et al. 2013), this represents an opportunity to explore a relatively unusual model of non-union EIV in Britain, during a period when the newly elected Labour government appeared to have warmer attitudes to trade unions after almost two decades of Conservative governments of leaving them out in the cold.

The chapter begins with an overview of the company and its history. The case study is then placed within the wider national and sectoral context. Having located WebBank within its internal and external context, the chapter then explores in some detail the evolution, structure, and operation of EIV, before providing an assessment of the outcomes and effectiveness from both a company and employee perspective. We conclude by considering some of the conditions associated with the success and failure of EIV, and present some of the general lessons which can be learned.

In order to present the story of EIV at WebBank over time, the material is based upon researcher interaction with members of the organization from 2004 until 2010, including a period of detailed fieldwork which was conducted on site during the period 2004 through 2006. This involved conducting detailed interviews with a range of senior and line managers, as well as HR specialists, employee representatives, and employees. Unfortunately, a further tranche of fieldwork planned for 2010, and agreed to by the UK Company Director, had to be abandoned due to difficult trading conditions in the business at that point. However, the Chair of the EIV structure nevertheless agreed to continue informal on-site conversations, and his contribution is gratefully acknowledged. This provided valuable insights into some of the challenges faced towards the end of the life of the business, and was supplemented by analysis of the local business and press reports which covered events at WebBank in great detail. The business subsequently closed in 2011.

FINANCIAL SERVICES IN THE UK

Firstly, it is important to clarify what is meant by the financial service sector. International classifications of the sector include commercial and investment banking, insurance, fund management, securities dealing, venture capital, and derivatives trading. Professional services such as accounting, legal services, and management consulting are normally excluded and considered instead to be part of wider business services. Financial services have long been an important part of the UK economy, with London generally considered to be one of the world's leading financial centres. The sector contributes around 10 per cent of GDP and employs more than 1 million people, mostly in London, the South East, and Scotland. The majority of employment in UK financial services is in banking (435,000 employees) and insurance (300,000 employees; CityUK 2010). Within the broad banking category, the sector includes a wide range of job roles from wealth managers and traders in investment banks, to customer service advisers in bank branches and call centres Indeed, financial services is the largest employer of call centre workers, with several pioneering the concept in the early 1990s.

Retail banking, as opposed to wholesale and investment banking, can be divided into three broad areas: core banking, secondary banking, and peripheral banking. Core banking consists of traditional banking products such as personal current and savings accounts. Secondary products include loans such as credit cards and mortgages, while peripheral banking services include products such as insurance and pensions which are outwith the domain of traditional retail banking offerings. There are three main types of organisation offering retail bank services in the UK. Retail banks, such as Lloyds, focus primarily upon accepting deposits and offering loans. Universal banks, such as Barclays and RBS, offer retail products but also have investment banking operations. Finally, building societies, such as Nationwide, are mutual organizations with a history which dates back to the Industrial Revolution as small local organizations which pooled funds to facilitate land and house purchases. Modern building societies now offer a wide range of financial products in addition to mortgages and compete directly with banks in the UK retail market.

COMPANY HISTORY AND BUSINESS MODEL

WebBank was launched in the late 1990s as one of the first movers into the telephone- and Internet-based banking arena in the UK. It was created by a major British financial service organization which was seeking to expand into the direct retail banking market. In this sense, it benefited from the experience of its parent organization in financial service provision, although the entry into retail banking represented diversification of its products and services. Up until the 1990s, retail banking had been dominated by the long-established "Big Four" UK clearing banks: Barclays, Midland Bank, Lloyds TSB, and National Westminster Bank. However, technological developments and the opportunity for telephone- and Internet-based banking meant the lack of an extensive high-street branch network was no longer necessarily a barrier to entry in consumer banking. WebBank was therefore one of the pioneers of the Internet-based banking model. Unlike the big-name clearing banks, besides a small official headquarters office in London, the company centred operations on a business park on the outskirts of a provincial city, traditionally associated more with engineering and manufacturing than financial services. Indeed, the 80-hectare business park was itself formerly an industrial area of the city, but was now redeveloped as a business park strategically positioned adjacent to the railway station and the national motorway network. The utilitarian, hangar-like exterior belied the contemporary designer interior. Interestingly, the centre only had one floor, ostensibly in keeping with desire for a more egalitarian work environment. A central atrium, housing a coffee shop, sofas, and informal "dens" and "sanctuaries" for relaxation, led out to vast, open-plan workspaces accommodating the 2,500 employees. The canteen was styled more like a chic noodle bar than a traditional workplace dining area, and the dress code was liberal: even the CEO was said to don shorts on hot summer days. The work environment was therefore quite different from that of the central London skyscrapers and high-street branches of its competitors.

However, it was not only the physical environment which made it different from established rivals. The workforce was generally young, with most employees under thirty-five, and with a high proportion eighteen to twenty-three, having joined straight from school or college. For many entry-level employees, WebBank was their first full-time employer, and for most, it was their first experience of working in the financial services industry. A typical entry-level position was as a customer service agent, handling the 12,000 telephone-based enquiries received by the centre each day. Further enquiries were received by Internet-based messaging services, and call agents would split time between answering telephone calls and replying to electronic messages. Most customer-facing employees worked variable shifts between the businesses core hours of 7 a.m. and midnight seven days a week, with specialist and professional staff working traditional office hours, and a skeleton graveyard shift ensuring twenty-four-hour customer service.

Led by a management team consisting of a CEO from the parent organization and a CFO from a rival Big Four bank, the raison d'être of WebBank was to create something fresh and innovative in the traditionally conservative and oligopolistic British retail banking market. As with many dot-coms, fast growth was a key aim, and the company launched a range of highly competitive products which were feasible because of the lower overheads. The bank rapidly established a large customer base, accumulating several million customers and several billion pounds in deposits in the first few years. The company aimed to create a brand which aligned with its pioneering approach, emphasizing innovative, market-leading products and distribution channels, as well as excellent customer service. As the customer based expanded, so did the product range, with the business eventually offering a suite of financial service products including insurance, mortgages, and investments. In 2000, the firm registered on the London Stock Exchange and broke into profit for the first time in 2001.

The new business also had a statement outlining its purpose and values:

- Our enduring purpose is to revolutionize customer experience of financial services driven through unleashing the power of people
- Our core values are honesty, integrity and respect for people
- We aspire to be vibrant, imaginative and fair in everything that we do
- We constantly look to offer customers products and services that put them in control of their money
- We respect our people's individuality and diversity, encouraging them to develop their careers in a stimulating environment
- Our shareholders own the business and must be fairly rewarded for their investment
- We work cooperatively with our suppliers and business partners and choose those who share our values and strive for mutual trust and benefit
- We behave as good neighbours in our local communities and as a responsible citizen
- We respect, protect and where possible enhance the quality of the environment

EMPLOYEE VOICE IN FINANCIAL SERVICES

Employee representation in British financial services has traditionally been characterized by competition between trade unions committed to industrial unionism and collective bargaining at a sectoral level, and internal staff associations representing employees working within a single bank. While staff associations were traditionally regarded as less "unionate" (Blackburn 1967) because of their lack of independence from employers and less adversarial relationships, this distinction has become increasingly blurred over time. Several staff associations have arguably become increasingly unionate, undertaking a collective bargaining function, affiliating to the Trade Union Congress, rebranding as staff unions, and even supporting industrial action (Waddington 2013). A series of mergers has also blurred the boundary between staff associations and unions. The main industrial union was known as the Banking, Insurance and Finance Union (BIFU), itself an evolution of the National Union of Bank Employees (NUBE) and the Bank Officers Guild (BOG). A new union, known as Unifi, was created in 1999 as a result of a merger of BIFU, the National Westminster Staff Association, and the former Barclays Group Staff Union. Unifi merged with Amicus in 2005, which has since merged again to form part of Unite. In contrast to much of the British private sector, union membership has been relatively robust (Gall 2008), and this has been explained in terms of employer support, employment in concentrated centres, and employment growth in the sector for most of the postwar period.

Most of the large financial service organizations in the UK have some form of collective voice through either external trade unions or internal staff associations. Indeed, in 2004, 72 per cent of financial service organizations recognized trade unions, and aggregate density was 32 per cent (Kersley et al. 2006: 119). By point of comparison, figures in private-sector manufacturing were 23 per cent and 21 per cent, respectively. Fifty-six per cent of financial services workplaces have a union density greater than 50 per cent compared to only 11 per cent in UK manufacturing. Density also tends to be significantly higher in banking than in insurance. In 2004, 85 per cent of financial services workplaces had arrangements for employee representation, meaning representation was available to 80 per cent of workers in the sector. Importantly, besides privatized public utilities, financial services is the only private sector industry in which union recognition is the norm in the UK (Kersley et al. 2006). Non-union employee representation of the type examined in this chapter remains unusual in this sector.

EIV AT WEBBANK: EVOLUTION, STRUCTURE, AND OPERATION

Rationale

The main system of EIV at WebBank was the Employee Forum, which was introduced two years after the bank launched. The impetus for an employee voice mechanism was said to have come from management, following two years of rapid growth, in terms of both customer and employee numbers. However, this also coincided with British and European policy debates around statutory trade union recognition and mandatory information and consultation, so debates about employee voice were on the agenda of many employers. There are various explanations for the creation of staff representation so soon after the opening of the bank. On the one hand, it could have been, as was claimed by HR managers, that an employee voice mechanism is simply a necessary part of any HR toolkit, and when organizations reach a certain size, indirect structures are needed in addition to direct EI structures. It could also have been partly because as, a completely new business, and with so many new employees constantly joining, there was a concern with developing effective communication channels. On the other hand, it could be viewed as an attempt to proactively construct an internal EIV system which potentially acted as a substitute for trade union recognition or mandated structures under impending European legislation. However, the forum preceded the Information and Consultation of Employees Regulations introduced in 2005 by five years, so it was not necessarily just a response to a changing legislative environment. Indeed, it may have represented a degree of institutional isomorphism, given that the senior management team already had much experience in the financial service sector, in which collective representation remains the norm. In this sense, a collective voice system might have been considered to be a normal part of organizational governance. Though management claimed to be ambivalent about trade union recognition, they did suggest that an internal staff forum has advantages such as greater understanding of the culture, universal coverage of employees working for the organisation, and no wider political agenda.

Evolution

At first, the employee forum consisted of three part-time employee representatives, and the agenda was said to have been heavily guided by a few senior management figures in association with the HR team. Consultation was said to typically occur after decisions had actually been made. Issues raised by the employee representatives were said to be fairly low level "tea and toilets" items, including the quality of the sausages offered in the canteen and the dislike of the handwash in the lavatories. After two years, the Chief Executive was said to have expressed disappointment regarding the effectiveness of the employee forum and proposed a need to reconsider how the business might improve it EIV mechanism. Interestingly, the same year, a British trade union had identified WebBank as a target for union organization and arranged some union publicity events in the vicinity of the centre. This is an important juncture given that union representation is the norm in the sector, and because it is unsurprising a 2,500-strong workforce would be an attractive prospect for union organizers. Management and employee representatives subsequently attended a range of meetings with the Trade Union Congress (TUC) Partnership Institute, which was set up to promote union–management partnership, as well as with the main trade union representing financial service workers. However, management admitted a skepticism regarding the appropriateness or desirability of trade union representation within WebBank, but were nevertheless intrigued by the notion of labour–management partnership which was dominating the broader public policy discourse in the early 2000s. At this point, contact was made with the Involvement and Participation Association (IPA), a not-for-profit organisation engaged in employment policy and consultancy and promotion of workplace partnership. Following advice from the IPA, a decision was taken to relaunch the employee forum, and this time a revised structure was devised by the employee representatives rather than the management team. Under the banner "Playing it Big," the representatives presented a new structure to the senior management team. In terms of structure, this required a new, expanded system of full-time employee representatives, supported by a network of part-time area representatives. It proposed a need for agreed facilities time, as well as a budget allocation to support forum activity such as training, equipment, travel, and conference attendance. In terms of process, the key change was a commitment to a genuine process of consultation, in contrast to before, when decisions were often communicated to employee representatives shortly before being announced to employees. The proposal for a new employee forum was accepted by the senior management team, and preparations for the "new" employee forum began.

Structure

The expansion meant the three full-time salaried employee representatives would be supported by twelve part-time representatives, who would each be allocated four hours per week for forum work. Their remit was to represent and communicate with employees who work in their particular section of the business. All employee representatives were appointed through a formal election process.

Structure of the WebBank Employee Forum

Employer chair	Chief executive
Employee chair	Elected full-time employee representative
Employee vice chair	Elected full-time employee representative
Full-time employee representative	Elected full-time employee representative
Management representatives	Two members of senior management team
HR representative	Nominated by employee chair
Forum secretary	Nominated by HR representative

The relaunch also meant the development of a formal Commitment Document, which stated the objectives and principles of the employee forum.

Aim: to represent the voice of all the banks' people, to make working life great, and to drive superior business results

1) Objectives

- To increase the level of employee involvement in change and business initiatives which affect employees using effective consultation

- To build and maintain effective relationships with all departments through consultation
- To represent independently and without prejudice the interests of Web-Bank people both collectively and individually

2) Primary principles

- Joint commitment of the employee forum and bank will ensure success
- Recognition by all of the legitimate roles, interests and responsibilities of those on the employee forum
- Transparency between the employee forum and the bank through effective consultation and information sharing
- Building trust between the bank and its people
- Employees have the right to be represented and have equal opportunities within the business
- Employees have exceptional training and effective development

3) Operating principles

- Act for the good of the bank and its people
- Stay within the overall context of the bank's strategy, support that strategy, and contribute to the bank's strategy
- Respect the principles of consultation

Operation of the EIV

In terms of approach, an emphasis was placed upon working, where possible, in a cooperative problem-solving manner rather than adversarial posturing. In part, this was inspired by the notion of labour–management partnership which was popular in policy and practitioner circles at the time as a preferred approach to workplace relations. It was suggested that while a nonpartnership approach often involves defending employer and employee positions in a mutually exclusive manner, partnership is more concerned with working together to find a mutually acceptable outcome to shared problems, with an overall aim of contributing to the overall success of the enterprise. However, such an approach was believed to require a high level of trust and respect between management and employee representatives to work effectively. The hope was that the outcomes of working together would result in decisions which were more balanced and fairer than they might otherwise have been. Representatives aimed to ensure management took into account the human implications of proposals and decisions, while management recognized that the employee representatives were not inherently antibusiness or antimanagement but aimed to promote and highlight the interests of the workforce. For some managers, this made the non-union employee representation (NER) system distinctive from some forms of union voice which they believed tended to be more politically and ideologically charged. Employee represen tatives recognized arguments that NER structures might be considered to be a weak alternative to—or a substitute for—trade union representation. However, they took issue with the view that unions by definition have more power, suggesting instead that systems of effective and ineffective representa tion can arise in both union and non-union contexts. It was the quality of the relationships forged between management and the representative rather than union/non-union status which was believed to be crucial. If the NER system was perceived by representatives and employees to be ineffectual, this may have generated interest in unionization as an alternative.

Nevertheless, it was clear that management retained the right to man age within the EIV structure. It was explicit in the Commitment Docu ment that the NER body was a consultative body, and consultation was defined as where "both parties' views are stated and heard before a deci sion is made. The perspective of each party is understood by the other but not necessarily agreed between them." The consultation framework was explicitly based upon the IPA Options Based Consultation model. Firstly, business objectives are identified. Management then identify potential options and consult with employee representatives. Employee represen tatives thus have the opportunity to respond and provide feedback at an early stage in the process. Management then regroup and devise a revised list of options which take account of the responses of employee representatives, justifying why the final decision was made as well as why alternative options were rejected. Decisions are then made and cascaded to employees.

Option-based Consultation Model (IPA)

1) Identify business objective
2) Consultation with representatives before decision is made
3) Decision made (by managers)
4) Communication of decision
5) Implement business objective

This approach meant the purpose of the forum was to consider, question, and challenge proposals, but management reserved the right to make the final decision. The relationship was described as assertive and challenging but not necessarily confrontational. However, operation of the employee forum changed over time, and the Marchington and colleagues (1992) framework is useful in demonstrating this evolution (see also Wilkinson et al. 2013).

Degree of Influence

Marchington and colleagues (1992) propose that degree of influence can be mapped on a continuum of participation from worker control at one end to managerial unilateralism at the other. In between the two extremes, they outline several intermediary positions, including information provision, communication, consultation, and codetermination. The WebBank forum appeared to have been gradually climbing the "escalator of participation." During the first few years, the focus was upon information and communication; however, it was soon realized by management and representatives that such an approach appeared to yield fairly limited benefits. Communication was also said to be late in the process, meaning little opportunity to influence proposals. It was clear that this evolved after the redevelopment of the forum into a more substantial consultation body. Though management retained the right to manage, the employee forum afforded the opportunity for representatives to influence decision making. While the forum was not a negotiating body, its role as consultation body was structured around explicit commitments to early consultation, opportunities to give feedback and influence proposals, and a commitment to transparency of decision-making processes.

Scope of Decision Making

The scope of decision making also evolved over time. Initially, the range of issues discussed by the forum was primarily concerned with immediate day-to-day operational issues relevant to employees. Many of these might be considered to be concerned with hygiene factors such as the nature of the work environment or lack of car parking. However, over time the scope of issues expanded to cover three main areas.

Organisational Change
Firstly, the forum was involved with issues concerning organizational change and work organization. Within this general category, a wide range of issues had been developed in consultation with the employees, and two are particularly illustrative of the evolution of the scope. Firstly, a proposed restructure of the technology centre, resulting in many staff changing roles, was deemed by forum representatives to have been based upon arbitrary selection criteria. A particular concern was that in some cases, there was a feeling that the selection process was based more upon personal relationships and loyalties than upon those most suited or qualified to carry out the roles. The employee forum representatives subsequently worked with the management team to devise criteria which were based upon the knowledge, skills, and attributes required to carry out the job rather than social relationships. A second example concerned the suspension of duvet days in the call centre. Duvet days, where employees could effectively take a day off at the last minute, were introduced as a potential way of reducing sickness and absenteeism rates. Each employee was allocated four such days on which they could request a holiday at the very beginning of that working day. In the run up to Christmas one year, management noted that absenteeism was a problem and that call targets were not being met as a result. A proposal

was made to end duvet days. However, representatives from the call centre believed that such as message would have been deemed unfair by employees with good attendance records and might be perceived to be a punishment of the majority because of the behaviour of a minority. It was predicted that a decision to cancel duvet days would have been badly received and only angered an already overstretched and demoralized workforce in the run up to Christmas. As a result of the consultation process, a more sensitive approach and communication resulted. It explained that because call answer times had fallen below the business targets, management had reluctantly deemed it necessary to suspend duvet days until service targets improved. The difference between the two situations may appear subtle, but for employee representatives, the more sensitive explanation avoided inflaming an already tense situation. On the other hand, management admitted that without forum insights, they would probably have taken a more factual and potentially heavy-handed approach.

Discipline and Grievance

The forum also provided voice to employees on an individual basis as part of the organizational discipline and grievance process. Many of the discipline cases occurred in the call centre operations, and it was noted that this appeared to be common across the industry, and indeed across call centre environments in general. Typical issues included timekeeping, absenteeism, and underperformance. In most disciplinary hearings, an employee representative would be involved, normally holding informal meetings with the employee and manager involved in advance of the formal meeting. As well as dealing with individual cases, the employee forum was involved in codesigning a new discipline and grievance procedure which was developed to ensure compliance with new statutory requirements in the UK. Employee representatives would normally aim to establish the nature of the problem and, in turn, the cause of the problem from both an employee and employer point of view. This mediation role, it was suggested, offered the opportunity for a third party to assess the situation from both sides. Representatives suggested that this improved the discipline and grievance process because it allowed identification of cases in which issues had arisen because of misunderstandings or personal issues, as opposed to cases where it was a deliberate misdemeanour by either party. It was believed this meant that such issues could in turn be dealt with in a more appropriate and sensitive manner.

Pay and Reward

A key difference from the collective bargaining associated with trade union representation is that the employee forum was not involved in the formal negotiation of pay. However, there was evidence to suggest that representatives had become gradually become involved in pay and reward consultations. Though the role was advisory, there was evidence to suggest forum feedback had been taken into account, resulting in subsequent policy changes such as the introduction of a holiday purchase scheme, alterations to the package of fringe benefits, and the administration of the company pension scheme.

Form

In terms of form, the NER structure worked in parallel with other, more direct voice mechanisms. For example, the company conducted monthly staff surveys, and employee representatives were given the opportunity to include questions which were considered to be useful to their own work and priorities. Other direct voice mechanisms included "fireside chats" between line managers and employees and annual "town hall" meetings. In addition, extensive use was made of electronic communications such as the intranet both to cascade information to employees and to solicit feedback and employee responses, with most web pages giving employees the opportunity to comment or discuss items. While these communication methods had no formal link to the forum, employee representatives did report some ad hoc involvement with these techniques.

Level

The level of issues discussed changed over time. In its infancy, the focus was upon low-level, day-to-day issues, although there was evidence to suggest that as the employee forum matured, representatives were increasingly involved in an array of issues spanning various organizational levels. There was also evidence to suggest that management were increasingly inviting employee representatives to get involved in more policy working groups and committees.

ASSESSMENT OF THE OUTCOMES

The main benefit for the company was the regulation of decision making the EIV system afforded, which was believed ultimately to result in better and more legitimate decisions. Management suggested that employee representatives provided valuable insights and constructive criticism regarding business proposals, in relation to both the nature of work processes as well as the overall climate of employee relations. This was believed to mean that oversights or alternative options could be identified at an early stage, and thus the voice process acted as a useful checkpoint and "sanity check" on management thinking. The employer was able to identify decisions which were better in the long-term. Without dialogue, decisions may have been based on short-term expediency rather than long-term business interests. Interestingly, management acknowledged that decisions based solely on "profit maximising" and "efficiency" are often inefficient because of the scant regard for equity outcomes. Such decisions were then met with resistance and opposition, whereas decisions resulting from compromise were met with greater levels of legitimacy and acceptability. In other words, there was recognition of a business case for employee voice.

Without employee voice, it was suggested that management may have devised proposals in good faith but nevertheless potentially missed or under-estimated potential employee relations flashpoints and the likely concerns of frontline workers. There was evidence to suggest that this was increasingly happening, with management engaging with the forum representatives earlier and in relation to a wider range of issues, because they perceived value in doing so rather than merely because they should. Another advantage for the company was they were operating within an EIV framework they had effectively codesigned rather than one which had been imposed as a result of statutory requirements. The threat of unionization loomed large, and therefore management had a vested interest in ensuring the NER system was deemed effective.

In terms of disadvantages from the company perspective, the key issue was primarily the cost (both financial and nonfinancial) required to develop and sustain an effective EIV system which would attract and sustain the buy-in of all actors.

For employees, the main benefit was access to some form of collective voice mechanism through which they could express their views and concerns to management. The importance of this must not be underestimated given the decline of collective voice and shift to direct voice in many UK workplaces, and especially those in the private sector. For many WebBank employees, this was their first full-time employment and, in turn, their first experience of collective voice mechanisms of any type. From this perspective, it might be supposed that such an employee demographic might be relatively open minded in relation to the benefits or role of non-union employee representation. It also offered an approach to representation which most said they preferred, namely a predominantly cooperative rather than adversarial relationship with management. While most employees were not especially interested in the EIV system on a day-to-day basis, most were aware of its existence and function, and elections of representatives were highly publicized events. To be clear, the employee forum did not offer full "job regulation," whereby representatives become authors of the rules that govern work, nor did it offer industrial democracy or the retaliatory power associated with trade unions (Hyman 2001). The EIV forum also never yielded "economic regulation" through the negotiation of terms and conditions collective bargaining.

Though there are clear problems with simply comparing union and non-union voice structures in general terms, it remains relevant given that an important question in judging the efficacy of the structure is how it might compare to other potential alternative voice mechanisms. The findings of Waddington and Whitson (1997) are useful in this respect in their study investigating the reasons British workers join trade unions.

The results revealed that by far the most common response (with 72 per cent respondents) was to get support if there was problem, followed by improvements in pay and conditions (36 per cent) and a belief in unions (16 per cent). A potential disadvantage is that while the forum aimed to offer as effective a voice as a union would, the forum had less legal support to offer. As the forum was focused more around promoting cooperation and employee welfare concerns, it could not offer employees specialist legal advice where a major conflict occurred and resulted in a disciplinary and grievance situation. An interesting result of this was evidence of some employees who reported satisfaction with the collective representation offered through the NER, but had also privately joined a trade union precisely for the peace of mind this affords in terms of potential recourse to independent individual representation.

The findings at WebBank appeared to confirm other research which has found that employees in non-unionised settings believe that a union would make little difference, as well findings which suggest that UK workers want collective representation characterized by cooperation rather militancy or confrontation (Bryson and Freeman 2006). Concerns were expressed regarding unions being too militant and antibusiness, and would generate conflict rather than improving employment relations.

RECENT DEVELOPMENTS AT WEBBANK

Since WebBank opened at the height the of the dot-com bubble in the late 1990s, there have been considerable changes in the UK and international financial service sector. After an initially impressive start, WebBank struggled to sustain its position in the intensely competitive UK retail banking market, and in 2003, the parent organisation attempted to sell the business. However, there was a lack of interest among competitors, who had responded by developing their own Internet-only brands offering enhanced products and services compared to their high-street offerings. Competitors included Intelligent Finance (Lloyds-HBOS), Cahoot (Santander), and First Direct (HSBC). For many customers, this offered the best of both worlds: the convenience of Internet banking combined with the security and peace of mind associated with a national branch network should things go wrong. Research has suggested that 77 per cent of consumers would not consider an online- or telephone-only bank (OFT 2010). Fear of fraud means many potential customers remain fundamentally suspicious of Internet banking, and the sector is also notorious for consumer inertia. For the dominant Big Five, this is good news, with high-street current accounts used as a gateway product with the opportunity for cross-selling or an array of products and services.

In 2007, the parent company decided to sell what was at that point a loss-making business to a U.S. financial service organisation keen to improve its foothold in the UK retail banking market. Shortly after, the implications of the global financial crisis (GFC) contributed to a sustained period of turbulence within the sector. Major banks including RBS received government support to ensure their continued viability, a situation which might have been quite unthinkable in the boom years. Another consequence of the GFC has been the consolidation and concentration in the retail banking sector, with fourteen mergers since 2008, including HBOS-Lloyds TSB and Alliance and Leicester-Santander. The new Big Five held an 85 per cent share of the personal current account market, 60 per cent unsecured loans, 62 per cent savings deposits, and 75 per cent of new lending in the mortgage market (OFT 2010). At the same, many international operators faced economic pressures in their domestic markets and scaled back international operations. The U.S. owner of WebBank was no exception and in 2010 took the decision to "reduce its portfolio of non-core operating businesses and assets." WebBank had clearly struggled and was making significant losses, and the employee forum also experienced intense pressure. It was perceived that the new American management team did not understand or appreciate the value or purpose of the employee forum. Many of the original senior management champions had left, and relationships between senior management and the forum representatives needed to be reconstructed. It was suggested that in some cases this had been possible, but that in others it had proved more problematic, exacerbated by a context of constant restructuring, high management turnover, cultural differences, and a tough business climate. Though access for a detailed investigation was understandably not forthcoming during this period, it was clear that in general, the employee forum members had felt sidelined and marginalized since the U.S. acquisition. In 2011, the business was sold in several parts (mortgages, savings, credit cards) to other competitor financial service organizations. The WebBank brand is still in use, albeit merely as a trading name, with the original WebBank business and centre employing 600 workers closed.

EIV IMPLICATIONS AND LESSONS

Several implications and lessons can be derived from a review of the WebBank experience of NER on a greenfield site.

The Importance of the Business Context

The EIV system at WebBank was created in a very young organization which was distinctive from others in the sector in terms of both its business and Human Resources Management (HRM) model. While the senior leadership team were veterans of the financial service sector, there was an opportunity to initiate and develop an EIV system from scratch in a fresh environment. This makes it quite different from many of its main competitors, which have a long history of operation and embedded traditions of HRM and must work within the constraints of ingrained employment relations systems. The latitude for management choice in this context was therefore greater than in long-established settings. As with much in HRM, given the relevance of contextual contingencies, it seems unlikely that a single best-practice EIV structure can simply be transposed from one organizational context to another. Nevertheless, several ingredients appear to be associated with positive evaluations of organizational processes and their absence associated with negative evaluations of EIV.

Clear Expectations of Purpose

To be effective, EIV requires a clear understanding of the purpose and rules of engagement. In particular, is the expectation that EIV will provide a process of codetermination and joint decision making resulting in industrial democracy, or is it more concerned with ensuring effective information and consultation and the opportunity to have a say? The expectations and responsibilities of actors at WebBank were expressed in the Commitment Document, and management and employee representatives were clear that the employee forum was a consultation body as opposed to a negotiating body and that within this framework, management retained the right to manage and, indeed, to make the final decision. This was not perceived to be a particularly problematic feature, because workers and employee representatives believed that the process of information and consultation delivered mutual benefits.

Clear Understanding of the Processes

Similarly, all actors need to have a clear understanding of the processes associated with achieving the objectives. In the case of WebBank, the meaning and process of consultation was made explicit by the detailed Options-Based Consultation' framework developed in conjunction with the Involvement and Participation Association.

High-Trust Relations among Organizational Actors

Strong working relationships between the key actors in the EIV process were identified as a key success factor underpinning the effectiveness of the structure. These were important at all levels and most notably between senior management and employee representatives, middle/line managers and employee representatives, and between representatives and employees. In this respect, positive informal working relationships were as important as the more formal processes associated with the formal infrastructure. A challenge was what happened when key actors who had acted as voice advocates and champions left the business, such as the departure of the inaugural CEO in 2006.

Legitimacy

Management must accept the legitimacy of the EIV system if it is to function effectively. This requires a subscription to the pluralist nature of workplace relations, where occasional conflict and disagreement is viewed as natural rather than evidence of troublemaking or a breakdown in communications. Management need to accept the constructive criticism offered by employee representatives and be open to exploring alternative perspectives, ideas, and viewpoints; indeed, these need to be positively encouraged. They also need to accept that not only are alternative views legitimate, but they also can potentially lead to better business decisions. Attempts to undermine, exploit, or constrain the representative body mean it is likely the body will deliver little for management or workers.

Transparency

In order to foster an environment of trust and confirm the legitimacy of the structure, a culture of transparency was required, with management actively consulting with employee representatives at an early stage on a whole range of business issues and proposals. While this required management to trust the representatives, especially when the information remained confidential and sensitive, it also served to consolidate trust, as representatives valued being entrusted and involved at an early stage.

Problem-Solving Approach

Actors regularly spoke in terms of problem-solving approaches, and there was evidence of innovative solutions being devised as a result. Rather than establishing and defending positions, the emphasis was upon working together to identify a mutually acceptable way forward through robust debate and accepting disagreements as normal.

Long-Term Perspective

Actors were required to take a longer-term perspective in relation to decision making rather than merely seeking quick fixes. In other words, a more strategic approach to HRM was required.

Employee Representatives

Employee representatives need to be standing for the right reasons and to be credible as the voice of employees. A key concern of management is that some representatives only stand for election because of a personal vendetta with the company or that they only represent the views of a vocal minority of workers. Employee representatives need to ensure that they are accepted by management as the legitimate and representative voice of all employees. They must also have interpersonal skills required to develop collaborative but influential relationships with management. These roles are likely to be challenging, and require adequate training for those assuming roles as representatives so that they are capable of engaging in debate and not merely opposing or criticizing. Representatives are increasingly required to challenge on the grounds of the business case, and this requires particular skills and approaches. As Terry notes, "success in consultation is perceived to rely on force of argument and technical competence rather than upon muscle" (Terry 2003: 493). While it might be relatively easy to decide which position to take in relations to distributive issues such as terms and conditions, it can be more difficult to decide what to support where more integrative matters are concerned (Terry 2003). A delicate balance has to be struck by representatives between being perceived as "too strong" and "too weak" (Ackers et al. 2004) by both management and the workers they represent.

Senior Management Support

Management support was central to the success of the EIV mechanism. In particular, the explicit support and regular involvement of the Chief Executive sent a strong signal about the relevance of the forum to the business. Without visible support from the top, a risk is that the EIV mechanism is viewed as a peripheral or tangential mechanism.

Middle Management Support

It is essential to get the buy-in of line managers who are actually responsible for implementing policy and managing people on a day-to-day basis. Yet middle management might not automatically support or understand the role of the EIV. They may view it as at odds with reality, restricting autonomy and slowing down decision making. They may also lack the skills and encounter difficulties reconciling competing and sometimes contradictory priorities. Finally, line managers might not be rewarded in accordance with their commitment or engagement to EIV and thus be driven by a narrower focus upon the achievement of "hard" business results. This can result in inconsistencies in the application of agreed-on policies and processes.

Employee Awareness and Support

A danger is that EIV becomes an arcane elite-level process of little relevance to workers. Of course, it is likely that most employees do want or need a detailed account of—or involvement with—forum activity. However, a lack of communication can lead to perceptions of inactivity, inertia, and irrelevance. Employees sought enough communications to allow them to follow the main business and employment relations "headlines" with clear signposts to further details should they require it. Importantly, employees supported collaborative rather than combative relationships with management.

Integration with the Wider Business and Governance Structures

EIV needs to be integrated into the overall management of the business. EIV also needs to be able to operate at a senior strategic level within the business but also capture the day-to-day dynamics of employment relations. The requires the engagement of all actors and not just a clique of staff formally involved with the employee forum. While it is easy to be dismissive of "tea and toilets," such issues are often key hygiene factors. The danger is the EIV becomes so involved in strategy that such issues—which really matter to employees—also fall off the agenda.

CONCLUSION

We can see that the relationships at the centre of the EIV are dynamic and susceptible to periods of energy and action as well as periods of relative inactivity. While a period of turbulence or organizational change may reinforce the value of EIV, when the environment stabilizes, it might be easy to forget or undervalue the structure. Equally, turbulence might consolidate and reinforce the efficacy of the structure, or it could potentially undermine its value. A key change in the operation of the WebBank EIV was the acquisition of the business by a U.S. organisation in 2007 and the perception that the new owners were less convinced by the value or relevance of the NER. As a result, senior and middle management support appeared to evaporate.

To be sustainable, the voice process needs to be seen to be delivering regular benefits to the parties involved. While this does not mean that all actors were happy with all of the decisions all of the time, there are clear risks associated with a structure which is not perceived to deliver any benefits for labour or management. For management, the benefits sought included constructive criticism and ideas about how business proposals could be improved. For labour, the benefits sought were primarily associated with ensuring organizational decision-making processes were transparent, fair, and well justified, and that improved employment relations outcomes were regularly achieved as a result. Voice which is not thought to have any "regulatory impact" (Hyman 2005) is unlikely to be sustainable.

REFERENCES

Ackers, P., M. Marchington, A. Wilkinson, and T. Dundon. 2004. "Partnership and Voice, with or without Trade Unions: Changing Management Approaches to Organizational Participation." In M. Stuart and M. Martinez-Lucio (eds.), *Partnership and Modernisation in Employment Relations*, pp. 20–39. London: Routledge.

Blackburn, R. M. 1967. *Union Character and Social Class: A Study of White-Collar Unionism*. London: Batsford.

Bryson, A., and R. Freeman. 2006. *What Do British Workers Want?* CEP Discussion Paper 731, July. London: LSE.

CityUK. 2010. "Economic Contribution of UK Financial Services 2010." www.CityUK.com.

Gall, G. 2008. *Labour Unionism in the Financial Services Sector: Fighting for Rights and Representation*. Aldershot: Ashgate Publishing Company.

Hyman, R. 2001. *Understanding European Trade Unionism: Between Market, Class and Society*. London: Sage.

———. 2005. "Whose (Social) Partnership?" In M. Stuart and M. Martinez-Lucio (eds.), *Partnership and Modernisation in Employment Relations*, pp. 386–411. London: Routledge.

Kersley, B., C. Alpin, J. Forth, A. Bryson, H. Bewley, G. Dix, and S. Oxenbridge. 2006. *Inside the Workplace: Findings from the 2004 Workplace Employment Relations Survey*. London: Routledge.

Marchington, M., J. Goodman, A. Wilkinson, and P. Ackers. 1992. *New Developments in Employee Involvement*. Employment Department Research Paper No 2. Sheffield, UK: HMSO.

OFT. 2010. *Review of Barriers to Entry, Expansion and Exit in Retail Banking*. Office of Fair Trade, no. 1282, November, accessed June 23, 2014. Available at http://webarchive.nationalarchives.gov.uk/20140402142426/.

Terry M. 2003. "Partnership and the Future of Trade Unions in the UK." *Economic and Industrial Democracy*, 24(4): 485–507.

Waddington, J. 2013. "The Views of Members towards Workplace Union Organization in Banking between 1999 and 2008." *British Journal of Industrial Relations*, 51(2): 333–54.

Waddington, J., and K. Whitson. 1997. "Why Do People Join Unions in a Period of Membership Decline?" *British Journal of Industrial Relations*, 35(4): 515–46.

Wilkinson A., T. Dundon, and M. Marchington. 2013. "Employee Involvement and Voice." In S. Bach and M. Edwards (eds.), *Managing Human Resources*, 5th ed., pp. 268–288. Oxford: Blackwell.

7 Partnership at Eurotunnel
Challenges for NER and Union Representation

Paul J. Gollan and Senia Kalfa

INTRODUCTION

This chapter presents the case of Eurotunnel, a private binational company that operates the Channel Tunnel that connects Britain and France. The chapter will present quantitative and qualitative research evidence that explores voice mechanisms in Eurotunnel and employees' satisfaction with those. It also details the partnership arrangement that Eurotunnel management entered with the Transport & General Workers Union (T&GWU) in 2000. Through our case study, we wish to demonstrate the following two points. First, ill-thought-out and poorly implemented non-union employee representation (NER) arrangements can lead to dissatisfaction and eventually to union representation. Second, partnership arrangements in dual-representation arrangements are rife with conflict and power plays. Through this case study, we are able to contribute significantly to the existing but limited literature that examines NER arrangements within the contexts of a partnership agreement.

The chapter is structured as follows. We begin with a presentation of company information and the methodology followed over the course of this research. We continue with a brief literature review on the topic of partnership. This is followed by the empirical data, presented in chronological order: we begin with the first wave of the research that was conducted in 1999, the second wave in 2002, and the third wave in 2010 through 2011. A discussion of the empirical findings follows.

METHODOLOGY AND COMPANY BACKGROUND

Eurotunnel manages the infrastructure of the Channel Tunnel and runs accompanied truck shuttle and passenger (car and coach) services between Folkestone in the UK and Coquelles in France. The company started operations through the tunnel on 6 May 1994. It is a market leader for cross-channel transporting, handling nearly 50 per cent of passenger traffic. Eurotunnel also earns toll revenue from other train operators: Eurostar for rail passengers and English, Welsh and Scottish Railway (EWS) and the Societé Nationale des Chemins de Fer Français (SNCF) for all rail freight which use the Tunnel—and for coaxial and digital cable links through the tunnel. It operates 24 hours a day, 365 days a year. Since its opening, more than 325 million people have travelled through the tunnel, a figure which includes cars, shuttles, and trucks as well as Eurostar passengers. In addition, more than 300 million tonnes of goods have also been transported, with 88 per cent carried on trucks loaded onto Eurotunnel Truck Shuttles and 12 per cent on goods trains of the rail freight operators (Eurotunnel Group 2012).

Eurotunnel has the lease to operate the Channel Tunnel link between Britain and France until 2086. The company has a complex structure consisting of two legal entities to meet requirements in the UK and France. The UK Head Office is in Folkestone (Longport), with a separate office nearby for some administration activities and the call centre. Between 1993 and 2005, Eurotunnel employed approximately 1,400 staff in Britain. However, in 2005, Eurotunnel management announced a round of voluntary redundancies which left the workforce at approximately 850 staff.

Our research was conducted solely on the British operations of Eurotunnel over a period of approximately thirteen years (1998–2011). The overall purpose of the research was to examine the impact of legislative changes in the UK regarding increasing union representation rights and the introduction of the European Information and Consultation Directive and ICE regulations.

For the purposes of this research, employee surveys, focus groups, and interviews were conducted, in addition to an examination of company documents. A fundamental feature of the research design was to use a strategy that allows the flexibility of rich, deep, and complex factors to emerge from what are essentially dynamic processes (Dundon and Rollinson 2004). The emphasis on rich and detailed information in the case study approach by utilising both quantitative and qualitative approaches can be useful in explaining social processes and outcomes. While the interviews provide in-depth understanding of a particular given situation and focus groups can represent a collective response to questions that permit testimonies and narratives (Gephart 2004: 458), the use of a questionnaire can "bridge the gaps" of qualitative data and help facilitate the management of a mass of information and allow direct comparison between nodes of data or variables (Yin 1993; Dundon and Rollinson 2004). However, there are certain limitations to the case study approach; because it focuses on events within a particular context, it can be difficult to generalize from the results. Scott (1994: 30) argues that the case study should be seen as something different from general social surveys:

> Case studies are not about indicating how common a particular phenomenon is, but rather about helping to understand situations . . .

this means using the evidence of behaviour in particular enterprises to shed light upon issues which are common to a wide range of business organisations.

It can also be argued that a combination of methods provides the best means to understand the "delicate and intricate interactions and processes occurring within organizations" (Hartley 1994: 209) as a means to triangulate and thereby improve validity in analysing the results. While the interviews and observation provided explanations for why certain policies and procedures had to be adopted, the questionnaire provided factual information on employee perceptions and attitudes, for example.

The rationale for using Eurotunnel as a case study was the potential impact of the culturally and functionally diverse nature of its workforce representation arrangements in a single establishment. The case study also highlights the complexity of operating a uniform consultation structure across a highly diverse workforce. In addition, Eurotunnel's unique ownership and structure with a formal and established set of consultation procedures arguably makes this a critical case study.

LITERATURE REVIEW

In this section, we will briefly review some research on the notion of partnership. We limit our literature review in this manner for two reasons: first, the literature on NER has been extensively portrayed elsewhere in this book. Second, as Eurotunnel did undertake a partnership model with the T&GWU, it is important to understand the underpinnings of such an approach.

Partnership in Union Settings

Before briefly presenting the basics of partnership, it is important to underline the pluralistic assumptions upon which it is based. According to Budd and Bhave (2008), the pluralist employment relationship focuses on the bargaining mechanisms employers and employees use to advance their interests (sometimes conflicting and sometimes shared) in imperfect labour markets. For Kaufman (2005), a core pluralist value is that labour is not simply a commodity and, as such, Budd (2004) points to the fact that labour is entitled to equity and voice in the workplace. Trade unions are critical in the pluralist employment relationship due to the inequitable outcomes stemming from imperfect labour markets and unequal bargaining power; thus the role of unions is to level the playing field between and protect workers by being a counterweight to corporate power (Budd and Bhave 2008).

The notion of partnership was becoming particularly popular in the UK in the late 1990s to early 2000s, partly due to the quest of Labour governments to modernise workplace relations (Danford et al. 2005). Martinez Lucio and Stuart (2002a: 252) explain that modernisation incorporated, among other things, a move away from adversarial relationships between employers and trade unions to collaborative ones "on the basis of a common interest between capital and labour in enterprise performance and competitiveness." At the time, partnership was a welcome change in British industrial relations and was even advocated by the Trades Union Congress (TUC) as a sustainable and beneficial choice given the previous Thatcherite strategy of ignoring and weakening unions. Importantly, a number of scholars agree that the idea of social partnership was so prominent at the time due to its uptake by British businesses (Ackers and Payne (1998) identified.

The definition of partnership is somewhat elusive and has been subjected to interpretation. Guest and Peccei (1998) define partnership as commitment to a set of principles that exclude recognition of autonomous worker representation. McBride and Stirling (2002) define it as a description of the collective employment relationship. According to Haynes and Allen (2001), partnership in general entails having a relationship, whether economic or social, with an enterprise, which in turn implies commitment to this enterprise and some influence on its governance. Greater worker cooperation in creating higher productivity and greater organisational flexibility are is emphasised.

Scholars have focused primarily on the outcomes of partnership. A number of benefits for employees have been noted in the partnership literature, such as improved rewards and working conditions, more positive relationships with supervisors, enhanced employee consultation and involvement, and greater job security (Haynes and Allen 2001; Findlay et al. 2002). For businesses, partnership facilitates knowledge sharing and fuels the organisational learning process that leads to the creation of new products, processes, and forms (Wilkinson 2000) in addition to enhanced productivity and profitability and lower turnover and absenteeism (Trades Union Congress 2002).

The benefits of partnership for trade unions are a matter of debate. Oxenbridge and Brown (2002) highlight research (e.g. Guest and Peccei 2001; Kelly 2001) that claims the majority of the benefits of partnership to be for management. Depending on their frame of reference, scholars have presented social partnership either as a means to sustain union influence in the workplace (e.g. Munro 2002) or "as a unitarist ploy to further compromise the independence of unions from management and quicken their decline" (Ackers and Payne 1998: 533). For example, Martinez Lucio and Stuart (2002b) have argued that the rhetoric of partnership may appear attractive but entails inherent dangers for trade unionists. Similarly, Bacon and Storey (2000) as well as Marks and colleagues (1998) have argued partnership could displace unions through the introduction of consultative committees.

Partnership in Non-Union Settings

It should have been made obvious by now that the vast majority of the debate on partnership arrangements at work is focussed on the relationship between employers and unions. According to Johnstone, Ackers, and Wilkinson (2009), most policy and organisational definitions as well as academic research suggest "representative participation as the bedrock of partnership." In fact, for the TUC, partnership entails union presence axiomatically, a position which is opposed by the Confederation of British Industry and the Chartered Institute of Personnel & Development (Badigannavar and Kelly 2005). What is largely absent from the literature is an examination of partnership forms between employers and non-union representative bodies or even dual forms (Johnstone, Ackers, and Wilkinson 2010). In fact, in a recent article, Johnstone, Ackers, and Wilkinson (2009) identified only five papers on partnerships with non-union or dual arrangements. Johnstone and colleagues (2010) argue that this is because much of British industrial relations (IR) research focuses on unionised workplaces as well as because instances of non-union partnership are almost impossible to identify.

The findings of outcomes of partnerships in non-union settings are mixed. On the one hand, Dietz, Cullen, and Coad (2005) maintain that successful non-union partnerships are feasible. According to IRS (2000, in Johnstone et al. 2010), non-union partnerships are more "deep rooted" than are union structures, whereas Knell (1999, in Johnstone et al. 2010) argues there are negligible differences. For Upchurch and colleagues (2006), a non-union partnership allows limited employee voice and reinforces managerial prerogative, a phenomenon they termed "paradox of intention." Badigannavar and Kelly (2005) maintain that an argument for non-union representation and partnership could be that intense competition builds interdependency between employers and employees and bridges any issues that might divide them. In a similar vein, a firm which faces limited or no competition might be able to afford higher pay and good working conditions that unite employer and employee interests. However, through a case study of the non-union retail sector, they concluded that partnership in reality is characterised by discontent and disillusionment and puts the relationship between employers and employees under strain when they disagree over major issues.

Looking at these research findings through Budd and Bhave's (2009) models of the employment relationship, it could be argued that non-union instances of partnership fit within the unitarist model. According to these authors, the unitarist employment relationship assumes that employers and employees share common interests. "This model of the employment relationship . . . focus[es] on creating policies that simultaneously benefit employees and employers" (Budd and Bhave 2009: 57). Therefore, given the assumption of interdependency of employers' and employees' interests that underpins non-union partnerships, it would be reasonable to argue that this version of partnership is almost diametrically opposed to more traditional union–employer partnerships. This case allows us to explore the impact these fundamentally different conceptual bases have on the success of partnership.

For Johnstone, Ackers, and Wilkinson (2009), existing research on partnership faces the following challenges. First, there is a lack of evidence regarding workers' experiences of partnership. Second, taking into consideration the context of the partnership agreement as well as the relationships surrounding the negotiations is crucial for a solid evaluation of partnership (267). Finally, there is a need to understand more about partnership as a process before judging its outcomes. The Eurotunnel case presents a unique opportunity to fill these gaps in the existing literature.

REPRESENTATION AT EUROTUNNEL (UK)
1992 TO 1999: NER BEGINNINGS

As part of an early policy decision to integrate and harmonize the UK workforce, the Eurotunnel (UK) Company Council (CC) was established in December 1992 as the sole channel of employee representation. The CC was broadly similar to the enterprise committee (or *comité d'entreprise*) under French legislation. Importantly, the CC was the company's communications forum and had three main aims: to give information and consult on matters of common concern to employees; to manage the social and welfare budget equal to 1 per cent of payroll (approximately £250,000–350,000 per year);[1] and to represent all employees at Eurotunnel, including informal bargaining and negotiation over pay and conditions.

The CC consisted of eight employees who were democratically elected through a secret ballot every two years from all eight constituencies: technical engineering, shuttle services, tourist division, train crew, freight division, corporate (administration), technical railway, and the call centre. Each department also elected a deputy, who would stand in for the CC rep when s/he was unavailable. All representatives were permanent employees with at least one year's service and on permanent rather than temporary contracts. They could, however, be full-time or part-time employees (Gollan 2002). Rules allowed twenty hours a month to be spent on council business by representatives and deputies, although this was not strictly enforced. Minutes were published through noticeboards, newsletters, and the company's intranet. In 1995, the CC was granted membership in the Industrial Society (now known as the Work Foundation[2]) and was the first works council to ever gain such recognition. It was stated in the council's 1995 information leaflet: "What this means is our representatives can go on courses and get access to the most up-to-date advice about working practices, dismissal procedures, contracts of employment, maternity, paternity, health and safety" (Gollan 2002: 52).

As stated in its constitution, the CC consulted on all matters and issues of concern to employees, such as operational changes, shift rosters, workplace change, investment strategy, terms of employment, and financial and performance data. However, personal issues and grievances were excluded from the discussion unless they raised issues that had wider implications for the entire workforce. Meetings were held approximately once a month and were attended by all representatives and their deputies, the senior executive or chief operating officer who chaired the meeting, and the human resources director. Any other senior managers could be invited to participate when the need arose: for example, Occupational Health and Safety (OHS) matters required the OHS Officer/Manager. Sub-committees dealt with the spending of the sports and social budget (Gollan 2002).

1999 Employee Survey Results

An employee survey was undertaken in December 1999 to January 2000 with the objective of revealing employee attitudes towards the CC and their views on the role a trade union might play at Eurotunnel. The survey involved a self-completion questionnaire consisting of twenty-seven questions and was distributed by the CC reps to employees of all sections. The findings are based on 123 responses, from 400 questionnaires (approximately 32 per cent response rate). In addition, focus groups were held to highlight and discuss themes raised in the completed questionnaires. Each interview lasted approximately thirty to ninety minutes. In addition, interviews over the period were conducted with the senior managers and the human resources director of Eurotunnel. The following themes were unearthed.

Council Effectiveness

When asked how often they talked to their representative, only 5 per cent of respondents stated "very often," with 20 per cent stating "fairly often." Importantly, 75 per cent indicated that they spoke to their section's rep rarely or not at all. More worryingly, 3.5 per cent did not even know their representative. Furthermore, 55 per cent indicated that council representatives were helpful in keeping them up to date with developments at Eurotunnel. However, 45 per cent felt that the reps were not helpful at all. Thirty-six per cent of respondents thought the council was effective in representing general employee interests. One respondent suggested, "The company council are good in relation to the social side of things but lack the muscle or determination on the most vital issues. That way union representation may improve things with management thinking first before they act."

Interestingly enough, the chief employee representative at the time seemed to share this opinion: "Generally, I would say the company council is not so effective really. Many employees are waiting until the union comes in to solve their problems."

Attitudes to Management

As an indicator of trust in management, employees were asked to what extent they believed the information they were given. Some 44 per cent reported they did not believe management at all or only a little. The lack of trust was also highlighted by an earlier survey Eurotunnel management had conducted in 1998, in which 52 per cent of the respondents argued management was more inclined to talk not listen, 51 per cent suggested general communication was bad, and 58 per cent stated that they received information in the last minute.

As Table 7.1 indicates, disillusionment with management was rife. Employees were also asked how much influence they had over management, with 78 per cent stating they had none or little. This frustration was reflected in the following statement:

> Our department is undermanned. As a result it is impossible to create a rota that covers the operational requirements of the company and gives us a humane shift pattern. Techs are always required to be ultra-flexible within the shift pattern while managers neglect to fill vacancies. We get a new group leader every year and morale is low. Management do consult us on various issues but their hands are tied and nothing ever changes. The only way to get change, is to force change. WITH UNIONS!

Representation

A survey conducted at the time by Eurotunnel had suggested that up to half the employees would be willing to join a union should management recognise one.

Table 7.2 shows respondents' answers with regards to who they would prefer to represent them in different issues. The table shows that overwhelmingly, employees preferred union representation for grievance issues, work conditions, and pay and benefits, with the picture being less clear on OHS, job security, and training.

However, as Table 7.3 shows, employees still saw the council as having a role in Eurotunnel even if trade unions were recognised. As one employee

Table 7.1 Satisfaction with Management Information

	Very Satisfied	Satisfied	Not so Satisfied	Not Satisfied at All
Amount of information	4.2	22.5	56.7	16.7
Type of information	4.2	27.5	55	13.3
Timing of information	2.5	10.8	62.5	24.2

Table 7.2   Do you believe unions would improve your position over . . .

	Yes	No
Individual grievances	74.1	25.9
Work conditions	73.3	26.7
Pay and benefits	72.2	27.8
Health and safety	58.6	41.4
Job security	50.9	49.1
Training	44	56

Table 7.3   If trade unions were recognised in Eurotunnel, what role should the Company Council have?

	No Role	Information Role	Consultation Role	Don't Know
Pay and benefits	17.7	22.1	54.0	6.2
Introduction to new technology	12.4	32.7	46.0	8.8
Changes to working practices	15.0	24.8	54.9	5.3
Staffing issues, including recruitment and redundancies	17.7	26.5	50.4	5.3
Employee grievances	21.4	20.5	52.7	5.4

summarised, "I feel the company council could co-exist with the union presence but at present they lack the experience and knowledge for representation in all areas."

UNION RECOGNITION AND REPRESENTATION AT EUROTUNNEL (UK): 2000 TO 2004

In 1999, the CC and the Industrial Society conducted a survey of Eurotunnel employees as a means to gauge employee views towards union recognition. The survey found that an overwhelming majority of the employees were in favour of trade union recognition. Additionally, the results indicated that employees did not believe that the CC as it was constituted was an effective body in representing employees over pay and conditions of employment.

Another important influence was the union recognition requirements under the provisions of the Employment Relations Act 1999. It was felt by management that the legislation could be a catalyst for a number of diverse and complex union-based arrangements within Eurotunnel (Gollan 2006). In March 2002, a general framework for informing and consulting employees in the European community was formally adopted and came into force. This directive applied to undertakings or businesses in Member States with at least fifty employees (or establishments with twenty employees or more) and required them to inform and consult their employees in good time about issues directly affecting work organization, job security, and employment contracts regarding terms and conditions. More specifically, the directive put employers under a legal obligation to inform their staff on an ongoing basis about matters such as firm performance and strategic planning.

At the time, commentators had suggested that this proposal implied the establishment of national-level works councils in the UK or, at least in non-union establishments, some form of NER (Gospel and Willman 2002, 2003), although the directive offered a substantial degree of flexibility in relation to the shape of information and consultation arrangements. For the UK, the directive required organizations to have much more extensive employee consultation processes than were in place. The European Commission (1998) stated that the aim of the directive was not only to keep employees informed of management decisions but also, more broadly, to provide, as a social objective, enhanced employee rights and increased employee involvement over a range of enterprise issues.

The Commission had suggested that this proposal complemented existing national and EU provisions and legislation and sought to "fill the gaps and inadequacies that have been identified in the long process of consultation." In other words, the proposal was seen by the Commission as building upon the "piecemeal" nature of existing community law, enhancing the impact of the existing directives on collective redundancies and safeguarding employees' rights in the event of transfers of undertakings. It was argued that creating a general framework for employee information and consultation at the EU level would make these legislative provisions more effective, comprehensive, and workable. The Commission also highlighted that "consultation between employer and employee [should be] based on a dialogue and exchange of views," including decisions likely to lead to substantial changes concerning work organization and contractual relations and an "attempt to seek prior agreement on the decision concerned" (European Commission 1998).

Within this legislative context, a partnership agreement was finalized in June 2000 between Eurotunnel management and the Transport & General

Workers Union (T&GWU), which gave the union negotiation rights for the entire Eurotunnel workforce regardless of their membership status,[3] confirmed the acceptance of the existing consultation framework, and established a joint management–trade union forum. It was suggested by Eurotunnel management that the company was in favour of the partnership agreement as a means to assist the organizational change process. In addition, any conflict could be resolved through a formalized conflict-resolution procedure.

At the time that Eurotunnel management signed the agreement with the T&GWU, the then director of HR indicated that the impetus for recognition was the industrial action undertaken by train drivers, who were members of a rival trade union, Aslef, which had created organisational upheaval and crisis (Gollan 2003). Aslef had been lobbying Eurotunnel for many years to gain recognition. From August 1997, Aslef worked in tandem with the T&GWU in order to bring about joint recognition; however, Eurotunnel management decided to recognise only one of them, and these two parties signed the agreement discussed earlier. As a result, Aslef initiated a ballot among its members which approved a series of discontinuous twenty-four–hour strikes. The first of these strikes took place on 20 November 2000 and it was considered important due to the company's £6.5 billion debt and the perishable nature of service delivery, with industrial action costing potentially millions of pounds a day in lost revenue (Gollan 2007).

The agreement created two representation structures:

- A modified **Company Council** with eight representatives which represented all employees at Eurotunnel and which met six times a year as opposed to twelve. After union recognition, deputies were not expected to attend CC meetings, although they would stand in for the rep if she or he was unavailable. The role of the CC also remained largely the same, with the exception of negotiation over pay and conditions, which was now a union issue. While CC members could be independent members of the union, they could not be acting as a union representative "carrying out union services" (HR Director). The HR Director was actually concerned with the union trying to populate the CC with its members.
- A joint **trade union forum** represented union members at Eurotunnel, covering all issues of concern, including negotiations over companywide pay levels. Eurotunnel has eight union reps, elected in their sections every two years, who meet bimonthly and are allocated twenty hours a month for union activities, with the amount of time doubling for the two senior reps.

The importance of the partnership agreement and working with the CC was voiced by one T&GWU official, who stated:

We are a pragmatic union and we would complement it. We would not want to bypass or undermine it. We, as a union, could enhance the role of the company council. The recognition agreement is a new, significant development for Eurotunnel and the T&G. We see this agreement as a model agreement, looking at it as a basis of a very good example of best practice.

At the time of union recognition, the HR Director hoped that within six to twelve months, Eurotunnel might be able to move toward a single, unified negotiation body with a partial merger of the CC and the T&GWU. In our last discussion in November 2011, this objective had not yet been achieved.

2002 Employee Survey Results

In December 2002, an employee survey was undertaken eighteen months after union recognition. The objective of the survey was to ascertain how Eurotunnel employees' views and opinions toward management and representation since union recognition and to examine the likely success of the new dual union and NER arrangements. It was distributed to all UK employees (1,367 employees) and was attached to employees' pay slips by the CC. Some 552 completed questionnaires were returned, representing around 40 per cent response rate of the total UK workforce. The survey covered all eight constituencies at Eurotunnel and was broadly representative of all employees at Eurotunnel. The survey consisted of a self-completion questionnaire of thirty-one questions. In addition, at the end of the questionnaire, employees were invited to make open comments about their work environment in relation to several issues, such as management, employee consultation, and representation. This yielded some 253 open comments, providing additional depth to employee responses (Gollan 2006).

The themes raised in the questionnaire included work involvement, personal involvement in the consultation process, information received from management, the extent of voice and influence, union relations, CC effectiveness, and management relations. In addition,[4] focus groups were held with CC and union reps and interviews were conducted with senior management to highlight and discuss themes raised in the completed questionnaires. The intention of this research strategy was to assess the feedback on and satisfaction with the effectiveness of consultation structures in representing and communicating the interests of employees to management and the degree of satisfactory outcomes that were achieved. This formed a basis for ascertaining the structure's contribution to general organizational productivity and effectiveness and to management and employee relations.

Table 7.4   Information from Management

		How satisfied are you with the information management gives you?			
		Very Satisfied	Satisfied	Not So Satisfied	Not Satisfied at All
Amount of information	Union respondent	1.1	39.4	41.1	18.3
	Non-union respondent	3.5	49.1	38	9.4
Type of information	Union respondent	1.1	39.4	43.4	16
	Non-union respondent	2.4	45.8	42.9	8.9
Timing of information	Non-union respondent	0.6	20	52.6	26.9
	Non-union respondent	1.9	35.3	47.7	15.1

Information and Consultation

Similarly to the findings of the 1999 survey, the vast majority of respondents were dissatisfied with the level information they had. Table 7.4 shows the level of satisfaction with information dissemination—further, the findings are separated between union and non-union respondents.

Table 7.4 shows that neither CC representatives nor union representatives had been effective at communicating with the workforce over workplace issues. Further, the lack of trust had not been repaired since 1999. In the question: "To what extent do you believe the information you are given by management?" 46 per cent of union respondents and 30 per cent of non-union respondents suggested they did not believe the information from management.

Representation

In 1999, the survey results had shown that the majority of employees were in favour of union representation. In 2002, trade union effectiveness was questionable, with half of union respondents arguing the union was effective in representing employee interests and the other half claiming the opposite. Trade unions had less support from non-union members, with only 23 per cent of respondents suggesting that they had been effective.

The perceived ineffectiveness of the union among non-union respondents was summed up in the following quote:

Table 7.5 Improvement since Trade Union Recognition

| | Since trade union recognition, do you believe the trade unions have improved your position over the following issues? | | | |
| | Yes | | No | |
	Union Respondent	Non-Union Respondent	Union Respondent	Non-Union Respondent
Pay and benefits	21.6	6.1	78.4	93.3
Work conditions	22.6	5.8	77.4	94.2
Health and safety	27.5	7.3	72.5	92.7
Training	8.4	7.7	91	97.3
Employee grievances	33.7	7.3	66.3	92.7
Job security	22.2	4.3	77.8	95.7

The trade unions are ineffective because they are inexperienced, unused to [the] legal side of work practices and gullible. The human resources director can run rings around them. The management will always protect themselves and despite procedures put in place, i.e., suggestion scheme, etc., they appear to protect their own corners and pay lip service to the employees.

Interestingly, around 60 per cent of non-union respondents in the survey suggested that the CC should retain a consultation role over pay and benefits, changes to working practices, staffing issues, and employee grievances. This contrasts with 30 to 40 per cent of union respondents who suggested the CC should maintain a consultation role even with union recognition. Few non-union respondents believed that the CC should have no role (less than 10 per cent), although this was higher among union respondents, with around one in four stating the CC should have no role. One non-union respondent suggested, "The idea of the CC is a good one. They want the same benefits as anyone else, but they don't have the power to achieve a great deal. They need to evolve with the company and be given more power on certain issues. Management need[s] to accept them and inform them more than they do now. Work with them not against them."

Management and Employee Relations
It could be argued that perceptions of management behaviour may have implications for the effectiveness of NER voice arrangements and can act as catalysts for increased union presence and activity. Thus, it is important

Table 7.6   Representing General Employee Interests

| | How effective do you believe the CC and the trade union have been in representing employee interests? | | | |
| | Company Council | | Trade Union | |
	Union Respondent	Non-Union Respondent	Union Respondent	Non-Union Respondent
Very effective	1.1	5.5	9.9	1.5
Effective	13.7	36.5	41.3	21
Not so effective	48.6	37.9	40.7	44.6
Not effective at all	36.6	20.1	8.1	32.9

to gauge employees' perceptions of management relations and the level of influence in the decision-making process.

In response to the question "In general, how would you describe relations between managers and employees at Eurotunnel?" only some 23 per cent of union respondents indicated "very good" or "good" compared to the more favourable response from non-union respondents (38 per cent). The overwhelming majority indicated that management and employee relations were not good.

A comment from one respondent reflected these findings:

> Disciplinary procedures are meted out all too readily at Eurotunnel . . . with the result that employees have little respect for middle management. Those in positions of higher management frequently abuse their privileges, so that morale is generally lacking in the workplace.

In relation to the opportunity to influence management decision making, nearly all union respondents indicated they did not have the opportunity. Interestingly, a sizable proportion of non-union respondents thought they could influence decision making, with 35 per cent and 20 per cent, respectively, suggesting they could influence changes to working practices and the introduction of new technology.

Survey respondents were given the opportunity to provide open-ended comments at the end of the questionnaire. Respondents voiced strong opinions on Eurotunnel management and what needed to be done for improvement. The results confirmed that respondents held largely negative views about management, highlighted the lack of communication and consultation from management, and suggested that this resulted in low morale and a lack of trust in Eurotunnel management. These comments from respondents would seem to support the survey findings more generally.

Table 7.7 Comments in Order of Frequency

In order of importance	Comments	Number of responses
1	Low morale due to bad management	65
2	Lack of communication with management	44
3	CC ineffective	42
4	Pay/pensions and promotion	28
5	Negative attitudes toward trade unions	26
6	Positive attitudes toward trade unions	12
7	Define roles for trade union and CC	11
8	Positive attitudes toward the CC	8
9	Shift issues	7
10	Miscellaneous	6
= 11	Positive attitudes toward Eurotunnel	5
= 11	French/English issues	5
12	Planning and facilities	4
= 13	Health and safety	2
= 13	Subcontractors	2

DEVELOPMENTS AT EUROTUNNEL BETWEEN 2005 AND 2011

Between 2009 and 2011, we conducted periodic interviews with management and trade union and company council representatives so as to continue exploring the employment relationship as it unfolded at Eurotunnel. In 2011, Eurotunnel also conducted an internal survey so as to identify employee perceptions on management style, training, and communications as well as employees' level of engagement. We were given access to these findings, and we draw upon them in our analysis.

The findings will show that the relationships among the trade union, management, and the company council had, in fact, deteriorated since 2004. Three events contributed to that effect. First, in October 2005, the company announced 850 redundancies (774 full-time-equivalent) in an effort to alleviate an increasing debt which at the time stood at £6.4 billion

(BBC News 2005). These left the UK workforce at 780 full-time-equivalent staff (Eurotunnel Group 2005). Second, in 2007, the T&GWU merged with Amicus, the second-largest trade union in Britain at the time, to form Unite the Union (henceforth Unite), which is now the largest trade union in Britain and Ireland with 1.5 million members (Unite the Union 2012). The merger led to a change in leadership, which contributed significantly to adversarial relationships among the three stakeholders. Third, in 2010, Eurotunnel management went through a disciplinary process with an employee who was eventually dismissed. As the employee was a union member, the union took an active role in his disciplinary process, and the negative relationship between *Unite* and management was exacerbated.

Our interviewees almost unanimously identified the 2009 wage negotiations as the catalyst for the power struggle among the trade union, management, and the company council. The negotiations took three months (February to May), as management and Unite could not agree on the percentage of wage increase. Whilst the union wanted a 2.5 per cent increase (CC reps, 31 July 2009), management was willing to give 1.45 per cent (Commercial Operations Manager, 31 July 2009). According to the Commercial Operations Manager, the majority of the workforce resented the union for stalling the negotiations: "The biggest source of friction we've had has been over the fact that the union has been stalling the pay negotiations when they are the minority of the staff."

In fact, the union density in Eurotunnel at the time of the 2009 interviews was a matter of debate. While union representatives we interviewed claimed the number was approximately 45 per cent of the workforce, the company council reps interviewed claimed to know "for a fact that they've got about 22 per cent of staff." The difference could be membership as opposed to bargaining rights—in a later interview, the HR Director (11 August 2010) claimed that membership was approximately 22 per cent but the union had bargaining rights for approximately 70 per cent of the employees.

These negotiations aggravated not only the relationship between management and the trade union but also the relationship between the union and the company council. The Commercial Operations Manager (31 July 2009) attributed that deterioration to the new senior union representative, also known as the convenor, who took a much more combative stance towards the company council. In fact the chief company council rep, who was invited to the pay talks, was "kicked out every time he spoke" (Commercial Operations Manager, 31 July 2009). The chief council representative recalls: "[The convenor] hated us . . . I had a blazing row with her in the pay talks because she said: you're not here to speak" (31 July 2009).

The Company Council representatives we interviewed attributed the failing relationship between them and the union to the fact that "they [the union] think we have no part to play" (Senior CC rep, 31 July 2009). In fact, they questioned the whole process of union recognition by maintaining that the council was neither involved nor consulted at the time. They also argued against the validity of the survey conducted in 1999 which sought to gauge whether staff was in favour of union recognition. Whilst acknowledging the legal framework that Eurotunnel had to comply with at the time, they were disappointed at the limited role the company council was given in the pay and conditions negotiations, which effectively saw them relying "on who the convenor is" (CC rep, 31 July 2009).[5]

On the other hand, the union representatives interviewed, who saw the role of the council as that of a social function organiser, were disgruntled with the Council's "interference" with pay negotiations. In that way, the council was seen to be invading the union's territory. In the words of the union commercial representative:

> They're constantly trying to talk about terms and conditions. If we could have a clear segmentation: "that is our part and it is not discussed in any of your meetings"; then we could work better together. You know it is them fulfilling their role which is not the same as ours and us doing our job so to speak. Like I said they want the more power, they want to do what we do as well but they haven't got those things to debate about.

The union reps further attributed the troubles they faced in their relationship with the council to the HR Director who, in their mind, consciously tried to create rivalry between them and the CC in order to "divide and rule." In our August 2010 interview with the HR Director, he mentioned he was aware that the union perceived him as the "puppeteer" and the council reps as the "puppets." As expected, he dismissed any claims to that effect. However, he acknowledged that recognising the T&GWU was a "knee-jerk reaction to the employment regulation that was coming." As such, he instead attributed the poor relationship between the two representative bodies to the fact that "their existence together in this organisation has always been inconclusive. It's always been a very fragile relationship, a fragile truce dare I call it." He recalled an incident in which the Eurotunnel lawyer asked him to:

> complete the statement: Eurotunnel has industrial relations problems because . . . I went silent . . . but the answer I gave to that was because the relationships between all of the parties are immature . . . under developed, in a sense. The structures we put in place were ill thought through originally because we replicated what was happening in France . . . but what we didn't think about is how are you going to deal with it if it's a minority union or they're representing a handful of people? I think what we've got here is immaturity . . . the structures are immature . . . the groups are immature.

The pay negotiations continued to trouble Eurotunnel in 2010 and, as a result, the relationships among the competing stakeholders were "at an all-time low" (HR Director). The HR Director, at the time of the interview three months into the negotiation process, explained that management was "pushing for a multi-year deal this year," which the union did not accept. Initially, to support their position, the union conducted a consultative ballot, which "in the UK, is kind of testing the water [before conducting a] full blown ballot." He pointed to the "inflammatory" language used by the union, likening it to "propaganda," which he believed was a regional mandate not limited to Eurotunnel: "Regional officials are probably picking up that they've got to show resolve and a backbone."

Interestingly enough, in our August interview, the HR Director portrayed their efforts to negotiate with the union as an attempt to help them:

> If we proceed on continuing a dialogue or a process with you guys without implementing this pay deal, actually your credibility in this organisation is going to get shot to pieces. It's all very bad anyway. People are frothing at the mouth with regard to this.
>
> (11 August 2010)

After stalling developments for a while, the union proceeded in conducting an official ballot. In that process, the union density at Eurotunnel became public knowledge: Unite had 243 members or 25 per cent of the workforce. Of those, 140 voted in the ballot regarding the pay deal, with the results being as follows:

- 140 voted against the pay deal
- 55 voted for and 85 against strike action
- 83 voted for and 57 against action short of a strike (HR Director interview, 19 November 2010).

As a result, the pay deal was rejected by the union, but management proceeded with it anyway. According to the HR Director, the 83 individuals who wanted to take some form of industrial action "represent 34 per cent of union membership and only 10 per cent of the entire workforce" (HR Director interview, 19 November 2010). As such, the HR Director argued that management decided to proceed with the pay package, an action he claimed was received with thanks from the majority of the workforce, who "understand that people are losing jobs out there. I'm not going to argue about having a pay rise when I could very well find myself in the same kind of situation."

The industrial action that Unite members decided upon was

> an overtime ban within an organisation that does not really do a lot of overtime, so that was about as threatening as a toothless tiger in a

chimp cage, a ban on call out and strict work to rule. I mean we went through a week of purported action in October and we kind of came through that thinking well nothing really happened.

(HR Director interview, 19 November 2010)

The power struggle between the company council and the union continued well into 2010, with the HR Director recalling an incident in which the "national-level representative . . . said look, what is this company council? You've got to recognise that we're the representative body here, you deal with us, you give us the credibility, you don't deal with a sort of third-rate . . . organisation that's sponsored by the company." The fractious relationship between the union and the company council was detrimental to the majority of the workforce according to the HR Director, who became "the silent majority."

In the meantime and as briefly mentioned earlier, the company decided to take disciplinary action and, in the end, terminate an individual's employment at Eurotunnel. As this person was a union member, Unite took an active role in the proceedings, with events escalating after the person being fired. The cumulative effect of all these incidents is that "there is damage in relationships and how you start to construct the future—things like trust and all that kind of good stuff are very much out of the window" (HR Director interview, 19 November 2010).

In May through June 2011, Eurotunnel hired a private consultancy that specialised in employee relations to conduct a survey and identify employee perceptions on management style, training, and communications as well as employees' level of engagement. The survey was distributed to all 800 employees and had a 60 per cent response rate (479 completed returned questionnaires). Table 7.8 shows the levels of employee satisfaction reported, with the last row capturing what the consultancy firm claims to be the level of Eurotunnel employees who are truly engaged.

Table 7.8   Levels of Employee Satisfaction

Percentage employees who are . . .	
Satisfied with job . . .	72%
. . . and motivated	42%
. . . and satisfied with Eurotunnel as an employer	42%
. . . and loyal to Eurotunnel	40%
. . . and would recommend Eurotunnel as an employer	39%
. . . and proud they work for Eurotunnel	38%

Survey conducted by Harris Interactive—reproduced with the permission of Eurotunnel management.

Table 7.9 shows the outcomes of the survey; the areas with the lowest percentage were identified as the areas for action and were clustered in the following three categories: communication, change management, and career development. Table 7.10 summarises the open comments in the survey.

We interviewed the HR Director approximately one week after the company had received these results. For him, this survey highlighted that "the

Table 7.9   2011 Eurotunnel Survey Outcomes

Order of Importance	Drivers of Motivation/ De-Motivation	Net Agree 2011
1	My work gives me a feeling of personal accomplishment.	56%
2	I am treated with respect at work.	56%
3	I speak favourably about Eurotunnel to people outside work.	73%
4	I am satisfied with the career development opportunities open to me at Eurotunnel.	27%
5	Manager treats people equally.	62%
6	I am well trained in customer service skills.	51%
7	There is a good system for identifying and dealing with health and safety issues.	62%
8	Manager does a good job managing poor performers in my team.	39%
9	Change is communicated well at work.	30%
10	Eurotunnel takes notice of what employees have to say.	20%
11	Customers are treated well when things go wrong.	35%

Survey conducted by Harris Interactive—reproduced with the permission of Eurotunnel management.

Table 7.10　Open-ended Comments—Eurotunnel Survey 2011

Topic	Representative Quote
Unions	I resent the unions, which only represent a small fraction of the workforce, having a disproportionate input into pay negotiations.
Listen	I wish that higher-level management would listen to the people on the ground and do the job week in week out.
Career and Anglo-Franco relations	No opportunity for advancement, no change in job content, therefore same job, same salary until retirement, no motivation. Generally, French staff are promoted instead of UK staff. Car allowances have not increased for 10 years. French management style is incompatible with UK staff. If I could afford it, I would willingly retire early.
Agency staff	I have concerns about the number of agency staff working at Eurotunnel. They have no allegiance to Eurotunnel and are not treated the same as Eurotunnel staff, which has an impact on morale for all.
Uniform	The new uniform is embarrassing to wear and the worst one we have ever had.
Succession planning	Company rather stagnant—no new blood or fresh ideas for many years due to block on external recruitment. Workforce aging together, experience levels in next 10 years a worry.
Too many managers	In recent years has been an increase in middle management with less focus on ground staff. A lot of middle management finding difficult to find tasks too do and a lot of doubling up.

Survey conducted by Harris Interactive—reproduced with the permission of Eurotunnel management.

relevance of unions is being brought into question . . . since things such as poor pay, or poor OHS are not problems at Eurotunnel." While at the time the management team was still considering potential courses of action, they were planning on addressing staff comments about not being listened to and their "personal development and growth being ignored" as well as communicating change better. However, they had not yet come up with plans to that end.

DISCUSSION

The research undertaken at Eurotunnel provides an opportunity to explore the effectiveness of union and non-union arrangements as well as to assess employees' attitudes toward the CC and the trade union. Regarding the effectiveness of NER arrangements and union representation, the views of survey respondents and interviewees would suggest that the CC had been essentially ineffective as a representative body due to the very limited role played in the decision-making processes. It would appear that the CC's primary role was based on a management agenda to provide information on performance or "business" issues (improving quality, productivity, customer service, and/or sales), to communicate the benefits of change, and to persuade employees of the need for such change rather than to address employees' concerns and meet their expectations. Given that until union recognition, the CC was the sole body representing employee interests at Eurotunnel, this finding is important because it explains the prevailing lack of trust between management and employees. Not only did CC representatives not have enough power to be a truly successful representative body, but also management did not actively acknowledge that employee concerns can be different from those of management. In doing so, management helped weaken the CC, which led to increasing levels of frustration and created an environment for greater trade union activity.

Interestingly, the research findings also seem to indicate that while the majority of employees were in favour of union recognition at Eurotunnel, they were not yet convinced that union representation by the T&GWU would achieve greater benefits for employees. Moreover, many non-union employees at Eurotunnel remained convinced that the CC should continue to represent the workforce, with its role ranging from serving as an information channel on some issues to a genuine negotiation body with greater power than existing arrangements on others.

The experience of Eurotunnel would also suggest that some employees were reluctant to abandon NER arrangements altogether, providing management with more diverse and complex representation arrangements. This could be seen as a failure of management and the T&GWU/Unite to convince employees of the merits of a single channel of trade union representation. For management, this dual-representation arrangement could raise concerns regarding employees' acceptance of management decisions and undermine the effectiveness of organizational change initiatives due to the increased complexity of dealing with a number of representation arrangements, contributing to greater decision-making complexity and longer time frames for conflict resolution.

One of the reasons for management to establish NER arrangements at Eurotunnel was a desire to have a more direct relationship with employees without the mediating forces of a "third party" through union representation. In this endeavour, Eurotunnel's union substitution approach failed to stop the forces for unionization, the catalyst for which was the Aslef presence in the train crew section of the workforce. Consequently, the maintenance of NER arrangements was very much dependent on the threat of unionization. However, the findings at Eurotunnel would also seem to suggest that an important underlying driver in the unionization process was management's ambivalent behaviour toward employees' views and concerns rather than any potential financial advantage for employees gained by unionization. Importantly, dissatisfaction over certain issues considered by employees as important and the lack of trust between management and employees appear to have been an even more critical impetus to the unionization process. Significantly, although their expectations were high prior to union recognition, many non-union employees were not totally convinced that unions alone would solve these issues. Only when management was perceived as unresponsive did the union become more of a catalyst for collective action.

The terrain of partnership politics presents us with a complex set of challenges. In our view, the future of the Eurotunnel partnership was doomed from the start. First, the roles of the two representative bodies were never clearly defined, which led to them arguing over which one is the more legitimate body to represent the interests of Eurotunnel employees. Second and more importantly, the success of partnership arrangements is predicated on trust between stakeholders; however, our findings demonstrated that employees distrusted management and the information they disseminated, that management distrusted the unions, and the unions and the CC distrusted each other.

To an extent, this conflict between the two representative bodies was beneficial for Eurotunnel management and the pursuit of their interests. While employees were given inefficient voice mechanisms, Eurotunnel management pushed for its own agenda, as demonstrated by the wage negotiations. Our case study also highlights the critical role that the HR Director, the senior CC rep, and the senior union representatives have in ensuring the success of a partnership. Given the combative relationship among all three individuals, it is of no surprise that the partnership was in a stalemate.

CONCLUSION

Overall our results would suggest that employees were dissatisfied with both the NER and union arrangements at Eurotunnel. Furthermore, neither arrangement appeared to address employees' expectations in providing effective employee voice. There may be a number of reasons for and potential implications from this important finding. One possible explanation could be that the external environment (Eurotunnel's financial situation, cost cutting, competition, etc.) had restricted the management's ability to address the concerns of employees no matter how capable, motivated, or willing the management is in developing good employee relations. This could be seen as a basic pluralist industrial relations critique of human relations that voice lacks effectiveness if the external environment is negative. The second explanation is that management lacked the capability and experience to address and deal with the complexity of employees' concerns through either the NER or union arrangements. Third, employees have high expectations that cannot be met under the prevailing financial conditions by either the CC or the trade union due to their limited influence over the organizational decision-making process. And finally, employees' perception of a lack of independent voice in the CC as well as in the union due to the union–management partnership arrangements and failure to act on employees' concerns has further undermined the legitimacy, authority, and trust in both arrangements.

An important issue to emerge from the research is that the Eurotunnel arrangements have failed in two respects: in terms of communication, both the union and CC have failed to meet employee expectations, and in terms of providing an effective voice and involvement mechanism, they have also failed to address issues of concern to employees. Perhaps an important conclusion to be drawn from the case study is that constraints such as profit pressures and the trauma of cost cutting in difficult market conditions can poison employer–employee relations and, without legal support and financial resources, pits the employee representatives and management in an adversarial struggle.

While this study is focused on a single company, it could potentially have far-reaching implications for employers, unions, and government policy regarding the structures needed for providing effective consultation and representation. Overall, the evidence in this case would suggest that there were two main drivers for the development of greater voice arrangements—regulatory change due to new trade union recognition laws and employee pressure for greater voice. In addition, three important conditions can be identified that have influenced the effectiveness of the voice arrangements at Eurotunnel—managerial attitudes, employee expectations, and wider business pressures. Significantly, this research highlights the potential limitations and dangers for employers of not addressing the needs and expectations of workers. Given the devolution of decision making in many organizations and the greater focus on employee commitment and effective organizational change, these findings are of particular interest. They suggest that if employers wish to encourage an alignment of interests between employee behaviour and organizational goals, they need to place greater emphasis on giving employees a greater say in the decision-making process and on addressing the expectations of employees.

NOTES

1. This fund was set up for the benefit of the employees and may be used to arrange trips away and nights out as well as welfare support for families in need. The CC members are the only trustees (Gollan 2006).
2. The Work Foundation, previously the Industrial Society, is a not-for-profit organisation that aims to be the leading provider of research-based analysis,

knowledge exchange, and policy advice in the UK and beyond. As the Industrial Society, it campaigned to improve the quality of working life, emphasising practical training interventions that organisations could adopt to do that (Work Foundation 2013).
3. This practice is accepted by the Trade Union Congress. Unlike other countries, there is no union shop clause in the UK—such a clause is, in fact, illegal.
4. Sixteen focus groups with CC and union reps and fifteen interviews with senior managers and the HR Director at Eurotunnel were conducted in total throughout the research period.
5. Interestingly enough, one of the union reps we interviewed who was a member of the council prior to union recognition recalled how he and other council members were feeling the union was "invading our patch."

REFERENCES

Ackers, Peter, and Jonathan Payne. 1998. "British Trade Unions and Social Partnership: Rhetoric, Reality and Strategy." *International Journal of Human Resource Management,* 9(3): 529–50.
Bacon, Nicholas, and J. Storey. 2000. "New Employee Relations Strategies in Britain: Towards Individualism or Partnership? *British Journal of Industrial Relations,* 38(3): 407–27.
Badigannavar, Vidu, and John Kelly. 2005. "Labour–Management Relationship in the Non-Union Retail Sector." *International Journal of Human Resource Management,* 16(8): 1529–44.
BBC News. 2005. *Eurotunnel announces 900 job cuts.* 1 November 2012, http://news.bbc.co.uk/2/hi/business/4361732.stm.
Budd, John W. 2004. *Employment with a Human Face: Balancing Efficiency, Equity and Voice.* Ithaca, NY: Cornell University Press.
Budd, John W., and Devasheesh Bhave. 2008. "Values, Ideologies and Frames of Reference in Industrial Relations." In P. Blyton, N. Bacon, J. Fiorito, and E. Heery (eds.), *The SAGE Handbook of Industrial Relations,* pp. 92–113. London: SAGE.
———. 2009. "The employment relationship." In A. Wilkinson, N. Bacon, T. Redman, and S. Snell (eds.), *The SAGE Handbook of Human Resource Management,* pp. 51–70. London: SAGE.
Danford, Andy, Michael Richardson, Paul Stewart, Stephanie Tailby, and Martin Upchurch. 2005. "Workplace Partnership and Employee Voice in the UK: Comparative Case Studies of Union Strategy and Worker Experience." *Economic and Industrial Democracy,* 26(4): 593–620.
Dietz, Graham, John Cullen, and Alan Coad. 2005. "Can There Be Non-Union Forms of Workplace Partnership?" *Employee Relations,* 27(3): 289–306.
Dundon, T., and D. Rollinson. 2004. *Employment in Non-Union Firms.* London: Routledge.
European Commission. 1998. *Commission Adopts a Proposal for a Directive on Information and Consultation of Employees.* Brussels: European Commission.
Eurotunnel Group. 2005. *Annual Report.* Paris, France.
———. 2012. *Our Performance 2012* [cited 31 October 2012]. Available from www.eurotunnelgroup.com/uk/eurotunnel-group/operations/our-performance/.
Findlay, P., A. McKinlay, A. Marks, and P. Thompson. 2002. "Mutual Gain or Mutual Strain? Exploring Employee Attitudes to Partnership." In *20th Annual Labour Process Conference.* University of Strathclyde, Glasgow.
Gephart, R. P. 2004. "Editor's Note: Qualitative Research and the *Academy of Management Journal.*" *Academy of Management Journal,* 47(4): 454–62.

Gollan, Paul. 2002. "Management Strategies and Outcomes on Non-Union Employee Representation at Eurotunnel." *New Zealand Journal of Industrial Relations*, 27(1): 49–64.

———. 2003. "All Talk but No Voice: Employee Voice at the Eurotunnel Call Centre." *Economic and Industrial Democracy*, 24(4): 509–41.

———. 2006. "Twin Tracks—Employee Representation at Eurotunnel Revisited." *Industrial Relations*, 45(4): 606–49.

———. 2007. *Employee Representation in Non-Union Firms*. London: Sage.

Gospel, H., and P. Willman. 2002. *The Right to Know: Disclosure of Information for Collective Bargaining and Joint Consultation in Germany, France and Great Britain*. Edited by London School of Economics. London: Centre for Economic Performance.

———. 2003. "The Coming of Workplace Information Sharing and Consultation: What It Means for Employee Representation in Britain." *Perspectives on Work*, 7(1): 38–9.

Guest, G., and R. Peccei. 1998. *The Partnership Company: Benchmarks for the Future. The Report of the IPA Survey Principles, Practice and Performance*. London: Involvement and Participation Association.

———. 2001. "Partnership at Work: Mutuality and the Balance of Advantage." *British Journal of Industrial Relations*, 39(2): 207–36.

Hartley, J. F. 1994. "Case Studies in Organisational Research." In C. Cassell and G. Symon (eds.), *Qualitative Methods in Organisational Research*, pp. 208–29. London: Sage.

Haynes, Peter, and Michael Allen. 2001. "Partnership as Union Strategy: A Preliminary Evaluation." *Employee Relations*, 23(2): 164–93.

Johnstone, Stewart, Peter Ackers, and Adrian Wilkinson. 2009. "The British Partnership Phenomenon: A Ten Year Review." *Human Resource Management Journal*, 19(3): 260–79.

———. 2010. "Better Than Nothing? Is Non-Union Partnership a Contradiction in Terms?" *Journal of Industrial Relations*, 52(2): 151–68.

Kaufman, Bruce. 2005. "The Social Welfare Objectives and Ethical Principles of Industrial Relations." In J. W. Budd and J. G. Scoville (eds.), *The Ethics of Human Resources and Industrial Relations*, pp. 25–59. Champaign, IL: Labor and Employment Relations Association.

Kelly, J. 2001. "Social Partnership Agreements in Britain: Union Revitalisation or Employer Counter-Mobilisation?" In M. Martinez Lucio and M. Stuart (eds.), *Assessing Partnership: The Prospects for and Challenges of "Modernisation,"* pp. 79–86. Leeds, UK: Leeds University Business School.

Marks, A., P. Findlay, J. Hine, A. McKinlay, and P. Thompson. 1998. "The Politics of Partnership? Innovation in Employment Relations in the Scottish Spirits Industry." *British Journal of Industrial Relations*, 36(2): 209–26.

Martinez Lucio, Miguel, and Mark Stuart. 2002a. "Assessing Partnership: The Prospects for and Challenges of Modernisation." *Employee Relations*, 24(3): 252–61.

———. 2002b. "Assessing the Principles of Partnership: Workplace Trade Union Representatives' Attitudes and Experiences." *Employee Relations*, 24(3): 305–20.

McBride, Jo, and John Stirling. 2002. "Partnership and Process in the Maritime Construction Industry." *Employee Relations*, 24(3): 290–304.

Munro, Anne. 2002. "'Working Together—Involving Staff': Partnership Working in the NHS." *Employee Relations*, 24(3): 277–89.

Oxenbridge, Sarah, and William Brown. 2002. "The Two Faces of Partnership? An Assessment of Partnership and Co-Operative Employer/Trade Union Relationships." *Employee Relations*, 24(3): 262–76.

Scott, R. 1994. *Willing Slaves? British Workers under Human Resource Management*. Cambridge, UK: Cambridge University Press.

Trades Union Congress. 2002. *Partnership Works: A TUC Report*. London: TUC Partnership Institute.

Unite the Union. 2012. *2012* [cited 1 November 2012]. Available at www.unitetheunion.org/default.aspx.

Upchurch, Martin, Mike Richardson, Stephanie Tailby, Andy Danford, and Paul Stewart. 2006. "Employee Representation and Partnership in the Non-Union Sector: A Paradox of Intention?" *Human Resource Management Journal*, 16(4): 393–410.

Wilkinson, F. 2000. "Cooperation, the Organization of Work and Competitiveness." In L. Clarke, D. D. Gijsel, and J. Janssen (eds.), *The Dynamics of Wage Relations in the New Europe*, pp. 279–94. Deventer: Kluwer.

Work Foundation, The. *Our history 2013* [cited 8 January]. Available at www.theworkfoundation.com/Impact/Our-History.

Yin, R. 1993. *Application of Case Study Research*. Beverly Hills, CA: Sage.

Part III

Canada

8 A Century of Employee Representation at Imperial Oil

Daphne G. Taras

INTRODUCTION

Imperial Oil has continuously operated North America's most significant and well-developed non-union representation plan. After almost 100 years of using a non-union system, the Canadian company remains firmly committed to developing non-union representation vehicles to satisfy the need for managers to interact with employees and employees' desire for voice and influence over their working lives. The choices made by Imperial allow us to examine why formal non-union practices persist over many generations despite the dramatic economic booms and busts that are endemic of the "oil patch" and even after fundamental shifts in business practices following a massive merger. How did non-union voice thinking become so entrenched within the Imperial culture?

The chapter begins with the legal context and shows that Canada's permissive legal environment allows Imperial to be one of a number of major Canadian companies that openly practice non-union representation. Because Imperial's non-union plan is so formal and derived from industrial relations precepts of representation and collective voice, it is imperative to first put to rest our readers' curiosity over how such a plan can be lawfully practiced in Canada, a country that provides significant protections to unions through a mature collective bargaining regime. The next major section provides a contemporary portrait of Imperial Oil as a business so that its significance, its stressors and challenges, and its place in a larger industry can be understood. We then go on a journey through history to chronicle the evolution of Imperial's Joint Industrial Council (JIC), borne in the aftermath of the U.S.–based Ludlow Massacre of 1914 and with a crystal-clear provenance such that 100 years later, the system would be instantly recognizable as the Rockefeller Plan, invented by William Lyon Mackenzie King and disseminated throughout North American industry.

The information presented about the company and its history and the workings of non-union systems was drawn mainly from primary sources. Over a ten-year period from 1993 to 2003 and then again for a few months in 2011 through 2012, I interviewed a total of about 130 workers, managers, and union officials across many of Imperial's sites. I had an unusual degree of access to documents, handbooks, and even Imperial Oil's archives. I am permitted to use the company name as long as I respect confidentiality of sources.

After reviewing the history, we move to a section on the challenges posed to Imperial by the ExxonMobil merger and the ushering in of a new decade of innovation of non-union systems, particularly in the new business support centers that exist as giants within the burgeoning call center industry of the Maritimes. Finally, there is a section that distills the analysis into simple lessons about why this particular company is an ardent modern practitioner of a system of representation that some readers might think of as anachronistic and the vestige of a bygone era. Yet the system managed to adapt to an entirely new industrial setting from where it had first originated. In a book that explores a variety of case studies of plans that have enjoyed longevity, the recent reinvigoration of Imperial's non-union plans both is stimulating and provides a real-time test of how non-union plans can adapt to new circumstances.

The Legal Context for Non-Union Representation

To fully appreciate this chapter, it is necessary first to set the legal context. Canadian law is silent as to the practice of non-union representation. As long as non-union plans do not thwart union organizing, companies are permitted to operate their plans without oversight or interference by collective bargaining laws, statutes, or government policies. Non-union employees who prefer to represent their own interests either as individuals or in groups can meet and deal with their employers on any topic salient to the employment relationship, including wages and working conditions. However, in sharp contrast to the unionized sector in Canada, the non-union arena is unregulated (except for basic employment standards such as hours of work, health and safety, and so on) and little understood and has tended to escape sustained scrutiny. A Canadian non-union system can closely emulate a union in all respects, but as long as it does not purport to be a union or go head to head with unions during organizing, it can freely exist (Taras 1999). Indeed, non-union systems can have handbooks or documents that are exceedingly similar to collective agreements. The legal status of such handbooks would be as individual contracts of employment applied to collectives of workers, with final recourse to a company's internal dispute-resolution vehicles and then to the courts. In the unionized sector, collective agreements are protected by labor laws and overseen by arbitrators and labor boards, with courts showing considerable deference to the expertise of labor relations professionals.

Imperial is not the only major Canadian private-sector employer to use formal non-union plans. Here are three other noteworthy examples.

(1) The second-largest airline in Canada and ninth-largest airline in North America is Westjet. For its 9,000 employees, Westjet operates an employee-management system whose most recent permutation is the Pro-Active Communications Team (PACT).

(2) Within Canada's automotive parts manufacturing industry, Magna International is the third-largest auto parts supplier in the world, with more than 80,000 employees worldwide. Magna uses an "Employee Charter" to deal with its non-union employees, who are entitled to use their Employee Advocate to solve problems. A Fairness Committee and a variety of techniques align workers with corporate goals. Until 2007, unions were viewed as "incompatible" with the complex system of rights and rewards (Lewchuk and Wells 2007: 121). To the astonishment of labor relations specialists, Magna and the Canadian Auto Workers Union in 2007 entered into an unprecedented agreement titled Framework of Fairness that basically conferred voluntary recognition to the union and integrated the CAW into the Magna human resource system, with the union giving up the right to strike and adapting itself to the Magna model (Malin 2010; see also Canadian Auto Workers 2013). Overnight, a coherent and long-standing non-union model was transformed to a type of hybrid labor relations system.

(3) In the steel industry, ArcelorMittal Dofasco uses a proactive team approach for its 5,000 employees. The culture, known as the Dofasco Way, had been used since 1912, and Dofasco was the first Canadian manufacturer to introduce profit sharing in 1938 (Harshaw 2000, Storey 1983), although companies in other industries commenced profit sharing earlier, and Imperial Oil began its own plan in 1920. The Dofasco Way continued after the 2006 purchase of Dofasco by Europe-based steelmaker Arcelor (which at the time also merged with Mittal Steel; see www.Dofasco.ca website). There are complaints that some elements of the relationship have been eroded with the pressures of global competition (Arnold 2013). In an unusual move, ArcelorMittal Dofasco invited the United Steelworkers to meet its employees in 2008, as other ArcelorMittal locations are represented by the Steelworkers (Van Alphen 2008), but the union was not able to win sufficient support to certify the workforce.

These three examples show that non-union plans can be deeply engrained in the company's ethos, as in the Dofasco Way and Magna's Charter. Moreover, it does not matter in which jurisdiction the company's head office is situated—federal in the case of Westjet or provincial, with the province of Ontario for both Dofasco and Magna and the province of Alberta for Imperial. With regard to non-union plans, the same permissive climate permits these plans to be created and continue.

There is no doubt that Imperial's non-union plans would have been labeled "company unions" and banned in the United States by the 1935

Wagner Act's Section 8a2 applied in tandem with Section 2(5). American firms such as Polaroid, with large, formal, and well-developed non-union plans similar to those practiced by Imperial, were forced to disband their plans (see LeRoy, Chapter 13, this volume; Gibb and Knowlton 1956; Koch et al. 1989). The overarching reason for the ban was contextual: in the throes of the Great Depression, large national unions were expected to help raise the economy out of its doldrums (Kaufman 1996, 2000). Almost a decade later, Canada made a deliberate departure from the American approach. When Canada finally prepared its own Wagner Act equivalent in 1944, the Depression was a thing of the past and the paramount economic concern was stoking industrial production for World War II. Harmonious labour–management dealings were encouraged, and any form of worker–management participation was endorsed. Cooperative relations were the key; adversarial relations, such as those advocated by the more radical unions, would be overtly discouraged, and such unions would not be certified as fit to bargain. (These and more reasons are enumerated in Taras 1997a: 37–40). In short, there is no serious legal impediment to the open practice of "company unions."

The Company

At one time, Imperial was the single dominant energy company, and now it is part of a cluster of large, integrated firms. Once an Ontario-based firm, Imperial is now headquartered with almost all the other oil and gas enterprises in Calgary, Alberta. Today, Imperial is Canada's second-largest integrated petroleum firm, having actually fallen slightly from decades of holding first place. It is Canada's only industrial company with a AAA rating from Standard & Poor's, and it has increased its annual dividends eighteen years in a row. Its 2012 capital and exploration expenditures total $5.7 billion, and its earnings were $3.8 billion on revenues of over $31 billion ($ Can; hovering around parity with $ US). It is 69.6 percent owned by the American firm Exxon. In 1989, Imperial purchased Texaco Canada at a cost of $5 billion.

Today Imperial is Canada's largest petroleum refiner, and it has a leading market share in coast-to-coast networks that include 1,850 service stations. It is a complex organization with a variety of activities that span the length of Canada. It has refineries in Dartmouth, Nova Scotia (200 employees), Nanticoke (260 employees), and Sarnia (1,000 employees), refineries in southwestern Ontario, and a large Strathcona (450 employees) refinery in Edmonton, Alberta.

For most of its history, Imperial operated fairly autonomously from Exxon, but the 1999 ExxonMobil merger—at that time, the largest business merger in the world—has had ripple effects into Canada and has fundamentally altered Imperial Oil's business strategy and workforce planning. The merger originated in the United States. The Exxon Mobil Corporation reunited the descendent companies of John D. Rockefeller's Standard Oil trust—Standard Oil Company of New Jersey (Exxon) and Standard Oil Company of New York (Mobil)—that had been broken in 1911 by order of the U.S. Supreme Court in a landmark decision that established the logic of antitrust interventions as public policy (U.S. Supreme Court 1911).

The merger brought together Imperial's retail brand Esso (a phonetic version of pre–1911 Standard Oil initials) with Mobil Canada and created opportunities to test Imperial's resolve to manage its workers using complex structures of non-union representation.

In Canada, about two years after the merger, a formal operations agreement was put into place. Imperial Oil became a supplier of human resource expertise based on full cost reimbursement. When Exxon and Mobil merged, the companies changed their organizational design from a geographic basis to functions. The merged company's production, distribution, marketing, and human resources offices were housed in the former Mobil location at Fairfax, Virginia. Before the merger, Imperial Oil's human resources and industrial relations operated almost entirely autonomously. After the merger, Imperial reported more closely to the ExxonMobil offices. As a Canadian manager recently told me, "today there is much more communication with Exxon than ever before. If we are bargaining with any union, we can review our discussions with a 'pair of cold eyes' [in ExxonMobil] and that is very helpful." With the merger, Imperial's human resources professionals in Canada have an industrial relations center of expertise that didn't exist before the merger, and it is headed by an executive located in Mobil's former head office in Fairfax, Virginia. It is noteworthy that ExxonMobil is amalgamating its many enterprises into one location and anticipates moving its head offices to a Houston, Texas, campus by 2015 (Bhattarai and Heath 2012). In the early 1990s, I called Exxon to ask their industrial relations department for their sentiments on Imperial Oil's continued use of a form of employee representation that could not be practiced in the United States. The American senior managers knew nothing about Imperial's industrial relations; that certainly is no longer the case today.

Figure 8.1 documents the company's net income since 1960.[1] The top line in the chart is an inflation-adjusted value, derived from taking the nominal value of the income divided by the Consumer Price Index (CPI) of the same year. The chart also shows a calculation using 1970 as the base year and takes the inflation-adjusted value adjusted for the CPI of the base year. The impact of the ExxonMobil merger on income is significant, but earnings per share in Figure 8.2 have not shown the same growth—adjusted for inflation, the earnings per share (EPS) tend to fluctuate around a rather flat trend line. Of course, the earnings do not include dividends or other adjustments to shareholder returns.

Imperial is very involved in the development of the Canadian oil sands, the world's largest *in situ* deposit of oil and a total deposit second only in size to that in Saudi Arabia. Imperial was a founder and remains a 25 percent owner of Syncrude Canada, which mines and upgrades oil sands in the Athabasca region of Alberta. Imperial's Cold Lake operation is the world's

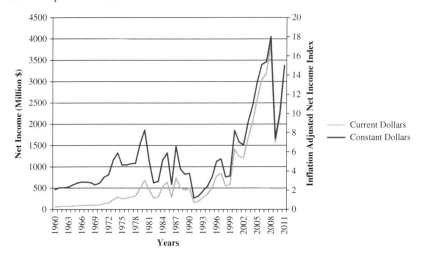

Figure 8.1   Imperial Net Income 1960–2011

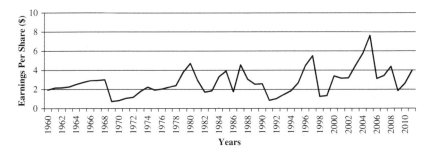

Figure 8.2   Imperial Earnings Per Share 1960–2011

largest thermal *in situ* heavy oil operation, encompassing four plants over a 780-square-kilometer area of oil sands in the mideastern area of Alberta.

Because of opportunities opened up with the growing technological mastery of the Canadian oil sands, the company is in a major expansion phase, with most costs committed to a single oil sand project at Kearl, north of Ft. McMurray in Alberta. The first development phase at Kearl was $12.9 billion, and the site commenced operations by 2013 and will grow its capacity each year for the next few years. It was sanctioned for development in 2009, at a difficult time in the global economy. The lease has approximately 4.6 billion barrels of recoverable bitumen (heavy oil that must be diluted or heated in order to flow). Kearl is 71 percent owned by Imperial, which is the operator, and 29 percent owned by ExxonMobil Canada. It is being developed with the intention of becoming Canada's largest mine, intended to produce up to 345,000 barrels per day. Site construction is achieved through a variety of contractors, including Fluor, with more than 19,000 workers involved in the megaproject. Kearl will become a camp-based project, using a rotational shift schedule and company-provided accommodations. Fly-in, fly-out schedules allow workers to assemble at Kearl while having family lives elsewhere in Canada. Indeed, the shift of employment into the many Alberta-based megaprojects has caused the eastern-most provinces of Canada to bemoan that Alberta's recruitment problem has become other regions' retention problem.

Imperial also has more than eighty years of Arctic experience and has been exploring for oil and natural gas in the Beaufort Sea in an Ajurak-Pokak joint venture with ExxonMobil and BP.

EMPLOYMENT PATTERNS

Recruitment of quality employees has always been a part of the culture of Imperial. Every October, all managerial, professional, and technical employees hired within the previous year are flown to Calgary for the Corporate Orientation Seminar, consisting of more than three days of learning and networking.

While attention is paid to employee quality, the industry has had steady declines in the number of full-time employees as a result of technological breakthroughs, as well as the use of subcontracted employees for megaproject building phases. Therefore, though income and activities of the company can grow dramatically, there is an opposite trend in the company's workforce evident in Figure 8.3.[2] For example, in 1975, Imperial's Strathcona refinery was built adjacent to Edmonton, and it replaced obsolete refineries in Edmonton, Regina, Winnipeg, and Calgary. Many years ago, I interviewed the president of the Energy and Chemical Workers Union, and he predicted this exact phenomenon, that for every barrel of oil produced, there would be fewer and fewer permanent employees and that his job with the union was to keep workers safe and push for high wages and good-quality jobs with training opportunities. Decreases in employment arose also from successive waves of dramatic downturns in international oil prices, in tandem with the desire to maintain value for shareholders (Weston, Johnson, and Siu 1999).

Instability in the industry, known for its boom and bust cycles, has a direct bearing on employment levels. For example, between 1991 and 1996, Statistics Canada tables show a loss of almost one in three workers (Statistics Canada, Employment (Survey of Employment, Payrolls and Hours [SEPH]), Table 281–0024–4,14). However, much of the decline in the workforce during bust periods is in head office workers and a reduction in oil service work. At a company like Imperial, wage earners (a term used by Imperial to denote industrial relations' "rank and file" as compared to salaried employees) are likely more buffered from bust cycles but are also more vulnerable to long-term attrition due to technological advances. We see this in Figure 8.3. Imperial was not

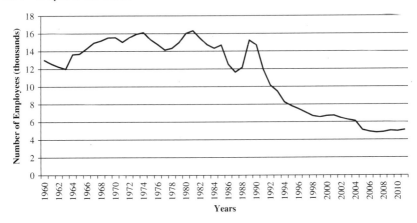

Figure 8.3   Number of Imperial Employees 1960–2011

alone in employment contraction. Between 1980 and 1992, one study tracked employment at eight major oil companies as falling from 800,000 to 300,000 (72 percent reduction), with headquarters staff at six major oil companies reduced from 1988 to 1992 from 3,000 to only 800 (Cibin and Grant 1996).

Imperial Oil is less unionized than the industry or its competition. The entire oil and gas sector's union coverage is low and is declining. Compared to a national union density rate of 32 percent (and today at 29.6 percent), oil and gas had only 12.3 percent unionization in 2006. Unionization in oil and gas extraction is about 9 percent, and gas station workers have less than 5 percent unionization (data from Calvert and Cohen 2011: 41–4).

The characteristics of Imperial's petroleum industry workforce that are salient to the study of labor relations are:

(1) Wage earners are highly trained and are well regarded within the industry and are treated with some deference by management. They are the elite of blue-collar workers.

(2) In this continuous-process industry, highly trained workers are integral to the flow of product through vast investments in capital equipment. There is little ability to substitute for the expertise of these workers; they are mission critical.

(3) Workers are quite savvy about gaining information about wages and working conditions of competitors in the industry. Most workers are far removed from customers but are keenly aware of workplace conditions in competitors.

(4) Workers have a sense of efficacy such that they are comfortably able to contact unions to obtain information about wages, and they have access to national wage and working condition surveys. Unions cooperate in supplying information because they are interested in organizing Imperial and because they can use information about Imperial

to leverage matching wages from unionized competitors with whom they bargain.

From a strategic human resource perspective, labor relations challenges must be solved in ways that meet these key industry attributes for large, integrated players like Imperial:

(1) The total cost of labor is a relatively minor (less than 20 percent) component of total operating cost, but the ramifications of human error are substantial, especially in safety-sensitive environments in the oil sands and the refineries. Labor cost is not much of a preoccupation in this industry relative to the attentiveness to the internationally set price of oil and gas.

(2) Because of the capital-intensive nature of the industry and the inherent risks of petroleum production, companies are acutely aware of safety. At Imperial, there is a campaign known as Nobody Gets Hurt, and the 2012 annual report records that there were no lost-time safety incidents. Although 19,000 new workers were introduced to the Kearl site, only one contractor experienced a lost-time incident, and the lost-time rate for the site is .01, which compares to a province of Alberta oil and gas industry average of .50 (Imperial Oil 2012: 4.)

(3) Product pricing can be passed on to consumers. When global oil prices rise, consumers pay more at the pump. When prices fall, there often are downsizings at the main head offices, among white-collar workers, and in petroleum exploration. However, relative to these cycles of booms and busts, employment by production workers is stable although declining as productivity improves due to improvements in technology and equipment.

(4) Although the petroleum industry is one of the least unionized settings in North American industry, the threat of unionization and the consequences of strikes and industrial unrest can be dire. There is evidence that firms will pay a premium to workers to keep unions at bay (Taras 1997b). As one manager put it to me many years ago, "if you have potential to unionize, err on the side of giving too much."

(5) There has developed an *entente cordiale* among companies such that they rarely poach each other's workers. Companies try to develop their own in-house training and certification or cooperate with technical colleges to train workers and promote them for their efforts. While many companies stress their desire to retain their skilled wage-earner workforce, Imperial has one of the strongest internal labor market approaches in the industry. Most employees I interviewed began their careers at Imperial and had never been employed elsewhere.

(6) There are formidable barriers to entry into the refining and production parts of the industry. The junior firms encircle the integrated firms, specializing instead in exploration and development or services,

and often their hope is to be acquired by the larger firms and hence be well compensated for their business risks.

(7) Mechanisms for information sharing have developed in this industry (Taras 1997b: 191). For example, twice a year, a number of key industrial relations managers meet at Red Deer, Alberta, to share information about wages and working conditions. These meetings started in the early 1950s and continue. They are legal. (Companies cannot "conspire" to fix product prices, but the law permits them to coordinate wages and conditions, just as unions are permitted to pattern bargain.)

Given these conditions, we can develop a compelling portrait of highly skilled and confident workers being extremely well compensated by companies with an interest in remaining union free and having the capacity to meet or exceed union wages with no compelling concern over the affordability of this strategy. These workers are an elite group, and their per-capita productivity would be astonishing if the industry used measures only based on workers' efforts, but there are so many other expenses and investments involved that it simply is not part of the industry norms, and it would be misleading to measure productivity in this manner.

What is most interesting from the perspective of this volume is why, when radical and unanticipated change in conditions for the firm—including fluctuating oil and gas prices, technology enhancements, and new discoveries—that "punctuate the equilibrium" (Gersick 1991), with all the implications for breaking "the grip of inertia" (Romanelli and Tushman 1994), was there so little volatility over a century of the practice of non-union representation? This is the question for us.

Company History with Non-Union Employee Representation

Now that the reader is familiar with the industry, let us take a journey to visit the origins of Imperial's non-union system and trace its evolution. I wrote a treatment of this subject (for Canada—Taras 2000—and so too did Rees for the United States [2007, 2010] and Kaufman [2003]), and I will provide only the highlights. The interested reader may wish to read the more comprehensive accounts, including first-hand observations by Mackenzie King ([1918] 1973) and McGregor (1962) and a critical account by Gitelman (1988), and also see Rees (2010) for his excellent account based on opening the archives of Colorado Fuel and Iron (CF&I) Company.

The genesis of the Imperial Oil system is easily traced and is unusually well documented. The Rockefeller family had significant coal mine holdings in Pueblo, Colorado, over which the family was absentee owner. In 1914, conditions for the Rockefeller-owned CF&I's workers were miserable, the laws of the State of Colorado were not followed by managers (although CF&I was considerably better than some of the worst offenders in the

industry), and the Communist-influenced United Mine Workers gained support from workers. In a company town, in order to strike, workers and their families moved outside the perimeter of company control into a tent city. Gunfire broke out repeatedly, culminating in a fire and the suffocation of women and children huddled in a safety burrow underneath their flaming tent. Known as the Ludlow Massacre, this 1914 loss of life led to the most significant public relations challenge to the Rockefellers in their family history.

The linkage to Canada begins early. The former Canadian deputy minister of labor was in a hiatus from politics and was hired as a special consultant to the Rockefellers to craft a solution to warfare in the mines. William Lyon Mackenzie King had a PhD from Harvard and for many years had been investigating and mediating major Canadian labor disputes. He had written all early labor statutes in Canada. After being contacted by John D. Rockefeller Jr., Mackenzie King wrote a letter on August 6, 1914, in which he presented a full depiction of the philosophy and workings of the non-union plan that came to be known as the Rockefeller Plan, the Colorado Plan, or the joint industrial council (JIC). This was not the first company union plan to be adopted in American industry, but it did contain features that were unique to Mackenzie King's labor relations logic. Mackenzie King abhorred recognition strikes, and he urged JDR Jr. to sidestep recognition by embracing the "principle of Collective Bargaining between capital and labour . . . which will afford opportunity of easy and constant conference between employers and employed with reference to matters of concern to both." He wrote that a "line must be drawn between those who are 'paid salaries' on the one hand, and those who 'earn wages' on the other" (King, 6 August 1914, National Archives of Canada MG 26J1, Vol. 24). The two groups would meet in a joint industrial council. Workers would have the right to select their own representatives from the category of wage earners (a term that is still used at Imperial Oil today). Mackenzie King urged JDR Jr. to accept that there must be no discrimination against union activists: "Every employee has the absolute right openly to belong to a labor union or not, as he pleases . . . [but] all have the right of representation, and not only those who are organized" (King [1918] 1973: 284, from US 64th Cong., 1st sess., doc 859).

This precise plan was embraced by JDR Jr. and was rapidly disseminated throughout American industry via the Rockefeller interests. With encouragement and companionship from Mackenzie King, JDR Jr. visited the mines, was personally won over by the plan, and became an ardent supporter. The underlying rationale was to:

Aim primarily at affording a guarantee of fair play in determining, in the first instance, the conditions under which men would be obligated to work and the remuneration to be paid, and secondly, the carrying out of these conditions in a spirit of fair play.

(King [1918] 1973: 284, from US 64th Cong., 1st sess., doc 859)

An equal number of "elected" wage earners would meet with "selected" managers in order to create an atmosphere of respect and joint problem solving. The issue of union recognition was adroitly sidestepped: even union supporters could be elected, but the intent was to prevent them from hijacking the JIC. Mackenzie King became a labor relations mentor to Rockefeller and a close friend. Eventually, Mackenzie King became Canada's longest-serving prime minister, seeing Canada through much of the depression, World War II, and postwar rebuilding. The plan was designed to elicit voice and be a system of representation (Taras 2003).

Rees studied CF&I archival materials and found revealing trends in the implementation of the plan. Skilled workers appreciated that they were being heard and that the company was improving their conditions, but less-skilled workers, often immigrants and non-whites, did not achieve the same empowerment or gains (Rees 2010: 3). His conclusion is that the JIC plan was neither a panacea nor was it so flawed that it should be condemned. Rees (2007) concludes that even though management clearly was self-interested in establishing the JIC, there were documented gains to workers that call into question the notion that this particular form of company union was a "sham" or a "fraud" (in the words of the iconic union organizer Mother Jones, quoted by Rees 2007: 457). There were genuine achievements, and Rockefeller, under the steady tutelage of Mackenzie King, became an ardent proponent of employee representation. JDR Jr. did genuinely spread tenets of the Progressive movement and forced the adoption of the Rockefeller Plan throughout the family's industrial empire. Many unionists balked, objecting to these ersatz union-like forms of representation as shams. However, in the context of the times, with most industrialists staunchly opposed to any dilution of managerial authority, JDR Jr. was quite an iconoclast—not to the point of recognizing radical unions, but taking the lesser step of joint dealing with employees. Oddly, American Federation of Labor President Samuel Gompers first took the same position as Mackenzie King that the joint industrial council plan could break down the resistance of owners to unions, that it would be a first step along a path toward industrial relations enlightenment. Gompers concluded that "Whenever men meet together to talk over working conditions and ways of betterment, there enters into their lives an incalculable opportunity for progress. Mr. Rockefeller is laying the foundations upon which real unions will be developed" (quoted in Rees 2010: 8).

The CF&I JIC plan was adopted by Standard Oil (New Jersey). Earlier, in 1898, Standard Oil purchased the majority share of Imperial in Canada, and through this cross-border ownership, the JIC moved into Canada. There was sporadic union organizing of Imperial in Canada, but the company refused recognition. The fledgling JIC got off to a "rocky start" in 1919, as the union infiltrated the JIC and put its salary demands on the table at the first JIC meeting (Grant 1998: 83).

In response to this and future union organizing threats, the company began to consider methods to anticipate employee demands and improve conditions before the eruption of discontent. Aided by the professionalization of the HR function and the adoption by the company of a number of welfare capitalism features (e.g., insurance, training, profit sharing, high benefits, and so on), conditions for workers using JICs began to pull ahead of those negotiated by unions. Indeed, there began a long-standing practice of matching and then exceeding union rates, and this tactic became a key feature of the success of the JIC to both management—which wanted to avoid unions and was willing to pay premiums to achieve this objective—and to workers, who benefitted from the offers put on the table by management.

Taken in isolation from other HR practices, the JIC might appear as an elaborate union substitution plan. However, this would not do justice to a larger HR strategy. In 1919 and 1920, the company introduced an eight-hour working day, life insurance policies, pension plans, and a benefit program to support workers with illnesses or injuries. The 1920 employee share-purchase plan was heavily subscribed (Grant 1998: 88). In 1932, Imperial was the second Canadian company to adopt the five-day work week; in 1937, the company introduced paid holidays; 1939 brought a company savings plan; in 1953 the company hired a full-time industrial hygienist to address health and safety concerns; and the company was an early innovator in compressed work weeks and flexible hours in the 1970s (Imperial Oil 1991).

What gains did Imperial achieve through early adoption of progressive practices? Imperial gained a stable workforce that believed that the company would provide "cradle-to-grave" protections and employment. Imperial had the first pick of prospective employees. The company developed a reputation in the petroleum industry for its leading practices. From my years of interviews of petroleum firms, I found that when Imperial's competitors were considering new developments, they would ask "well, what would Imperial do?" or say "Let's call Imperial" (Taras's 1993 interviews). The quality of Imperial workers and facilities was demonstrably better than those of other employers. I recall quite clearly being on the road to attend to my research interviews at various Imperial gas plants, and I took a wrong turn in the remote Alberta back-country and stumbled into a gas plant. "This can't be Imperial," I thought, "because it doesn't have a sign saying how many thousands of days without industrial accidents, and it doesn't sparkle with cleanliness, and the receptionist is surly." I was right; it wasn't an Imperial plant.

With the rise of the petroleum industry in the period after the 1990s, Imperial now has a number of competitors that are using the same HR strategy, and there has been erosion of Imperial's first-mover advantage. But the company remains a top employer, and the strategy is to develop talent. For example, Imperial recruits on campus and presents the following opportunity: "You have probably been told to expect multiple employers over the course of your career. How would you feel about multiple careers with a single employer?" (Imperial: www.imperialoil.ca/Canada-English/Files/People/employer.pdf, accessed summer 2013). The company offers Early Professional Development for new university graduates and considerable training opportunities for wage earners. Skeptics might say that Imperial is willing to pay a high price to remain non-union, but this interpretation does not do justice to the complexity of the HR strategy. Avoiding unions is desirable, but so too is a premier-quality workforce. Relative to other companies in the same industry, Imperial tends to hire juniors and promote from within, so that senior and influential people are completely socialized by the norms that prevail inside Imperial.

Organizational Structure and Operations of Non-Union Representation

Imperial runs a large, multitiered, and formal non-union system. At the top of the corporation, above the level of the JIC, are the executives who set companywide decisions on compensation structures and benefits and who make decisions about investments and restructuring. They do receive feedback from the District JIC and occasionally modify their plans. The company has a complex JIC System Guide that is used to train and guide JIC operations. To illustrate the formality of the system, I will outline the upstream JIC system that covers non-union workers in gas plants.

The upstream JIC system is two tiered, and it exists below the corporate level. The highest JIC level is the District JIC. Its mission, widely disseminated in JIC agreements, is that the JIC works together "in an open and honest dialogue on any subject of importance to the Employees and the Company. Through trust and cooperation we can all achieve excellence." Between sixty-five and eighty delegates attend meetings a number of times annually in Edmonton. Elected wage-earner representatives meet with about equal numbers of selected management-side delegates. Attending the meetings are Human Resource Management staff. The meetings are managed by four cochairs, two from the worker side and two managers, and agendas for meetings are set by this group of four, again with assistance from HR. The District JIC begins its meetings by sharing information—"quick hits"—and then handles issues that affect all operating areas. For example, shift differentials, work schedules, training, and issues involving benefits plans are reviewed. Minutes are taken and distributed afterwards. I examined the minutes within the Imperial Oil archives and also had access to minutes spanning many decades. About half the District JIC agenda consists of information items. When I attended the District meetings over a three-year period, I observed that the JIC received numerous presentations, such as alternations to the benefits package or applications of the job rebalancing (transfer) program. The presentations were informative and thorough, and delegates had the opportunity to ask questions and receive answers that helped them return to their local worksites with concrete knowledge. Worker delegates also can make presentations, and various committee reports are scrutinized. The District JIC is empowered to create subcommittees, populated by an equal number of worker representatives and managers.

The District JIC committees are answerable to the District JIC. The two most powerful committees are the Job Evaluation Team (JET) and the External Wage Team (EWT). JET examines pay classifications, and EWT gathers and analyzes Imperial's wages and working conditions in relation to industry norms. Each committee is privy to significant confidential information. Committees meet on an ad hoc basis at different locations. The committees are so entrenched in Imperial's planning that even when a remote operation in Norman Wells, near the Arctic Circle, unionized in 1993, the local union negotiators insisted in continuing to use the JET and other vestiges of their non-union JIC past, to the consternation of their national union (Taras and Copping 1998). Parenthetically, the Norman Wells site decertified a few years later and returned to the JIC fold.

There are local JIC committees, or site committees in the downstream divisions, that generally meet once a month. They deal with locally sensitive issues such as special compensation for remote locations, employee recognition, specific work schedules, and other ways of removing irritants and maintaining a well-run workplace. On average, there is one elected wage earner per fifteen workers. Elected JIC wage earners are paid for their time engaged in the JIC.

Delegates are encouraged to receive skill development, and there are a variety of courses for which delegates can register. New delegate training seminars take place at least once per year and are heavily attended. I was at the February 1995 two-day new delegate seminar, and the topics were the expected roles, key capabilities, how to improve communication, and meeting management skills. At the request of the wage earners, there also was a session on negotiation skills.

One of the most interesting aspects of the JIC system throughout Imperial is the creation of local JIC written agreements. They tend to be small, cerlox-bound documents of about 6 inches high and 4 inches wide, mimicking many collective agreements in the unionized sectors whose size allows workers to keep the agreements in coverall pockets. Most agreements have a mission statement that promotes cooperation. For example, the Sarnia Manufacturing Site (a member of the products and chemicals division) has in its 2011 agreement this mission:

> The Company and Elected Delegates shall maintain an effective relationship that promotes the business success of the Sarnia site and the employment security and well being of the employees, through open and honest dialogue. (Article 1, 1.01, page 6)

The Sarnia agreement continues to describe the purpose of the JIC as:

> a system whereby management and wage employees through the elected delegates will:
>
> • Discuss business objectives and their relationship to wage employees,
> • Discuss management's perspective on wage employee issues,

- Discuss the concerns, aspirations and objectives of wage employees, and
- Through a mutually agreed principled negotiation process, resolve all issues that relate to hours of work, rates of pay and working conditions in a way that balances the needs of wage employees and the business
- Discuss other matters/issues that are of importance or interest to wage employees.

(Article 1.02, page 6)

This agreement also contains a work-now, grieve-later directive (Article 1.03e), and a three-step grievance process culminating in a decision by head-office executive management. Occasionally, Imperial Oil has taken grievances to third-party arbitrators for resolution, but this is very rare.

JIC agreements are lengthy and complex, and an unsophisticated observer ought to be forgiven for confusing these agreements with union–management collective agreements. Again using the Sarnia site, the agreement is sixty-five pages long and then has another eighty-four pages of appendices. The similarity to collective agreements is especially evident in attention to wage rates, postings, and extremely detailed specifics of vacations, leaves, and other working conditions.

The JIC system has open pay practices, whereby detailed charts and tables exist within JIC agreements showing hourly wages by year, wage progression, the impact of training, and years within job phase. In the large Sarnia site, seniority matters a great deal, and the JIC agreement has many provisions dealing with the accumulation of seniority, the loss of seniority, and how the Seniority Committee oversees seniority. There are distinctions between site seniority and department seniority, and if many employees are hired at once, there is a random selection process run by the Seniority Committee to determine placement on the department seniority list (Article 8: 47–54). However, in order to successfully bid for positions, employees must have the "required qualifications" before seniority becomes the selection mechanism.

In addition to the JIC, there are a number of noteworthy variants. At Cold Lake operations in Alberta, a Forum model emerged in 1977 as an alternative to the JIC. There was more of a town hall approach used in the Forum. Over the years, the Cold Lake operation became more strongly affiliated with the JIC and then formally became part of the JIC. Given the importance of the Cold Lake operations, a Cold Lake worker became the third worker co-chair within the JIC system.

The Dartmouth Refinery in Halifax, Nova Scotia, has a separate "System of Employee Voice/Representation" called a Management–Employee Relations Committee (MERC) with its own complex collective-agreement–like Wage Employee Handbook of almost 200 4 × 6-inch pages. Five management representatives, matched by an equal contingent of employee representatives, meet to discuss terms and conditions of employment. Like the JIC, the body is cochaired by a manager and a designated employee. There is an Employee Concern Resolution Process.

A perplexing issue for Imperial has been its relationship with the Dartmouth refinery, which has been described to me as "iffy" for many decades. The Dartmouth Refinery has been operating since 1919 and is considered to be quite inefficient and in need of upgrading. It produces 88,000 barrels a day. It employs about 200 people, of whom 140 would be considered wage earners, plus 200 contractors. It is considered a small site in the pantheon of Imperial operations, and there are not many significant workplace issues other than the normal concern for payment options for safety boots and healthy options for overtime meals. Dartmouth compensation is better than the regional norms. The initial trigger to poor relations was layoffs in the early 1990s. The surrounding shipyard community is relatively highly unionized, and the local workforce is somewhat more militant than comparable sites that Imperial runs elsewhere. When layoffs resulted in permanent job losses, the relationship between worker reps and managers in the JIC deteriorated to the point that the JIC became dysfunctional. Imperial managers made a decision to abolish the JIC, which was a significant event that still resonates. A manager concluded that "We truly struggled; It comes down to trust. There is very little turnover there, and there are long memories." The company tried an employee forum, but it did not receive much participation from wage earners. There were rumors of union activities. Instead of moving to individual dealing with employees, the company concluded that it needed to overhaul its approach and hired a consultant to perform a needs assessment. He created a Management–Employee Relations Committee (MERC). Worker votes would result in representation, in a similar fashion as the JIC. However, there continued to be a lack of participation, and the system is one of the least functioning non-union plans within Imperial. Nevertheless, the MERC process did produce a lengthy handbook with features of a collective agreement. The company has been frustrated that it has been unable to restore a healthy relationship using any type of formal non-union system.

Perusing the Dartmouth Refinery's Wage Employee Handbook for 2010 (the equivalent of other sites' JIC agreements), the strained relations are evident. There is no mission statement at all and no pretense that the MERC has urged cooperation or "open and honest dialogue." The Introduction tells us that the purpose is to "document in one convenient place" all the practices of the site. Distribution of the document is classified for "Imperial Oil Use Only." The next section of the handbook goes immediately into "Process for Resolution of Issues" and describes that the Employee Concern Resolution Process (ECRP) can be found on the "Employee Voice" website (Article 1.1). There are Rules Compliance Guidelines (Article 1.2). The next provisions deal with "Decision Criteria for Workforce Reduction" (Article 1.3). This site's tensions are captured in the terse language and the organization of issues.

Imperial Oil announced in spring 2012 its intention to either sell the Dartmouth refinery or transform it into a "tank farm" that simply stores product that has been refined elsewhere (Taylor 2013a, 2013b). Not surprisingly, the first substantive item in the handbook is "Decision Criteria for Workforce Reduction," which guides the elimination of jobs through the following sequence: first, removal of probationary and fixed-term employees; second, employees with performance-related probation; third, if employees have the ability to do the work and unique or specialized skills, the seniority principles prevail, with reasonable efforts made to transfer employees or retrain them and move them to other sites within Imperial Oil. Once an employee has met performance expectations in previous assessments, receiving a classification of Valued Contributor, performance should not be a factor in determination of the order of job termination (Article 1.3: 6–7). Ultimately, Imperial was unable to find a buyer and is in the process of converting the Dartmouth refinery into a terminal operation. Imperial chairman and CEO Rich Kruger acknowledged that "closing the refinery is a difficult decision for our employees and the local community. We will make every reasonable effort to minimize the impact." Surplus capacity will be decommissioned, and conversion is underway (Imperial, newswire, 19 June 2013).

Imperial embraces "open-door communication" in the company's Code of Ethics. The Operations Integrity Management System and other policies promote accountability, urge commitment to safe practices, and encourage employees to communicate their concerns. For whistle blowing (although the company does not use this term in its policies, preferring to stress using the open door and seeking "advice"), the company has an English Ethics Adviser in Calgary and a French Ethics Adviser in Montreal. The company also accepts confidential complaints and even anonymous complaints. Imperial promises that "No action will be taken against employees for voicing concerns in good faith" and assures employees that management cannot take or threaten actions unless the employee "acts with wilful disregard of the facts."

MODERN PERMUTATIONS

One of the most fascinating phenomena at Imperial is how the JIC system morphs to suit rapidly growing subsidiary enterprises. The idea of non-union plans is much more "nimble" (in the words of a Vice President) than I would have anticipated from examining how formalized it had become in my research findings in the 1990s (Taras 2000). Where the JIC was found to be too formalized and complex, a number of modifications were made to make it more "JIC-lite" to suit new surroundings. For example, at the Moncton, New Brunswick, ExxonMobil Business Support Centre, the company created a Forum system. A manager described it this way:

The Forum is semantics. They didn't want to have all the trappings and bells and whistles of the JIC. They wanted a homegrown system. The Forum sounds better for admin people, who don't want to be thought of as 'wage earners' like the production folk.

The Moncton operation had a management champion who was transferred from operations, where he had enjoyed and nurtured the JIC system. After about forty people were hired, Imperial thought about a JIC–like structure, and the Moncton manager asked for advice from senior head office HR managers, who promoted a formal system. As the Moncton operation grew by the rate of about 200 new employees per year, the manager knew there was a need for consistency, standards, and training. People hired were very young. The Forum could bring common issues together and resolve any irritants. When another though smaller business support center was established in St. John, New Brunswick, it replicated the Forum system.

The province of New Brunswick has become a mecca for call center development in Canada, with a bilingual workforce and a low average turnover. The province has more than 100 call centers, with more than 20,000 employees in that industry sector (McFarland 2007: 4). There have been organizing drives by the Teamsters for Purolators sites, by CAW for UPS, by CEP for Phonettix Intelecom, and by PSAC for Accenture, with varying degrees of success and failure. At times, call centers have been closed or relocated, perhaps due to union organizing (McFarland 2007). The Teamsters successfully organized the Purolator Courier administrative center in Moncton, but failed to unionize Purolator's call center in 1995. The Canadian Auto Workers undertook a difficult organizing battle at UPS in Fredericton. Imperial's business support centers are not quite call centers, as they do not engage in direct marketing. They are part of an inbound system in which people call the centers for business support, for example, with repairs, credit issues, and business processes. However, they do bring together a large number of people into a setting that is an attractive target for unions. The Steelworkers and Canadian Auto Workers have targeted a number of major call centers for organizing, but there have been no formal organizing attempts at the Imperial centers.

In the postmerger environment, having highly trained, satisfied, and motivated employees working at the business services centers is one of the ways Imperial can prove that it is deeply integrated into Exxon and a vital part of a worldwide system. Unlike oil workers, who are far from the final customers, the workers in business centers interact with customers and must solve issues to the entire satisfaction of customers. Although fundamentally different in so many respects from oil workers, the business center workers also are critical to the company's success. They need training, a positive attitude, and good interpersonal skills.

THE MOTIVES AND PURPOSES BEHIND
NON-UNION REPRESENTATION

From the perspective of Imperial managers, to keep unions at bay is clearly a desirable—and by and large, an achievable—outcome. In this regard, Imperial Oil is no different than most of the other companies in the same industry (Taras 1994, Basken 2000). The company has been quite successful at limiting the spread of unionization even once a plant or two have become unionized. For example, the large Edmonton-based Strathcona refinery has been unionized for decades, and the remote Norman Wells refinery was briefly unionized in the 1990s and the union has since been decertified (Timur, Taras, and Ponak 2012). Although there might be one or more locations unionized, Imperial never had more than 5 percent unionization. Imperial had always used the strategy of matching or exceeding union wages, and in an industry with relatively few workers and large profits, management "generosity" did not appreciably harm the bottom line. The effect of wage matching and union pattern bargaining led to almost no variability in wages for the same position (Taras 1997b).

Even as early as the 1920s, Imperial and similar companies were savvy about eliminating economic incentives for unionization. When a group of Steelworkers came in 1920s to the Turner Valley oilfields to build a refinery, the Royalite Oil Company quickly offered its oilworkers the Steelworker package of wages and more attractive hours of work, aborting a union organizing drive. In 1950, after enduring a one-month strike against Shell operations in Burnaby, British Columbia, the oilworkers managed for the first time to break through the Imperial Oil wage barrier. Imperial responded by unilaterally topping the Shell settlement for its non-union workers, and the lesson was clear: Imperial workers would always get the benefits of unionization without any of the costs, whether ill will at the workplace, tense strikes, or simply payment of dues.

In the mid-1960s a wave of union unrest threatened the entire Canadian petroleum industry, and strikes by the Energy and Chemical Workers Union (ECWU) came close to generating a general strike in the province of British Columbia (described in Jamieson 1968: 420). After a difficult 1969 strike, both union and company management were exhausted, and there developed an unwritten *entente cordiale* in the industry as a whole: "Pay the pattern, smooth out regional differences, and there will be no surprises from either side."[3] Hence, in the petroleum industry, there is a complementarity that exists between unions that use Imperial's predictable matching as a strategy to drive up wages in all its collective agreements across the industry and Imperial's workers' desires to get the benefits of unionization without paying dues. As the union president of the Energy and Chemical Workers Union told me in 1991,

In the early 1940s our bargaining strategy was an organizing strategy. We delivered wage increases that way—actually to all employees, not just unionized. In some respects it is good to have Imperial Oil. It is less costly to have a show at the Imperial gates than to have a strike.

The tendency of the company to eliminate economic incentives to unionize has created the phenomenon that Imperial managers sometimes complain of as an "entitlement mentality" among workers. Workers are socialized to make their demands persuasively, and with full awareness that the company can afford enhancements to employment conditions. I saw workers ask for home computer networks and computer allowances and make their request seem plausibly connected to company interests. It is difficult for managers to say no (although they did with regard to home computers). The JIC feels good; it has a convivial tone, and so it is not unusual for workers to be treated especially well. After a while, the costs of running non-union escalate, not by any single deliberate decision but by the cumulative effect of small acts of appreciation by management. In the Norman Wells refinery, the company's efforts to stop the flow of "entitlements" fed into the hostility that led to unionization (Taras and Copping 1998). I have always enjoyed the metaphor given to me by an IR specialist at another major company, when he commented on Imperial's JIC: "It is like inviting a pet bear into the house. You keep sweets in your pocket as a reward, and you never turn your back."

Two main reasons underlie union avoidance. First, although today the industry's labor climate is currently fairly calm, we must develop amnesia about the decades of acrimony. There were generations of serious—even lethal (with the death of workers on picket lines in the 1960s)—strikes. This is an extraordinarily capital-intensive industry, and work disruptions and strikes create complex challenges to product throughput imperatives as well as legitimate safety concerns for those who operate equipment and processes. During the years of intense union organizing and lengthy strikes of between one and four months in the 1950s and 1960s, companies relied on layers of foremen and supervisors to monitor plant unrest and also, in the event of strikes, to operate the plants as replacement workers. In effect, the industry had to be double-staffed. With peaceful labor relations, new forms of work design, including job enlargement and job rotation, were introduced into plants. These designs needed remarkably few foremen and supervisors, and so there is difficulty operating plants during periods of labor unrest. Many plants work within legal requirements for particular workers who have achieved certification in specific technical aspects of the job. Historically, the first-line foremen and supervisors had been promoted from the shop floor and would have been adept at running the plant, but eliminating this level in the hierarchy created a gap that few of today's managers can fill.

Imperial is an attractive target for union organizing, particularly because of its iconic stature. It would be a real coup for a union organizer to penetrate Fortress Imperial. The company knows that the union has a strategy of cooperating and sharing data with worker representatives in the JIC system. I have numerous examples from archives of information sharing. The union's idea was to impress workers by demonstrating the union's superior skills, cross-company knowledge, and bargaining resources. To entice JICs and other non-union systems to affiliate with the union as a first step, the ECWU constitution and bylaws enabled alternative arrangements for associations and mergers (Taras 1994: 155), showing that the union was prepared to enter a period of courtship and even an engagement in order to win the JIC vote.

Second, managers simply dislike adversarialism and are averse to being scrutinized by unions. This is an industry that is quite American influenced, in a province with Canada's lowest union density. The city of Calgary tends to be politically conservative. Many managers and senior executives in the oil and gas sector are viscerally opposed to unions (Taras 1997b). Further, a great many managers of plants and refineries are engineers, and they have told me they are frustrated with the delays that they believe would be necessary to seek union members' assent. They don't like the idea of being "frozen" by multiyear collective agreements, and they intensely dislike the rigidities of collective agreements. (Of course, this is somewhat ironic, since the JIC agreements are quite rigid as well, albeit with a gloss of easy movement into cooperative solutions papered as appendices to the main agreements. But when I examine collective agreements in the energy sector, I see a great many of them containing memoranda of understandings as well.) Managers find the notion of formal bargaining to be stressful, and they would rather deal with non-union employee committees. Managers also are particularly hostile to the idea that non-Imperial employees—union officials from the national union—could intrude on company business. They do not want "third parties" preventing harmonious relations with workers.

It should be noted that in the rare circumstances in which Imperial sites have become unionized, for example, Strathcona and Norman Wells, the company has reacted with grace and professionalism. The union officials have told me they have had far worse companies to deal with in the oil and gas sector. Imperial managers are "not so much anti-union as pro-JIC" (Taras 2000: 290). It is quite common that non-union delegates and leaders of non-union systems, if dissatisfied with outcomes or processes, will actually lead the unionization drive and then become the leaders of the union local (Timur, Taras, and Ponak 2012).

The non-union systems at Imperial are not simply about union avoidance. There is an equally or, for many managers, even more compelling vision of a harmonious workplace. The system allows employee voice, and the company has, time and again, found that hearing suggestions from employees creates incremental but vital fine tuning of new developments. For example, when the company changed its employee database to an SAP system, employees made valuable suggestions that improved the execution and effectiveness of the new system. Managers recall many times thinking, "Jeez, we didn't think of that. Right, let's look at that."

Manager delegates genuinely believe both publicly and privately that the non-union systems create cooperation and an integrative approach to problem solving. They believe that worker delegates learn sound managerial ways of thinking, that somehow wage earners will be inculcated with an appreciation of company values and aspirations through their participation in the JIC or other non-union system. In other words, the non-union systems are an extension of the care and consideration given to employees, the attention to training and good selection, and the respectful treatment required to keep highly skilled employees satisfied that they matter to the company.

The JIC larger meetings are pleasant. They allow different operations to provide briefings as to their recent challenges. Workers inform each other as to developments throughout the Imperial operations. They socialize together. They enjoy themselves. They have a welcome break from the usual job duties and are well treated in their major meetings together.

The JIC lately has not had major changes or difficulties. Management reports that it has reached a steady state, in which it is simply "business as usual."

Success Factors and Strains

There is nothing haphazard or accidental about the embeddedness of non-union representation at Imperial. The company is vigilant about removing any economic incentive for workers to unionize. But it is not so simple; the complete strategy also involves information sharing. Not only are Imperial wages above union rates, but worker delegates have access to industry-commissioned wage surveys that in most companies would be confidential to HR staff. Workers can verify information, and they can help the company make decisions through the EWT committee. The degree to which wage earners are given access to the specifics of competitor companies' compensation structures is extraordinary.

Managers who run the system tend to appreciate it. They work effectively with the wage-earner co-chairs. Meetings are regularly scheduled and minutes are taken, so there is a continued expectation built into the system that it is permanent. The HR specialists support the JIC system in ensuring meetings are well run, documents are produced, information is provided and distributed to the appropriate levels, and there is respect for requests.

Money is spent. Resources are allocated to ensuring meetings go smoothly. Flying workers to Edmonton multiple times per year, having them stay in a hotel, feeding them, and supporting them is daunting and requires logistical expertise. Committees meet and solve issues, and their work is lauded at the District JIC.

But removal of economic incentives and a well-run non-union system have not prevented pockets of unionization within Imperial. Management style at the local level is a success factor. As a result of the 1993 unionization of the Normal Wells site (described in Taras and Copping 1998), Imperial decided to pay more attention to the human side of the managerial equation. No longer would engineers be promoted to managerial positions based merely on their education and professional expertise. Their ability to work effectively with people would be assessed, and they would be offered training and support to eliminate managerial styles that might erode cooperative relations with employees. The company, under the now-retired HR executive, determined that modern workers were resistant to command-and-control managerial styles.

Attention to managerial style was a prudent step for Imperial. In my earlier research, I found that workers were not naïve about their non-union systems. Instead, they were wily strategists. They learned the rhetoric of collaboration, and they were skilled at framing issues in ways that seemed genuinely integrative. However, behind closed doors, in their premeetings (to which I was invited for a number of years), they were more positional. They would spend time determining the tactics that would make them most persuasive to managers. I found that a significant number of wage-earner delegates and the constituents they represent believe they are engaged in bargaining. What management sees as an "entitlement mentality" is really the effect of workers' talents at securing gains. While in a unionized workplace, the workers might enhance their power by forceful displays or strike votes, by contrast, in a non-union setting the workers become more powerful by seeming to be collaborative and seeking solutions that are a "win-win" when their real interest is simply their own "win" (Taras 2000: 241.) Workers could easily recall their victories to me, and they told me that the JIC must deliver periodic wins so the non-union system does not become a "toothless dog." Worker delegates are adept at using the union threat, and the best delivery of the union threat is through subtlety. Workers would casually mention a site within Imperial that unionized, or that they felt their constituents might be restive and calling the union.

Cultivation of employee voice is a condition for the success of non-union plans. Managers must encourage employees to raise concerns, and their issues must be treated respectfully. While major strategic decisions are made at the corporate executive level, their implementation can be influenced by the JIC. For example, the JIC makes recommendations on benefit plans, on the rollout of policies, and a wise manager listens carefully and crafts victories for the JIC when possible.

For Imperial's non-union systems to succeed, workers must have faith in their representatives. Although new delegates have trepidation about their roles, the company does provide training so that they learn corporate matters, as well as issue analysis and effective communication. Further, by selecting worker cochairs to comanage the JIC, they perceive they have more input into the non-union system. They told me they tend to select co-chairs they perceive as courageous, articulate, and trustworthy.

Strains emerge when the systems are not tended to with care. There have been years during which the senior managers responsible for chairing or cochairing the JIC system were inattentive, and the system can provide few benefits if it is not cultivated. Workers can become apathetic about the system, and delegates of lesser quality or skill can be elected. Then when a new senior manager is promoted, the task of rebuilding the non-union system can be daunting. It takes many years to rebuild vitality.

Another strain of running non-union systems is the hypervigilance required of management. The open-door policy and the requirement for managers to be continuously receptive to worker delegates can be exhausting. Some wage-earner delegates are relentless in raising issues, and managers find it difficult to issue an unequivocal refusal that might shut down the relationship. This empowers workers to continue their subtle campaign of bargaining while seeming to be seeking a "win-win" outcome.

For senior managers, an additional strain is their need to sideline other management delegates so that they can hear from workers. Midlevel managers find themselves stranded at the District level. While there is a semblance of democracy with equal numbers of management and worker delegates, the real game that is played is between all the workers and the most senior manager at the meetings, as he has the highest decision-making authority. One top manager told me that "The purpose of the JIC is to hear from wage earners, not from supervisors, and not from human resources people." Conditions can be uncomfortable for foremen and supervisors, as the non-union systems allow wage earners to leap over levels of management hierarchy to voice concerns.

IMPLICATIONS OF IMPERIAL: WHAT EXPLAINS THE LONGEVITY OF THE NON-UNION REPRESENTATION SYSTEM?

I have been studying Imperial Oil for almost two decades, interviewing dozens of managers and employees over those years, always alert to the question of why the company remains an ardent practitioner of formal non-union representation plans. It is tempting to conclude that the company can afford its preference for a complex form of non-union voice. Indeed, most oil companies could afford such expenditures on employee representation, but the point is that they do not use it with the vigor of Imperial. PetroCanada is highly unionized. Other major companies use individual dealing and only modest forms of non-union practices such as focus groups, surveys, and open-door policies.

There is no single compelling answer as to why Imperial supports its non-union model, but rather, there is a group of interrelated factors:

(1) There is an embedded culture of support for the JIC and other formal systems of representation. They are part of the history and there is an incumbency effect that favors these plans. To move away from them would require a commitment to another form of dealing, and the company is content with what it already knows. This tendency to support the status quo is exacerbated by the fact that most managers

begin their careers with Imperial and progress through the ranks, so that they are socialized into the system, and it is taken for granted that this is the Imperial way of doing business. "Other companies look at me like I'm crazy," said a manager, "but we have convinced ourselves that this system is what we value, that it creates open and honest communication, and it is what we do at Imperial for success."

(2) The Human Resources Department and its tentacles of HR managers embedded in plants and refineries throughout the country have a role in supporting the system. When managers are promoted into line positions that cause them to become management co-chairs within the JIC or other systems, the senior members of the Human Resources Department brief them on the advantages of the system and encourage them to use it effectively. For example, when a senior production manager was promoted from the Cold Lake Forum system into the JIC upstream system, the (now-retired) HR Vice President commented, "I could sense he wasn't quite sure about the JIC animal for production ops, but we encouraged him. When the [two worker co-chairs] came to me and said supervisors weren't giving enough time for the reps to attend to JIC business, I talked to [the senior line manager], and the problems were resolved."

(3) The employees grew up in the system and see how the JIC works. The system "breeds itself" as successive generations of workers are elevated to becoming JIC representatives and cochairs. Just as managers spent entire careers within the Imperial fold, so too did its wage-earner workforce. Many JIC worker reps end up as supervisors, as their leadership skills are discovered and rewarded by career advancement within Imperial. When last I examined seniority at Imperial among wage earners, petroleum workers had an average of more than eighteen years.

(4) There is extensive complementary training. New delegates are trained. The subteams of workers who oversee job classification systems receive training and see company data. Because information is shared with workers, there is more trust in the representation systems. As one manager put it, "they see our data; they know we aren't smoking them on the numbers. It is so smooth; it isn't management always defending decisions; it is members of a joint compensation team that includes workers."

(5) There have been downturns and changes in the industry. When downsizing happened after the Texaco merger in 1989 to 1990, and then additional industry softness in 1992, 1996, and 1998, workers were involved in the "rebalancing process." The idea of "rebalancing" arose within the JIC system, and the company and its worker reps sought solutions that would prevent layoffs, including transfers and retraining opportunities. Workers participated in finding solutions that helped other workers. When benefits are adjusted, sometimes even rolled back, workers are involved in fine tuning so that they

minimize the negative effects on them. Managers are respectful of workers' insights into how to actually implement policies and plans. It is noteworthy that the company did try to remove "entitlements" and started cutting labor costs, but the JIC system itself was not on the chopping block. Instead, the JIC became an ally in the company's efforts to reduce costs and preserve productivity.

(6) Wages and benefits are high, and there is no economic advantage to unionization. Indeed, with the payment of union dues, workers would have to drop their take-home pay in order to be unionized at the prevailing union rates in the industry. For example, at the Sarnia refinery in Ontario, the lowest-paid trainees earn a regular rate of more than $30 an hour, and within a few years of training, base hourly wages rise to more than $43 an hour. Top classifications earn more than $50 an hour, and employees can earn various premiums for working at height, doing engineering duties, having shift differentials, and of course, doing overtime work (Imperial Oil 2011). Rank-and-file workers' wages are openly available in the various JIC agreements and handbooks, including wage progression systems from year to year. There is little compensation secrecy among the "unionizable" of Imperial's workforce. The company is aware its compensation is attractive enough to withstand scrutiny by employees who might be shopping for a better deal.

The company's commitment to its JIC systems is sufficiently strong that it even tries to protect non-union representation when properties are divested. For example, when a large operation at Judy Creek in Swan Hills, Alberta, was sold to Pengrowth Energy in 1997, Imperial strongly recommended that the acquiring company keep the JIC in place and use it to manage employee relations. Some of the managers at that site moved to Pengrowth, and Imperial managers were "concerned" that their former employees should be protected. Pengrowth migrated everything from Imperial at the time, including its representation policies. The Swan Hills employees worked with Pengrowth to found a new JIC.

Now we turn to why the company continues to implement non-union plans, even in workforces outside the traditional, highly skilled oil and gas rank and file. Managers who were transferred to senior positions in the Maritime service centers come from Imperial and were socialized in the history and benefits of joint dealing. Here again, mobility within Imperial's internal labor force strategy acts to reinforce the use of non-union systems. Forced to speculate about the future of these service centers, it would not surprise me if they developed the highest wages, best benefits, and longest job tenures in the call center communities. Just as Imperial and other integrated petroleum firms tended to treat their workers as part of an industrial elite, so too will the service centers invest in selection, training, compensation, and customer-relations skills.

Imperial Oil has made an extraordinary commitment to non-union representation, and worker voice and influence is one component of a larger system of human relations designed to encourage business success. When the non-union system works well, workers are partners rather than adversaries. Their voice is cultivated and their issues are resolved. They are adept at making their needs known, and they do engage in subtle bargaining. Certainly these elite workers are not pawns of management; neither are they brainwashed to abandon their own agendas. Managers are given the opportunity to hear from workers, and management obtains greater knowledge of worksite concerns. The workforce is effectively managed. Although these non-union plans are enterprise based, they have access to information that allows them to consider industry conditions. Imperial continues its commitment to innovating non-union systems by extending its openness to employee voice even to the Maritime service center setting.

As I reflect upon Imperial's century of experience with non-union systems, I am struck by the simplicity of the original vision of Mackenzie King in 1914 that there must be a mechanism "which will afford opportunity of easy and constant conference between employers and employed with reference to matters of concern to both" (King, 6 August 1914, National Archives of Canada MG 26J1, Vol. 24). And the interesting development after the ExxonMobil merger is that rather than the parent company's influence weakening non-union representation within Imperial, instead, voice mechanisms are growing roots in new and non-traditional workplaces.

NOTES

1. I am indebted to Kaleigh Zerr for her research assistance in analyzing company performance and employee numbers. The charts were developed using the Wharton Data Platform applied to the CompuStat Database. CompuStat begins in 1950, but a decision was made to exclude the first decade of data as there were too many flaws, gaps, and inconsistencies.
2. Figure 8.2 includes all employees of consolidated subsidiaries (both domestic and foreign) and all part-time and seasonal employees. It excludes consultants, contract workers, and employees of unconsolidated subsidiaries.
3. Interview with ECWU Union President Neil Reimer, 1991.

REFERENCES

Arnold, Steve. 2013. "The Dofasco Way." theSpec.com, June 2, 2013, accessed July 2013.

Basken, Reg. 2000. "My Experience with Unionization of Nonunion Employee Representation Plans in Canada." In Bruce E. Kaufman and Daphne Gottlieb Taras, eds., *Nonunion Employee Representation: History, Contemporary Practice and Policy*, pp. 487–497. New York: M. E. Sharpe.

Bhattarai, Abha, and Thomas Heath. 2012. "Exxon Mobil Moving Fairfax Operations to Houston in 2014, Taking 2,100 Jobs." *The Washington Post, Capital Business*, June 6. Available at www.washingtonpost.com/business/capitalbusiness/exxon-moving-fairfax-operations-to-houston-in-2014/2012/06/06/gJQA7o00IV_story.html, accessed May 2014.

Calvert, John, and Marjorie Griffin Cohen. 2011. "Climate Change and the Canadian Energy Sector: Implications for Labour and Trade Unions." Canadian Centre for Policy Alternatives. Available at www.policyalternatives.ca/sites/default/files/uploads/publications/National%20Office/2011/10/Climate%20Change%20and%20Energy%20Sector.pdf, accessed May 2014.

Canadian Auto Workers. 2013. "CAW-Magna Timeline." Available at caw.ca/assets/pdf/MagnaTimeline.pdf, accessed May 2014.

Cibin, Renato, and Robert M. Grant. 1996. "Restructuring Among the World's Leading Oil Companies, 1980–92." *British Journal of Management*, 7(4): 283–307.

Dofasco-ArcelorMittal. 2013. "Who We Are" and "History." Available at www.dofasco.ca, accessed July 2013.

Gersick, C. J. G. 1991. "Revolutionary Change Theories: A Multilevel Exploration of the Punctuated Equilibrium Paradigm." *Academy of Management Review*, 16(1): 10–36.

Gibb, G. S., and E. Knowlton. 1956. *History of Standard Oil Company (New Jersey)*. New York: Harper and Row.

Gitelman, H. M. 1988. *The Legacy of the Ludlow Massacre: A Chapter in American Industrial Relations*. Philadelphia: University of Pennsylvania Press.

Grant, Hugh M. 1998. "Solving the Labour Problem at Imperial Oil: Welfare Capitalism in the Canadian Petroleum Industry, 1919–1929." *Labour/Le Travail* 41(Spring): 69–95.

Harshaw, Mark. 2000. "Nonunion Employee Representation at Dofasco." In Bruce E. Kaufman and Daphne Gottlieb Taras (eds.), *Nonunion Employee Representation: History, Contemporary Practice and Policy*, pp. 463–68. New York: ME Sharpe.

Imperial Oil. 1991. *Story of Imperial Oil*. Toronto: Imperial Oil
———. 2012. "Responsible Growth." Summary Annual Report. Calgary, Alberta: Imperial Oil.

Imperial Oil, Dartmouth Refinery. 2010. *Wage Employee Handbook*. Dartmouth, Nova Scotia: Imperial Oil.

Imperial Oil, Sarnia Manufacturing Site, Products and Chemicals Division. 2011. "Joint Industrial Council Agreement." April. Sarnia, Ontario: Imperial Oil.

Jamieson, S. M. 1968. *Times of Trouble: Labour Unrest and Industrial Conflict in Canada 1900–66*. Report of the Task Force on Labour Relations. Ottawa, Ontario: Government of Canada.

Kaufman, Bruce E. 1996. "Why the Wagner Act? Reestablishing Contact with Its Original Purpose." *Advances in Labor and Industrial Relations*, 7: 15–68.
———. 2000. "The Case for the Company Union." *Labor History*, 41(3): 321–50.
———. 2003. "Industrial Relations Counselors, Inc.: Its History and Significance." In B. E. Kaufman, R. A. Beaumont, and R. B. Helfgott, *Industrial Relations to Human Resources and Beyond*, pp. 31–114. New York: M. E. Sharpe.

King, William Lyon Mackenzie. 1914. "Letter to John D Rockefeller," August 6, 1914. National Archives of Canada MG 26J1, Volume 24.
———. [1918] 1973. *Industry and Humanity*. Reprint. Toronto: University of Toronto Press.

Koch, Marianne, David Lewin, and Donna Sockell. 1989. "The Determinants of Bargaining Structure: A Case Study of AT&T." In David Lewin, David B. Lipsky, and Donna Sockell, eds., *Advances in Industrial and Labor Relations* (Vol. 4), pp. 223–51. London: JAI Press.

Lewchuk, Wayne, and Don Wells. 2007. "Transforming Worker Representation: The Magna Model in Canada and Mexico." *Labour/Le travail*, 60(Fall): 107–36.

Mallin, Martin H. 2010. "The Canadian Auto Workers-Magna International, Inc. Framework of Fairness Agreement: A U.S. Perspective." *Saint Louis University School of Law Journal*, 54: 525–63.

226   *Daphne G. Taras*

McFarland, Joan. 2007. *Vulnerable Jobs in the New Brunswick Call Centre Industry.* Paper delivered at the New Brunswick and Atlantic Studies Research and Development Centre Conference, Town and Country: Exploring Urban and Rural Issues, New Brunswick, St. Thomas University.

McGregor, F. A. 1962. *The Fall & Rise of Mackenzie King, 1911–1919.* Toronto: Macmillan Co.

Rees, Jonathan. 2007. "What if a Company Union Wasn't a 'Sham'? The Rockefeller Plan in Action." *Labor History*, 48(4): 457–75.

———. 2010. *Representation and Rebellion: The Rockefeller Plan at the Colorado Fuel and Iron Company, 1914–1942.* Boulder: University Press of Colorado.

Romanelli, E., and M. L. Tushman. 1994. "Organizational Transformation as Punctuated Equilibrium: An Empirical Test." *Academy of Management Journal*, 27(5): 1141–66.

Storey, Robert H. 1983. "Unionization Versus Corporate Welfare: The Dofasco Way." *Labour/Le travail* 12: 7–42.

Taras, Daphne Gottlieb. 1994. "Effects of Industrial Relations Strategy on Selected Human Resource Practices: Canadian Petroleum Industry." PhD dissertation. University of Calgary, Faculty of Management.

———. 1997a. "Why NonUnion Representation is Legal in Canada." *Relations industrielles/Industrial Relations*, 52(4): 761–80.

———. 1997b. "Managerial Objectives and Wage Determination in the Canadian Petroleum Industry." *Industrial Relations*, 36(2): 178–205.

———. 1999. "Evolution of Nonunion Employee Representation in Canada." *Journal of Labor Research*, 20(1): 31–51.

———. 2000. "Contemporary Experience with the Rockefeller Plan: Imperial Oil's Joint Industrial Council." In Bruce E. Kaufman and Daphne Gottlieb Taras, eds., *Nonunion Employee Representation: History, Contemporary Practice and Policy,* pp. 231–58. New York: M. E. Sharpe.

———. 2003. "Voice in the North American Workplace: From Employee Representation to Employee Involvement." In B. E. Kaufman, R. A. Beaumont, and R. B. Helfgott (eds.), *Industrial Relations to Human Resources and Beyond,* pp. 293–329. Armonk, NY: M. E. Sharpe.

———. 2006. "Nonunion Representation and Employer Intent: How Canadian Courts and Labour Boards Determine the Legal Status of Nonunion Plans." *Socio-Economic Review,* 4(2): 321–36.

———, and Jason Copping. 1998. "The Transition from Formal Nonunion Representation to Unionization: A Contemporary Case." *Industrial and Labor Relations Review*, 52(1): 22–44.

———, and Bruce E. Kaufman. 2006. "Nonunion Employee Representation in North America: Diversity, Controversy and Uncertain Future." Industrial Relations Journal, 37(5): 513–42.

Taylor, Roger. 2013a. "Imperial Oil refinery has lots of potential." *Chronicle Herald, Business.* Available at thechronicleherald.ca/business/1052256-taylor-imperial-oil-refinery-has-lots-of-potential, accessed May 2014.

———. 2013b. "Imperial's Dartmouth refinery will probably soon be history." *Chronicle Herald Business.* Available at thechronicleherald.ca/business/374449-taylor-imperial-s-dartmouth-refinery-will-probably-soon-be-history, accessed May 2014.

Timur, A. Tarik, Daphne Taras, and Allen Ponak. 2012. "Do Pre-Existing Nonunion Representation Plans Matter when Employees Unionise?" *British Journal of Industrial Relations*, 50(2): 214–38.

U.S. Supreme Court. *Standard Oil Co. v. United States*, 221 U.S. 1 (1911).

Van Alphen, Tony. 2008. "Dofasco Invites the Union to Gauge Worker Interest." *The Toronto Star,* March 20, 2008. Available at theStar.com, accessed July 2013.

Weston, J. Fred, Brian A. Johnson, and Juan A. Siu. 1999. "Mergers and Restructuring in the World Oil Industry." *Journal of Energy Finance & Development*, 4(2): 149–83.

9 Non-Union Employee Representation in the Royal Canadian Mounted Police
Resistance and Revitalization

Sara Slinn

INTRODUCTION

The Royal Canadian Mounted Police (RCMP) is an iconic Canadian institution with its roots in paramilitary peacekeeping on Canada's frontier in the 1800s but which has developed into a large, sophisticated organization operating domestically and abroad. The RCMP is a complex organization that continues to be strongly influenced by its paramilitary origins while it is also faced with a quickly evolving and expanding mandate in circumstances of limited resources. Throughout its history, the RCMP has been characterized by reluctant and grudging change prompted by crises, grassroots RCMP member discontent, and, especially in recent years, pressures from legal challenges and public inquiries.

The issue of RCMP member workplace representation has been a contentious one for much of the organization's history, with the federal government and RCMP consistently opposing independent employee representation or unionization. The impetus for the non-union employee representation system that the Force initially implemented and much of its subsequent development was the Force's desire to remain free of unions. The Force's response has evolved from explicit legal prohibition from unionizing or involvement with labour organizations to introduction of a management-controlled non-union system as the exclusive form of RCMP member employee representation in the face of widespread RCMP member rebellion against the Force's managerial practices to statutory enforcement of that exclusive system and, in recent decades, strong resistance to legal challenges of this exclusion of other forms of employee representation.

This chapter begins with a brief introduction to the RCMP and an overview of police labour relations in Canada. An outline of the development of non-union representation in the RCMP is followed by an explanation of the current RCMP non-union representation system (the Staff Relations Representation Program or SRRP) and its interaction with the RCMP's broader labour relations system, including Pay Council, the Mounted Police Members' Legal Fund, and the grievance and discipline systems. The chapter closes with some thoughts on the current state and future of non-union representation in the RCMP.

RCMP OVERVIEW

The RCMP has a force of 18,617 police officers, accounting for 26.8 per cent of the 69,438 police officers in Canada (Canadian Centre for Justice Statistics 2011: Table 2–1). Public policing in Canada operates at three levels: federal, provincial/regional, and municipal, with the majority of policing occurring at the municipal level. The RCMP provides policing at the federal level.[1] At the provincial/regional level, there exist the Ontario Provincial Police, the Sûreté du Québec, and the Royal Newfoundland Constabulary (operating in specific areas of Newfoundland and Labrador). Most municipalities have established municipal police forces. In addition to its primary role as a federal police force, the RCMP also provides provincial/regional and municipal police services through policing agreements where that jurisdiction does not have its own force.[2] Such agreements currently exist with eight of the ten provinces and the three territories, and approximately 190 municipalities, 184 Aboriginal communities, and several international airports (RCMP 2006). Even where a municipality has its own police service, the RCMP may also be called in to assist local forces when necessary (Hall and de Lint 2003: 222). Overall, RCMP members make up 21.4 per cent of the country's 45,630 municipal police officers and, at the provincial/regional level, RCMP officers represent 65.5 per cent of the country's 16,913 provincial and regional police officers (Canadian Centre for Justice Statistics 2011: Table 2–1).

The RCMP is organized into fifteen divisions, each approximating provincial boundaries and each led by a commanding officer. The national headquarters is located in Ottawa, the nation's capital. Divisions are grouped into one of four larger geographic regions: Pacific, Northwestern, Central, and Atlantic regions, each headed by a Deputy Commissioner (RCMP 2012a). The Commissioner is the highest authority in the RCMP, reporting to the federal Minster of Public Safety and the federal Treasury Board as the employer.

The RCMP is also organized into five business areas: federal services, criminal intelligence, contract policing, national police services, and corporate infrastructure (RCMP 2006). The RCMP is responsible for enforcing federal law throughout Canada (including national security, immigration and passport control, drug enforcement, economic crime, and protection of state officials and visiting foreign dignitaries). The RCMP also provides police support services (such as forensic analysis, criminal records information, and technological assistance) to forces throughout Canada. The RCMP also has an international role, including responsibility for managing deployment of Canadian police officers to international peace missions. RCMP officers have participated in these missions since 1989 and, beginning in 1995, police officers from Canadian municipal, provincial, and regional police services also have participated in these missions (RCMP 2012b).

Historically, the RCMP and its predecessor organizations (discussed in what follows) were central to the country's security and intelligence operations and regularly targeted left-wing political organizations and their supporters, including labour organizations.[3] The RCMP's traditional role in suppressing labour activities has, as will be addressed, contributed to the Force's reluctance to permit members to participate in mainstream forms of collective employee representation systems.

POLICE LABOUR RELATIONS IN CANADA

Police associations have a long history in Canada, which can be traced back at least to the beginning of the twentieth century, when police in several large Canadian cities formed associations and which continue in operation to this day (Forcese 1999: 103). A surge in police association activity occurred in the 1960s and 1970s, prompted by police officers' relatively poor compensation and working conditions against the backdrop of widespread legislative change granting public-sector workers access to statutory collective bargaining schemes.

Canadian public-sector labour relations were transformed in the 1960s and 1970s. Responding to pressure from increasingly militant public-sector workers and their associations, between 1960 and the mid-1970s, statutes were passed across the country extending access to statutory schemes of collective employee representation and bargaining to much of the public sector, including provincial and municipal police forces. The 1967, the federal Public Services Staff Relations Act (PSSRA) is generally regarded as the catalyst for this transformation, and by the late 1970s, most Canadian public-sector workers at the municipal, provincial, and federal levels were able to unionize and access statutory collective bargaining systems, including municipal and provincial police. During this period, police associations became more militant and aggressive, achieving significant monetary and non-monetary gains in bargaining, although rarely resorting to strikes (Jackson 1986: 5–6, 87). Currently, 74.7 per cent of public-sector workers in Canada are covered by a collective agreement (Statistics Canada 2011).

Police associations, with statutory authority to act as the independent representative of their members in bargaining and administering collective agreements, either through statutory designation or union certification process, are the norm in Canada. Currently, all municipal and provincial/regional police forces are covered by collective bargaining legislation, as is the other federal non-military police force, the Railway Constables (Canada 1996: 49).[4] In contrast, members of the armed forces do not have access to a statutory collective bargaining regime (Canada 2003a: ss. 2(1)).

In some Canadian jurisdictions, police are included within the general labour relations legislation. However, police bargaining is more commonly governed by separate labour legislation. This separate treatment reflects the widespread understanding that some common elements of labour relations schemes, such as work stoppages, are not appropriate or desirable for the police context. Such concerns tend to focus on the distinctive character and public importance of police work and the unique treatment of discipline in police organizations (Canada 1996: 49).

Not only have the majority of municipal and all provincial police forces unionized pursuant to these statutory schemes, producing more than 250 unionized police forces across the country, but policing is one of this country's most highly unionized occupations (Lynk 2006: paras. 44–5). Therefore, the RCMP is unique amongst Canadian police forces in that its members remain statutorily prohibited from either unionizing or choosing non-statutory independent collective workplace representation and are explicitly excluded from existing federal public-sector collective bargaining legislation (Canada 2003a: s.2(1)(d)). Instead, RCMP members are subject to a statutorily imposed non-union representation system that is not independent from management (Canada 1988: s.96).[5] The most significant differences between police and non-police labour relations lie in the treatment of bargaining impasse resolution and discipline. Most, although not all, jurisdictions prohibit police strikes or lockouts.[6] Where permitted, police work stoppages are substantially restricted, such as by Saskatchewan's requirement for exhausting the statutory conciliation process as a precondition to a work stoppage or British Columbia's essential service restrictions on work stoppage activity. Police strikes are rare and are regarded as something that "cuts to the very heart of the police–public relationship" (Jackson 1986: 128). Collective bargaining legislation applying to police—whether it is a separate statute or the general legislation—tends to substitute compulsory third-party interest arbitration for work stoppages as a bargaining dispute resolution mechanism. In some jurisdictions, arbitration may be triggered at the request of one party, while in others it requires the request of both parties or is at the discretion of the Minister of Labour.

A second difference lies in the treatment of discipline. Statutory codes of conduct for police generally remove discipline from the scope of bargaining and, therefore, from collective agreements. These codes establish disciplinary processes and penalties and ensure management retains control over discipline. However, police associations and negotiations may still have a role in discipline that falls outside these codes (Canadian Police College 1980: 102), and collective agreements commonly provide for police association representation for officers involved in the disciplinary process (Lynk 2006: para.56).

Overall, police collective agreements strongly resemble those for other occupations. Lynk's review of a representative sample of Canadian police collective agreements indicates that these agreements typically include comprehensive provisions dealing with working conditions; grievance procedures reflecting the "industrial model" of multistage grievance processes for non-disciplinary matters, including neutral third-party binding arbitration;

and general provision of a right to association representation in grievance and disciplinary proceedings (2006: paras. 59–67).

Police labour relations are regarded as relatively harmonious with constructive relations between police associations and management and with associations being well regarded by the public (Anderson 1980; Canadian Police College 1980: 119; Jackson 1986: 96). The distinct nature, culture, and organization of police work sets it apart from other occupations, and this has also influenced the structure and tenor of labour relations that have developed in this sector (Canada 1996; Canada, Department of the Solicitor General of New Brunswick 1992; Drennan 2003; Jackson 1986: 94). Distinguishing features of police work include long hours and shift work in dangerous and stressful environments, exposure to social problems, frustration with the judicial system, and significant public and departmental scrutiny and criticism. This social and professional isolation and shared hazards and difficulties engender strong camaraderie among police (Canada, Department of the Solicitor General of New Brunswick 1992: 35–7; Jackson 1986: 94–5), and the authoritarian personality associated with policing has been found to be a product of on-the-job socialization.[7]

The structure and character of management in police organizations are also distinct. Management is dominated by former officers drawn from the ranks who continue to identify strongly with their subordinates (Jackson 1986: 96; Van Maanen 1984). Second, unlike most workplaces, management structure is bifurcated: while day-to-day operational authority rests with the chief of police, policy and budget authority are located with governmental authorities or a board of police commissioners (Jackson 1986: 94). Consequently, collective bargaining takes place between the police association and the government or board, allowing management to remain neutral or even support the police association on particular bargaining issues (Jackson 1986: 94–5).

Nonetheless, tensions do exist, particularly around the question of the appropriate distribution of power between management and associations, and some senior officers and managers tend to regard associations as illegitimately usurping management's authority and jeopardizing its ability to discharge its obligations to the public (Canadian Police College 1980: 97; Drennan 2003; Jackson 1986: 88).

An interesting feature of some Canadian police labour relations systems is the restriction or prohibition of individual officer or police association affiliation with or membership in umbrella labour organizations or trade unions.[8] It is for this reason that most police have formed independent police "associations" rather than "trade unions." The explanations offered for these prohibitions centre on the concern that if permitted to directly or indirectly affiliate with organized labour, the ability of police to exercise "fair and impartial law enforcement," such as with respect to policing picket lines, will be compromised (Jackson 1978: 37).

These explanations reflect a dim view of trade union activities but are representative of police management and government views. Both historically and currently, police at all levels in Canada are involved in controlling and maintaining peace during labour disputes and picketing. Indeed, some contend that controlling labour was a key reason for the creation of both the Northwest Mounted Police (from which the RCMP arose) and the Ontario Provincial Police in the late nineteenth and early twentieth centuries (Hall and de Lint 2003: 221). Nonetheless, there does not appear to be evidence that a labour threat to impartial policing is a legitimate contemporary concern.

DEVELOPMENT OF NON-UNION EMPLOYEE REPRESENTATION IN THE RCMP

Non-union representation in the RCMP has developed over many decades, and five distinct eras can be discerned: prohibition, suppression and substitution, a resort to legal challenges, revitalization or retrenchment of the program, and the current period of revitalized legal challenge. As explained further in what follows, introduction and early development of non-union representation in the Force resulted from internal pressures expressed in RCMP members' open rebellion against oppressive, militaristic management in the context of a rapidly changing society, labour relations environment, policing practices, and consequent threat of unionization. By the mid 1980s, the limits of change that could be realized from internal member pressures appeared to be exhausted, and supporters of RCMP unionization turned to legal channels. These efforts created a significant and sustained external legal threat of unionization, pushing the Force to modify its non-union representation system and avoid unionization by better responding to RCMP members' needs. After a decade of calm, this external legal threat has reemerged.

Era of Prohibition

From the very beginning of the RCMP and its predecessor organizations until the early 1970s, the federal government and RCMP management maintained a position of uncompromising denial of any form of workplace representation for members, which was reinforced by statutory prohibitions and sanctions.

The RCMP was created in 1920 by the effective merger of two federal police forces: the Royal North West Mounted Police (dating from 1873) and the Dominion Police (established in 1868; Canada 1920; King 1997: 51–2). Reflecting the paramilitary nature of these forces and their primary role in establishing order in Canada's frontier—including suppressing labour unrest—the attitude of the government and Force Commissioners was that of explicit prohibition on any form of collective employee action or association with labour organizations. This period in history, and particularly the post–World War I era, was marked by significant and destabilising labour unrest in many countries, making policy makers fearful of public uprisings threatening the state. These events included police strikes and incidents of police refusing to control labour demonstrators. Consequently, during this period, governments sought to suppress police unionism (Forcese 1999: 103).

In 1918, members of both predecessor forces and, subsequently, the RCMP were expressly prohibited by an Order in Council (OIC) from engaging in any form of collective labour activities, including joining or associating with an array of labour or employer organizations, and violators were subject to instant dismissal (Canada 1918).

This OIC remained in force for almost six decades, until 1974, and the government included a similar prohibition in the Rules and Regulations governing the RCMP, introduced in 1945 (Canada 1945: s.31(a), 1981). These prohibitions arose from government's concern that allowing Force members to be identified with one side of a labour dispute would compromise the Force "Members might refuse to obey the command to subdue labour uprisings, or to fill in for a striking local police force, if their allegiance to their fellow employees came into conflict with such a command" (Canada 1918; *Delisle* 1999: para. 93).

Until the mid-twentieth century, collective bargaining was overwhelmingly a private-sector phenomenon in Canada. Few public-sector workers had access to statutory collective bargaining, although even during this time the broad, sanction-backed prohibitions imposed on RCMP members were exceptional. However, by the late 1970s, most Canadian public-sector workers at the municipal, provincial, and federal levels, including police, were able to unionize and access statutory collective bargaining systems. Meanwhile, the RCMP underwent little change and retained its historically paramilitary practices.[9]

Although the 1967 PSSRA established a comprehensive statutory collective bargaining scheme for most federal government and public-sector workers, it explicitly excluded RCMP members (Canada 1967: s.2(1)(e) "employee"). The Preparatory Committee on Collective Bargaining in the Public Service had recommended that RCMP members be excluded on the basis that the nature of the Force's duties and its militaristic code of conduct were inconsistent with participation in an employee association, raising the familiar concern about divided loyalty and obeying orders (Canada, Preparatory Committee on Collective Bargaining in the Public Sector 1965). In contrast, the 1968 Woods Task Force report recommended extending collective bargaining to private and public police officers, subject to limitations on work stoppages and substitution of binding arbitration (Canada 1969: paras. 439–40). Nonetheless, RCMP members were excluded from federal public- and private-sector labour legislation

(Canada 1967, 1972). The federal government and RCMP management remained determined to deny RCMP members collective employee representation, and the issue of RCMP member unionization did not come to the fore until 1972.

Suppression and Substitution: Origins of Non-Union Employee Representation

This uncompromising ban on labour activity began to yield to and was ultimately unable to wholly resist the broader social and public-sector labour relations changes of the 1960s and 1970s, which ignited RCMP member militancy and resulted in establishment of, first, an *ad hoc* RCMP staff representatives program in 1972, replaced by the Division Staff Relations Representatives program (DSRRP) in 1974.[10]

By the early 1970s, government and the RCMP Commissioner were no longer able to deny RCMP members' growing discontent and interest in an employee association. Widespread member dissatisfaction and frustration, centering on overtime and transfer policies and allegations of unfair and arbitrary discipline and dismissals, led members to complain publicly in the media about their working conditions and lack of grievance mechanism (Hardy and Ponak 1983: 89; Reed 1984: 86). During the late 1960s, joint operations between RCMP and other police forces became common, and this close contact with other police officers highlighted for RCMP members the relative arbitrariness of RCMP management in regard to discipline and transfers and the inferiority of their own working conditions, compensation, and benefits (Reed 1984: 86; RCMP 2003: 10).

The triggering event for creation of an RCMP employee representation system is commonly identified as a July 1972 *Maclean's* magazine article written by a former RCMP corporal, Jack Ramsay (Ramsay 1972). Ramsay excoriated RCMP management and its system of military discipline and its effect on members. He described the "tyranny" and "caste system" of RCMP management, criticising RCMP rules as "more appropriate to a penal colony than a police force" and "a throwback to a military age" (Ramsay 1972: 22, 68). Ramsay also painted a stark picture of members' vulnerability in dealing with management in the absence of an employee association, contending that "Every member knows that if he complains, he'll be labelled a trouble-maker. . . Policemen in other forces have their associations. The Mounted policeman has no one. He's alone" (1972: 20).

Ramsay's article captured the attention of government and the Force. Members of the Opposition in Parliament called for an independent commission of inquiry, creation of an ombudsman for RCMP members, and independent review of RCMP disciplinary procedures and the Commissioner's Standing Orders (CSOs) (Canada, Commissioner of the Royal Canadian Mounted Police. 1974; Deukmedjian 2002: 48).

Responding to Unrest: The Ad Hoc *Representation System*

In an effort to diffuse this tide of dissatisfaction and pressure and the attendant growing support among members for unionization, the Force quickly established an *ad hoc* representation scheme consisting of annual meetings between member representatives and RCMP management to discuss staff matters (Reed 1984: 149; RCMP 2003: 10; Sawatsky 1980: 233–4). Although most representatives were appointed by Division Commanding Officers instead of being elected by members, it appears that may have been a matter of expediency rather than of design (Reed 1984: 150–1). However, management made it clear that these meetings were for the purposes of communication, and the representative system was a vehicle for neither individual member complaints nor negotiations (Reed 1984: 151–2). Three annual meetings were held under this system between 1972 and 1974.

This *ad hoc* program proved ineffective. Although issues were discussed at the annual meetings, no resolution was reached on any matter (RCMP 2003: 11). The Commissioner's insistence that meeting minutes be confidential further inflamed member discontent and dissent (RCMP 2003: 11). Hardy and Ponak attribute the program's failure to three key weaknesses: workload, as representatives' responsibilities were supplementary to their regular duties; a single representative per division was inadequate for some larger divisions; and the program lacked a formal structure for communicating member issues (1983: 90). Member representatives indicated that the program lacked credibility among members because of the lack of co-operation and support from management, including Commanding Officers, lack of cooperation with Treasury Board, and members' fear of management reprisal for lodging grievances (Reed 1984: 153).

This *ad hoc* program has also been criticized as avoiding the underlying causes of member dissatisfaction and reflecting an attitude that the discontent was due to "a few troublemakers" rather than wider problems within the Force (Sawatsky 1980: 232). Nonetheless, this *ad hoc* system provided the foundation for the current employee representation system.

Capitulating to Rebellion: The Division Staff Relations Representatives Program

The real turning point came in May 1974, when RCMP members held meetings in British Columbia, Ontario, and Québec to discuss establishing an association. Hundreds (and, in Ottawa, thousands) of members attended the meetings. Votes were conducted at some of these meetings, and the results demonstrated overwhelming support for repeal of the 1918 OIC and pursuing an association (Sawatsky 1980: 229). The federal Solicitor General attended the Montreal meeting and pledged to seek to remove the 1918 OIC and improve RCMP officer compensation (Sawatsky 1980: 230).

This show of determination moved Commissioner Nadon to quickly call for two *ad hoc* representatives' meeting to be held that month (Reed 1984; Sawatsky 1980: 236). The solicitor general opened the first meeting, stating that while the government wanted to improve morale, it wasn't interested in an RCMP union but supported the existing *ad hoc* representation system (Reed 1984: 154). At the second meeting, RCMP management announced members would receive a substantial pay increase and overtime pay (Sawatsky 1980: 235). The 1918 OIC was repealed soon thereafter (Canada 1974).

Commissioner Nadon agreed to meet with *ad hoc* member representatives to hear members' concerns, propose a fourteen-point framework for a more formal consultation program, and undertake a study into employee associations (*Delisle* 1999: para. 23; RCMP 2003: 11). Representatives held a referendum on this proposal and reported "overwhelming acceptance" in all except Québec's "C" Division association (RCMP 2003: 11).

The Commissioner created a fact-finding group in May 1974 to assess "the effects, advantages and disadvantages, of police associations on operations, personnel, and management" and appointed Staff Sergeant Middleton to produce a report (Middleton 1974: i, v). In the resulting report, however, Middleton sought to distance himself from the fact-finding group's favourable views of police associations. He also drafted the modest report recommendations, which he described as: "the product of my personal analysis of the material at hand" rather than reflecting the views of the group (Middleton 1974: vi).

Meanwhile, in the foreword to the report, Commissioner Nadon expressly opposed an association: "I wish to make the Force's position very clear; the Force is opposed to the formation of an association or union of members and this position has been made known to our Minister" (Middleton 1974: i). The Commissioner also rejected several of the report's recommendations, notably those suggesting investigating an association, because the Force was already implementing the DSRRP (Middleton 1974: i–ii).

The new DSRRP was governed by the Commissioner's Standing Orders (Division Staff Relations Representatives Program) and the Force's administrative policy manual. The DSRRP was monitored and coordinated by RCMP management through the Staff Relations Program Office, which was administered by a commissioned officer, the staff relations program officer (SRPO), who was selected by and reported directly to the Commissioner, and the program was subject to bi-annual review by the RCMP (RCMP 2003: 30, 60).

The DSRRP included member representatives from each division (DSRRs) elected to two-year terms, with no term limit. DSRRs' salaries were funded by Division Commanding Officers from each division's budget, and DSRRs returned to the regular force upon leaving office (Hardy and Ponak 1983: 90–1; RCMP 2003: 11). The communication and consultation structure was also improved to involve four consultation processes: (1) authorizing more contact and consultation between DSRRs and management, (2) permitting DSRRs to attempt informal grievance resolution and to offer assistance and advice in the formal grievance process, (3) including DSRRs on committees as members, observers, or liaisons, and (4) holding semi-annual conferences of DSRRs and senior RCMP officials to consider nationally relevant issues, although the Commissioner retained final decision-making power on all issues (Hardy and Ponak 1983: 91–3).

Treasury Board and the RCMP's Compensation Branch determined RCMP member compensation. The branch, assisted by the Pay Research Bureau, made annual compensation recommendations to Treasury Board based on comparator police forces. Two DSRRs, appointed liaisons to the RCMP's Pay and Compensation Committee, had no role in preparing the recommendation but simply received updates on the compensation decision-making process. These updates were not to be disclosed to other representatives or members, who received only the final decision (Hardy and Ponak 1983: 93).

The DSRRP was the subject of several critical assessments. The most favourable evaluation was offered by Dennis Forcese in 1980. He compared the DSRRP favourably with police associations across Canada, noting that it "may by its advocates be described as a mode of 'worker participatory democracy'" and that it "has placated membership, preserved the RCMP esprit, and has done so at no inconvenience to the public" (1980: 118). Forcese attributed the success the program had in offering participation to RCMP members to two factors: what members and DSRRs characterized as the "constant latent threat" of unionization and management goodwill (Forcese 1980: 113).

In Forcese's view, DSRRs had achieved significant input into management decisions and perhaps more than in unionized police forces with less cordial management relations (Forcese 1980: 114). Even regarding compensation and benefits, he concluded the DSRRP had some influence due to DSRRs' close monitoring of police salaries, creating member expectations which then influenced decision making by the Compensation Branch (Forcese 1980: 177). Forcese also found some improvement regarding discipline and management actions and reduced fear of reprisals for bringing complaints (Forcese 1980: 117, 118).

Writing in 1983, Hardy and Ponak offered the most critical assessment of the DSRRP, concluding that it reflected many shortcomings common to federal government consultation systems (94–5). Specifically, it suffered from ambiguous terms of reference, addressed limited issues, provided no input on compensation, was only advisory in nature, and operated with secrecy, weakening its role as an employee association (Hardy and Ponak 1983: 94–5). The authors suggested broadening DSRRs' roles on committees, revising the compensation process to permit representative participation and possibly fact finding or arbitration, and outside review of grievances (1983: 95).

However, they were sceptical that, in the long run, such changes would stave off members' demand for collective bargaining and warned that member dissatisfaction and pressure for bargaining were growing and that management would eventually have to choose between "strongly resisting, with the help of existing legislation, any union campaign or of taking a hands-off stance and permitting events to run their course" (Hardy and Ponak 1983: 96).

Similarly, Gary Reed characterized the DSRRP as a system that coopted internal dissent into the Force's existing structure, was simply senior management's response to the threat of unionization, and simply operated as a means for management to receive feedback from members, which the Force had previously lacked (1984: 161, 175, 183). Reed contended that "[w]hat power the DSRRs do have is derived from the electoral process and the lingering fear of an association. That power is, incidentally, quite considerable and represents a major constraint on management" (1984: 183).

Finally, as part of the Challenge 2000 program review exercise discussed in what follows, the DSRRP surveyed a sample of RCMP members. Although the survey report concluded that, overall, the DSRRP served RCMP membership well, the specific responses reveal a mixed portrait of the program (Pollara 2001: 8). Although the survey found the DSRRP was widely known by members and accessible, it also found that its communication, effectiveness, and representation of minority groups within the Force were lacking. Survey responses also demonstrated a substantial level of dissatisfaction with the DSRRP and negative perceptions of the program's effectiveness, including substantial concern that DSRRs had no influence or were too close to management (Pollara 2001; see Tables 9.1, 9.2, and 9.3).

Resort to Law

Since 1974, a central and persistent figure in establishing independent associations and efforts to access unionization for RCMP members has been

Table 9.1   Satisfaction with DSRRP

	Very Satisfied	Somewhat Satisfied	Neutral	Not Very Satisfied	Very Dissatisfied	Don't Know/ Refused
			(%)			
Satisfaction with Services of the DSRRP	15	32	30	14	8	1
Satisfaction with the Degree of Consultation	5	20	34	26	12	3

Source: Pollara 2001: 12, 44.

Table 9.2 Effectiveness of DSRRP and Pay Council

	Very Effective	Somewhat Effective	Neutral	Not Very Effective	Not at All Effective	Don't Know/ Refused
	(%)					
DSRRP effectiveness at representing members	8	28	36	20	7	n/a
DSRRP effectiveness at dealing with management						
Divisional management	3	19	40	27	7	n/a
Headquarters management	2	17	42	28	8	n/a
Perceived effectiveness of Pay Council	3	19	45	21	9	3

Source: Pollara 2001: 45, 49, 51.

Table 9.3 Reasons Members Would Not Seek DSRR Assistance

	%
No reason would not seek DSRR assistance	63
Reasons would not seek DSRR assistance	
DSRRs have no impact/influence	18
DSRRs too close to management	14
Don't know my DSRR	8
DSRRs not easily available	8
Don't trust my DSRRs	7
Don't feel comfortable with DSRR	5
DSRR not experienced enough	3
Don't like my DSRR	2
Don't support the DSRRP	2
Don't know/refused	4

Source: Pollara 2001: 45, 49, 51.

Gaétan Delisle. Delisle joined the RCMP in 1969 and, before retiring in 2009, spent more than thirty years as an elected representative in the RCMP non-union representation system, established and presided over several independent RCMP member associations, and has been the driving force behind an ongoing series of legal challenges to the Force and its non-union representation system between 1986 and 1999.

Beginning in the early 1970s, several independent RCMP member associations formed for the purposes of representing members in collective bargaining and gaining access to unionization. The early associations had little traction (*Delisle* 1999: para. 106), and the first significant association was formed in 1979: the national Association of 17 Divisions (17 Divisions). Beginning in the mid-1980s, a number of other independent associations emerged: L'Association des Membres de la Division "C" in 1985 (Division "C," later renamed L'Association des Membres de la Police Montée du Québec, or AMPMQ); a regional association in Ontario in 1990; in 1994 the "E" Division Members' Association in British Columbia (later the British Columbia Mounted Police Professional Association, or BCMPPA); the Capital Region Association in 1995; the Mounted Police Association of Ontario in 1998 (MPAO); and, in 2010, the Mounted Police Professional Association of Canada (MPPA) was formed as an association of the BCMPPA, AMPMQ, and MPAO.

Faced with the RCMP's steadfast refusal to recognize any independent association, Delisle and the associations resorted to legal means to compel the RCMP to achieve their goals. They made repeated attempts between 1986 and 1999, first to secure certification of associations under existing collective bargaining statutes to legally require the RCMP to recognize certified associations as the exclusive bargaining agents for RCMP members, later turning to charter litigation to have statutory exclusions from existing collective bargaining legislation struck out as contrary to the Charter, and trying to amend the Canada Labour Code (CLC) to include RCMP members (Canada 1997).

What Delisle and the associations were seeking was formal standing for the associations to negotiate collective agreements, including compensation; to have access to an independent procedure for grievances; to have a voice on issues such as pensions, scheduling, discipline, and the Force's rules; and to address alleged anti-francophone discrimination (Robinson 1987; Slotnick 1986).

Government and RCMP management objections to RCMP access to statutory collective bargaining in these cases—as they do today—centred on arguments that unionization would threaten the RCMP's ability to operate as a stable, reliable, and neutral national police force and that because of the Force's unique character, there would be no substitute for its services if RCMP members engaged in a work slow-down or full strike (MPAO 2009: para.82). The government has argued that the Force's national police services (such as national identification and forensic services), international responsibilities, national security roles, and availability to provide services when another police force or prison guards strikes could not be fulfilled by another police force or the armed forces (*Delisle* 1990a: 60–1, 1997: para. 7, 1999: para. 113; MPAO 2009: para. 82). The Force has also expressed concern that unionization would interfere with the RCMP policing picket lines during labour disputes (Slotnick 1986). The government and RCMP maintain these objections today.

Although Delisle had established the 17 Division association to become the certified union for RCMP members nationwide, he soon concluded that it was too difficult to organize on a national basis (Cordon 1995). In 1985, he formed a provincial association in Québec, Division "C," as part of a plan to first certify associations in various provinces under collective bargaining legislation, then later establish a national union for RCMP members (Maser 1986; The Ottawa Citizen 1986; Shalom 1986).

In 1986, Division "C" filed an unsuccessful application with the Canada Labour Relations Board (CLRB) for union certification under the Canada Labour Code (CLC) to represent RCMP members in Québec (L'Association des Membres de la Division "C" 1986). Eighty-seven per cent of Québec RCMP members had signed membership cards in support of this application (The Ottawa Citizen 1986).

A pivotal change in the Canadian legal environment had occurred in 1982: adoption of the Canadian Charter of Rights and Freedoms (Charter) and in particular the s.2(d) Charter guarantee of the freedom of association (FOA). The Charter supersedes all other laws such that any law or other state action inconsistent with the Charter may be declared invalid. The Canadian labour movement had initially been optimistic about the potential for the Charter—particularly the FOA—to protect and enhance labour rights. This optimism was short lived; in spring 1987, the Supreme Court of Canada (SCC) issued three concurrent decisions, commonly known as the labour Trilogy, explicitly ruling that the Charter FOA did not protect collective bargaining or strike activity.[11] Nonetheless, RCMP members and their independent associations launched several Charter-based legal challenges, persisting in their efforts even after the Trilogy was issued.

The CLRB decision to uphold the exclusion of RCMP members from statutory collective bargaining legislation prompted Delisle and the associations to refocus their efforts on challenging the constitutionality of these statutory exclusions as contrary to RCMP members' Charter rights and freedoms and amending the exclusionary legislation.

In 1987, Delisle, then also AMPMQ president, challenged the provisions of the PSSRA and CLC excluding RCMP members from collective bargaining regimes as unjustifiable violations of RCMP members' Charter freedoms of association, expression, and equality rights. However, relying on the Trilogy, majorities of the Superior Court in 1989, the Québec Court of Appeal in 1997, and the SCC in 1999 rejected these claims (*Delisle* 1990a, 1997, 1999). Having exhausted the possibilities of Charter assistance, this SCC decision marked the end of legal challenges to the RCMP's non-union status for nearly a decade.

The only remaining channel for Delisle and the associations was to change the law, and they pursued numerous unsuccessful attempts to pass private members' bills to either remove statutory prohibitions on RCMP unionization or provide separate RCMP collective bargaining legislation (Canada 1997, Bill C-336; Canada 2003b, Bill S-24; Canada 2004, Bill S-12; Canada 2005, Bill S-23; Canada 2006, Bill C-392; Canada 2009, Bill C-437).

Delisle and his efforts have had a divisive influence within government and the RCMP, eliciting both fierce support and opposition among RCMP members and management and within the SRRP. Many regard Delisle as a troublemaker who has been difficult to deal with because of the strong support he enjoys from the great majority of RCMP members in Québec who joined his independent associations and elected him as DSRR or Staff Relations Representative (SRR) for decades (*Delisle* 2002: para. 21).

A troubling reflection of the RCMP's determination to resist the rise of independent associations, unionization, and, perhaps, its frustration with Delisle and his collaborators personally are reports of reprisals, including discipline, suffered by RCMP members who participated in supporting, establishing, and operating independent member associations (*Delisle* 1990a, 1999: paras. 103–5). Pointing to use of the CSO prohibition on alternative programs and application of Code of Conduct standards to prevent unionization to bring disciplinary proceedings against RCMP members who participated in supporting, establishing, and operating alternative member associations, two Justices in the 1999 SCC decision concluded that RCMP management had subjected members to practices that would likely have qualified as prohibited unfair labour practices under the PSSRA (Canada, Commissioner of the Royal Canadian Mounted Police, 1997 s.3(2); *Delisle* 1999: paras. 103–5).[12]

Delisle himself claims to have experienced harassment, retaliation, and a series of internal RCMP investigations as a result of his association activities (*Delisle* 1997: para. 3). In particular, Delisle identifies his expulsion from the DSRR Caucus and the discipline he received as a result of political activities.[13] In 1990, Delisle, then a DSRR, was voted to be expelled from the DSRR Caucus by other DSRRs for "misconduct and irresponsibility." The federal court, in granting an interim injunction returning Delisle to the caucus, concluded that this expulsion was clearly related to his unionizing efforts (*Delisle* 1990b).

Shortly thereafter, in 1993, the Commissioner introduced a CSO prohibiting DSRRS from engaging in activities "prejudicial to the goals and objectives of the DSRRP" or promoting "alternative programs in conflict with the non-union status of the DSRRP." Delisle contends that this change was in response to the federal court ruling (Delisle 1998: paras. 27, 32). The following year, Delisle and two other DSRRs were disciplined under this CSO for attending and participating in a panel discussion at the first meeting of the "E" Division Member Association (*Delisle* 1999: para. 104).

Revitalization or Retrenchment?

Once again, in the face of serious threats to the existing DSRRP in the form of Delisle's legal challenges and a real threat of unionization, between 1987 and 2003, the RCMP and DSRRP engaged in a series of efforts to protect the program.

A joint committee was created at the 1987 annual management–DSRRP conference to review the DSRRP. The resulting report, issued in October 1988, found unclear and differing expectations existed about the program and attributed this to widespread lack of member awareness of the original framework proposed in 1974, which had never been enshrined in policy (RCMP 2003: 12). Following the report's recommendation, in December 1988, the Commissioner expanded the original fourteen-point framework to twenty-two points and included these in a separate section of the RCMP Administration Manual (RCMP 2003: 12). The following year, the DSRRP was formalized when the RCMP Regulations were amended to require the RCMP to "provide for representation of the interests of all members with respect to staff relations matters" (Canada 1988: s.96).

In 1998, driven by concern that Delisle's Charter challenge might succeed at the SCC, the Commissioner approved the DSRRP's request to undertake what became the Challenge 2000 Review, with its final report issued in December 2003 (RCMP 2003: 14–5). Tasked with determining "the strongest and most effective possible system of representation," it ultimately recommended maintaining the DSRRP instead of an independent association (RCMP 2003: 16). In addition to renaming the program the Staff Relations Representatives Program (SRRP), the review led to some substantive changes to the program (the SRRP is outlined in detail in a later section).

One of the most significant changes was reorganization of the program's legal foundation and governing instruments. At the time of the Review, the DSRRP was founded on RCMP Regulation s. 96 and the CSOs and policies located in a chapter of the RCMP's administration manual. The review led to a formal SRRP constitution being adopted in 2002 (RCMP 2003: 36) and a written agreement between the Commissioner and the SRRP in October 2002, and RCMP Administration Manual provisions relating to the program now dealt with in the Constitution and Agreement were removed (RCMP 2003: 7, 27, 50; Canada 2003).

The program changes arising from the *Review* do reflect some elements that the report expressly attributed to pressure from members supporting formation of an association and collective bargaining rights. For instance, recognition that failure to address sustained member dissatisfaction could result in a member uprising such as seen in the 1970s underlay the Commissioner's agreement to a limited third-party external process for unresolved issues (RCMP 2003: 17, 59–60).

Moreover, some changes resulting from the review seem to reflect a common desire by management and the SRRP to limit dissent—particularly dissent that might foster support for an association. The report indicated that a great majority of Sub-representatives, current and past DSRRs, and all Commanding Officers surveyed agreed that "senior management should be asked to express its support [for the SRRP] as being the only representative labour relations program that would be recognized by the RCMP" (RCMP 2003: 31). The report attributes this largely to "the perceived need for members' interests to be expressed by a single national voice in order to be treated seriously by management" (RCMP 2003: 31). Similarly, the report explains that, because the SRR Caucus is expected to make reasonable efforts to "permit differing views to be submitted and argued in its meetings and in its other forms of deliberation," enforceable sanctions are needed for any SRR or Sub-representative for violating the constitution or other specified criteria (RCMP 2003: 45).

Discomfort with the idea that the SRR program might take on any characteristics of a conventional police association is apparent in views expressed in the review report about membership dues. The report explained that introducing dues "could subtly change the nature of the Program and lead to a more adversarial relationship with management" and noted that overwhelming majorities of current and past DSRRs, Commanding Officers, and Sub-representatives surveyed indicated that financial contributions by members were unnecessary and contrary to the best interests of the program (RCMP 2003: 29).

Revitalized Legal Challenges

In 2007, the legal landscape changed significantly when the SCC in the Health Services and Support—Facilities Subsector Bargaining Association (2007) decision rejected the Trilogy, instead ruling that the Charter FOA protects collective bargaining. This startling decision was widely regarded as offering tremendous potential for unions and workers to use the FOA to protect and substantially extend collective bargaining rights. This decision revitalized the labour movement within the RCMP. After nearly a decade with legislative change as the only possible route to securing recognition and bargaining rights, Charter litigation once again offered an opportunity for the independent RCMP associations to achieve their goals.

Shortly after the SCC decision was issued, the MPAO and BCMPPA launched a new Charter challenge. In April 2009, the Ontario Superior Court ruled on this case, concluding that the statutory entrenchment of the SRRP as the sole bargaining vehicle for RCMP members was an unjustifiable denial of RCMP members' FOA rights (*MPAO* 2009). This decision was based on the court's findings that the SRRP is not an independent association formed or selected by RCMP members and that "the interaction between the SRRP and management cannot reasonably be described as a process of collective bargaining" (*MPAO* 2009: para. 60). The court provided an eighteen-month grace period before the offending legislative provision would be of no force and effect. The court found no violation of RCMP members' equality rights and denied the claim that prohibitions on RCMP members' communication violated their FOA and freedom of expression rights.

For a time, it appeared that independent RCMP associations had finally succeeded in using the law to achieve access of a bargaining regime outside of the existing non-union representation system, if not necessarily gaining bargaining rights or statutory recognition for existing independent RCMP member associations. However, the government responded to the Court ruling by introducing a bill which, if passed, would have complied with the ruling yet avoided the possibility of any of the independent associations gaining collective bargaining rights for RCMP members. In June 2010, as the grace period was running out, government introduced Bill C-43 (Canada 2010). Bill C-43 would have provided RCMP members with a mechanism to opt for representation by a certified bargaining agent determined by the Public Service Labour Relations Board, with the default being a new non-union joint consultation system, increased Commissioner authority over hiring, discipline, termination, and promotion decisions, and a restructured grievance and discipline system. However, Bill C-43 was never passed, dying on the order paper when Parliament was prorogued in March 2011.

In April 2011, the associations' success was undermined when the Charter landscape changed once again. The SCC issued the *Ontario (Attorney General) v. Fraser* decision, which has been interpreted as significantly limiting the scope and application of the Charter FOA to collective bargaining. Relying on this decision, the Ontario Court of Appeal in 2012 overturned the earlier superior court decision, concluding that imposition of the SRRP does not meet the necessary legal standard of rendering the exercise of RCMP members' FOA "effectively impossible" and, therefore, does not violate the Charter FOA (*MPAO* 2012). The court pointed to three factors supporting its decision. First, RCMP members have been able to form voluntary associations, such as those bringing this legal challenge. Second, the SRRP offers an extensive consultative process between management and SRRs allowing RCMP members an opportunity to reach collective goals through associational activity. The court ruled that independence from management and opportunity for employees to choose their representative are not necessary characteristics for an employee representative organization to be constitutionally adequate. Finally, the Legal Fund, by providing legal representation to its members in workplace-related matters, supports and complements the SRRP (*MPAO* 2012: paras. 121–36). In reaching this conclusion, the court described the Legal Fund as "entirely self-governed, independent and autonomous, with independent, democratically elected directors and officers" (*MPAO* 2012: para. 132). This characterization is addressed next. The associations were granted leave to appeal this decision to the SCC.

Charter jurisprudence is in a period of rapid change, and it is impossible to predict whether the SCC's ruling in this appeal will finally grant the independent associations access to bargaining rights or whether it will mark the definitive conclusion to decades of litigation over RCMP member representation rights.

CURRENT STAFF RELATIONS REPRESENTATION PROGRAM

Since 2002, operation of the SRRP has been governed by the Constitution and Agreement between the SRRP and the Commissioner (Royal Canadian Mounted Police Staff Relations Representative Program [SRRP] 2012a, 2012b).[14] The Constitution now explicitly recognizes the SRRP as the "official labour relations program for representing members" and formalizes the SRRP's purpose as:

> [T]o promote mutually beneficial relations between Force management and the wider membership. To such ends, the SRR Program is mandated to provide members across the RCMP with fair and equitable representation in labour relations matters and to facilitate their participation in the development and implementation of Force policies and programs.
>
> (2012a: Arts. 4.A, 2)[15]

The review report emphasized the importance of senior management's introduction of the word "participation" into the purpose clause, contending that it "involves an important step beyond simply being consulted and informed about management's plans or decisions" and that it is meant to demonstrate that the Commissioner and senior management are willing to facilitate such a process (RCMP 2003: 36). This commitment to participation is echoed in the Agreement (2012b: Arts. 8–10, 25–27). Nonetheless, final decisions remain with management, although the Commissioner has agreed to consider, with SRRP Caucus, referring unresolved issues to a third party for advice (SRRP 2012b: Arts. 25, 36).

The SRRP involves full-time SRRs and part-time Sub-representatives elected by members within their own division or zone, the Program Office Administrator, and other SRRP staff (SRRP 2012a: Art. 5, 2012b: Art. 3). There is at least one SRR per division and at least two Sub-representatives per division or zone, and currently there are forty-one full-time SRRs and approximately 150 Sub-representatives (SRRP 2012b: Arts. 4–6, Appendix A).

The SRRP Caucus, the collective body of all SRRs, meets four times a year and is responsible for submitting an annual report to members and the RCMP's Senior Executive Committee and for establishing a number of national committees and subcommittees focusing on specific projects, paralleling the national RCMP policy centres (SRRP 2012a: Arts. 6, 9, 13, 18). Regional, headquarters, and divisional caucuses are composed of SRRs and Sub-representatives from the relevant region or division and are the program contact points for management. These caucus members attend division management meetings involving issues affecting members' terms and conditions of employment (SRRP 2012a: Arts. 10, 11).

The National Executive Committee (NEC) is composed of two SRRs elected by SRR Caucus for three-year terms and who constitute the National Executive (NE) and five Regional Caucus Chairs consisting of one SRR from each of the four regions and from national headquarters elected to the NEC for one-year terms by members in those areas (SRRP 2012a: Arts. 8, 9, 2012b: Art. 16). NE is the presiding body of SRR Caucus and the governing body of the SRRP between SRR Caucus meetings (SRRP 2012a: Art. 8.F). It is also the formal contact point between SRR Caucus, its committees, the Commissioner, RCMP senior management, and the Minister of Public Safety. The NE normally attends and participates in meetings of the RCMP Senior Management Team and the Commissioner may allow the NE to participate in these meetings upon invitation (SRRP 2012a: Arts.8.G-I, 2012b: Art. 17, 19, 20).

Following the Challenge 2000 Review, the RCMP modified the program structure and governance. This included replacing the SRPO position, selected by and reporting to the Commissioner, with a Program Office Administrator (POA) selected by and accountable to the SRRP Caucus (RCMP 2003: 60; SRRP 2012a: Art. 5, 2012b: Art. 3). A further measure of independence was RCMP management agreeing to set an annual, negotiated budget for the SRRP, with the potential for additional funding where the SRRP can make a "business case" for it (RCMP 2003: 7; SRRP 2012b: Arts. 11–12). Nonetheless, the POA is responsible for ensuring the SRRP budget is managed according to Treasury Board directives and is administratively accountable to the budget approval authorities (SRR 2012b: Art. 13).

Responding to the 2001 survey findings that communication with members was a key weakness of the DSRR, management agreed to provide the SRRP with free access to its communication systems and allowed the SRRP to issue a national newsletter "representing the majority view of the Caucus" (SRRP 2012b: Art. 32(c)). However, significant, explicit restrictions are placed on external communications by the SRRP and RCMP members. Notable is the obligation on the SRRP not to "communicate with the Media, Minister of Public Safety, Parliament, Senate or the general public concerning RCMP policing programs or activities or in matters involving provincial or federal law enforcement or security policy without the permission of the Commissioner" (SRRP 2012b: Art. 33). Limited exceptions exist for NE or SRRs with permission from NE to communicate with the media, Minister of Public Safety, Parliament, Senate, or the general public on behalf of the SRRP and RCMP members regarding matters relating to terms and conditions of employment and work, including requiring that "communications regarding differences with management will be made only after full consultation has been exhausted" and that copies of all media advisories and notice of news media interviews be provided to the Commissioner (SRRP

2012b: Art. 34).[16] As explained in the review report, though referring to the more restrictive limits on communications that existed under the original 2002 Agreement, this is a "very important new policy without which it is difficult to imagine that the Program could be effective" (RCMP 2003: 44). These limitations exist alongside the long-standing s.41 RCMP regulation limitation on member communications providing that "a member shall not publicly criticize, ridicule, petition or complain about the administration, operation, objectives or policies of the Force, unless authorized by law."

Eligibility, nomination, and election requirements and procedures for SRRs and Sub-representatives are governed by provisions of the RCMP Administration Manual and are unchanged from the time of the DSRRP. To be eligible for nomination, an RCMP member must ensure that acting as an SRR or Sub-representative won't lead to "any actual, apparent or potential conflict of interests," in accordance with the requirements of the RCMP Act (Canada 1985a: s.37(d); RCMP n.d.: Part XVI, s. 2.1.3). Proposed candidates are also required to declare any outside activities that may violate the conflict-of-interests prohibition, "including any offices held in any organization that represents or provides representation to members of the RCMP or any other police force or their personnel" (RCMP n.d.: Part XVI, s. 2.2). These limitations appear to be clearly directed at and could well disqualify RCMP members holding office in one of the independent RCMP associations or in the umbrella police association organization, the Canadian Police Association, which supports the efforts of the independent associations.

THE BROADER RCMP LABOUR RELATIONS SYSTEM

A comprehensive discussion of the current RCMP employee representation system must also address the broader RCMP labour relations system which includes Pay Council, the Legal Fund, and the grievance, discipline, and non-disciplinary sanction systems (referred to here as "grievance and discipline" systems). This section describes each component of the labour relations system, noting the SRRP's role—or absence of role—in each.

Pay Council

Treasury Board holds the ultimate statutory authority to determine RCMP members' compensation (Canada 1985b, s.22) and, until the Pay Council was established in 1996, RCMP members lacked any formal system for input into compensation decisions.

Pay Council is composed of a neutral Chair, two SRRP representatives, and two management representatives. Pay Council solicits input from RCMP members and formulates a recommendation on pay and benefits to present to the Commissioner. If the Commissioner accepts this recommendation, it is then reviewed by the Minister of Public Safety. If the Minister approves the recommendation, then it is presented to Treasury Board on the Commissioner's behalf. Treasury Board then determines RCMP member pay and benefits. As Pay Council itself has noted, this process puts the Commissioner in a difficult position, both acting as employer representative and making compensation requests on members' behalf (RCMP Pay Council 1997: 1.1).

Notably, Pay Council does not directly negotiate or consult with Treasury Board, the final decision maker, but simply makes non-binding recommendations to the Commissioner based on consensus and collaboration (*Meredith* 2011: para. 15, 2013: para. 82). As such, its role "cannot be considered wholly equivalent to collective bargaining" (*Meredith* 2011: para. 72). Nonetheless, the existence of Pay Council has recently been characterized as one of the key features of the RCMP labour relations system permitting RCMP members to exercise their Charter FOA (*MPAO* 2012). In light of this, it is interesting to note that the 2001 DSRRP survey revealed little familiarity with Pay Council among RCMP members (and the Pay Council system has not changed substantially since that time), and less than a quarter of responding members characterized Pay Council as effective (Pollara 2001: 50–51; see Table 9.2).

Although RCMP compensation has remained in the range of the top three or four comparator forces and so it may be argued that Pay Council has served RCMP members well, the non-binding nature of the Pay Council process has recently come under scrutiny. In December 2008, after approving compensation increases, Treasury Board significantly reduced RCMP compensation increases without consulting Pay Council. This change was reflected in federal public-sector wage-control legislation passed shortly thereafter. The Federal Court of Appeal has held that this did not violate RCMP members' Charter FOA (*Meredith* 2013). These events highlight the tenuous nature of Pay Council mechanism.

Mounted Police Members' Legal Fund

The Legal Fund was established in 1997 by a group of DSRRs as a non-profit corporation for the purpose of providing legal funding to resolve issues between Legal Fund and the government which affect the members' "dignity or welfare" in cases where such funding is not available through an existing RCMP or government program (Legal Fund 2012a: 10). The creators of the Legal Fund recognized that a necessary element of member representation was missing from the DSRRP and remains absent from the SRRP: the ability to provide RCMP members with external legal opinions and legal representation. The SRRP is only permitted to request legal opinions from the Department of Justice. Treasury Board or the Commissioner receives and decides these requests, and there is no opportunity for funding legal representation for members. In some cases, prior to the existence of the Legal Fund, RCMP members had resorted to "passing the hat around," collecting donations from RCMP members to fund legal defences for members in employment-related civil and criminal matters.

The Legal Fund regards itself as "part of the overall labour relations regime within the RCMP" offering an "insurance policy" for members, providing private legal opinions and representation for qualifying Legal Fund members (Brown 2009: 4–5; Legal Fund 2005, 2012a: 7; *MPAO* 2012: para. 133).[17] The types of legal matters it has most commonly become involved in include assault, harassment, defamation, disability, promotion, and malicious prosecution (Legal Fund 2012a: 2). The Legal Fund has also intervened in recent cases addressing the nature of Charter protection of collective bargaining.[18] The Legal Fund also launched a Charter claim challenging government action limiting RCMP member compensation in disregard of the Pay Council process (*Meredith* 2011, 2013).

The Ontario Court of Appeal, in the MPAO Charter case discussed earlier, credited the Legal Fund with playing an important role in the ability of RCMP members to engage in collective pursuit of workplace goals and, therefore, to exercise their Charter FOA (MPAO 2012: para. 132). The court appeared to give great weight to its characterization of the Legal Fund as an independent organization, describing it as "funded exclusively by the dues of its members, and is entirely self-governed, independent and autonomous, with independent, democratically elected directors and officers" (*MPAO* 2012: para. 132). However, with the exception of financial independence, the court's description is difficult to tally with the realities of the structure and operation of the Legal Fund. The Legal Fund's governance, membership requirements, and limitations, conditions, and procedure for Legal Fund members to receive funding indicate that the organization and its operations are intertwined with the SRRP and RCMP, and membership and its benefits are not available to all RCMP members.

Unlike the SRRP, the Legal Fund is financially independent of the RCMP, obtaining its resources from dues paid by its members (Legal Fund 2005: Art. 5.04). Charging Legal Fund members $4 per pay period, the Legal Fund has accumulated significant resources and reports having spent more than $5.6 million on legal fees on behalf of Legal Fund members over the first fifteen years of its existence (Legal Fund 2012a: 4, 2012b).

Although the Legal Fund's bylaws state that it is "separate and apart from the RCMP and the Office of the Commissioner of the RCMP" (Legal Fund 2005: Art. 2.0), its governance and decision making, as established by these same bylaws, are necessarily connected with the SRRP and RCMP management. The Legal Fund is governed by a board of directors, executive committee (EC), and division boards. Each of these bodies is composed exclusively of and elected or appointed by SRRs and/or SRR Sub-representatives. Among the requirements for qualifying to be a director are that a Legal Fund member must be SRR of an RCMP division meeting specific requirements in terms of the proportion of members in the division who are also Legal Fund members (Legal Fund 2005: Art. 6.03). Directors are elected by voting members at annual meetings (Legal Fund 2005: Arts. 6, 7, 9). However, only Legal Fund directors, SRRs, and SRR Sub-representatives hold voting rights (Legal Fund 2005: Art. 5.03). The EC consists of five Legal Fund directors appointed by the board of directors (Legal Fund 2005: Arts. 12, 15). The Legal Fund has also established a division board for each RCMP division, made up of SRRs and SRR Sub-representatives, who must also be Legal Fund members (Legal Fund 2005: Art. 11).

Legal Fund membership is voluntary but is not necessarily available to all RCMP members covered by the SRRP. To be eligible to apply to join the Legal Fund, an RCMP member must be eligible to vote for representatives under the SRRP and "interested in furthering the objects of the Legal Fund" (Legal Fund 2005: Art. 5.01). The board of directors (composed entirely of SRRs) makes membership decisions *in camera*, without the applicant present, and gives no reasons for its decisions (Legal Fund 2005: Arts. 5.02, 6.04). Nonetheless, a majority of RCMP members appear to have joined, and the Legal Fund reports it has more than 16,000 regular and civilian members (Brown 2009: para. 13).

Full Legal Fund membership privileges are available only to SRRs and certain SRR Sub-representatives. Two classes of members exist: voting and non-voting members. Voting members include only Legal Fund directors, SRRs who are Legal Fund members, and SRR Sub-representatives who are on a Legal Fund division board (Legal Fund 2005: Art. 5.03). All others are non-voting members who do not receive notice of Legal Fund meetings and who may only attend meetings at the board's invitation (Legal Fund 2005: Arts. 5.03, 16).

An applicant for funding must have been a Legal Fund member at the time of the incident and must have exhausted internal RCMP or government avenues of assistance (Legal Fund 2012a: 7). The funding application must be approved by a division board, then an Applications Review Committee (ARC), and then the EC. An ARC is appointed for each request for funding and consists of one member appointed by the EC from among its members, two directors appointed by the division board (excluding directors serving on the board), and one Legal Fund member appointed by those directors who are SRRs or SRR Sub-representatives from the applicant's division (Legal Fund 2005: Art. 13). The bylaws do not appear to provide for review of ARC rejections. The EC's decision is final, binding, and not subject to review (Legal Fund 2005: Arts. 11.03, 13). Division boards, the ARC, and the EC are composed entirely of SRRs and SRR Sub-representatives. Consequently, the approval process for Legal Fund support for legal opinions or representation is controlled exclusively by SRRs and SRR Sub-representatives.

The Legal Fund offers its members important legal services that are lacking from the SRRP and are commonly offered by police associations. In this regard, it makes a valuable contribution to the broader RCMP labour relations system. However, if, as the courts have concluded, the SRRP cannot be regarded as institutionally independent of the RCMP, then, given the complete integration of SRRs and SRR Sub-representatives into the Legal Fund governance and membership and funding decisions, it follows that the Legal Fund cannot be regarded as independent of RCMP management, either (*MPAO* 2012: para. 128).

Grievance and Discipline Systems

The RCMP grievance and discipline systems are complex, regulated by the RCMP Act, the Code of Conduct, the RCMP Administration Manual, and Commissioner's Standing Orders and divided into distinct, separately regulated processes. These systems have been the subject of several reviews and reports in recent years and are subject to ongoing revision (Brown 2007; Canada 2007; RCMP Pay Council 2005).[19]

Grievance procedures permit members to grieve a decision, act, or omission in administration of the Force personally affecting the member, provided that no other official redress process is available (Canada 1985b: Part III). A designated RCMP officer decides grievances, and a member may appeal this decision to the Commissioner. If the grievance falls into one of five specified categories, then the Commissioner must refer the matter to the External Review Committee (ERC) before deciding the matter unless the Commissioner grants the member's request to not do so (Canada 1985b: s.36, 2011: 6).[20] The ERC is an independent tribunal established by Parliament, in operation since 1988 (Canada 1985b, 2011: 35). The ERC's review may include recommendations, but this is the extent of its authority. The Commissioner's decision can be appealed to the federal court.

Separate processes exist for formal and informal discipline. Informal discipline is imposed by supervisors. The Commissioner makes rules governing appeals and designates senior officers to hear appeals, and only specified sanctions may be appealed. There is no further appeal (Canada 1985b: s.42). Formal discipline is handled by an "appropriate officer" who decides whether the matter will go to hearing before a three-officer adjudication board appointed by the Commissioner. The affected member may have representation from outside legal counsel or from a member representative (RCMP Adjudicative Services Branch 2009: 13). Appeals of board decisions are first reviewed by the ERC. The Commissioner makes the final decision on the appeal but is required to consider the ERC's findings and recommendations (Canada 1985b: Part II).

Suspensions, discharge, and demotion are subject to separate, non-disciplinary processes. Any member suspected or convicted of a disciplinary offence may be suspended (Canada 1985b). A Commanding Officer's suspension decision cannot be appealed. In the case of discharge and demotion, the Commanding Officer initiates the process, and the affected member can request that a discharge and demotion board, composed of three senior officers, hear the matter. Appeal of a board's decision is to the Commissioner, who generally first refers such appeals to the ERC for review before deciding (Canada 1985b: Part V, 2011: 7). In the case of both disciplinary and non-disciplinary processes, the Commissioner makes final decisions on appeals, although further appeal may be available to federal court (Canada 1985b: Part II, V, 2011: 7).

The ERC sees itself as playing a crucial role in RCMP labour relations, "help[ing] to maintain fair and equitable labour relations" and providing "sound guidance in RCMP employment and labour relations matters" (Canada 2011: 3). However, the ERC's role is limited to reviewing and issuing findings and recommendations regarding appeals of specified types of grievances, non-disciplinary, and certain formal disciplinary matters. It cannot initiate a review; this depends on the Commissioner referring a matter to the ERC, which the Commissioner is not required to do in all matters and, in all cases, the final decision rests with the Commissioner (Canada 2011: 3–5).

Although the grievance, discipline, and sanction systems do not explicitly provide for SRRP or Legal Fund representation of affected members in the procedures, members may be represented or assisted by another member in presenting a grievance, in proceedings before most boards, in preparing written representations in response to a notice of discharge or demotion served on a probationary officer, or appeals of informal or formal discipline (Canada 1985b: s.41.1). This appears to allow an SRR or Sub-representative or someone from the Legal Fund or even from an independent association to act as representative provided they are also an RCMP member. However, SRR governing documents do not address member representation in such forums, and the 2001 Pollara survey indicated that conflict with a supervisor, discipline, and working conditions were not among the matters most commonly raised by members with DSRRs (Pollara 2001: 11). This suggests that the DSRRP—and now the SRRP—plays a limited role in this core labour relations function.

In contrast, the Legal Fund indicates that it may agree to fund representation for Legal Fund members in matters including discipline, suspension, dismissal, civil or criminal actions, or public complaints (Legal Fund n.d.). However, as noted, the Legal Fund is only required to fund its own members, membership is not necessarily available to all RCMP members, and funding decisions are final, binding, and non-reviewable decisions of Legal Fund committees (Legal Fund 2005: Arts. 11.03, 13). Therefore, the availability of Legal Fund representation is not clearly similar to the type of representation offered by police associations and holds the potential for arbitrary, discriminatory, or bad-faith refusal of funding for representation without recourse for the RCMP member.

In sum, the SRRP plays a limited and highly circumscribed role in broader labour relations functions in the RCMP. Its most defined role is with respect to Pay Council and the Legal Fund, and its least defined roles are with respect to grievance and discipline, although the non-independent and non-universal Legal Fund may come to play an important representative role in member representation in the grievance and discipline system.

CONCLUSION

Daphne Taras and Bruce Kaufman (2006) have identified four "faces" of non-union employee representation as reference points for evaluating such representation systems. The first is an evolutionary face, offering improved economic conditions for workers and greater workplace democracy, representing a starting point for unionisation to develop. Second is a unity-of-interest face, in which the representation system is regarded as a component of the employer's human resources system and is intended to achieve a harmonious workplace with worker interests aligning with the employer's goals. Third is the union-avoidance face, in which the purpose of the employee representation scheme is to reduce or eliminate demand for unionisation through tactics of suppression and substitution. Finally comes the complementary face, in which non-union representation is regarded as a complement to—rather than a substitute for—union representation, with each having separate areas of influence and responsibility.

The history and experience of the SRRP and its predecessor programs suggest that this non-union employee representation system wears a Janus face. One aspect is the union-avoidance visage, looking back across the RCMP's history of consistent efforts to suppress RCMP members' attempts to gain representation by an independent association or unionization. Unlike most other employers, legal prohibitions and restrictions were available to government and management and liberally used to suppress and substitute for independent representation. Where complete suppression was impossible—either because of vigorous internal dissent or external legal threats—management and government responded by allowing a more substantial non-union representation system to emerge incrementally in order to satisfy members sufficiently to defuse momentum for unionization. Thus has emerged as the second aspect of the SRRP, its complementary face. This has produced the current SRRP and the related organization, the Legal Fund.

As detailed earlier in this chapter, the SRRP offers a degree of consultation and participation in managerial decision making, with a limited role for input into compensation and RCMP policies and a limited representational role in grievance and disciplinary proceedings. The SRRP, however, remains dependent upon the goodwill of management to permit it to operate, and all final decisions remain in the hands of the RCMP Commissioner and government. Therefore, although the SRRP has evolved, its essential nature as a substitute for independent employee representation or unionization persists. Therefore, the RCMP remains an anomaly among Canadian police forces, where the norm is for independent police associations to enjoy access to statutory collective bargaining regimes, often including interest arbitration rather than work stoppages as dispute resolution mechanisms and negotiating wide-scope collective agreements.

The futures of both the RCMP and the SRRP are in flux. In recent years, the RCMP has been widely described as an organization in crisis. It has faced a number of embarrassing incidents, some leading to inquiries and reports. These reports offer strong criticism of the RCMP's managerial culture and practices and speak of the frustration and overwork of RCMP members, criticising the lack of protective structures and practices in place for members.[21] In short, the RCMP is an organization in a period of rapid and difficult transition on numerous fronts, and the SRRP is again a subject of intense internal and external scrutiny and pressure.

The results of a recent RCMP poll of its employees offer some insight into aspects of RCMP employees' workplace experience, suggesting that it continues to be an environment fraught with managerial shortcoming, yet with an intensely dedicated and loyal workforce. Less than half of respondents agreed that they are consulted appropriately on decisions affecting their work, that RCMP employees are treated fairly, or that they are respected and trusted, while just over half reported being kept well informed about matters important to them. Especially troubling is the 19 per cent of employees who indicated that they had been verbally harassed or tormented while at work, with many identifying the harasser as a direct supervisor, superior, or coworker. There also appears to be significant discontent with management training and the capabilities of senior RCMP leaders—which was also one of the dissatisfactions underpinning the call for a member association in the 1970s. The survey results reveal RCMP employees have little faith in the value of their complaints or feedback. Nonetheless, respondents also indicated a tremendous level of commitment to ensuring the success of the RCMP and pride in being an RCMP employee (RCMP 2009; see Table 9.4).

Looking ahead today leads to a conclusion that is startlingly similar to the conclusion Hardy and Ponak reached in 1983: that even if the RCMP

Table 9.4 Selected Results of RCMP Employees' Workplace Experience Poll, National Responses

	Disagree	Neither Agree nor Disagree	Agree
		(%)	
I am consulted appropriately on decisions and actions that have an impact on my work.	38	18	45
At the RCMP, employees are treated fairly.	34	21	45

(*Continued*)

Table 9.4 (Continued)

	Disagree	Neither Agree nor Disagree	Agree
		(%)	
At the RCMP, employees are respected and trusted.	28	23	49
I am kept well informed about matters that are important to me.	25	23	52
The RCMP prepares supervisors/ managers well for their supervisory/managerial responsibilities.	51	24	25
The RCMP develops capable senior leaders with the right competencies to carry out executive responsibilities.	46	28	26
Employees' complaints are dealt with effectively.	34	29	37
I believe that action will be taken based on the results of this survey.	49	28	24
I am proud of the work carried out in my work unit.	5	8	86
I am strongly committed to making the RCMP successful.	2	7	92
	Yes	No	I'd rather not answer
During the past 12 months, were you verbally harassed or tormented, while you were at work?	19	74	6
If a friend of yours told you she/he was interested in working in a job like yours, what would you tell her/him? I would:	(%)		
Strongly recommend it	62		
Have doubts about recommending it	24		
Advise against it	7		
Don't know/no response	8		

Source: RCMP 2009.

modifies the SRRP to address some of the concerns over its limited form of consultation, this may defuse the current push for full collective bargaining rights but is unlikely to permanently silence these demands (96). In the wider, difficult circumstances in which the RCMP currently finds itself, it may be of great value to the organization and a real opportunity to improve the functioning of this troubled workplace if management allowed the complementary aspect of its non-union representation system to fully emerge by allowing a more independent and empowered employee representation association to develop and help govern the workplace.

NOTES

1. At the federal level, there also exist the Canadian National Railway and Canadian Pacific Railway Police Services, the Canadian Forces Military Police, and smaller security services such as the House of Commons Security Service. However, these do not provide general police services and are not addressed in this chapter.
2. If a municipality does not provide its own policing, it may enter into an agreement with the RCMP or a provincial force to provide these services.
3. In 1984, these functions were transferred to the newly established Canadian Security Intelligence Service (CSIS). This change followed the recommendations of the McDonald Commission Report (Canada 1981) that security intelligence be performed by a separate, non-police agency.
4. Another federal police force, the Ports Canada Police, was also unionized, although this force was disbanded in 1997.
5. Separate treatment of RCMP members is due to specific provisions of the Public Service Labour Relations Act (Canada 2003a) and the RCMP Regulations (Canada 1988). Although section 5 of the PSLRA provides that "Every employee is free to join the employee organization of his or her choice and to participate in its lawful activities," ss. 2(1)(d) excludes "a person who is a member or special constable of the Royal Canadian Mounted Police or who is employed by that force under terms and conditions substantially the same as those of one of its members" from the statute's definition of "employee" for the purposes of labour relations rights, including access to the statute's collective bargaining system. Meanwhile, s. 96 of the Regulations mandates a non-union representation program to apply to RCMP members.
6. Police work stoppages are prohibited for: Alberta, Ontario municipal and provincial forces, Winnipeg police force, Newfoundland and Labrador municipal police, Prince Edward Island, and municipal and provincial police forces in Québec but permitted in British Columbia, Manitoba, Saskatchewan and Nova Scotia and for the Royal Newfoundland Constabulary (see Lynk 2006).
7. See Forcese (1999: 153–56) for a comprehensive review of this research.
8. Police in Alberta are prohibited from joining trade unions other than police associations. Similarly, Ontario municipal and provincial police and the Québec provincial police force members may form associations but may not join trade unions or labour organizations. Royal Newfoundland Constabulary officers may form an association which is permitted to affiliate specified umbrella labour organizations (see Lynk 2006).
9. See Deukmedjian (2002) and Reed (1984), generally, for an account and evaluation of the development of RCMP managerial practices and its intersection with RCMP labour militancy.

10. The DSRR was also commonly referred to as the "Div-Rep" program.
11. The Trilogy consists of *Re Public Service Employee Relations Act (Alta.)*, [1987] 1 S.C.R. 313; *PSAC v. Canada*, [1987] 1 S.C.R. 424; and *RWDSU v. Saskatchewan* [1987] 1 S.C.R. 460.
12. The Ontario Court of Appeal recently rejected the AMPMQ's claim that management conduct constituted unfair labour practices on the basis that no such claim could be made in the absence of a Charter right to collective bargaining (*MPAO* 2012: para. 140).
13. RCMP Regulations (Canada 1988: S.57(1)) prohibited RCMP members from engaging in political action. In 1995, Delisle was suspended without pay for insubordination for refusing to obey a direct order to withdraw his candidacy as mayor for a municipality in Québec. Delisle brought a successful legal challenge, and that Regulation was declared to be void and inoperative as contrary to the Charter (*Delisle* 1998, 2002).
14. The Constitution and Agreement have been revised periodically since their inception, most recently in 2012, likely in response to the ongoing Charter litigation.
15. The corresponding provisions in the original (2002) constitution contained different language. It described the SRRP as "as the system and program of choice for management–employee relations for members of the RCMP" and used the term "staff relations" instead of "labour relations."
16. This description is drawn from the 2012 version of the Agreement, which includes significantly looser restrictions on communications than did the original Agreement signed in 2002.
17. The Legal Fund also provides members with a variety of nonworkplace benefits to members, such as group banking plans (Mounted Police Members Legal Fund 2012a: 7).
18. The Legal Fund acted as an intervener in both the SCC *Ontario (Attorney General) v. Fraser* case (although the RCMP did not), arguing in favour of less expansive Charter protection for collective employee representation (*Ontario (Attorney General) v. Fraser* 2011; Brown 2009: para. 21), and in the recent Charter challenge to the SRRP, supporting government's position against several RCMP members' associations bringing the challenge (MPAO 2009, 2012).
19. At the time of this writing, Bill C-42 (2012) proposes, among other changes, to significantly reform discipline and grievances relating to misconduct and to grant the commissioner greater investigatory and dismissal powers.
20. Eligible categories are interpretation and application of governmentwide policies applying to members; pay withheld during suspension; interpretation and application of the Isolated Posts Directive and Relocation Directive; or administrative discharge on specified grounds.
21. These reports include Brown 2007; Canada 2007; Duxbury 2007; and Université de Montréal 2008.

REFERENCES

Adams, Roy J. 2008. "The Human Right of Police to Organize and Bargain Collectively." *Police Practice and Research: An International Journal*, 9(2): 165–72.
Anderson, John C. 1980. "The Employer–Employee Relationship in Police Labour Relations." In *Conflict and Cooperation in Police Labour Relations*, B. M. Downie and R. L. Jackson (eds.). Ottawa: Canadian Police College, 183–215.
Brown, David A. 2007. *A Matter of Trust: Report of the Independent Investigator into Matters Relating to RCMP Pension and Insurance Plans*, June 15,

Ottawa: Office of the Independent Investigator into RCMP Pension and Insurance Matters.

Brown, Murray E. 2009. Affidavit submitted to the Supreme Court of Canada (Court File No. 32968), September 14.

Buckie, Catherine. 1989. "RCMP Chief Says He'll Live with a Union if Court Orders It." *The Gazette*, September 23, A4.

Canada. 1918. Order-in-Council PC 1918–2213.

———. 1920. *An Act to Amend the Royal Northwest Mounted Police*, S.C. 1920 Ch. 28.

———. 1945. *Rules and Regulations for the Government and Guidance of the Royal Canadian Mounted Police Force of Canada*, C. Gaz, 1577.

———, Preparatory Committee on Collective Bargaining in the Public Sector. 1965. *Report of the Preparatory Committee on Collective Bargaining in the Public Service* (A. D. P. Heeney, chairman), July. Ottawa: Queen's Printer.

———. 1967. *Public Services Staff Relations Act*, S.C. 1966–67, c. 72.

———, Task Force on Labour Relations. 1969. *Canadian Industrial Relations: The Report of Task Force on Labour Relations* (H. D. Woods, chairman). Ottawa: Privy Council Office.

———. 1972. *Canada Labour Code, 1972*, SC 1972, c. 18.

———, Commissioner of the Royal Canadian Mounted Police. 1974. *Commissioner's Standing Orders (Division Staff Relations Representatives Program)* (made pursuant to the *Royal Canadian Mounted Police Act*, RSC 1985 c R-10 s 21(2)).

———. 1974. Order-in-Council PC 1974–1339.

———, Minister of Supply and Services, 1976. *Report of the Commission of Inquiry Relating to Public Complaints*. Internal Discipline and Grievance Procedures within the Royal Canadian Mounted Police. Ottawa: Government of Canada.

———. 1981. Order-in-Council PC 174/1981.

———, Commission of Inquiry Concerning Certain Activities of the Royal Canadian Mounted Police, 1981. *Third Report: Certain R.C.M.P. Activities and the Question of Governmental Knowledge* (Justice D. C. McDonald, chairman). Ottawa: Minister of Supply and Services.

———. 1982. *Canadian Charter of Rights and Freedoms*, Part I of the *Constitution Act*, 1982, being Schedule B to the *Canada Act 1982* (UK), 1982, c 11.

———. 1985a. *Canada Labour Code*, RSC 1985, c L-2.

———. 1985b. *Royal Canadian Mounted Police Act*, RSC 1985, c R-10.

———. 1988. *Royal Canadian Mounted Police Regulations, 1988*, SOR/88–361.

———, Department of the Solicitor General of New Brunswick. 1992. *Policing Arrangements in New Brunswick: 2000 and Beyond*. Prepared by Alan Grant, Solicitor General of New Brunswick, Fredericton, Canada: Department of the Solicitor General, Province of New Brunswick.

———, Human Resources Development. 1996. *Seeking a Balance: Review of Part I of the Canada Labour Code* (Andrew C. L. Sims, chairman). Ottawa: Minister of Public Works and Government Services.

———, Commissioner of the Royal Canadian Mounted Police. 1997. *Commissioner's Standing Orders (Representation)* (SOR/97–399), August 5. Available at http://canlii.ca/t/l9sx (accessed 28 June 2012).

———. 1997. Bill C-336, *An Act to amend the Royal Canadian Mounted Police Act*, 1997. 2nd Sess, 35th Parliament, 1997.

———. 2003. *Commissioner's Standing Orders Repealing the Commissioner's Standing Orders (Division Staff Relations Representatives Program)* (SOR/2003–325), September 23. Available at www.gazette.gc.ca/archives/p2/2003/2003-10-22/html/sor-dors325-eng.html (accessed 14 June 2012).

———. 2003a. *Public Service Labour Relations Act*, SC 2003, c 22.

260 *Sara Slinn*

——. 2003b. Bill S-24, *An Act to Amend the Royal Canadian Mounted Police Act (Modernization of Employment and Labour Relations)*, 2nd Sess, 37th Parl, 2003 (first reading 23 October 2003).

——. 2004. Bill S-12, *An Act to amend the Royal Canadian Mounted Police Act (Modernization of Employment and Labour Relations)*, 3rd Sess, 37th Parl, 2004 (first reading 12 February 2004).

——. 2005. Bill S-23, *An Act to amend the Royal Canadian Mounted Police Act (Modernization of Employment and Labour Relations)*, 1st Sess, 38th Parl, 2005 (first reading 1 February 2005).

——. 2006. Bill C-392, *An Act to amend the Public Service Labour Relations Act (RCMP Members and Special Constables) and the Royal Canadian Mounted Police Act*, 1st Sess, 39th Parl, 2006 (first reading 7 December 2006).

——, Task Force on Governance and Cultural Change 2007. *Rebuilding the Trust: Report of the Task Force on Governance and Cultural Change in the RCMP* (D. A. Brown, chairman). Ottawa: Task Force on Governance and Cultural Change. Available at www.publicsafety.gc.ca/rcmp-grc/_fl/tsk-frc-rpt-eng.pdf (accessed 13 June 2012).

——, Minister of Public Safety. 2008. *Ministerial Directive on the RCMP Disciplinary Process*, January 28.

——. 2009. Bill C-437, *An Act to amend the Royal Canadian Mounted Police Act (Labour Relations)*, 3rd Sess, 40th Parl, 2009 (first reading 16 September 2009).

——. 2010. Bill C-43, *The Royal Canadian Mounted Police Modernization Act*, 3rd Sess, 40th Parl, 2010 (first reading 17 June 2010).

——, House of Commons Deb. 2010. *Royal Canadian Mounted Police Modernization Act* (Bill C-43), December 13, 40th Parl, 3rd sess, No 119, col. 1250–1255 (Stockwell Day, President of the Treasury Board and Minister for the Asia-Pacific Gateway).

——. 2011. *Royal Canadian Mounted Police External Review Committee 2010–11 Annual Report*. Ottawa: Minister of Public Works and Government Services. Available at www.erc-cee.gc.ca/reports-rapports/annual-annuel/pdf/2011-eng.pdf (accessed 1 March 2013).

——. 2012. Bill C-42, *An Act to amend the Royal Canadian Mounted Police Act (Enhancing Royal Canadian Mounted Police Accountability Act)*, 1st Sess, 41st Parl, 2011 (first reading 20 June 2012).

Canadian Centre for Justice Statistics. 2011. *Police Resources in Canada 2011*. Ottawa: Statistics Canada. Available at www.statcan.gc.ca/pub/85–225-x/85–225-x2011000-eng.pdf (accessed 1 March 2013).

Canadian Police College. 1980. *Conflict and Cooperation in Police Labour Relations: The Proceedings of a Symposium on Canadian Police Labour Relations Held at the Canadian Police College, Ottawa, Canada, December 4–7, 1978*. Prepared by B. M. Downie and R. L. Jackson. Ottawa: Canadian Police College.

Cordon, Sandra. 1995. "Mountie Defies Superiors in Battle to Form Union." *Toronto Star*, February 12, A11.

Delisle, Gatéan Delisle. 1998. *Factum of Appellant submitted to the Supreme Court of Canada (Court File No. 25926)*.

Deukmedjian, John Edward. 2002. "The Evolution and Alignment of RCMP Conflict Management and Organizational Surveillance." Unpublished PhD dissertation. University of Toronto, Toronto, Ontario.

——. 2003. "Reshaping Organizational Subjectivities in Canada's National Police Force: The Development of RCMP Alternative Dispute Resolution." *Policing and Society*, 13(4): 331–48.

Drennan, James W. 2003. *Police Leadership and Labour Relations: A Reform Perspective*. Toronto: Emond Montgomery Publications Ltd.

Duxbury, Linda. 2007. *The RCMP Yesterday, Today, and Tomorrow: An Independent Report Concerning Workplace Issues at the Royal Canadian Mounted Police*. Ottawa: Royal Canadian Mounted Police.

Forcese, Dennis. 1980. "Police Unionism: Employee–Management Relations in Canadian Police Forces." *Canadian Police College Journal,* 4(2): 49–127.
———. 1999. *Policing Canadian Society,* 2nd ed. Scarborough, Canada: Prentice Hall Allyn and Bacon.
Gazette, The. 1989. "Union Ban Violates Rights: Mountie." September 13, A4.
Hall, Alan, and de Lint, Willem. 2003. "Policing Labour in Canada." *Policing and Society: An International Journal of Research and Policy,* 13(3): 219–34.
Hardy, J. Fred, and Ponak, Allen. 1983. "Staff Relations in the Royal Canadian Mounted Police." *Journal of Collective Negotiations in the Public Sector,* 12(2): 87–97.
Jackson, Richard L. 1978. "Police Labour Relations in Canada: A Current Perspective." In *Conflict and Cooperation in Police Labour Relations: The Proceedings of a Symposium on Canadian Police Labour Relations Held at the Canadian Police College, Ottawa, Canada: December 4–7, 1978,* p. 7. Hull, Canada: Canadian Police College.
———. 1986. "Canadian Police Labour Relations in the 80's: The Environmental Concerns." *Canadian Police College Journal,* 10(2): 86–138.
Kealey, Gregory S., and Reginald Whitaker, Committee on Canadian Labour History. 1989. *Royal Canadian Mounted Police Security Bulletins.* St. John's, Canada: Committee on Canadian Labour History.
King, Mike. 1997. "Policing and Public Order Issues in Canada: Trends for Change." *Policing and Society: An International Journal of Research and Policy,* 8(1): 47–76.
Lynk, Michael. 2006. Affidavit submitted to the Ontario Superior Court of Justice (Court File No. 06-CV-311508PD2), February 22.
MacDougall, Kevin. 2000. "Nonunion Employee Representation at the Royal Canadian Mounted Police." In Bruce E. Kaufman and Daphne Gottlieb Taras (eds.), *Nonunion Employee Representation: History, Contemporary Practice, and Policy.* Armonk, NY: M. E. Sharpe, Inc., 477–82.
Maser, Peter. 1986. "RCMP in Quebec to Move toward Unionization." *The Ottawa Citizen,* February 8, A12.
Matas, Robert. 1998. "RCMP Bracing for Possible Job Action in B.C. after 5 Year Pay Freeze." *The Globe and Mail,* January 6, A4.
Middleton, J. P. 1974. *A Study Report on Police Associations.* Ottawa: Royal Canadian Mounted Police.
Mounted Police Members Legal Fund. 2005. *Mounted Police Members Legal Fund Bylaws,* September 12. Available online at http://en.mplegalfund.com/mplf-bylaws/ (accessed 14 June 2012).
———. 2010. *Canadians Don't Want the Mounties Unionized.* Available online at http://en.mplegalfund.com/index.php?s=nanos (accessed 14 June 2012).
———. 2012a. *Members First: The Official Newsletter of The Mounted Police Members' Legal Fund* (Fall 2012).
———. 2012b. *Legal Fund Brief.* Unpublished document, available online at http://en.mplegalfund.com/wp-content/uploads/2012/06/Legal-Fund-Brief.pdf (accessed 1 March 2012).
———. (n.d.). *FAQs.* Available at http://en.mplegalfund.com/faq/ (accessed 14 June 2012).
Ottawa Citizen, The. 1986. "Mounties in Quebec Take Formal Union Request to Labor Board." February 13, A14.
Paton, Richard. 1985. *The Internal Communications Officer: "Manager in the Middle."* Unpublished.
Pollara. 2001. *A Study of the Division Staff Relations Representative Program (DSRR).* Unpublished.
Ramsay, Jack. 1972. "My Case Against the RCMP: End of a Career, End of a Dream." In *Maclean's,* July: pp. 19–74. Toronto: Maclean-Hunter Ltd.

Reed, Gary Edward. 1984. "Organizational Change in the RCMP: A Longitudinal Study." Unpublished PhD dissertation. Simon Fraser University, Burnaby, British Columbia. Available at summit.sfu.ca/system/files/iritems1/6346/b16558911.pdf (accessed on 26 January 2013).

Robinson, Jennifer. 1987. "Mounties Challenge Federal Law." *The Montreal Gazette*, May 7, A5.

Royal Canadian Mounted Police (RCMP). 1974. *Meeting of Division Representatives and Commanding Officers Held at Headquarters, Ottawa, Minutes of May 8 & 9, 1974*, pp. 10, 22–29, 46. RCMP Headquarters Library, Ottawa.

———. 1978. *Commissioner's Comments on DSRR Program*, Vol. 1, 1978, 6, 8.

———. 2003. *SRR Challenge 2000: Review Final Report*. Ottawa: Royal Canadian Mounted Police.

———. 2006. *Corporate Facts*. May 10, available at www.rcmp-grc.gc.ca/fs-fd/corporate-collectif-eng.htm (accessed 18 June 2012).

———. 2009. *Results: RCMP Employee Opinion Survey 2009*. August 31, available at www.rcmp-grc.gc.ca/surveys-sondages/2009/emp/empl2009_result-eng.htm (accessed 14 June 2012).

———. 2010. *Staff Relations Representative (SRR) Program: Role*. February 16, available at www.rcmp-grc.gc.ca/srr-rrf/role-eng.htm (accessed 14 June 2012).

———. 2012a. *Organizational Structure*. January 17, available at www.rcmp-grc.gc.ca/about-ausujet/organi-eng.htm (accessed 14 June 2012).

———. 2012b. *International Peace Operations*. June 21, available at www.rcmp-grc.gc.ca/po-mp/index-eng.htm (accessed 21 June 2012).

———. (n.d.). *Administration Manual*, as amended.

Royal Canadian Mounted Police Adjudicative Services Branch. 2009. *Management of the RCMP Disciplinary Process 2008–2009 Annual Report*. Ottawa: Royal Canadian Mounted Police. Available at www.rcmp-grc.gc.ca/pubs/adj/ann-08–09/report-rapport-eng.pdf (accessed 14 June 2012).

Royal Canadian Mounted Police Pay Council. 1997. *1997 Annual Report*. Ottawa: Royal Canadian Mounted Police.

———. 2005. *Pay Council Review of RCMP Internal Discipline System: Final Report and Recommendations*. Ottawa: Royal Canadian Mounted Police.

Royal Canadian Mounted Police Staff Relations Representative Program (SRRP). 2012a. *RCMP Staff Relations Representative Program Constitution*, as amended.

———. 2012b. *Agreement between the Commissioner of the Royal Canadian Mounted Police and the Staff Relations Representative Program*, as amended.

Sawatsky, John. 1980. *Men in the Shadows: The RCMP Security Service*. Toronto: Doubleday.

Shalom, Francois. 1986. "Request Submitted to Labor Board." *The Globe and Mail*, February 13, A8.

Slotnick, Lorne. 1986. "Quebec Mounties Leading Union Drive." *The Glove and Mail*, July 30, A5.

Statistics Canada. 2011. "Unionization 2011." *Perspectives on Labour and Income*. Ottawa: Statistics Canada. Available at www.statcan.gc.ca/pub/75-001-x/2011004/article/11579-eng.pdf (accessed 1 March 2013).

Taras, Daphne G., and Bruce E. Kaufman. 2006. "Non-Union Employee Representation in North America: Diversity, Controversy and Uncertain Future." *Industrial Relations Journal*, 37(5): 513–42.

Tibbetts, Janice. 1999. "No Union for RCMP, Supreme Court Rules." *Edmonton Journal*, September 3, A9.

Université de Montréal, Research Group on Language, Organization and Governance. 2008. *Rebuilding Bridges: Report on Consultation of Employees and Managers of the Royal Canadian Mounted Police—C Division*. Prepared by

D. Robichaud, C. Benoit-Barné, and J. Basque, 5 November. Montréal: Research Group on Language, Organization and Governance. Available at http://dispersingthefog.com/report-1.pdf (Accessed 13 June 2012).

Uppal, Sharanjit. 2011. "Statistics Canada Unionization. 2011." *Perspectives on Labour and Income*, 23(4). Available at www.statcan.gc.ca/pub/75-001-x/2011004/article/11579-eng.pdf (accessed on 26 January 2013).

Van Maanen, John. 1984. "Making Rank: Becoming an American Police Sergeant." *Urban Life*, 2–3: 155–76.

Wills, Terrance. 1995. "Mounties Demand Right to Form Union." *The Gazette*, February 8, B1.

Windsor Star, The. 1987. "RCMP to Test Labor Law." September 12, A4.

Case Law

Canada (Attorney General) v Meredith, [2013] FCA 113.
Delisle c Canada (sous-procureur général), [1990a] R.J.Q. 234.
Delisle v Canada (RCMP), [1990b] 39 F.T.R. 217.
Delisle c Canada (sous-procureur général), [1997] 144 D.L.R. (4th) 301 (Qc CA).
Delisle c Canada (Procureur général), [1998] R.J.Q. 2751 (QSSC).
Delisle v Canada (Deputy Attorney General), [1999] 176 DLR (4th) 513 (SCC).
Delisle c Canada (Procureure générale), [2002] J.Q. no 202 (QCCS).
Health Services and Support—Facilities Subsector Bargaining Assn. v. British Columbia, [2007] 2 SCR 391.
L'Association des Membres de la Division "C" and The Royal Canadian Mounted Police, [1986] 14 CLRBR (NS) 46.
Meredith v Canada (Attorney General), [2011] FC 735.
Mounted Police Association of Ontario v Canada (Attorney General), [2009] O.J. No. 1352 (ONSC).
Mounted Police Association of Ontario v Canada (Attorney General), [2012] ONCA 363 (leave to appeal allowed, [2012] SCCA No 350).
Ontario (Attorney General) v. Fraser, [2011] 2 SCR 3.

10 From Non-Union Consultation to Bargaining in the Canadian Federal Public Service

Expanding the Bounds of Employee Representation through the NJC

Richard P. Chaykowski

INTRODUCTION

The evolution of industrial relations in the federal public service has been unique in two main respects.[1] First, early in the twentieth century, prior to the establishment of a legislative framework that provides employees with the right to form unions and collectively bargain, federal government employees established a variety of associations that sought to represent the employment interests of employees to the government (as employer). This occurred in the absence of any formal legislation or other legal regulations to establish these associations.[2] Some major segments of the federal work-force, such as the postal employees, have been organized into associations since the earliest days of the Canadian labour movement, although a major proportion of federal government employees remained unorganized, and many employees elected not to be members of any association.[3] Overall, from early on in the twentieth century, there was a fairly high degree of employee organization in some form.

Second, based upon a British model, the federal government and staff associations developed and institutionalized the National Joint Council (NJC) in 1944. At the time, this was a unique and quite effective forum for employee representation and consultation between staff associations and the government over a broad range of employment-related matters— and this council has remained a major pillar of the employment relations framework in the federal government. There remains no analog to the NJC in any other Canadian public-sector jurisdiction, nor is there a con-sultative council with similar scope and effectiveness in any private sector industry.[4]

In the period up to 1967, there was no formal legal mechanism by which a staff association could be recognized as the legal bargaining agent for employees. The Public Service Staff Relations Act of 1967 fundamen-tally transformed federal public-sector employment relations by making collective bargaining and arms'-length unions the centrepiece of labour relations. Whereas prior to 1967 the NJC was a joint forum for the various staff associations and employers, following the introduction of unionization and collective bargaining rights in 1967, the NJC became a joint forum for the newly formed unions (which were the successors to the staff associations) and government employers. In addition, the federal government employers continued to work with the Civil Service Commission (later the Public Service Commission) to implement various human resources management practices.

At the time, there were serious questions raised regarding whether the unionized labour relations system would simply replace the NJC entirely[5] or whether there was a meaningful role that the NJC, as a joint consultative forum, could play alongside the collective bargaining system in a way that complemented it. Nonetheless, since then, labour relations have effectively been conducted through the NJC as well as through the traditional mechanism of collective bargaining.[6] In fact, the longevity and success of the NJC since its inception in 1944 emphasises several important lessons regarding joint councils and non-union forms of employee representation: joint forums can support meaningful consultation and cooperation between employers and alternative forms of employee representation (e.g., associations or unions); joint forums can be viable institutional mechanisms to support improvements in the terms and conditions of employment; joint forums can be viable over long periods of time, especially when they are institutionally supported; and associations and joint forums can provide constructive preconditions for other forms of employee representation that may evolve, including unions and collective bargaining.

During the period since unionization and collective bargaining was introduced in 1967, successive governments continued to engage in tactics such as wage freezes, back-to-work orders, or suspension of interest arbitration, which have been characterized as "government unilateralism"[7] and which in any event have served, by definition, to circumvent and weaken the collective bargaining process and framework. On the one hand, during periods of high conflict and strained labour relations, the parties were oftentimes reluctant under these conditions to engage in consultation and cooperation at the NJC; but, on the other hand, the parties also recognized that the NJC offered an alternative forum to achieve at least some progress in labour relations. Government actions undertaken since 2000 to strengthen the mandate and resources of the NJC have provided fresh impetus to its role in facilitating consultation and cooperation between unions and their employers and in improving the terms and conditions of employment. In fact, given the ongoing tendency of the government to place constraints on the collective bargaining process through *ad hoc* measures, there remains the potential for the relative role of the NJC in overall labour relations to be enhanced even further, as the parties seek to use the NJC to fill at least a part of the labour relations void thus created.

Throughout the recent history of labour–management relations in the federal public service, the main factor determining the effectiveness of the labour movement in affecting the terms and conditions of employment has been the legislative regime. While the other main environmental factors (i.e., the legal, political, economic, and organizational factors) have had an impact, it was the political/legislative context which had been determinative of the fortunes of the labour movement in the federal public service. Prior to 1944, staff associations facilitated voluntary consultations with management, but they had no legal standing in the labour relations system. The establishment of the NJC in 1944, through government action, then significantly increased staff association effectiveness as representatives of employee interests because it provided a formal, institutional mechanism by which the staff associations could advance the interests of employees. Then in 1967, the establishment of formal unions and bargaining rights through legislation facilitated the transformation of staff associations to unions, providing organized labour with full legal standing and even greater prospects for advancing the interests of organized labour through collective bargaining.

In this century, the legal context appears to be emerging as a second major environmental factor that will impact industrial relations in the federal public service. The advent of the Canadian Charter of Rights and Freedoms (Charter) and subsequent landmark Supreme Court of Canada (SCC) labour cases, including *BC Health Services*[8] and *Fraser*,[9] regarding freedom of association and the related right to collectively bargain, appear to have substantially altered the labour relations landscape in Canada. On the one hand, the recent decisions in *Fraser* and in *RCMP*[10] appear to strengthen the legitimacy of non-union forms of employee representation; still other cases before the courts involve challenges to the right of government to exclude matters from the scope of collective bargaining (e.g., the current exclusion of pensions from federal public service collective bargaining) and to invoke back-to-work legislation in the federal jurisdiction.

It is likely that the constitutional developments with a more direct bearing on the legitimacy of non-union forms of representation and collective bargaining and the right to strike will continue to evolve through the longer term. As these legal issues become more clearly resolved, they may have important implications for broader labour relations policy, and they could also have an impact on the conduct of labour relations in the federal public service of Canada. For example, if non-union forms of employee representation (e.g., associations) are deemed legitimate and sufficient, then some employees may opt for a form of non-union representation and seek participation in the NJC. Whether such alternative forms of non-union representation are accepted at the NJC could impact the efficacy and centrality of the NJC in the longer term—as well as the roles of the NJC and collective bargaining in relation to each other. Furthermore, if collective bargaining and the right to strike are further strengthened, then this could, if only on the margin, affect unions' interest in the NJC.

In the next section, I briefly summarize the historical development of non-union representation and consultation in the federal public service, including the establishment of the NJC. In the third section, I consider the role of consultation and the NJC since collective bargaining rights for public service employees were established in 1967. The final section considers the current labour relations system in the federal public service and the potentially transformative role that legal developments may play in shaping the relative roles of the NJC and the collective bargaining process in labour relations. It concludes with observations regarding the factors affecting the longevity of the NJC and the role of the NJC in relation to non-union forms of employee representation.

THE HISTORICAL DEVELOPMENT OF NON-UNION REPRESENTATION IN THE FEDERAL PUBLIC SERVICE OF CANADA[11]

Growth of Staff Associations and Non-Union Consultation

The earliest forms of collective associations among federal civil service employees took root in the late 1800s and became more widespread by about 1900 in the form of various more formal associations than previously existed. By the early 1900s, there were a substantial number of associations, variously organized along departmental lines across regions or craft lines across regions or, in some cases, across departments but concentrated in a particular region. Then in 1909, two of the larger umbrella associations (the Civil Service Association of Canada and Civil Service Association of Ottawa) joined approximately twenty-one other associations to form a new overarching association, the Civil Service Federation of Canada.[12] Other major associations were soon formed, including the Professional Institute of the Public Service of Canada (PIPSC) in 1920 (including professional employees) and the Amalgamated Civil Servants of Canada in 1921 (including mostly postal employees).[13] During the period leading up to World War II, membership in associations expanded as employee interest in collective representation increased, and the associations consolidated their formal structures. The associations were employee generated so that membership was voluntary and not all employees chose to join an association. The associations were financially supported by voluntary dues payment.

The associations increasingly engaged in consultations with the government with a view to obtaining improvements in various terms and conditions of employment. However, the government, as employer, managed the workforce and set the terms and conditions of employment (including classifications, recruitment, and promotions) through the Civil Service Commission, which was established in 1908.[14] The government unilaterally set rates of pay and determined any pay rises. In this context, staff associations made "representations," typically to the Civil Service Commission, with "cap in hand," with little or no leverage to extract enhancements in employment terms and with little incentive for the government to offer improved conditions or pay (except in instances in which the improvement might match personnel or other management objectives). Employees were, not surprisingly, increasingly dissatisfied with the lack of substantive input into the process of determining terms and conditions of employment, and there were instances of industrial unrest, including, for example, a strike by postal workers in 1924 related to pay increases.[15]

This period of labour relations may be characterized as one of employee–employer consultation. Importantly, during this period, the staff associations were generally disadvantaged in labour relations in relation to the employer and especially weakened in terms of presenting their positions in consultations by several key factors. First, these civil service staff associations were neither established nor formalized under legislation and therefore had no rights under law as employee organizations, nor had they legal rights to bargain on behalf of their members (or others eligible to join a staff association but who had chosen not to become a members of a staff association).[16] Second, the associations represented, collectively, only about half of all civil service employees, so they suffered from both a lack of full legitimacy as employee representatives and limited financial resources.[17] And third, there was a lack of cohesion in their priorities and positions and generally a fairly high degree of interassociation competition.[18] The labour relations system could only change through legislation, and successive governments were unwilling to consider this option.

Founding of the National Joint Council

Interest among federal civil service associations in the formation of an industrial council of associations with the federal government (as employer) coincided with the broader interest in industrial councils in Canada that evolved across industries after World War I. As examples, industrial councils were formed in the private sector in the rail and construction industries and in the Saskatchewan public service (in 1920).[19] However, government resistance to the idea of a joint council and the preference of PIPSC, a major staff association, for its own council with the employer, resulted in little progress being made in establishing a joint council.

Even so, the main model the civil service associations looked to potentially emulate were the Whitley Councils in Great Britain.[20] These councils were established in 1919 across the British civil service with: (i) executive powers, which required the government to abide by decisions made by the council;[21] (ii) the authority to address the issue of compensation;[22] and

(iii) complementary committees established at the establishment, local, and national levels.[23] A highly modified version of the Whitley Councils established in the British civil service was proposed for Canada in 1928 in a private member's bill in Parliament, but the initiative to implement such a council failed when the government of Mackenzie King fell.[24] Over the next decade, little substantive progress was made towards establishing a joint council. However, by advent of World War II, the staff associations had finally become unified in their support for establishing a joint council, and the federal government's general opposition to establishing a joint council in the federal civil service had diminished, as it sought to promote labour–management cooperation and industrial peace across industries in order to ensure continuous wartime production.[25]

In Canada, the main legislative efforts to establish some version of the British Whitley Council in the Canadian federal civil service coincided with Liberal governments under the leadership of Mackenzie King, first in 1928 and then in 1944. The support of King, which appeared at first "equivocal" because of a reluctance to cede government authority, was likely determinative because King had previously been Minister of Labour and was both knowledgeable and experienced in labour relations and supportive of an industrial relations model that included employee representation.[26] The Canadian version of the British Whitley Council—the National Joint Council of the Public Service of Canada—was established by Parliament in 1944 by Order-in-Council PC3676, with Treasury Board confirming the constitution of the NJC in 1945.[27] This significant step forward in the industrial relations system was, therefore, a product of the political and governmental context.

The initial structure of the NJC consisted of both employer-side and staff-side members, with a Chair (employer side) and Co-Chair (association side) with a General Secretary as administrative head. The NJC was constituted as a bipartite organization, with representation from each of the member staff associations (originally eight staff association leaders or their designates) and employers (originally six senior management officials).[28]

While there were several smaller government employers, the main government representative at the NJC was Treasury Board. As the overwhelming largest and most influential employer-side member, their positions would tend to set the employer-side pattern in discussions. On the staff side, the number and form of the staff associations changed considerably over the years, as various staff associations reorganized and engaged in mergers. Much of the basic work on specific issues would be conducted by a series of area-specific working committees (e.g., travel regulations, working conditions) that were bipartite. As a functional matter, the NJC operated by consensus; but since most recommendations made by the NJC had some implications for spending, they had to be subsequently accepted by Treasury Board before being put into practice by either Treasury Board, the Civil Service Commission, or Governor General in Council.[29]

The NJC and the Limits of Consultation

The Canadian model for the NJC had several critical characteristics that differentiated it from the British Whitley Councils:[30] (i) the NJC did not have executive powers, only the authority to consult and advise; (ii) the NJC was established only at the national or service-wide level, with no provision for complementary joint councils at either the departmental or workplace levels;[31] and (iii) the NJC was precluded from consultations regarding pay (and other personnel matters reserved for the Civil Service Commission, such as merit, selection, promotion, and so forth).

The first characteristic meant that the NJC was intended to be strictly advisory in nature and not a decision-making organization.[32] Consequently, while the associations could discuss, consult, and advise over any employment-related matter at the NJC table, final decisions were vested with the government:

> Moreover, no formal mechanism had emerged which authoritatively determined the right of associations to speak on behalf of employees at the federal level or which protected the right of employees to join and participate in associations. However, it was not the lack of a legal mechanism for regulating relations between the Civil Service Commission and the employee associations which proved to be the fatal deficiency in this system. Rather, it was the fact that the Civil Service Commission had the power only to recommend to the federal government that the terms of employment agreed upon in consultation be implemented.[33]

This would lead to continued demands and pressure by the staff associations for full collective bargaining rights, which had just been granted to private-sector employees with the enactment of Order-in-Council PC1003 in 1944.

The exclusively national scope of the NJC was a significant departure from the British model, which included departmental councils. The lack of departmental councils was considered a major ongoing limitation that compromised the overall effectiveness of the NJC model:

> Probably the least successful aspect of the experience of the Canadian public service with joint consultation has been the failure to establish effective departmental joint councils. Most students of Whitleyism in the United Kingdom agree that the departmental councils provide a more useful and effective employer-employee mechanism than the National Council.[34]

Frankel (1956: 521) concludes that one explanation for this failure was that "if the staff associations were sufficiently strong and united in their desire for departmental councils it would be only a matter of time before they achieved them."

The third characteristic regarding the inability to consult over matters related to pay was rooted in the more fundamental concern that recommendations made by the NJC would not infringe on the powers or decisions of government.[35] The principle of protecting the ultimate right of Parliament and the government of the day to function unrestricted was not seriously challenged at the time. The main practical issue in this respect was control over the pay of government employees; the government wanted to ensure that no entities other than Parliament could constrain the financial obligations of the government of the day. This determination by the government to control decisions over pay only served to further reinforce the desire of staff associations, including their leaders and members, to achieve full rights to form unions and collectively bargain.

More specific concerns about the NJC also surfaced over time. These difficulties included the lack of a mechanism to resolve impasses; significant time delays extending from the initial stage of a recommendation being forwarded by the NJC to the government to its acceptance by the government through to its final implementation; and the lack of a grievance mechanism that applied to NJC policies in the workplace.[36] Finally, a recurring concern of the staff associations was that the government resisted using the NJC as a forum within which to address matters of compensation and the realization that the government was not prepared to relinquish *any* decision-making authority regarding matters related to pay.[37] The government did make serious proposals to engage in joint consultation, notably regarding compensation matters, outside of the NJC, including proposing that the Civil Service Commission and the staff associations consult and make recommendations.[38] However, this process appeared even weaker than the option of discussing compensation matters through the NJC. In any event, neither route would have altered the fact that final authority over compensation matters was vested in the government as employer.[39] Furthermore, holding out the prospect of an additional consultation process likely only served to further exacerbate the dissatisfaction felt by the staff associations.

Within the structural and practical constraints imposed by the various limitations on its powers and resources, the NJC made considerable progress in advancing the terms and conditions of employment of public-service employees. While the actual achievements of the NJC were subject to distinct ebbs and flows over time, the range of issues covered was extensive, including:[40]

- Health and safety (e.g., working conditions, construction)
- Workplace standards
- Technological change
- Medical insurance plans
- Retirement issues (e.g., employment after age 65)
- Overtime premiums

- Work-week reduction to five days and forty hours
- Moving/relocation expenses; and
- Voluntary revocable staff association dues deduction.

For the staff associations, the agreement to allow the deduction of association membership dues was a particularly important NJC achievement. Following initial consideration by a committee, the NJC approved a proposal for "voluntary revocable" dues check-off in late 1951; the check-off of Professional Institute fees was initiated in January of 1954.[41] This basic accomplishment provided a firm basis for the future activities of the employee associations:

> The achievement of the check-off had the immediate effects both of providing the staff associations with a more reliable financial basis for their operations and of freeing voluntary membership effort for redeployment in activities other than collecting dues. In the longer run it is doubtful whether any other single event in the fifties played a greater part in enabling the staff associations to develop and prepare themselves for the demands which were to be placed upon them in the next decade.[42]

In 1958, the government announced that it would bear the full cost of administering membership dues check-off.[43,44] The establishment of a firm financial foundation for the activities of associations, well in advance of the introduction of formal collective bargaining rights in the 1960s, likely contributed to their ability to transform themselves from "associations" into effective "unions."

During the two decades following World War II, when employees of the federal government did not have the rights to form unions, the NJC was the main institution by which the staff associations sought to make representations to their employers to improve the terms and conditions of employment of government employees. Through a formal consultative process at the NJC, the staff associations "informally negotiated" and consulted to obtain improvements over a broad range of employment conditions, and the functioning of the NJC as an institution and the process of labour–management consultation matured.

However, association leaders were very conscious of the critical limitations inherent in the NJC model, especially the refusal of the government to discuss matters related to compensation and, more fundamentally, the limited nature of a consultation process in which the government had final authority. Employee leaders understood that overcoming these crucial limitations of the NJC would involve attaining the rights to form unions and bargain collectively.[45] Fundamental dissatisfaction with the critical limitations of the NJC model, combined with broader pressures across jurisdictions to provide bargaining rights to public-sector employees, created significant pressures on the federal government to consider providing bargaining rights to federal public-service employees. In 1963, the federal government struck the Heeney Committee (Preparatory Committee on Collective Bargaining in the Public Service) to consider all aspects of providing public-service employees with the rights to form unions and collectively bargain.[46]

TRANSITION FROM NON-UNION REPRESENTATION TO DUAL PATHS OF COLLECTIVE BARGAINING AND UNION–MANAGEMENT CONSULTATION

The Formation, Administration, and Scope of Bargaining Rights

In 1967, the federal government enacted the Public Service Staff Relations Act (PSSRA). This act provided federal government employees with a broad range of employee rights to unionize and collectively bargain with their employers and established the new functional framework for the conduct of union–management relations.

Under the new PSSRA, for purposes of collective bargaining, there were multiple employers on the government side: the employers included Treasury Board, which represented the main governmental departments and employed the vast majority of workers, as well as several separate government employers that corresponded with distinct agencies, boards, councils, or commissions. Originally, there appears to have been no underlying, principled approach to determining which agencies ought to be considered as separate employers and which ought to be represented by Treasury Board[47]—the precise number and specific entities included as separate employers have changed over time as the government has reconfigured departments, boards, and agencies and undertaken privatization of some of its operations.

Prior to 1967, the staff associations attempted to represent as large a proportion of employees as possible, although some employees chose not to become formal members of an association. With the introduction of unionization rights in 1967, the staff associations that existed prior to 1967 basically "converted" to unions and all employees (except "excluded" employees within the meaning of the new PSSRA) within the newly defined bargaining units were represented by the new unions, and the leadership of the staff associations for the most part became the leaders of the newly established unions. For example, just prior to 1967, a large number of staff associations amalgamated (including the large Civil Service Federation and Civil Service Association of Canada) to form the Public Service Alliance of Canada (PSAC), which became the overwhelmingly largest union after 1967.[48] The PSAC was followed in size by the Professional Institute of the Public Service of Canada (PIPSC), which had originated in 1920 as an association. These two major unions were complemented by a variety of smaller unions.[49]

The content of the PSSRA reflected the now–commonly established general Wagner-style framework for the conduct of union–management relations in Canada, including the typical requirements that unions be certified, bargaining units be well defined, unfair labour practices be prohibited, and negotiations be conducted in good faith. The PSSRA established an administrative body, the Public Service Staff Relations Board (PSSRB), to administer the act, including the establishment of bargaining units, the functioning of collective bargaining, and the handling of interest and rights disputes.[50]

Importantly, the PSSRA provided unions, upon certification, with the choice of either of two options in the event of an impasse in negotiations: compulsory arbitration or conciliation (with the implied right to strike). In addition, the PSSRA provided for the designation of essential employees who are not permitted to withdraw their labour services in the event of a work stoppage, with the PSSRB given the role of adjudicating any disputes between the parties regarding the list of employees to be designated.[51]

Equally important in terms of the eventual effectiveness of the collective bargaining process were the restrictions placed upon the scope of bargaining. Many key employment issues were statutorily excluded from the scope of collective bargaining, including job classifications, promotions, layoffs,[52] and, notably, pensions, which were governed separately under the Public Service Superannuation Act (PSSA); this act provided for a form of joint consultation, which was also subject to the previous criticisms raised by the unions regarding the range of consultation initiatives put forward by the government over previous decades.[53]

The Structure and Functioning of the NJC Following Unionization

Since the staff associations that existed just prior to 1967 converted to unions under the new PSSRA, the basic employer and union membership composition in the NJC after unionization broadly mirrored the employer and staff association membership arrangement in the NJC just prior to the PSSRA. Consequently, since there was also a fairly smooth transition in association—union leadership, the actors at the table prior to 1967, remained essentially the same. However, a key issue is why the unions decided to maintain their support for the NJC when collective bargaining appeared to hold the greatest prospect for the substantial advances:[54]

> The obvious question arose in 1967: would there be a role for the NJC in the collective bargaining system which had just been introduced? It was widely agreed that there were matters which, in practical terms, could not be resolved on an individual basis with more than a hundred separate bargaining units. The Council's constitution was amended to reflect the new realities and its membership enlarged to include all certified bargaining units.[55]

NJC regulations and directives were deemed to be in the collective agreements so that the previous gains made at the NJC were protected.[56] While the unions were clearly focused on the prospects for major gains through collective bargaining, their continued participation in the NJC had no immediate cost or disadvantage; and the unions understood that the NJC could complement the collective bargaining system in practical ways, such as in addressing servicewide issues for which it would be in the interests of the unions and their members to have standard policies and outcomes across bargaining units.[57] In this way, the NJC served as a "common table" across unions and employers that could achieve gains for both in certain aspects of the employment relationship across bargaining units.

As was the composition prior to 1967, there were several employers on the government side, with Treasury Board predominating, and this configuration has remained essentially the same through to the current time. By 2012, the federal public service employed roughly 275,000 employees, with Treasury Board as employer for about 200,000 (with about 86 percent of these covered by a collective agreement).[58] The current complement of employers is presented in Table 10.1, Panel A. On the union side, the two main unions, PSAC and PIPSC, continue to dominate in terms of overall number of members represented, although each union has held only one seat at the NJC. The current composition of unions on the employee side of the NJC is presented in Table 10.1, Panel B.

The NJC currently operates, administratively, in ways that are essentially similar to its functioning when the unionization of employees occurred:[59] the NJC has a formal decision-making council that is composed of all members from both the employer and union sides, meets quarterly, and works by consensus; the council also has a standing executive committee, which is composed of three members from each side and administers council activities; the NJC is supported administratively by a General Secretary and Secretariat. The main labour relations work of the NJC is carried out by a set of standing committees, each of which is focused on a particular aspect of labour relations and employment, including the following:[60]

- Foreign Service Directives
- Government Travel
- Isolated Posts and Government Housing
- Joint Employment Equity
- Occupational Health and Safety
- Official Languages
- Relocation
- Service-Wide Committee on Occupational Health and Safety
- Union-Management Relations
- Workforce Adjustment
- Dental Care Plan Board of Management
- Disability Insurance Plan Board of Management

Table 10.1   Membership of the National Joint Council, 2011

Panel A: Employer Members
Treasury Board of Canada Secretariat Canadian Food Inspection Agency Communications Security Establishment Canada National Research Council of Canada Office of the Auditor General of Canada

Panel B: Union Members
Public Service Alliance of Canada Professional Institute of the Public Service of Canada Association of Canadian Financial Officers Association of Justice Counsel Canadian Air Traffic Control Association, CAW Local 5454 Canadian Association of Professional Employees Canadian Federal Pilots Association Canadian Merchant Service Guild Canadian Military Colleges Faculty Association Coast Guard Marine Communications Officers CAW-Canada Local 2182 Communications, Energy and Paperworkers Union of Canada Local 588-G Federal Government Dockyard Chargehands Association Federal Government Dockyard Trades and Labour Council (East) Federal Government Dockyard Trades and Labour Council (West) International Brotherhood of Electrical Workers, Local 2228 Professional Association of Foreign Service Officers Research Council Employees' Association Union of Canadian Correctional Officers – CSN

Source: National Joint Council. *General Secretary's Annual Report 2010–2011*. (September 22, 2011). Accessed at: www.njc-cnm.gc.ca/doc.php?sid=74&lang=eng on July 3, 2012.

The Dual Paths of Labour Relations: Cooperation and Consultation through the NJC and Collective Bargaining

The advent of the PSSRA was a watershed in federal public-service labour–management relations. It held out the promise of fundamentally transforming labour–management relations by providing employees with a more effective option than consultation—and a legislatively sanctioned framework within which to negotiate over a broad range of terms and conditions of employment. In so doing, however, the PSSRA also held the distinct possibility of marginalizing the NJC. This prospect followed from the fact that the unions viewed the consultation process through the NJC as, ultimately, one sided in terms of there being a process of "submissions" regarding changes to terms and conditions of employment and, on the other hand, unilateral because the ultimate decisions regarding change were vested with management—whereas the new collective bargaining regime was bilateral.[61]

In the post–1967 period, the industrial relations system was therefore characterized by two broad tracks: one included ongoing management-led personnel/ human resource management responsibilities as well as singular initiatives (which may include consultation and joint committees, e.g., the joint Advisory Committee structure required for pensions under the PSSA or the joint consultation committee established in 1978 by the Public Service Commission); and labour relations, including the union–management consultation through the NJC, and collective bargaining.[62] These elements of the federal public-service industrial relations system are depicted, over time, in Figure 10.1.

In the area of human resource/personnel matters, the government, as employer, exercised authority over matters related to recruitment, appointments and staffing, and merit through the Public Service Commission. Aside from these ongoing personnel matters, the government, as employer, also introduced a wide variety of particular human resource management initiatives into federal government workplaces over the decades. These initiatives, such as the highly publicised Public Service 2000 (PS2000), were intended to effect organizational change that would increase productivity and lower costs. They were often inspired by private-sector initiatives that aimed to introduce innovative human resource practices into workplaces. Attempts such as PS2000 to "modernize" the public service were led by management and met with suspicion by the unions and therefore generally failed to engage them.[63] Public-service human resources management responsibilities and practices were further overhauled in the early 2000s, resulting in the 2005 Public Service Employment Act.

In the labour relations domain, collective bargaining became the centrepiece of the labour relations system. As anticipated, the unions made a

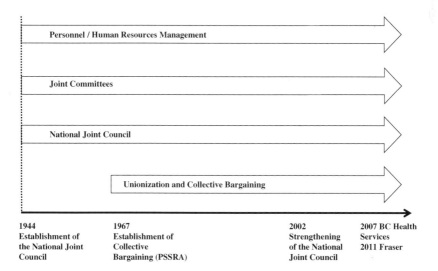

Figure 10.1   Industrial Relations in the Canadian Federal Public Service, 1944–2012
Source: Based upon Chaykowski (2002b: 75, Figure 1)

variety of gains over successive rounds of negotiations. Importantly, collective bargaining was viewed, increasingly, as limited because of two fundamental restrictions. First, there were a considerable number of important monetary (e.g., pensions) and nonmonetary issues (e.g., job classifications, promotions) which the parties were precluded, statutorily, from bargaining over, as noted. Had this restriction been, in and of itself, the full extent of the limitations imposed upon the collective bargaining system, it likely would not have diminished the elevated view of the unions of the collective bargaining route over the consultative route represented by the NJC.

However, layered over this restriction was a second significant constraint: government actions became, over time and with frequency, extremely intrusive into both the process and machinery and the outcomes of collective bargaining. This government intrusiveness occurred in a wide variety of ways over time, including[64] successive governments imposed employment outcomes through such means as wage controls or the imposition of settlements/agreements; and governments have otherwise short-circuited the established labour relations process through the imposition of back-to-work legislation, the suspension of interest arbitration, or unilateral claw-back of the pension surplus. While the precise motivations for successive governments to engage in unilateralism are difficult to ascertain, the ultimate effect has, regardless, been to significantly limit the efficacy of the collective bargaining system, particularly from the viewpoint of the unions.

Alongside this long-term collective bargaining context, characterized by incremental progress achieved through successive rounds of collective bargaining but significantly limited by ongoing government intervention, the unions and employers continued to advance labour–management relations and employment outcomes through the NJC. As examples, the unions achieved early gains at the NJC across a range of benefits (e.g., health care, cost sharing of premiums) and, more generally, achieved enhanced labour–management relations by addressing a range of issues through principled, problem-solving approaches.[65]

These advances were achieved despite the periodic and ongoing challenges to the NJC that arose, such as the willingness of the unions to attempt to take unresolved issues out of the NJC forum over onto the collective bargaining table, ongoing time delays, and the lack of a dispute-resolution process for impasses at the council.[66] Instead of deterring the unions, the experiences in fact led to a series of significant reforms to the structure and operations of the NJC:[67]

> By the end of the 1970s, the functioning of the NJC had undergone fundamental changes in three areas: the introduction of a grievance procedure that applied to NJC directives, including a provision for the binding third-party resolution of grievances that remained unresolved after the final stage of the grievance procedure; the creation of a mechanism to facilitate the resolution of impasses in consultation, utilizing a third party to make non-binding recommendations; and the establishment of

a procedure for the referral of items between the NJC and the collective bargaining spheres.

Despite these reforms and the ongoing overall commitment of the parties to the NJC, there were periods during which considerable strain in the labour–management relationship threatened the viability of the NJC.[68] Nonetheless, neither the unions nor the employer side were prepared to abandon the NJC, which, during some periods, remained the only meaningful forum for the conduct of labour relations and a significant vehicle to achieve advances in employment outcomes:[69]

> The importance of the National Joint Council to public service labour management relations was highlighted between 1991 and 1996, when public service bargaining was suspended but NJC discussions were explicitly exempted. Since 1999, the NJC has:
>
> * reached agreement on the Public Service Health Care Plan and established a Trust to jointly manage this plan;
> * negotiated childcare allowances;
> * renegotiated the Public Service Dental Care Plan and resolved foreign service issues related to the plan; and
> * developed a consultation framework to work toward a complete overhaul and modernization of the Travel Directive.

Recent policy developments have added considerably to the viability of the NJC. In 2001, the federal government initiated a broad effort to overhaul the conduct of human resources management (HR) and labour relations (LR) in the federal public service.[70] The government reforms drew upon the work of a series of commissions that had been established to analyze and assess the current state of HR and LR in the public service and make recommendations regarding possible reforms, including the:[71]

* Advisory Committee on Senior Level Retention and Compensation
* Advisory Committee on Labour-Management Relations in the Federal Public Service; and
* Task Force on Modernizing Human Resources Management in the Public Service.

The Advisory Committee on Labour-Management relations in the federal Public Service (the "Fryer Committee"), which was appointed in 1999, produced its final report and recommendations in 2001.[72] The Fryer Committee report included specific recommendations aimed at significantly strengthening the role and viability of the NJC:[73]

* making the NJC the main vehicle to achieve greater cooperation, "codetermination," and "codevelopment" between the parties, including codevelopment of staffing, classification system, the pension plan

- joint management of a newly established Compensation Research Bureau through the NJC
- recognition of the NJC as an independent organization; and
- enhancing NJC funding.

The result of the broader human resources and labour relations reform process was the Public Service Modernization Act, 2003 (PSMA), which primarily consisted of two new statues, the Public Service Labour Relations Act (PSLRA, replacing the PSSRA for public-service LR) and the Public Service Employment Act (focused on public-service HR), both of which came into effect in 2005.[74] The new PSLRA embodied a wide range of changes that

> provide for a labour relations regime in the public service based on greater cooperation and consultation between the employer and bargaining agents. It requires the establishment of labour-management consultation committees, enables co-development, enhances opportunities for conciliation and provides for negotiated essential services agreements.[75]

The new PSLRA also updated the labour relations board, dispute resolution procedures, unfair labour practices, managerial exclusions, and grievance handling and permitted two-tier bargaining, among other changes.

While not adopting the full set of Fryer Committee recommendations, the new PSLRA strengthened the NJC in several important ways. These reforms, while not resulting in any major shift in the role of the NJC in labour relations, have further institutionally strengthened the NJC and have served, if only marginally, to make the NJC more of a centrepiece of labour relations. First, the PSLRA formally acknowledged the NJC, thereby finally institutionalizing it within the labour relations legislative framework. Second, the PSLRA supported the NJC as the main option of the parties for the new emphasis in the Act upon consultation and codevelopment, thereby formally enhancing its role and its relevance as a labour relations institution.[76] Third, the PSLRA provides for ongoing, secure finding for its operations by explicitly making administrative support a part of the mandate of the new Public Service Labour Relations Board.[77] The expanded, renewed role of the NJC is reflected in its current mandate, which is to contribute:[78]

> to effective labour relations and human resources management on many fronts:
> - by co-developing public-service wide terms and conditions of employment through "NJC Directives";
> - by co-developing public service wide health care coverage;
> - by providing joint management of health care plans;

- by developing and reviewing occupational health and safety policies and providing advice and leadership to departments and agencies in this field;
- by resolving employee grievances (NJC directives) and appeals (dental and disability benefits);
- by providing a forum for information-sharing, consultation and co-development on other policies and initiatives (e.g., employment equity, official languages);
- by sponsoring other activities to build relations among the parties.

In 2009, the federal government enacted the Expenditure Restraint Act, which limited the annual pay increases of federal public-service employees over the period from the 2006 to 2007 through 2010 to 2011 fiscal years. This legislation imposed strict limits upon the pay increases that could be negotiated through collective bargaining, continuing the trend of successive governments to override the collective bargaining process:[79]

> The purpose of the Expenditure Restraint Act is to control expenditures by setting, as opposed to bargaining, increases in the rates of pay of unionized and non-unionized federal public service employees until 2010–11.

However, the legislation exempted pay increases arising from NJC recommendations.[80] The legislation therefore had the effect of, on the one hand, restraining the potential gains of employees through collective bargaining but, on the other hand, permitting gains made at the NJC table. This recent legislation again serves to reinforce the practical limitations of collective bargaining in federal public-service labour relations.

The NJC has proven itself to be a resilient institution, becoming a forum of choice for certain types of issues. This occurred for several basic yet quite different reasons. First, as the unions' and employers' experience with collective bargaining grew, it became apparent that there were significant and ongoing limitations to the collective bargaining framework. These limitations arose from both the legislative restrictions on the right to bargain over certain aspects of the employment relationship and the ongoing tendency for successive governments to engage in unilateralism in labour relations. The role of collective bargaining has therefore remained constrained over time, with the political context remaining as a major underlying factor giving rise to these limitations. Second, the NJC continued to be a forum within which the parties achieved incremental and tangible gains in terms and conditions of employment and in building constructive labour relations. These outcomes have been valued by both the unions and the employers. One tangible result of this support has been the institutional strengthening of the role and institutional structure of the NJC through the recent reforms to the federal labour relations legislation. Third, the parties were able to successfully adapt and modify the consultation process and mechanisms at the NJC to achieve an improved forum and process for consultation and what has been, in effect, a degree of codetermination. The net result is that, despite periodic tensions between the consultation and collective bargaining spheres, the overall conduct of labour relations through the dual paths of consultation and collective bargaining has a track record of successful coexistence and complementarity.

THE CONTEMPORARY SYSTEM OF PARALLEL CONSULTATION AND COLLECTIVE BARGAINING: THE EMERGING ROLE OF CONSTITUTIONAL DEVELOPMENTS

The Political/Governmental Context for Federal Public Service Labour Relations and Prospects for Change

The overall labour relations system and specific terms and conditions of employment in the federal public service have been primarily a function of the legislative regime and government *ad hoc* actions. The cumulative effect of the industrial relations developments over the past several decades, including various legislative changes and the progressive strengthening of employee organizations, has been the incremental strengthening of the NJC as a joint consultative mechanism and as a pillar of the overall labour relations framework in the federal public service. The weight of the descriptive evidence suggests that, because gains through collective bargaining and its mechanisms (including strikes) proved increasingly ineffective in the face of government restraints and unilateralism, the NJC became a *relatively* stronger institution; it yielded steady, if only incremental, gains for the unions. If the political/legislative context remains the main determining factor in federal public-service labour relations, then an extrapolation of past trends would suggest that the NJC will likely continue to become increasingly important and effective over time.

The broader Canadian labour relations system may, however, be on the cusp of significant transformation brought about by recent major SCC decisions in a series of Charter cases that will have the effect of altering the legal context. While the main factor shaping labour–management relations in the federal public service and the success of unions in achieving gains in the terms and conditions of employment has been the nature of the legislative regime and government *ad hoc* actions, changes in the legal context are producing new constraints on governments, thereby becoming major contextual factors affecting the industrial relations system. These SCC decisions, as well as decisions in related cases, directly affect labour relations in the federal public service by determining the viability of collective bargaining and the limits of government restraints and unilateralism as well as the effectiveness and centrality of the NJC.

The Emerging Legal Context

The recent evolution of SCC decisions involving freedom of association and the right to collectively bargain have begun to redefine the basic concept of what constitutes legitimate forms of employee representation. Taken together with decisions that have addressed the issue of Charter protection of the right to collectively bargain, the decisions also stand to define the viability and scope of collective bargaining as a process. In what follows, I consider three aspects of the changing legal context.

The Direction of the SCC Charter Decisions since the 1980s[81]

In the 1980s, the Trilogy of SCC Charter decisions regarding freedom of association affirmed that this Charter protection did not extend to collective bargaining and the right to strike;[82] subsequently, in *Delisle* (in 1999) and *Dunmore* (in 2001), the SCC essentially again held that these activities were not afforded Charter protection.[83] The landmark SCC decision in *BC Health Services* was a turning point because

> It overruled the Trilogy decisions and recognized a constitutional "right" of collective bargaining under section 2(d), while leaving open the issue of the right to strike.[84]

The more recent 2011 SCC decision in *Fraser*, which involved the legitimacy of non-union forms of employee representation, appears to have broadened the legal scope for what may constitute legitimate forms of employee representation:

> The Fraser decision opens up the possibility of exploring mechanisms other than traditional collective bargaining that would enable employer-employee negotiations, as long as those negotiations are "meaningful" and are conducted by the parties in "good faith." From a policy standpoint, there may be a variety of labour relations models that satisfy these criteria and do not involve replicating the standard Wagner-model machinery.[85]

At the federal level, a related case regarding the legitimacy of an existing form of non-union employee representation and the right of employees to form a union involves Royal Canadian Mounted Police officers. In 2012, the Ontario Court of Appeal, relying heavily upon the SCC decision in *Fraser*, ruled in *RCMP* that the non-union form of representation (association) generally available to the members was sufficient to fulfill the Charter rights of employees; that is, the government was not obligated to afford RCMP members with the traditional Wagner-type machinery. The key issue is the extent to which this line of cases provides a substantial basis in law for a wide variety of non-union forms of employee representation.

New Constraints on Government Actions

The SCC decisions in *BC Health Services* and *Fraser* have, apparently, had other important side effects on governments. In the cases of both Ontario and the federal government, as examples, these decisions appear to have recently had a chilling effect on the willingness of governments to impose wage settlements or freezes. In Ontario in 2011, the government imposed a wage freeze on non-unionized employees in the broader public sector through the Public Sector Workers Compensation Restraint Act but also declared that "All existing collective agreements will be honoured";[86] instead, the government decided only to recommend that unions and management negotiate wage freezes among unionized employees.

In 2012, the federal government imposed back-to-work legislation (Bill C-33) on employees of Air Canada. In response, the affected unions, including the International Association of Machinists and Aerospace Workers and Air Canada Pilots Association, commenced a Charter challenge to the legislation.[87] Aside from the specific legal grounds for the challenge in such cases, the actions of government may generally be challenged as causing "substantial interference" with the Charter rights of employees. Should these cases achieve a significant degree of success, then the court decisions could also have a chilling effect on the tendency of governments to engage in unilateral actions that override existing key aspects of the collective bargaining machinery or that limit or impose employment outcomes.

The Scope of Collective Bargaining

A major concern of the federal public-sector unions has been the exclusion of a wide range of monetary and nonmonetary issues from the scope of collective bargaining. Following the decision in *BC Health Services*, the Canadian Association of Professional Employees together with PIPSC launched a major Charter challenge regarding the exclusion of pensions and nonmonetary matters (e.g., staffing) from collective bargaining in the federal public service.[88] Success in these cases would significantly expand and strengthen the role of collective bargaining in the federal public service.

Impact of Changes in the Legal Context

While the full impact of these Charter cases has yet to fully play out, they appear to have already substantially altered the labour relations landscape in Canada. Interestingly, the recent decisions in *Fraser* and in *RCMP*, which provide an expanded view of what constitutes legitimate forms of employee representation, may eventually strengthen the legitimacy of non-union forms of employee representation, including in federal public-sector labour relations. The NJC, although now a successful model of union–management consultation, could become even more broadly developed as a forum for consultation between new non-union employee organizations (e.g., associations), unions, and the employers—thereby returning somewhat to its roots as a forum for representation between the employer and non-union associations.

Perhaps even more intriguing is the prospect that these decisions, should they continue to be upheld, will encourage other (non-union) organizations to utilize the NJC type of model as a basis for alternative forms of employee representation to conduct negotiations with one or more employers. The main requirements, that negotiations be conducted in a "meaningful" manner and in good faith, could be fulfilled within the context of a variety of institutional arrangements. A cursory assessment of the impact of these decisions might suggest that unionization and collective bargaining may be weakened by encouraging non-union forms of employee representation. But the more likely prospect would be greater legal and, possibly, policy support for alternative forms of employee representation and not necessarily the diminution of unions and the existing collective bargaining framework.

Furthermore, court decisions in favour of unions regarding the legitimacy of back-to-work legislation could serve to significantly constrain governments from undertaking unilateral actions that interfere with either collective bargaining or the right to strike. Constraining government's capacity to engage in "unilateralism" and expanding the scope of permissible areas of bargaining would considerably strengthen the role and relevance of collective bargaining generally, but especially in the federal public service.

Therefore, the growing number of legal cases regarding Charter rights and the general leaning of the decisions suggest that, at the least, the current federal public-service labour relations model of dual paths of consultation and collective bargaining will be maintained. However, the respective roles of the NJC and collective bargaining in federal public service labour relations both stand to be strengthened by the recent court decisions. While it is uncertain whether one path would eventually be more advantaged than the other by these decisions, the collective bargaining route has the prospect of being significantly enhanced.

THE ENDURING INSTITUTIONAL STRENGTH OF THE NJC

Recent legal and legislative developments in the federal public sector highlight the importance of these factors in determining employment outcomes and, more broadly, in shaping the labour relations system. The NJC originated as a forum for consultation between non-union associations and the employer long before the right to unionize and collectively bargain existed for federal government employees. The labour relations legislation of 1967 granting these rights was a major policy inflection point. At that time, it was uncertain what the impact would be on the NJC. There were widespread concerns that the NJC would simply become marginalized or, eventually, become defunct.

From the viewpoint of labour, the transition to unionism was successful, as the associations converted into unions and the leadership supported and led the conversion. Indeed, the long and growing track record of success of the associations in the period leading up to 1967 and their success in consultation with the employer through the NJC likely positively supported this transition process. The associations existed and grew prior to the establishment of the NJC in 1944. The NJC provided the associations with a formal and meaningful—albeit limited—mechanism within which they could represent the interests of employees to the employer.

Once employees achieved full bargaining rights, the NJC received a new constitution and continued as a forum between the newly formed unions and employers. There were episodes of tension between the collective bargaining and consultation routes and periods of very poor labour relations that threatened the viability of the NJC. However, since its inception as a forum for consultation between (non-union) associations and the employer, through the later period of union–employer consultation, the NJC was quite successful in yielding incremental positive gains for employees.

The success of the NJC may be traced to several key factors. First, it facilitated meaningful consultation that, arguably, at times touched upon "codetermination" of certain issues. Second, the NJC provided a practical mechanism to find solutions to servicewide issues, the coordination of certain employment outcomes, and the creation of cohesive human resource and labour relations policies and practices across departments and bargaining units. This occurred where it was in the interests of both the associations and later the unions to do so. Third, during the period following 1967, the NJC promoted discussion and dialogue over a range of issues "in term"—that is, between periods of actual collective bargaining. This function appears to have yielded periods of improved labour relations relationships as well as instances of other more tangible employment-related outcomes. This role was therefore a very positive one that was valued by the parties. Fourth, the NJC and collective bargaining proved, in practice, to be more complementary in nature than they were substitutes. The parties appeared to increasingly recognize this dynamic, which was supported even further in the legislative reforms of the early 2000s and as reflected in the new PSLRA.

NOTES

1. In this analysis, I take federal government employment to include all employment in government departments, agencies, boards, and other Crown corporations. Note that the number, type, and extent of government control over these organizations have changed considerably over the course of the past century.
2. See: Arthurs (1968–69).
3. See: Knowles (1955a; 1958).

4. In recent decades, the Canadian government supported the development of sector councils. These councils consist of employers and, where an industry is unionized, representation from the major unions, to address primarily industry-level human resource issues, such as the supply of skilled workers, worker adjustment in the event of layoffs, and training and development of the workforce. These councils tend to function cooperatively within an industry/sector but do not address matters of terms and conditions of employment. See Chaykowski (1998) and Gunderson and Sharpe (1998).

5. With the exception of "excluded" employees, virtually the entire federal public service was unionized. Aside from some senior managers and confidential employees (about 3 percent in the early 1970s), employees of the RCMP and Armed Services, as examples, were excluded from the right to form unions and collectively bargain; see Kruger (1974: 321). Following 1967, the NJC became a joint forum for the unions and employers.

6. Source: Chaykowski (2002a: 392, Figure 1); a discussion of the nature of the interrelationship between these two mechanisms is also provided. Also see Chaykowski (2002b).

7. See Swimmer (2002).

8. *Health Services* is the Supreme Court decision in *Health Services and Support-Facilities Subsector Bargaining Ass'n v. British Columbia*, 2007 SCC 27, [2007] 2 SCR 391.

9. *Fraser* is the Supreme Court decision in *Ontario (Attorney General) v. Fraser*, 2011 SCC 20, [2011] 2 SCR 3. My reference to the Supreme Court decision in *Fraser* means the majority decision written by Chief Justice McLachlin and Justice LeBel.

10. *RCMP* is the Ontario Court of Appeal decision in *Mounted Police Association of Ontario v. Canada (Attorney General)*, 2012 ONCA 363 (2012.06.01).

11. The analysis in this section draws upon Chaykowski (2000) and Chaykowski (2002b).

12. Sources: Chaykowski (2000: 332); and see Johnston (1953) and Rump (1939a, 1939b, 1939c).

13. Sources: Chaykowski (2000: 332); and Knowles (1955a, 1958).

14. See Hodgets and colleagues (1972: 26, 56–57). The Civil Service Commission was established under the *Civil Service Amendment Act*.

15. Source: Hodgets and colleagues (1972: 121–27).

16. See: Arthurs (1968–69).

17. Aside from certain management employees who might be precluded from joining a staff association, not all employees had an interest in joining a staff association, so that membership was incomplete.

18. Source: Hodgets and colleagues (1972: 174–75, 195); and Chaykowski (2000: 332).

19. See *International Labour Review* (1921: 60).

20. These Councils were named after John Whitley, who chaired the committee that recommended that these joint councils be created across British industries, including the British civil service; see Barnes (1974: 7–8).

21. Sources: Hodgets and colleagues (1972: 194) and Barnes (1974: 13).

22. Sources: Barnes (1974), Frankel (1956: 514–15), and Rump (1972: 14).

23. Source: Barnes (1974: 9).

24. See Barnes (1974: 19–23), Rump (1972: 8), Frankel (1956: 509), and Knowles 1955b: 6).

25. See Rump (1972: 8) and Barnes (1974: 25, 27).

26. See Barnes (1974: 19) and Chernow (1998: 588–590). Also see Barnes (1995) on King's initially limited but gradually increasing support for a constrained version of the British Whitley Council for Canada's civil service.

27. Source: Rump (1972: 8, 12).
28. See Rump (1972: 10). Staff associations would be represented by the leaders, while employers would be represented by senior government officials. For example, in the late 1950s, the employer-side representatives on the NJC included (Frankel 1956: 511): "among others, the Chairman of the Civil Service Commission, the Secretary of the Treasury Board, the Deputy Minister of Labour, and the Clerk of the Privy Council."
29. Source: Frankel (1956: 514).
30. See Barnes (1974; and Islay 1944: 779).
31. More precisely, the NJC constitution actually did provide for the possibility of forming departmental councils but they were never, in practice, established (Frankel 1956: 520):

    The constitution of the N.J.C. clearly provides for the creation of departmental councils, but there has been no positive experience with them. A first attempt to set up such a council was made in 1948 in the Department of Mines and Resources. This was a promising beginning. The Department even went so far as to set up regional joint councils for its branches. However, before this experience could mature, it came to an end.

32. Source: Hodgets and colleagues (1972: 194).
33. Source: Arthurs (1968–69: 975).
34. Source: Frankel (1956: 520).
35. Source: Hodgets and colleagues (1972: 194).
36. See Frankel (1956), Edwards (1974), and Barnes (1974).
37. See Chaykowski (2002a: 398).
38. See Chaykowski (2002b: 77–78) for discussion of the development of the proposal to provide joint consultation over compensation matters.
39. See Hodgets and colleagues (1972: 270, 274–75).
40. Sources: Barnes (1974: 64–6, 60, 85, 114–33) and Rump (1972: 16).
41. Source: *Professional Public Service*, Vol. 32, No. 9, September 1953: 1. Also see Barnes (1974: 60).
42. Source: Barnes (1974: 61).
43. Source: *Professional Public Service*, Vol. 38, No. 4, April 1959: 18.
44. That the government should assume the full cost of administering check-off was originally recommended by the NJC. [Source: *Professional Public Service*, Vol. 38, No. 6, June 1959: 15.]
45. See Johnston (1954: 2).
46. See Arthurs (1968–69).
47. Source: Arthurs (1968–69: 979). In 1967, for example, the National Film Board was considered as a separate employer, but the National Energy Board was not (see Arthurs 1968–69: 979 at fn 26). Currently, the National Research Council Canada is included as a distinct employer, reflecting the contemporary composition of Boards at the federal level of government.
48. The Public Service Alliance of Canada was formed in July 1966 as a result of the merger of the following sixteen organizations:

    • Civil Service Federation of Canada
    • Civil Service Association of Canada
    • Canadian Agriculture National Employees Association
    • Canadian Air Services Association
    • Canadian Immigration Staff Association
    • Canadian Marine National Employees Association
    • Canadian Taxation Division Staff Association

- Customs and Excise Officers Association
- Department of Justice Employees Association
- Department of National Health and Welfare Employees Association
- Department of Veterans' Affairs Employees National Association
- Federal Public Works Employees Association of Canada
- National Defence Employees Association
- National U.I.C. Association,
- Research Council Employees Association and
- Treasury Staff Association of Canada.

Source: *Memorandum Constituting and Creating the Public Service Alliance of Canada*, July 9, 1966 (mimeo).
49. See Chaykowski (2000: 335).
50. See Arthurs (1968–69), Finkelman and Goldenberg (1983), and Finkelman (1974).
51. See Arthurs (1968–69) and also the discussion therein.
52. See Ponak and Thompson (1995: 431).
53. See Finkelman and Goldenberg (1983: 230–31) and Chaykowski (2002b: 80).
54. For example, this sentiment is reflected in the comments of Claude Edwards at the founding convention of the Public Service Alliance of Canada in 1966 (see Edwards 1966).
55. Source: Barnes (1995: 15).
56. Source: Barnes (1995: 15).
57. The final report of the Advisory Committee on Labour Management Relations in the Federal Public Service ("Fryer Committee") emphasizes:

> With the introduction of collective bargaining in 1967, the scope of the NJC's activities was narrowed, but it remained a useful forum for collaborative efforts over the ensuing decades, especially as the relations between the parties deteriorated at the bargaining table. Over the years, the NJC has become a particularly useful forum for addressing service-wide issues such as the Foreign Service Directive, the Bilingual Bonus, the Travel and Relocation Directives and the Health Care and Dental Plans. It also played a key role in the extension of the Workforce Adjustment Directive, initially negotiated by the government and the Public Service Alliance, to the entire public service. (Canada 2001: 40)

Also, see Edwards (1974: 8) on the importance of the NJC in addressing servicewide issues.
58. Source: Treasury Board (2011: 10–11).
59. Source: National Joint Council. *General Secretary's Annual Report 2010–2011.* (September 22, 2011). Accessed at: www.njc-cnm.gc.ca/doc.php?sid=74&lang=eng on July 3, 2012.
60. Source: National Joint Council. *General Secretary's Annual Report 2010–2011.* (September 22, 2011). Accessed at: www.njc-cnm.gc.ca/doc.php?sid=74&lang=eng on July 3, 2012.
61. See Edwards (1966: 4).
62. Sources: Finkelman and Goldenberg (1983: 228–30) and Chaykowski (2002b: 80). The Public Service Commission was established in 1967 as the successor to the Civil Service Commission.
63. Chaykowski (2002b: 79–80) provides a description of some of the union reaction and labour relations repercussions of PS2000.
64. Source: Swimmer (2002). Government intervention and unilateralism in dealing with the process and machinery of federal labour relations and in the

public sector more generally is provided in Canada (2000: 22–25), Swimmer (1995), and Panitch and Swartz (1984).

65. See Chaykowski (2000: 339) and Chaykowski (2002a: 404).
66. See: Chaykowski (2000: 338–39).
67. Source: Chaykowski (2002a: 400–01).
68. Barnes (1995: 15) observes that periods when the labour relations were highly dysfunctional critically affected the sustainability of the NJC.
69. Source: Canada (2001: 40).
70. The first major set of concerns regarding HR and LR were raised in a report issued by the Auditor General that was highly critical of the current state of HR and LR in the federal public service (see Treasury Board 2011: 16).
71. See Treasury Board (2011: 16–17).
72. See Canada. *Working Together in the Public Interest: Second Report of the Advisory Committee on Labour-Management Relations in the Federal Public Service* (Ottawa: Treasury Board, 2001).
73. Source: Fryer Report (Canada 2001), Recommendations 3–7 and 24–29.
74. The PSMA also created amendments to the Financial Administration Act and the Canadian Centre for Management Development Act (now the Canada School of Public Service Act; see Treasury Board 2011: 5–6).
75. Source: Treasury Board (2011: 21).
76. Section 11 of the PSLRA states: "Co-development of workplace improvements by the employer and a bargaining agent may take place under the auspices of the National Joint Council or any other body they may agree on."
77. Specifically, Section 17 of the PSLRA states: "The Board's mandate includes the provision of facilities and administrative support to the National Joint Council."

    Prior to 2005, the funding for the NJC was from the Public Service Staff Relations Board (Canada 2001: 41); however, this responsibility does not appear to be a formal part of the mandate of the PSSRB, which would make funding to the NJC uncertain; nor is the NJC identified in the PSSRA.
78. Source: National Joint Council. *General Secretary's Annual Report 2010–2011.* (September 22, 2011). Accessed at: www.njc-cnm.gc.ca/doc.php?sid=74&lang=eng on July 3, 2012.
79. Source: Treasury Board (2011: 35, fn 45).
80. Specifically, the Expenditure Restraint Act states (Section 4) that:

    Any reference in this Act to additional remuneration does not include any additional remuneration that is provided for by a directive, policy, regulation, agreement or other instrument issued or made (a) on the recommendation of the National Joint Council and with the employer's approval.

81. The following discussion of SCC cases follows Chaykowski and Hickey (2012: 89–92). Interestingly, the original PSSRA specifically included the employees' right to "freedom of association;" see Arthurs (1968–69: 986). However, it has been legal challenges to violations of freedom of association and associated rights, rooted in the Charter, that are redefining the system of unions and collective bargaining.
82. The Trilogy refers to:

    (i) *Reference re Public Service Employee Relations Act* (Alberta), [1987] 1 S.C.R. 313
    (ii) *Retail, Wholesale and Department Store Union, Locals 544, 496, 635 and 955 v. Government of Saskatchewan*, [1987] 1 S.C.R. 460
    (iii) *Public Service Alliance of Canada v. Canada*, [1987] 1 S.C.R. 424

83. See: *Delisle v. Canada (Deputy Attorney General)*, (1999) 3 SCR 1016; and *Dunmore v. Ontario (Attorney General)*, (2001) 207 D.LR. (4th) 193.
84. Source: Labour Law Casebook Group (2011: 697).
85. Source: Chaykowski (2012: 301).
86. Source: Ontario, *2010 Ontario Budget. Budget Papers. Open Ontario: Ontario's Plan for Jobs and Growth* (Toronto: Queen's Printer) at 51–52.
87. Source: V. Lu. 2012. "Air Canada Machinists Launches Charter Challenge over Back-to-Work Law." *Toronto Star* (April 02). Accessed at www.the star.com/business/2012/04/02/air_canada_machinists_launches_charter_chal lenge_over_backtowork_law.html on April 22, 2014.
88. Source: Canadian Association of Professional Employees. (n.d.). *CAPE Annual Report 2010–2011* (Ottawa, ON: CAPE) at 14.

REFERENCES

Arthurs, H. W. 1968–69. "Collective Bargaining in the Public Service of Canada: Bold Experiment or Act of Folly?" *Michigan Law Review*, 67: 971–1000.

Barnes, L. 1974. *Consult and Advise: A History of the National Joint Council of the Public Service of Canada 1944–1974.* Kingston, ON: Industrial Relations Centre, Queen's University.

———. 1995. "The National Joint Council—Fifty Years On." *The Worklife Report*, 9(5): 14–15.Canada. 2000. *Identifying the Issues.* First Report of the Advisory Committee on Labour Management Relations in the Federal Public Service, pp. 22–25. Ottawa: Catalogue Number: BT22–70/2000.

Canada. 2001. *Working Together in the Public Interest.* Advisory Committee on Labour Management Relations in the Federal Public Service. Final Report (June 2001).

———. 2009. *Expenditure Restraint Act.* S.C. 2009, c. 2, s. 393. (Amended November 25, 2010).

Chaykowski, R. 1998. "The Role of Sectoral Initiatives in the Canadian Industrial Relations System." In Morley Gunderson and Andrew Sharpe (eds.), *The Emergence of Sector Councils in Canada*, pp. 295–315. Toronto, ON: University of Toronto Press.

———. 2000. "Advancing Labour–Management Relations Through Consultation: The Role of the National Joint Council of the Public Service of Canada." In B. Kaufman and D. Taras (eds.), *Nonunion Employee Representation: History, Contemporary Practice, and Policy*, pp. 328–47. Armonk, NY: M. E. Sharpe.

———. 2002a. "Prospects for the National Joint Council in the Renewal of Labour–Management Relations in the Canadian Federal Public Service." *Canadian Labour and Employment Law Journal*, 9(3): 387–414.

———. 2002b. "The National Joint Council and the Development and Future of Labour–Management Consultation in the Canadian Federal Public Service." *Workplace Gazette*, 5(3): 71–86.

———. 2012. "Canadian Labour Policy in the Aftermath of *Fraser.*" *Canadian Labour and Employment Law Journal*, 16(2): 291–312.

———., and R. Hickey. 2012. *Reform of the Structure and Conduct of Labour Relations in the Ontario Broader Public Service* (report to the Commission on the Reform of Ontario's Public Services). Industrial Relations Series. Kingston, ON: Queen's University.

Chernow, R. 1998. *Titan: The Life of John D. Rockefeller, Sr.* New York: Random House.

Edwards, C. 1966. "Address to the Founding Convention of the Public Service Alliance of Canada." *Civil Service Review*, (December): 2, 4, 6, 40.

Edwards, Claude A. 1974. "The Future of Public Service Unionism." *The Civil Service Review*, XLVII(3): 6–10.

Finkelman, J. 1974. *The Rationale in Establishing Bargaining Units in the Federal Public Service of Canada*. Reprint Series no. 25. Kingston, ON: Industrial Relations Centre, Queen's University.

———., and S. Goldenberg. 1983. *Collective Bargaining in the Public Service: The Federal Experience in Canada*. Montreal: Institute for Research on Public Policy.

Frankel, S. 1956. "Staff Relations in the Canadian Federal Public Service: Experience with Joint Consultation." *Canadian Journal of Economics and Political Science*, 22(4): 509–22.

Gunderson, M., and A. Sharpe (eds.). 1998. *The Emergence of Sector Councils in Canada*. Toronto, ON: University of Toronto Press.

Hodgets, J., W. McCloskey, R. Witaker, and V. Wilson. 1972. *The Biography of an Institution: The Civil Service Commission of Canada*. Toronto, ON: University of Toronto Press.

International Labour Review. 1921. "Control of Industry: Joint Councils in Canadian Industry." 3(3): 56–63.

Islay, J. 1944. *Dominion of Canada Official Report of Debates House of Commons*. Vol. 1: 778–79. Ottawa: King's Printer.

Johnston, V. 1953. The CSAO and the Federation." *Civil Service News*. March: 2–3.

———. 1954. "The Association in 1953." *Civil Service News*. January: 2–3.

Knowles, F. 1955a. "History of the Amalgamated Civil Servants of Canada." *Canadian Civil Servant*. June: 2–6.

———. 1955b. "History of the Amalgamated Civil Servants of Canada." *Canadian Civil Servant*. December: 9–10.

———. 1958. "Not to be Forgotten." *Canadian Civil Servant*. April: 2–6.

Kruger, A. 1974. "Bargaining in the Public Sector: Some Canadian Experiments." *International Labour Review*, 109: 319–31.

Labour Law Casebook Group. 2011. *Labour and Employment Law*. Eighth Edition. Toronto, ON: Irwin Law.

Panitch, L., and D. Swartz. 1984. "From Free Collective Bargaining to Permanent Exceptionalism: The Economic Crisis and the Transformation of Industrial Relations in Canada." In M. Thompson and G. Swimmer (eds.), *Conflict or Compromise: The Future of Public Sector Industrial Relations*, pp. 407–35. Montreal, PQ: Institute for Research on Public Policy.

Ponak, A., and M. Thompson. 1995. "Public Sector Collective Bargaining." In M. Gunderson and A. Ponak (eds.), *Union-Management Relations in Canada*, 3rd ed., pp. 415-54. Don Mills, ON: Addison-Wesley.

Rump, C. W. 1939a. "A History of the Civil Service Association and Reasons Why You Should Be a Member." *Civil Service News*, 17(2): 33–36.

———. 1939b. "A History of the Civil Service Association and Reasons Why You Should Be a Member." *Civil Service News*, 17(3): 65–70.

———. 1939c. "A History of the Civil Service Association and Reasons Why You Should Be a Member." *Civil Service News*, 17(4): 97–104.

———. 1972. "Employer–Employee Consultation in the Public Service: 1944–1972. A Review of the History, Functions and Achievements of the National Joint Council of the Public Service of Canada." *Civil Service Review*, 45(2): 6–16, 48.

Swimmer, G. 1995. "Collective Bargaining in the Federal Public Service of Canada: The Last Twenty Years." In G. Swimmer and M. Thompson. (eds.), *Public Sector Collective Bargaining In Canada*, pp. 368–407. Kingston, ON: Queen's University IRC Press.

———. 2002. "Putting the Fryer Committee Recommendations in Context." *Canadian Labour and Employment Law Journal*, 9(3): 313–34.

Treasury Board of Canada Secretariat (Treasury Board). 2011. *Report of the Review of the Public Service Modernization Act, 2003*. Cat. No. BT22–127/2011.

Part IV
United States

11 Employee Involvement and Voice at Delta Air Lines

The Leading Edge of American Practice

Bruce E. Kaufman

INTRODUCTION

This chapter examines the employee involvement and voice (EIV) system at Delta Air Lines, headquartered in Atlanta, Georgia (United States). Delta is currently the world's second-largest airline in terms of passengers carried and has approximately 80,000 employees. The company is the oldest surviving American airline, has a long-established reputation as a people-oriented employer, and operates what is probably the most highly developed and structured company-run EIV program in the United States. Relatively few of its domestic employees are covered under collective bargaining contracts, so the EIV system covers the great bulk of the workforce. Portions of the EIV system also cover international employees (about 10 percent of company employment).

The chapter begins with a brief overview of the company and its history. Then, to help locate the Delta experience in the broader frame of American management practice and labor law, the following section provides a thumbnail sketch of the development of corporate EIV programs in the 1920s, the role in them of non-union representational councils and forums, and their subsequent regulation under the Railway Labor Act and National Labor Relations Act. Since the structure and role of employee involvement at a company depends critically on its business model and associated human resource management (HRM) strategy, the chapter's next two sections describe both aspects at Delta and how they have changed in both planned and unexpected ways over the last four decades. A formal system of employee involvement and voice was begun at Delta in the mid to late 1990s, and the following section of the chapter chronicles why the company moved toward formal EIV, how the program was structured and implemented, and how it has evolved to the present time. Following is a short section that describes key features of the Delta EIV program as it exists today, and then a final section presents fifteen implications and "lessons learned" from this case study. Although this chapter is comprehensive in its coverage of the Delta case, readers may also wish to consult two earlier studies by this author for additional discussion (Kaufman 2003, 2012).

The story of employee involvement and voice at Delta is fascinating and full of insights and food for thought for researchers and practitioners alike. Among the food-for-thought items is whether the United States' labor law harms the nation's economic competitiveness by unduly restricting the ability of most companies to operate a Delta-style system of employee representational councils and forums. As the other chapters in this volume make clear, no other country so tightly constrains how non-union companies may provide involvement and voice to their employees.

The material for this chapter has been gathered from a large number of personal interviews with people from the front line to the CEO level at Delta Air Lines headquarters in Atlanta, extending from 1998 to the present time. In addition to on-site visits in Atlanta, numerous telephone interviews were conducted over the course of a decade with current and former Delta people around the country. In the most recent round of interviews, two question-and-answer (Q&A) sessions were held with the Delta Board Council as well as a wide range of structured interviews with managers and employees. Several Delta division-level employee councils flew volunteers to Atlanta for the interviews in order to provide a representative cross-section of perspectives. Included in the interviews were former Northwest managers and employees, including union leaders and members. Delta management graciously gave the author full access to company employees and permitted closed-door interviews where requested (no management personnel present). This chapter was reviewed by both Delta employee representatives and executives, but only a few factual revisions were suggested; hence the evaluations and conclusions that follow are completely those of the author. The cooperation of the company is gratefully acknowledged.

THE COMPANY

C. E. Woolman, principal founder, started the company as Delta Air Services in 1928 to sell crop-dusting services to Louisiana farmers. The company inaugurated passenger service in 1929 with a small plane that carried six people from Dallas, Texas, to Monroe, Louisiana, at 90 miles per hours (Lewis and Newton 1979). When Woolman retired as CEO of Delta in 1966, the airline employed 13,000 people, flew to dozens of cities in the eastern half of the country, and in many years reported the highest return on equity among major carriers.

Delta continued to grow over the next half century through internal expansion and a number of mergers and acquisitions. The latter include Northeast (1972), Western (1987), Pan Am (1991), and Northwest (2008). The Pan Am acquisition gave Delta significant international access to Europe and Latin America; the Northwest Airlines (NWA) merger greatly increased its presence in Asia. From 2008 through 2011, the combined Delta/NWA was the largest airline in the world, eclipsed only in 2012 with the merger of United and Continental.

The company enjoyed a steady upward trend in growth and profits through the 1970s and often ranked at the top of customer satisfaction surveys (Swiercz and Spencer 1992). After industry deregulation in 1978, measures of financial and operational performance deteriorated and also took on a more roller-coaster character. Some years in the 1980s and 1990s, the company reported record profits but in other years steep losses. Customer satisfaction also deteriorated, as did service quality indicators such as lost baggage and on-time arrival.

The decade of the early 2000s (2000–2009) was a nightmare for Delta and the rest of the airline industry that no person could foresee as the country headed into the new century. The worst event was the terrorist attack of 9/11 on the Twin Towers in New York City. The industry was shut down for several weeks, and Delta quickly lost more than a billion dollars; even after flying resumed, traffic growth was anemic, and more losses followed. Despite a gradual national economic recovery and several rounds of deep cost cutting at the company, Delta continued to hemorrhage money and by 2005 was facing a corporate debt nearing $30 billion. In September of that year, the company filed for bankruptcy.

Delta emerged from reorganization in 2007, but only after fending off a hostile takeover attempt by US Airways. Richard Anderson, the current CEO, was appointed to lead the company in 2007. He engineered the merger with Northwest (Anderson had some years earlier been CEO at Northwest) and slowly rebuilt the company's finances and relations with customers and employees, albeit hampered by additional obstacles such as large fuel cost spikes and the 2007 through 2010 financial panic and economic downturn.

Profitability returned in 2011 and climbed further in 2012. Currently the company employs more than 80,000 employees and flies more than 1,300 flights per day across six continents. At the time this chapter is written, the widespread feeling at Delta is that the company has turned the corner on a decade of disaster and is gaining altitude. One positive indicator is that in 2011, Delta ranked number one in *Fortune Magazine*'s list of the world's most admired airlines.

EIV IN THE UNITED STATES: HISTORICAL AND LEGAL BACKGROUND

Some historical and legal background regarding employee involvement and voice programs in the United States is important for fully appreciating the Delta story and its broader implications for practice and policy.

A former Delta Vice President of Personnel defined EIV as giving frontline employees "an opportunity to be heard and make a difference." A current Delta executive defined employee involvement as "employees are in on things." Other more detailed and academic definitions can be given (see Dundon, Wilkinson, Marchington, and Ackers 2004; Wilkinson, Gollan, Marchington, and Lewin 2010), but these short statements well sum up the main idea. EIV can be delivered as a form of either *direct* or *indirect* participation or a combination of the two. Direct EIV is when managers and an individual employee or small group of employees interact face to face, such as when an employee uses a company's open-door policy to discuss a workplace issue with a manager or a frontline production team meets with a supervisor before the beginning of a shift. Indirect EIV is when one or more employees represent others, such as on a plant council, employee forum, or dispute resolution committee (Gollan 2006a; Kaufman and Taras 2010). A well-developed EIV program typically features both direct and indirect channels, but as company size and breadth and depth of participation grow, so typically does the relative role of representational EIV.

A number of writers on modern management (e.g., Beer 2009; Lawler, Albers, and Ledford 2001; Walton 1985) portray EIV as a relatively recent innovation, discovered in the 1960s and 1970s as part of the development of what is now popularly called a "high-performance work system" (HPWS). (Other common labels are "high-commitment" and "high-involvement" work systems.) Like many other purported new ideas in management, EIV actually goes back a century and more to the birth of management as a specialized practice and the development of the personnel/industrial relations function in the modern business enterprise (Taras 2003).

A hundred years ago, management was done by strict command and control, and to solicit employees' opinions or to listen to their complaints, particularly at a group level, was regarded as a radical step and tantamount to abrogating the employer's right to manage (Harris 1982; Jacoby 1997, 2003; Kaufman 2008). Just as the traditional child-rearing model of that era held that "children don't talk back to parents" and "to spare the rod is to spoil the child," the traditional management model took a similar view toward employees. The job of managers is to think and plan and then tell employees what to do and how to do it; the job of employees is to listen, obey, and execute. Sometimes this command-and-control method of management was exercised with enlightened paternalism and a genuine concern for employees' well-being. In most cases, however, employers of that era had a hard-boiled attitude that labor is a commodity and should be purchased for as little as possible, used for maximum short-term advantage, and then discharged with no obligation when no longer needed or at the slightest provocation. A flood of non–English-speaking immigrants, cheap labor, no labor laws, and few unions facilitated this attitude. Perhaps difficult to appreciate from today's perspective, workers a century ago risked being fired for even asking how their pay was calculated or pointing out a safety hazard (Kaufman 2010).

The first organized employer initiatives in employee voice and involvement began in the 1910s, expanded rapidly in the 1920s, and then mostly died out in the 1930s (Nelson 1993, 2000). The EIV program at Delta is interesting in part because today it is the only large-scale example of what had existed in the 1920s at several hundred leading companies, including iconic names such as DuPont, General Electric, Goodyear, International Harvester, and Standard Oil (Kaufman 2000a, 2000b).

The most innovative but also controversial part of these early EIV programs involved the use of plant-/company-level employee councils. At first called works councils, by the 1920s these representational bodies were most often known as *employee representation plans* (ERPs; National Industrial Conference Board 1922, 1933). The plans typically formed employees into electoral districts, say by department or occupation, and allowed employees to select through secret ballot election fellow workers (say on a 1:200 basis) who would serve on a plant or company council with select executives and managers for monthly or quarterly meetings. Records of the period show that the councils discussed a broad range of topics, including those of interest to management (e.g., operational efficiencies, cost savings) and to employees (wages, hours, conditions). The councils often appointed permanent subcommittees to deal with specific areas, such as safety, employee benefit programs, and discipline/discharge cases, and also appointed *ad hoc* project teams for specific assignments (e.g., a survey of prevailing wages at competitor firms). The number of such ERPs slowly grew over the 1920s and by the end of the decade covered 1.5 million workers or about 5 percent of nonagricultural employment and 15 percent of manufacturing employment (Kaufman 2008: Table 5.1).

In most cases, the new EIV programs were not just a stand-alone development but, rather, were one component of a new management model (Kaufman 2000a; Leiserson 1928). The traditional "stick" model of command and control, hire and fire, and employer autocracy increasingly seemed to generate too-high direct labor costs from absenteeism and turnover, low productivity from disinterested and disaffected employees, and an adversarial relation conducive to strikes and unions. The new "carrot" model, often called at that time the *goodwill* strategy (Commons 1919), sought to lower labor cost, increase productivity, and incent cooperation by getting the employees on the company's side so they too were thinking about how to boost profits and satisfy customers. A happy by-product for the employers was that workers also lost interest in outside representation (Leiserson 1928).

To accomplish this transformation, these pioneer companies—often called at the time "welfare capitalists" (Perlman 1928)—created internal labor markets (ILMs) in which most hiring was at the entry level, job vacancies at higher levels were filled by internal promotion, and employees were promised job security—often for life—as a reward for loyalty and good performance (Jacoby 1997). Also part of the goodwill model were above-market wages, extensive benefit programs (health insurance, pensions), financial incentives (profit sharing, stock option plans), and promise of fair treatment in discipline and discharge.

A split developed, however, among goodwill companies regarding the place of EIV and, in particular, the collective voice part. Non-union companies of that period with a separate employment function typically called it either a personnel or industrial relations (IR) department (Kaufman 2008). At the time, the personnel label was typically adopted by companies taking a more paternalistic and individualized approach to employee relations; the IR label, on the other hand, was typically adopted by "corporate liberal" (non-union) employers who thought the goodwill model in a large multi-plant organization required some form of collective dealing with employees. Leading practitioners of the personnel goodwill strategy in the 1920s include Endicott-Johnson (see Zahavi 1988), Western Electric, and International Business Machines (IBM); leading practitioners of the IR goodwill strategy include all the iconic names listed earlier.

Going back to a distinction made earlier, the personnel companies practicing a goodwill HRM strategy relied on direct forms of EIV and, in particular, an employee-friendly and constantly visible and accessible chief executive, exemplified by Thomas Watson Sr. at IBM (Kaufman 2008). The CEO and his direct reports, using an open door and extensive face-to-face contact with the front line, made a more formal EIV channel unnecessary. The IR companies, on the other hand, combined direct and indirect EIV with an employee representation plan as the linchpin component.

Many modern management writers (e.g., Dulebohn, Ferris, and Stodd 1995) characterize the HRM function of the 1920s as primitive operations concerned mainly with payroll, company picnics, and union firefighting. At many companies of the period, this is an apt characterization; at leading welfare capitalist employers, on the other hand, the HRM function was highly developed, integrated, and a strategic player. This was particularly true at companies with extensive EIV and, in particular, employee representation plans since, of all parts of a corporate HRM program, these require the most hands-on, professional, and deft handling by senior management. Thus, one notes that in Balderston's (1935) list of the "best 25 HRM programs in the USA," three fourths of the non-union companies had some kind of collective EIV program.

In an astonishing fall from grace, the crown jewel of the goodwill model—the ERP—was prohibited as an "unfair labor practice" by the National Labor Relations Act (NLRA) of 1935 (Hogler and Grenier 1992; LeRoy 2000). This meant that the more than 400 employee representation plans in the country had to be dismantled lest they be challenged as a dominated "company union;" many were taken over by union activists and, with favorable rulings from the National Labor Relations Board (NLRB), transformed into independent unions (Jacoby 2000). Somewhat ironically, the relatively few welfare capitalist companies to escape the mass unionization of the 1930s were mostly those that avoided collective dealing with employees and instead pursued the paternalist/individual personnel approach.

Subsequent research (Moriguchi 2005) has shown that during the Great Depression decade of the 1930s, those companies that most seriously breached their implicit psychological contract with employees of job security, economic advancement, and fair treatment were most likely to be unionized. Companies that had formed ERPs and subsequently did large-scale wage cuts and layoffs during the Depression were particularly prone to unionization, as most of the companies cited ruefully found out. With successful ERPs and a partnership spirit in the 1920s, these companies were practically immune to union organization; in the 1930s, their employees grumbled but tolerated cutbacks and tightening up as long as the cuts were not too deep and repeated, were done with equal sacrifice among sharehold-ers, executives, and workers, and were implemented in a bilateral manner in keeping with the ERP process. However, the length and severity of the Great Depression forced companies to make repeated and quite deep cut-backs, and those that did not manage the process carefully and fairly (e.g., at International Harvester, the company ill advisedly choose to cut wages but maintain dividends) saw their employees angrily turn against them as untrustworthy "promise breakers" and use the ERPs as a launch pad for bringing in real unions (Kaufman 2008).

The ERPs' fall from grace and banishment by the NLRA was partly the result of the public and employee disillusionment with companies that preached partnership and mutual gain in good times but then made work-ers bear the brunt of sacrifices in hard times. But other factors also entered in. For example, President Roosevelt encouraged more unions as a two-pronged way to fight the Depression, with the idea that unions, through industrywide contracts, can stop a downward spiral of wage cuts and conditions (caused by excess supply in labor markets and overcapacity in product markets) that leads to a no-win "race to the bottom" and, second, unions, through collective bargaining, power can raise wages across indus-tries, which helps rebuild household income and gets consumer spending going again (Kaufman 2000a, 2000b). The non-union ERPs were portrayed by their critics as "employers' pets" and "toothless dogs" and thus lack-ing the power or market reach to perform either the wage-maintenance or wage-raising function. Another nail in the ERP coffin was that hundreds of companies, seeing that Roosevelt was encouraging more unions, rushed to set up ERPs as a quick and opportunistic way to forestall outside organi-zation (Bernstein 1970). Many in the Roosevelt administration and public at large regarded these ERPs as shams and one more example of corporate greed and duplicity. Finally, the non-union ERPs had become enemy number one of the organized labor movement, widely blamed by unions and their supporters for the substantial decline in workers' interest in union joining in the 1920s, and the leadership of the American Federation of Labor made its support of Roosevelt's labor program conditional on banning the non-union ERP option (Nelson 2000).

Thus, the ERPs' record of accomplishment a decade earlier—widely acknowledged as positive overall but checkered with success at some com-panies and failure at others (Leiserson 1928)—was mostly forgotten in the rush to spread independent labor organization across industry. Accordingly, the language put in the NLRA concerning non-union employee representation plans was highly restrictive and, in effect, outlawed any type of employee representational body—even if only a one-person ombud—that in any way engages in "bilateral dealing" (a broader concept than negotiation) with managers over wages, hours, conditions, or treatment of employees (Kaufman 1999; LeRoy 2000). In effect, the message to employees is (1) management cannot be trusted over the longer run to keep its promises and (2) if you want some kind of formal voice and involvement in the company, the way to get it is by joining an independent union.

Most major companies covered by the NLRA were unionized during the 1930s and 1940s, and after World War II, union density in core industries was often 80 percent and more. There is, however, one small and mostly ignored part of this story. The NLRA does not cover all private-sector industries; in particular, it does not cover railroads and airlines. These two transportation industries are instead covered under the Railway Labor Act (RLA) enacted in 1926—when ERPs still enjoyed greater public and political support. Seldom recognized or discussed, the RLA contains a more permissive stance on non-union representational councils and forums. It does not contain the NLRA's *per se* ban on non-union ERPs; rather, it allows companies to form and operate ERPs but only as long as their activities do not cross over into bargaining or interfere with employees' protected right to choose outside labor union representation (Estreicher 2000; Katz 2011).

Since ten of the eleven national trunk carrier airlines in the post–WWII era were mostly unionized, the RLA's more permissive stance on non-union ERPs was for decades a largely moot issue. The most important non-union exception in the industry was a small regional-based carrier located in Atlanta called Delta Air Lines and, as recounted in the next section, its founder and long-time CEO practiced the paternalistic-individualized personnel approach to employee goodwill and, therefore, eschewed collective forms of EIV. Outside of Delta, several trunk carriers at times experimented with non-union councils for certain employee groups that had not yet been organized, as did some small non-union regional carriers, but these were usually small and short-lived affairs and critically viewed by the RLA's administrative agency, the National Mediation Board (NMB).

This brief historical survey raises both an interesting question and observation as we transition to the Delta part of the story. The question is: How did Delta Air Lines evolve from a small, paternalistically run regional airline into the world's second-largest airline with the most advanced set of representational employee councils and forums in any American company? The corollary observation is that Delta exists today as the sole example in the United States of a major company with strong resemblance to the 1920s corporate liberal goodwill firms with employee representation plans. So viewed, Delta is a "one-of-a-kind" case study for investigation of the pros and cons of the EIV councils and forums that the nation chose to (mostly) ban with the NLRA in the Depression years of the 1930s. Of course, a drawback of studying a one-of-a-kind situation is generalizations have to be made with care.

DELTA BUSINESS MODEL AND HRM STRATEGY: PRINCIPLES VS. APPLICATIONS

The first book I am aware of written on the topic of employee involvement is by William Basset in 1919 called *When the Workmen Help You Manage*. Basset was a business consultant, and the book has always seemed to me to contain many well-grounded insights on EIV. Perhaps the most fundamental is on the second page of the Forward. There Basset tells readers: "The principles [of good management] do not change; the applications always change."

The next two sections of this chapter tell how Delta Air Lines somewhat serendipitously came to have a nation-leading EIV program. The story covers eight decades and is split into pre- and post-deregulation segments. But before embarking on it, "Basset's dictum" needs emphasis.

The management principle that has guided Delta Air Lines from its first day to the current day—albeit with some wavering in the 1990s and early 2000s—is this three-part value proposition: (1) an airline is mainly a customer service business, (2) superior customer service is a strategic source of competitive advantage because it permits charging a price premium and secures a loyal and therefore repeat customer base, and (3) essential to good customer service is a workforce with high morale and esprit de corps, strong sense of commitment to the job and company, and willingness to work as a team and go the extra mile. Of course, getting and maintaining a workforce with these attributes—as opposed to 80,000 "hired hands"—costs considerable money and management time and attention and in the end may not yield enough extra productivity and revenue to be a profitable investment.

An interesting part of the story to follow is how Delta successfully implemented this business model up to industry deregulation in 1978 and then struggled mightily and with only mixed success to readjust it to fit a completely different set of rules and competitive landscape post-deregulation. Although many other American companies decided by the 1990s that the employment/HRM component of this model (lifetime jobs, industry-leading wags, etc.) had become uneconomic and therefore mostly moved toward a different strategy (Cappelli et al. 1997), Delta ultimately chose to stay with it, albeit significantly reengineered and pruned back. Only a few short years ago when the company was in bankruptcy, its long-time employment model looked near dead; as recounted here, it has somewhat miraculously and phoenix-like gotten "back in the air" and flying again—or so it now seems when viewed in broad outline.

The other part of Basset's dictum also needs emphasis. Generically viewed, Delta has from Day 1 operated what is now called a high-performance work system (HPWS) with an employment component built on a high-commitment and unitarist (unity of interest) model. This assertion, however, flies in the face of much modern writing on the HPWS (e.g., Beer 2009; Huselid 1995; Kochan and Osterman 1994) since it is widely claimed to be a new discovery of the 1960s through 1980s. These writings, however, confuse application with principle. The principle, as described, is that companies get higher performance (*ceteris paribus*) with a more committed, enthusiastic, and cooperative workforce. Smart business leaders and writers on management have recognized this for a century and more, as have military leaders for several millennia (a nation being an organization and an army a workforce). These same leaders and writers, however, have also recognized that there is no "one best way" for getting this committed, enthusiastic, and cooperative workforce; that is, there are a number of different approaches (applications) that can get the job done, and these may well vary in effectiveness over time and across business situations. In particular, what we see in the Delta story is a constant adherence to the principle of unitarism but an evolutionary shift in how to achieve it from an individualist, paternalist, welfarist, command-and-control, and high-fixed-cost HRM model pre-deregulation to a reconfigured involvement, team, variable-cost, flexible, less hierarchical/silo structured, and more performance-attuned model post-deregulation (Kaufman 2012). Formal EIV, as we shall see, had no place in the former but a central place in the latter.

DELTA BUSINESS MODEL, HRM STRATEGY, AND EIV: PRE-DEREGULATION

The details of Delta's business model evolved from the late 1920s to the late 1970s, but the principles remained largely the same, partly because the founder, Mr. Woolman, remained at the helm for more than three decades and partly because the first several successor CEOs were long-time Delta executives schooled in the Woolman way of doing things (Lewis and Newton 1979).

Delta pursued growth and competitive advantage through several routes. One was to develop a secure and profit-generating base in the southeastern United States with Atlanta as the major hub and then gradually expand outward. This was an adroit and fortuitous move since Atlanta and the Southeast region experienced a long-term economic and population boom after World War II. Also helpful was that the Civil Aeronautics Board (CAB) limited entry into existing markets, such as Atlanta, and Delta's chief rival for Atlanta traffic was the increasingly troubled Eastern Airlines. Eastern had contentious relations with its unions and a reputation for indifferent service; finally, after several lengthy and bitter strikes, Eastern declared bankruptcy in 1991. With the help of Eastern's demise, along with earlier acquisitions such as Northeast Airlines, Delta acquired extensive north–south routes in the eastern half of the country, particularly on the profitable New York-to-Florida corridor.

Another part of the Delta business model was economy in operations. Mr. Woolman and immediate successors kept the airline largely debt free, early converted the airline to more popular and economical jet aircraft, invested only in new planes that were proven performers, and generated industry-leading productivity from its non-union workforce. Executive salaries and perquisites were also modest by industry standards.

The linchpin of the Delta business model, however, was its HRM strategy. The following three quotations from Woolman's speeches give the idea:

> For years, Delta flew planes similar to those of other airlines, at identical fares. Delta's success came not just from good operations and efficiency but above all from the friendly spirit of Delta and the way Delta employees handled the public.

> No one person is an airline. An airline is a team. It must be friendly, courteous, cooperative, efficient, and bound as closely as a devoted family.

> Good will pays dividends . . . and good will is an asset that won't show up on any balance sheet, but is the most important factor in operating a successful airline.[1]

The first quotation highlights Woolman's recognition that one route to competitive advantage is superior customer service and, in a service business such as airlines, high employee morale and commitment are crucial ingredients. The second quotation highlights the Delta emphasis on creating a cooperative team feeling among employees, framed by Woolman in a traditionally Southern cultural idiom as a "devoted family" (Whitelegg 2005). The third quotation could have come from any CEO of a 1920s welfare capitalist firm, for it speaks of the competitive advantage a company gains when it gets not only the eight hours per day of the employees' time but also the commitment of their hearts, minds, and energy (goodwill) to the job.

Delta Air Lines under Woolman became an exemplar of enlightened paternalism and positive employee relations. Another Woolman saying was "happy employees make happy customers make happy shareholders," and Delta went to considerable lengths to have happy employees. The company after WWII was typically the leader in pay and benefits among the major carriers, never made layoffs until the 1990s, offered lifetime jobs, made fair treatment a cardinal principle, and featured an oft-used "open door" for employees who wanted to talk to Woolman or other executives. According to company biographers, Woolman also kept in close contact with employees through "ceaseless swings around the Delta route system" and "the most enduring legacy of the Woolman era was the company's constant solicitude about perpetuating a phenomenon that over the years had come to be known as the 'Delta family feeling' " (Lewis and Newton 1979: 400).

A concomitant of Delta's solicitude about employees is that labor unions had little success in organizing its employees. The airline industry is one of the most strongly unionized in the United States, and during the post-war period, Delta stood out as a non-union anomaly. Woolman, like many entrepreneurs, was not a fan of labor unions. Lewis and Newton (1979: 57) observe, "In view of his southern background and highly paternalistic outlook, it is not surprising that Woolman believed labor unions unnecessary in a properly conducted enterprise." It was to his chagrin and disappointment, therefore, that the company's pilots chose early on (1935) to affiliate with the Air Line Pilots Association (ALPA). Only much later did one other small group of Delta employees, flight controllers, affiliate with an outside union. Although open about the fact it did not want unions, Delta under Woolman and successor CEOs took the high-road strategy to union avoidance by giving employees wages, benefits, and treatment comparable to or better than what unions could offer. Woolman's successor CEO, Tom Beebe, remarked on this subject, "Call it trite if you want to, but it works. We don't try to keep unions away. We just take care of our people" (quoted in *New York Times*, "Labor is Key to Delta's Profits," 4/28/1974). For most of the post-war period, the company did not have a single union election.

Management professor Fred Foulkes selected for study in the late 1970s twenty-six completely or mostly non-union companies with advanced positive employee relations programs. His findings and conclusions are published in book form as *Personnel Policies of Large Nonunion Companies* (1980). Although Foulkes does not indicate the names of participating companies, I understand Delta Air Lines was one. His study provides a number of additional insights regarding Delta's traditional employee relations model and the role of employee involvement and voice.

Given the historical analysis in the previous section, it is worth noting that Foulkes tells readers in the introduction that even in the late 1970s, it was a challenge to identify a significant number of large non-union companies because the tidal wave of unionization in the 1930s through 1950s had so diminished their ranks.

Although Foulkes does not directly say it, Delta and the other non-union companies he surveyed were in many respects similar to the large non-union "goodwill" employers of the 1920s—with one important exception. The similarity side is revealed in the parallel nature of their HRM programs. Common elements among Foulkes's twenty-six non-union companies are:

- Employment security through a no-layoff policy and carefully reviewed "last resort" termination
- Above-average pay and generous benefits; emphasis where possible on merit; and attention to fairness

- Outside hiring for entry-level jobs; promotion from within for higher-level jobs
- Emphasis on effective communication with employees and provision of feedback mechanisms (open-door policy, surveys, group speak-up meetings)
- An influential human resource function and careful/selective hiring
- An egalitarian culture with modest managerial status and compensation differentials

These six components, even if sometimes of a more underdeveloped or primitive nature, were also widespread among leading employers of the 1920s, as earlier described. All six were also central parts of the Delta HRM system into the early 1990s.

The one area of exception concerns the delivery of employee involvement and voice. One notes, to begin, that Foulkes uses the term "personnel" to describe the employment management approach of these companies. Recall from the previous section that a survey of top non-union employers in the early 1930s found most used some kind of collective voice, such as an ERP. Not by coincidence, in the 1970s—after the NLRA had been in effect for nearly half a century—the non-union companies surveyed by Foulkes had shifted course and were relying mostly on individual and small-group forms of participation and involvement, per the connotation of the "personnel" term. Not coincidentally, the employment function at Delta was called personnel.

More specifically, Foulkes (1980) notes that only two of the twenty-six companies "have employee representation communications devices" (283). Tellingly, he goes on to observe,

> One personnel director believes his company's employees' committee is very significant because top management listens to it and has great respect for it. However, he does admit that having elected employee representatives is of *questionable legality*, and that the company might be in trouble if it were challenged.
>
> (1980: 283, emphasis added)

It is speculation on the author's part, but I believe this company is Polaroid, and several years later its long-standing but modified ERP was indeed challenged and subsequently ruled by the NLRB to be an illegal company union (Kaufman 1999).

Delta was among the twenty-six companies in Foulkes' study that eschewed use of representational councils and forums, even though by being under the RLA it had the legal space to do what was denied to most of the other companies. Further, as indicated earlier, some other airlines, either small carriers or for particular work groups such as flight attendants at a major carrier, had experimented with non-union councils (Katz 2011).

Woolman, like Thomas Watson Sr. at IBM, was a committed individualist in employee relations and wanted no third party—not even an in-house third party—to stand between direct face-to-face manager–employee interaction.

Accordingly, the linchpin communication/feedback program at Delta in this period was the "personnel meeting" (described anonymously on pp. 288–89 of Foulkes's book). Every twelve to eighteen months several top managers convened a three- to four-hour meeting with workers at a particular location (e.g., flight attendants at the LaGuardia base), discussed the company's position and plans, described upcoming wage/benefit changes, and then took "no holds barred" questions and comments, with direct-report managers absent. The suggestions and complaints were written down, passed up the line, and acted upon where deemed meritorious.

The personnel meetings, although of a group nature, were a direct form of EIV. Long-term employees I interviewed at Delta could not recall any ongoing representational committee until the vice president of in-flight (flight attendants) formed a scheduling committee in the late 1980s. One flight attendant remarked on this lacuna, "Quite frankly, prior to the downsizing of the company [early 1990s], Delta people were quite content to be taken care of by management" (Cone 2000: 470).

Not only were Delta employees content to be taken care of, they were very grateful for it. In an unprecedented show of appreciation (precipitated by the company's refusal to follow other airlines and make large layoffs during the steep recession of 1981–82), Delta employees contributed $30 million to buy the company a new Boeing 767. The name given to the plane was *Spirit of Delta*, a visible and highly meaningful reference to the tight bond that had been created between company and employees.

Foulkes concludes from his study that what is fundamental to successful employee relations in a non-union environment is not a particular set of personnel practices or the direct versus indirect structure of the involvement and voice program (Basset's "applications"). Rather, the foundation rests on adherence to principles, such as a "climate of confidence, cooperation, and trust" (Foulkes 1980: 328) and "deep commitment and high consciousness . . . of their top managements of the overriding importance of the human element in an enterprise" (Foulkes 1980: 344). Delta management was singularly successful at this task, as symbolized in the *Spirit of Delta* gift from the employees. However, even as the "Delta family" celebration was in progress at the Atlanta hangar housing the plane, the economic foundation of the company was starting to erode and splinter and, with it, so did the company's ability to practice its traditional paternalistic and welfaristic style of employee relations. Although no one could foresee it at the time, Delta was getting ready to embark on a wrenching and near-fatal journey over the next three decades that required a fundamental reengineering of both its business model and HRM strategy, including the structure and role of employee involvement and voice.

BUSINESS MODEL AND HRM STRATEGY: POST-DEREGULATION

The American domestic airline industry was deregulated in 1978. Entry, pricing, and routes, once closely regulated by the CAB, became competitive decisions made in a free-market environment. The repercussions took years to fully work out, but the net effect was a profound and often wrenching transformation of the industry (Bamber, Gittell, Kochan, and Nordenflycht 2009; Johnson 2002; McKelvey 1988). Wages and benefits, earlier significantly above average in American industry, came under sustained competitive pressure and gradually ratcheted downward (Hirsch and Macpherson 2000). All the surviving legacy carriers also eventually went bankrupt, including Delta in 2005 (American was the last, doing so in 2011). Another unexpected development at Delta was creation of a broad-based and highly formalized EIV program. For purposes of smooth exposition, I break this part of the story into two parts and tell in this section the unfolding business events, changes to the Delta business model, and associated employment/HRM changes at the company from deregulation to now; the next section then provides a detailed description of the evolution, structure, and operation of the Delta EIV program.

After deregulation, new start-up carriers (e.g., People Express, Florida Air, Texas Air, ValuJet) quickly entered the market and began to compete with the legacy carriers, such as American, Continental, Delta, TWA, and United. Since a surplus of used passenger jets was available (many dozen at the time were parked on desert strips available for purchase/rent), as were experienced pilots and crew, the startups were able to get in the air with relatively modest investment. They also had much lower cost structures than the legacy carriers. This was partly due to lower labor cost; for example, most started out non-union, paid lower wages and benefits, and did not have the pension and medical obligations of the trunk carriers. (Southwest is the most notable exception, being a unionized carrier. See Gittell 2003.) They also adopted a different business model and in most cases only flew point to point on a select number of high-volume routes, thus avoiding both lower-volume small cities the CAB had forced the major carriers to serve and also the high fixed cost of a hub-and-spoke system, which Delta had earlier pioneered as a feeder device for its Atlanta center. At the same time, the legacy carriers—now free of CAB restraint on entry and routes—quickly started to expand into each other's markets.

The CAB had set minimum air fares so that the legacy carriers could earn a reasonable return with the expectation of quality service to passengers and service availability to marginal markets. Delta had prospered under this system because its HRM strategy, described in the previous section, provided the experienced and enthusiastic "we love to fly" employees who created the top-notch service for customers while, at the same time, its committed non-union workforce also gave it a distinct productivity advantage and thus lower operating costs relative to other unionized trunk carriers.

When regulation was removed, a number of these "pluses" disappeared or turned into "minuses," and profits soon began to shrink and, eventually, turn into losses. Air fares quickly started to fall and demand became more elastic (price sensitive), partly because the existing customer base now had more flying options but also because the composition of customers began to shift from price-insensitive business travelers to price-sensitive holiday and family travelers.

The new entrants with their lower cost structures and high-volume routes could make money at the lower ticket prices, but the legacy carriers could not, and hence their profit margins eroded and in a number of cases disappeared. Some legacy carriers (Braniff, TWA, Pan Am) soon went bankrupt and were either absorbed by other carriers or ceased operations altogether; the remaining legacy carriers, such as Delta, embarked on repeated rounds of cost cutting and various reconfigurations of their business models. A common response, for example, was to move the small-market business to subsidiary regional carriers and start an in-house discount carrier ("airline within an airline") on high-volume routes. Delta did both, in the former case with subsidiaries such as ComAir and Atlantic Southeast (both now sold off) and in the latter with its Song subsidiary (2003–2006). Both options were in part driven by the search for lower labor cost.

Figure 11.1 provides a snapshot view of the course of events at Delta from the late 1980s to the present time. The diagram charts earnings per share, the tenure and name of the CEOs, and the timing of major events.

Profit margins eroded in the 1980s, and Delta reported the first losses in decades. But things only came to a head in 1991 through 1994. CEO Ron

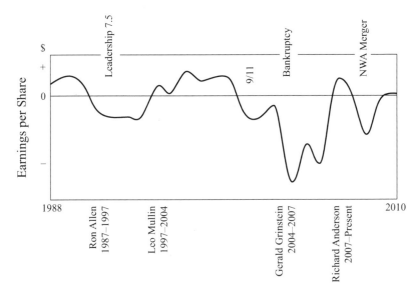

Figure 11.1   Delta Airlines: Earnings per Share, CEOs, and Major Events, 1988–2010

Allen, a relatively young, more aggressive, and risk-taking kind of leader (and also, unusual for an American corporation, from the personnel department), wanted to make Delta an international carrier and outbid United and American to secure the assets and routes of bankrupt Pan Am. Unfortunately, at the same time, passenger demand sank due to the recession of 1991 to 1992 and worries over the first Gulf War, while jet fuel prices spiked. Critics of the company also say that Allen and several earlier CEOs were too inbred and over their heads (Davis 1988).

As a result, Delta started to hemorrhage significant red ink in fiscal year 1991 ($506 million) and again in 1992 ($540 million). The first tangible threat to the traditional Delta family/goodwill model appeared at this point; in 1991 to 1992, Delta cut non-union wages and salaries 5 percent, laid off several hundred pilots (the union refused the 5 percent pay cut), and cut 6,200 jobs in other parts of the airline through attrition, elimination of part-time jobs, and early retirement. No layoffs were done among the non-union full-time workforce, however.

Large losses continued in 1993 and 1994, and the company felt forced to take additional cost-cutting measures. In 1994, Allen announced a new cost-reduction program called Leadership 7.5. The name comes from the goal of cutting Delta's average cost per seat-mile from 9.8 (an industry leader) to 7.5 (industry average) through $2 billion of savings. The largest savings came from an unprecedented reduction in force of 15,000 people, accompanied by more wage cuts, rollback of benefits, and abandonment of the strict promote-from-within policy. Allen described the company's strategy as "to be a high-value airline for the customer, but to do it at low cost" ("Delta Air to Pare Up to 15,000 Jobs," *The Globe and Mail*, 4/29/1994).

An airline stock analyst applauded Delta, saying its cost cutting was "now the most aggressive in the industry" (*San Antonio Express*, "Delta Air Lines Said Thursday It Will Cut," 4/29/1994), and indeed Delta staged a dramatic profit rebound for the rest of the decade. A newspaper, however, quoted a Delta insider as saying, "There was a breaking of the covenant" ("Delta CEO Sets Goal of Friendlier Skies," *USA Today*, June 1999), which another described as "employees feel betrayed . . . [and] fear the Delta family is dead" ("Delta Air's Allen to Quit," *Wall Street Journal*, 5/13/1997). In addition to all the give-backs, employees felt the program was abruptly announced, unilaterally imposed, and a sacrifice imposed on them because of Allen's ill-advised purchase of Pan Am. On top of it, Allen seemed dismissive about employees' concerns; when asked in a news interview about sagging employee morale he remarked, "So be it." Soon afterward, "So be it" buttons started to appear on the chests of Delta employees at ticket counters and on planes ("So Be It: Why Delta Air Lines Decided It Was Time for CEO to Take-Off," *Wall Street Journal*, 5/30/1997). Not coincidentally, as morale sagged, so did Delta's once-vaunted reputation for excellent customer service. By 1999, it had plunged from first to last among the legacy carriers.

Allen was forced by the board of directors to resign in mid-1997. Even though profits were high and rising in 1995 through 1997, Allen's distinct unpopularity with the workforce was tied to the tanking of morale and service quality. He had underestimated the push-back that came from unilaterally changing the psychological contract that Woolman and successors had so assiduously cultivated.

The promote-from-within policy had also applied to Delta CEOs but was abandoned in 1997 when the company hired an outsider, Leo Mullin, to take over from Allen. Mullin came not only from outside Delta but also from outside the airline industry (banking, utilities, McKenzie Consulting). Mullin was hired to do for Delta what Lou Gerstner had done at IBM—shake up, slim up, and turn around a company grown too inbred and behind the market curve. Gerstner undertook a dramatic multibillion-dollar cost-reduction program, including a major downsizing and reorientation of IBM's welfare capitalist–style HRM program (also featured in Foulkes's 1980 book). Mullin quickly signaled that the days of Delta's "till death do us part" lifetime employment model were also nearing an end. Symbolically, this was communicated by changing the name of the employment department from personnel to human resources and bringing in an executive from General Electric to run it; in terms of substantive change, the Delta ILM was opened up to much greater inflows and outflows, while some parts of the operations (e.g., cabin cleaning) were outsourced to lower-cost external vendors.

Ordinarily these actions would have ensured that Mullin got off to a rocky start with employees, who were still mostly longtime Delta veterans inculcated in the Woolman legacy. Mullin, however, partly got a "pass" because Allen had already broken the covenant and was the lightning rod for employee disaffection; further, in his first several years he undertook a number of actions that raised morale by improving sales and customer service. The company, for example, invested in new Boeing 777s, substantially refurbished its existing fleet, and improved baggage and departure/ arrival reliability. As Figure 11.1 indicates, Delta in the late 1990s started to again report healthy earnings. This led Mullin to make a series of HRM decisions that diverged from the new Gerstner model at IBM. While Gerstner continued to cut away at the traditional welfarist-lifetime IBM employment model, Mullin restored the pay and headcount reductions done under Allen's Leadership 7.5 program in an effort to further improve the damage to employee morale and commitment. Indeed, in a controversial move, he publicly pledged to employees to keep their pay "at or near the top of the industry" ("Delta Unveils Plan to Increase Pay," *Wall Street Journal*, 11/19/1998). Within two years, employment rebounded by 20 percent to 76,000 (partly due to acquisition of Atlantic Southeast), pilots got a new contract restoring their wages to 4.6 percent above the next-highest-paying company, and the non-union workforce got raises in 1997, 1998, and 1999.

The honeymoon started to sour in 2000 and ended in divorce in 2004, ironically because not only did Mullin soon find himself in an even worse profit crisis than Allen had a decade earlier, but he was equally ham-handed in the way he dealt with it.

Delta had a long history of relatively amicable relations with its pilots' union, but under Allen the relationship eroded. As earlier indicated, Mullin tried to restore peace by restoring the pilots to industry-leading pay, but the adversarial genie seemed to have escaped the bottle.

In 2000, ALPA demanded a further hike in pay, arguing that Delta's resurgence of profit justified an increase. In what appeared in hindsight to be a bargaining disaster (Mullin had no labor relations experience), the company caved in 2001 and agreed to a pay deal that not only maintained wages at an industry-leading position (senior captains now earned $300,000+) but in fact boosted pay 20 percent above the average for other legacy carriers and more than double the pay of pilots at hometown low-cost carrier AirTran. The agreement came, however, only after protracted acrimony and, finally, a work-to-rule slowdown by the pilots that forced cancellation of thousands of flights. This episode drove a further wedge between the company and its customer base. Internally, it further frayed the "we are a family" climate, put another dent in the morale of the rest of the Delta workforce, and seemed to signal the non-union employees that perhaps a union could indeed make a difference.

The pilots' bargaining snafu was nothing compared to what came next. The terrorist attacks of 9/11 sent the entire airline industry in a deep tailspin, and Delta was no exception. Within two weeks, the nation's airlines had cut the number of flights in half, more than 100,000 people were gone from the payroll, and losses exceeded $8 billion (Bamber, Gittell, Kochan, and von Nordenflycht 2009). The Delta president told the author in an interview that managing the company during the immediate aftermath of 9/11 was like piloting a plane through a thick fog bank with all the dials spinning. By the end of September, Delta cut employment by 13,000 (15 percent) and posted a $1 billion loss. Delta, however, was the last of the legacy carriers to make job cuts, and most (84 percent) were accomplished through voluntary separation and leave programs. Other companies, such as Northwest and US Air, invoked the "force majeure" clause in their union contracts, allowing them to nullify labor-protection language and institute immediate layoffs with no severance pay; on the other hand, several low-cost carriers, such as Southwest, made no layoffs (Gittell 2003).

The airline industry hoped for a cyclical rebound from 9/11 but instead was hit by more demand shocks (e.g., SARS epidemic, second Gulf War), supply shocks (e.g., surging oil prices), and intensified price competition from low-cost carriers. Delta began to hemorrhage money; losses mounted to $4 million a day and by 2004 cumulated to more than $5 billion. Several other network carriers (US Air, United) fairly soon nosedived into bankruptcy (Bamber, Gittell, Kochan, and Nordenflycht 2009). The Mullin executive team was faced with either working out dramatic cost savings or the likely prospect of a Delta bankruptcy.

The story of 2002 to 2004 at Delta was indeed more cost cutting, albeit with one additional upsetting event thrown into the mix. The headcount reductions of 2001 (16,000 total) were followed by another 8,000—approximately half through voluntary means and the other half through layoffs. Compensation and benefits for the non-union workers were cut back (10 percent pay/benefits cut, higher health care contributions, less vacation, eliminating health care coverage for new retirees). And the company went back to the pilots in 2003 and said the union must either roll back pilots' pay by $1 billion a year or the company would file bankruptcy. A major uncertainty, however, was fuel cost (about 25 percent of operating cost), which had gone up greatly and put a major squeeze on profitability. The company communicated to employees, in a sort of industry economics lesson, that the size of pay and workforce reductions was linked in a "sliding scale" manner to the price of oil—the more oil went above $60 a barrel, the larger had to be the offsetting cuts in labor cost ("Cost of Saving Delta: 9,000 Jobs," *Tribune Business News*, 9/23/2005).

Like Allen, Mullin gradually lost the support of the workforce and ultimately lost the confidence of the board because, in the words of an industry magazine ("Trust Seeker," *Airline Business*, 8/2006), the cost-cutting campaigns they initiated turned out to be "two of the worst-managed in US airline history" (pp. 49–50). Mullin then added insult to injury with two maladroit moves in the area of executive compensation. As frontline employees were taking big cuts, the company announced that sixty top executives had received $17 million in bonuses in 2002, and in 2003, Mullin was not only keeping his $795,000 base salary but was also getting a $1.4 million bonus (he later gave it back). Then, worse, even as employees grew increasingly fearful for the safety of their pensions, word hit the street that the company was spending an estimated $65 million for bankruptcy-proof "pension insurance" for thirty-three top executives—several of whom promptly took early retirement.

With Delta's financial condition hurtling out of control and employee discontent at an all-time high, the Delta board of directors forced Mullin to resign in late 2003. The goodwill HRM model appeared to be in shreds and perhaps mortally wounded. A Delta employee said, "You had an overwhelming reaction that bordered on a sense of betrayal" (quoted in "Changing Pilots," *Wall Street Journal* 10/4/2007).

Mullin was replaced in January 2004 by long-time board member Gerald Grinstein. Grinstein had been on the board since 1987 when Delta purchased Western Air Lines. As CEO at Western, Grinstein had restored profits and employee relations in a business turnaround situation and then, from 1989 through 1995, did much the same at railroad Burlington Northern. As a board member at Delta, he took the lead in forcing out both Allen and Mullin and was a consistent spokesman for employees and supporter of EIV.

Everyone realized fifteen years earlier that Delta had to lower its cost structure to compete in a deregulated marketplace, and yet after Leadership 7.5 and another decade of large cuts, Delta's cost per seat-mile remained at a ballooned 11 cents. The challenge facing Grinstein in early 2004, therefore, was how to cut $5 billion more from the cost structure, keep employees on board, and at the same time rebuild a reputation for superior service upon which a large part of Delta's competitive advantage rested. In many respects, Southwest and AirTran posed the same low-cost/high-quality challenge to Delta that Toyota posed to General Motors and Canon posed to Xerox.

Grinstein ultimately had to take Delta into bankruptcy in September 2005, but when he stepped down in 2007, the airline was clearly on a rebound. In a retrospective, a *Businessweek* article notes,

> Less than four years after being on life support, Delta is now the picture of health. Thanks to a management overhaul, a rigorous shift towards more profitable international routes, aggressive cost-cutting, and a shrewdly timed merger with Northwest Airlines [done by Grinstein's successor], Delta is now viewed by many analysts as the country's top-performing major carrier.
>
> ("How Delta Climbed Out of Bankruptcy," 3/14/2009)

As this quote indicates, the turnaround rested on a number of sweeping organizational changes along with further deep cuts for all stakeholders. The elements of the "new Delta," however, are best viewed as new operational spokes fitted to the traditional but freshly rejuvenated hub of employee partnership. Revealingly, this same article states, "Everything was built around Delta's paternalistic culture . . . the path to renewal and recovery was a willingness on the part of management and employees alike to make sacrifices."

Starting out as CEO, Grinstein observed that "the delicate social contract had been damaged and must be restored" ("Muted Celebration," *St. Petersburg Times*, 4/24/2004) and "We're in a service business where all you're selling is attitude and ability . . . [so] we have to show [Delta] people that we care about where they work, so that they will care too" ("Trust Seeker," *Airline Business*, 8/2006). In effect, Grinstein was recommitting the company to Woolman's original business model of seeking competitive advantage through quality customer service—with the price premium and repeat business base it creates—and to gaining this superior service through an HRM strategy that continued the Woolman emphasis on partnership, cooperation, and employee commitment, even if this traditional employment model had to be substantially reworked to fit in a deregulated marketplace and despite the fact many other companies (e.g., IBM in the computer business) had largely abandoned it altogether.

The most immediate and visible way Grinstein signaled disgruntled employees his commitment to restored partnership was in rearranging compensation. On the management side, he canceled the executive pension insurance program, capped his own salary at $500,000, took zero bonus and stock options, cut 41 percent from the compensation budget for executives (in part by forcing out people from the president on down), and ordered that no executive would receive a salary increase until the wages of frontline workers were restored to the industry average. On the employee side, he stipulated that on emergence from bankruptcy, workers get a 3.5 percent equity stake in the company, $400 million in pay raises and bonuses, and a profit-sharing plan designed to disburse at least 15 percent of pre-tax earnings. One tangible result of Grinstein's move toward renewed partnership was his ability to get the pilots' union in 2004 to accept more than $1 billion in concessions; shortly after emerging from bankruptcy, a Delta manager reported, "This is as inspired as I have seen the team in 17 years since I started at Delta" ("A New Dawn for Delta," *Airfinance Journal*, 3/2007).

By comparison, Northwest came out of bankruptcy four weeks after Delta, the CEO took a $26 million bonus, and employees received no equity but bankruptcy claims of $1 billion and a considerably less generous profit-sharing plan. In turn, the flight attendants' union blasted the Northwest CEO's bonus as "obscene, unfair, and out of spirit with any sense of shared sacrifice" ("Changing Pilots," *Wall Street Journal*, 10/4/2007).

A newspaper in 2007 spoke of the renewed "love affair between management and employees" at Delta and observed how this had translated into better business performance. In February 2007, the company announced it had earned the first annual operating profit since 2000. The article goes on to say,

> By the end of 2005, Delta's on-time performance had climbed to No. 5 among the 10 big carriers from last place. It rose to No. 3 for all of 2006 and the first half of 2007. Toni [X], a flight attendant . . . said changes under Mr. Grinstein began to restore morale, as did conference calls in which managers sought flight attendants' input.
>
> ("Changing Pilots," *Wall Street Journal*, 10/4/2007)

Grinstein retired in early 2007 having successfully navigated Delta's way through bankruptcy. Shareholders were wiped out, employees had taken steep pay and benefits cuts, and many thousands had lost their jobs, yet Grinstein was widely regarded as a hero who had saved the airline and brought the Delta family back together. A newspaper reported, "Grateful workers greeted Mr. Grinstein's retirement with five months of farewell dinners and a $25,000 ad in Delta's in-flight magazine" ("Changing Pilots," *Wall Street Journal*, 10/4/2007). True, the ad was not in the same class as a $30 million new plane, but it was nonetheless evidence that commitment had not entirely boiled away.

The board did a CEO search and passed over Delta insiders in favor of someone outside the company. To the concern and consternation of some inside Delta, they chose Richard Anderson, former CEO at Northwest Air Lines (2001–2004). Given Northwest's reputation for deeply adversarial labor relations and hard-nosed management, Anderson seemed an incongruous choice to follow Grinstein. However, the board appears to have made a wise choice, and at the time this chapter is written (mid-2012), Anderson is widely popular at the company and credited with adroitly leading the company through more turbulence (spiking fuel costs, the 2008–2010 financial crisis, merger with Northwest in 2008). In 2008 to 2010, Delta was the largest airline in the world (until the 2011 merger of United and Continental) and, after significant losses in 2008 to 2009, returned to modest profitability.

In a recent book on the airline industry, Bamber, Gittell, Kochan, and van Nordenflycht (2009) suggest that after the mid-1990s, Delta no longer practiced the commitment model. The more accurate reading is that Delta has partially repositioned the commitment model and has partially restored the breadth and depth of employee commitment, and it is impossible in today's environment to recreate the level/style of commitment achieved in the pre-1990s.

Anderson has, on one hand, assiduously linked the current Delta back to the traditional Delta of Woolman's era. His speeches are sprinkled with references to Woolman, he sits at Woolman's desk, every employee in 2008 received a booklet Anderson wrote called "Rules of the Road" in which Woolman is cited three times, a new $2.5 million Woolman Café was opened in 2009 at Atlanta headquarters, and every passenger on a Delta flight today is greeted before takeoff with a video featuring Anderson, who links the flight experience coming up to the "serve the customer" values passed down from founder Woolman.

The "Rules of the Road" booklet also heralds what has changed at Delta. It still strikes the "proemployee" and "partnership" themes. Section I lists seven "Basic Business Principles" (e.g., annual revenue growth of 7 percent, always fly safe), and if one counts lines, almost exactly half are devoted to employees and their interests ("the best employee relations," "employer of choice," "treating them with respect and dignity"). On the next page, Section II is devoted to "Connecting with our Business," and the second of three principles is vintage Delta: "Know Your People and Care for Them." However, a person knowledgeable of Delta's history also sees four distinct differences. First, Anderson's pledge about compensation shifts from "industry-leading" to "fair and appropriate;" second, the "family" term is missing, and instead one reads, "We run a meritocracy;" third, the old paternalistic "management by a few" is replaced by the title of Section VII, "People: Encourage Employee Involvement;" and fourth, job security shifts from a corporate entitlement to a performance-based reward ("people who meet goals get advanced" and "no 'new' jobs for nonperformers").

Thus, on one hand, as earlier claimed, the basic Delta business model has not changed; that is, it still strives for unitarism and uses unitarism to gain competitive advantage through premium pricing for superior customer service delivered by committed "go the extra mile" employees. On the other hand, the *basis* of unitarism and the commitment model *have* shifted. Much downgraded is the family, corporate welfare, paternalist, and lifetime job basis of employee commitment, and substantially in its place is a new psychological contract based on mutual performance and sharing of wins and losses, collaborative teamwork, reasonably secure jobs at a good place to work, and active voice and fair treatment.

As described shortly, Delta's EIV program is central to this new version of the commitment model. So also is a much-reconfigured compensation system. For Delta, bankruptcy had the beneficial effect of allowing it to put in place a lower-cost and more performance-contingent reward system than it otherwise could. Thus, the base pay level was lowered from "industry leading" to "industry average" but with new or expanded contingent forms of pay added to the system so *total* pay can still be industry leading if the company does well. Also, the pension system was revamped from defined benefit to defined contribution; unlike other bankrupt legacy carriers, however, Delta did not default on its nonpilot pension funds and, instead, resumed contributions after bankruptcy.

THE DELTA EIV PROGRAM: EVOLUTION, STRUCTURE, AND OPERATION

Organized employee involvement began at Delta in the last year of Allen's tenure as CEO. It took two forms. The first initiative was the creation of the Delta Board Council (DBC). In May 1996, the pilots' union requested a seat on the board of directors. The company compromised on a non-voting seat; management believed, however, it could not grant the pilots' request without also giving representation to the other 64,000 unorganized employees. So the DBC was created with a mission to serve as the "Eyes, Ears, and Voice of Delta people in the boardroom" (Cone 2000: 470). The council began with seven members from different non-union divisions of the company (e.g., Flight Attendants, Reservation Sales, Tech-Ops, Administrative Personnel), and initially three were selected by the DBC to attend the board meetings on a rotating basis. All DBC members began attending board meetings in 1997. Each DBC person was selected by division peers through an application and interview process, could be based anywhere in the Delta route system, and served a two-year term.

The second EIV initiative was formation of a Flight Attendant Forum (FAF). It was largely the impetus of the senior vice president of Delta's In-Flight division, Jenny Poole (a former flight attendant who worked her way up), and grew out of a prior flight attendant scheduling committee. The forum was a two-tier structure. Employees at each of Delta's sixteen flight attendant bases formed a local council with elected representatives (on a 1:100 ratio) to work with base management on local issues affecting flight attendants and In-Flight services (e.g., crew locker rooms, boarding procedures). Local bases them selected representatives (on a 1:1,000 ratio) to serve on a systemwide council headquartered in Atlanta. The System Forum met three times a year, had twenty-six people, met separately from management to formulate a consensus of what were the most pressing systemwide issues affecting In-Flight and flight attendants, and then met with senior management to present and discuss the issues. Topics could include anything affecting the In-Flight division, such as scheduling, per diem compensation, cabin food service, and work rules; off the table, however, were companywide personnel issues such as compensation and benefits.

The commitment model at Delta was at this point under significant strain. These EIV initiatives, however, did not originate as part of some larger strategic plan to put the commitment model back on track. Delta basically "backed into" formation of the DBC because of the pilots' contract and, once formed, was unsure what to do with it (other executives somewhat dubiously regarded it as "Allen's baby"). Likewise, the FAF had top-level approval but was not part of a new companywide HRM strategy. Thus, although EIV was later to become strategic at Delta, it did not start out this way.

Once created, both councils began to take on a life of their own that executives had not fully anticipated or perhaps entirely desired. The DBC's initial charter, for example, allotted each representative only eight days per year for council meetings and activities, plus additional time "as needed." The new DBC members, however, came to their positions charged up to "make a difference" for both company and employees and quickly pressed to expand their mission and resources. When the DBC was formed, neither Allen nor other executives could have anticipated that within a year, DBC members would have successfully lobbied for permission to fly around the Delta system on "city visits" in which two to three members held a day-long series of meetings with frontline employees and then reported back to Atlanta. A benefit of these fly-ins was that they helped break up an insulated "old boys" network and exposed a number of hidden poor performers in local base management; a drawback was that base managers quickly started to feel the DBC was an enemy threat and end run on their authority rather than a helpful colleague and constructive problem solver.

The FAF also had teething problems. Some employees were prone to turn the forum meetings into "bitch and moan" sessions that alienated managers; likewise, some managers alienated the employee representatives by too quickly going to "can't be done" and doing it with an attitude that mixed superiority, impatience, and excessive control.

The two EIV initiatives at Delta were not in response to an overt union threat, such as startup of a union organizing drive. As detailed earlier, Delta had long practiced a "make unions unnecessary" strategy, and until all the cutbacks of the 1990s, union organizers knew Delta employees were a lost cause. Even with all the cutbacks, the first union election in modern times was not until 2000 (ramp workers), and the union received only 17.3 percent of the eligible vote. Employee restiveness and dissatisfaction in In-Flight was, however, one motive behind formation of the FAF and, to the degree it resolved grievances and restored commitment, was a successful part of Delta's union-avoidance strategy. Similarly, the DBC had a direct link to unions to the extent it was pressure from the pilots' union for a board seat that motivated management to also give representation to the non-union workforce; however, the reactive and *ad hoc* nature of the DBC's formation points against a more immediately timed or strategically planned union-avoidance motive.

As detailed in the previous section, Allen was forced out in 1997 and Leo Mullin replaced him in 1998. By the end of Mullin's tenure, Delta had what can safely be described as the most formalized and highly developed EIV program in any American (mostly) non-union company. The program was a cascading set of councils, forums, and project teams that extended from the boardroom to the hangar floor. Ironically, the growth and development of EIV at Delta was again, for the most part, not part of Mullin's business or strategic HRM model but a combined product of a continued "backing into it" at the top level (CEO and president) and "push forward" by long-time Delta people from the vice president level down to the front line.

At the top remained the Delta Board Council. It continued to have seven members, but now the positions were full time (typically days, nights, and many weekends). Its role had expanded to six major functions:

- Give top executives an unfiltered "pulse of the company" view as seen from the front line.
- Communicate to the front line an unfiltered account of where the company is going and why.
- Represent the interests and perspective of employees to top management and the board.
- Serve as a consultant to management on new policy initiatives, particularly in the people area.
- Partner on or lead special projects (e.g., revision of the compensation review process).
- Conduct one to two days of site visits to Delta facilities around the world.

At the next level down were five divisional-level employee councils/forums (in parentheses number of represented employees in the year 2003): Flight Attendant Forum (19,500), Technical Operations Employee Council (9,500), Airport Customer Service Employee Forum (20,000), Cargo Partnership Council (1,450), and Reservations Sales Voice in Partnership (9,000). These groups (except Reservation Sales) held periodic meetings in Atlanta, where representatives (some peer elected, others peer selected) flew in from around the country/world for several days of caucuses and meetings with senior management. The mission of the groups was to identify problems and issues that could be jointly worked out to increase business effectiveness and employee satisfaction. Companywide pay and benefit policies were off the table, but on the table were a wide range of topics from relatively mundane (putting ATMs in crew lounges) to "big deal" items (e.g., maximum monthly flying hours, a peer-review termination panel).

The next level down was base-/city-level councils and forums. For example, each city with a reservation sales office or a flight attendant base had employee forum representatives chosen by peers. The local groups send up the line employee feedback on division-level issues (e.g., a policy/IT problem with booking a certain class of reservation), work with base managers on local issues (e.g., turning planes around faster), and provide a skip-level channel of communication to Atlanta on local managers who are either above or below the performance bar.

The bottom level was approximately one hundred continuous improvement teams (CITs) scattered across all parts of the company. Typically composed of volunteers at a base or facility, they tackled a specific issue or problem and recommend a solution to management. In Tech-Ops, for example, a team was formed to reduce the cost of engine overhaul so Delta could win more contract work.

For reasons described previously, the commitment model deteriorated further during Mullin's tenure and, indeed, threatened to disintegrate. After a near-death experience in 2003 to 2005, the commitment model rebounded at Delta and, arguably, what saved it was the EIV program and, behind it, certain board members, higher-level executives, and key employees who hung in as "partnership champions."

The most telling example of EIV's contribution to preserving the commitment model was Delta's force reduction immediately after 9/11. Other network carriers abrogated their union contracts and peremptorily laid off tens of thousands of employees within days. Although every day of delay cost Delta hundreds of millions of dollars, it took two weeks to partner with employee councils and work out six voluntary leave programs. The wage/benefit reductions in 2002 to 2003 were also worked out with the councils, thus avoiding some of the unilateral and surprise element Allen engendered with Leadership 7.5.

Skeptics of non-union councils and forums claim they only ratify what management wants to do in the first place and, in particular, they earn their way by helping sell employees on the need for pay cuts. The reality, at least at Delta, is considerably more complex and generally positive. Labor compensation at Delta was the highest in the industry and had to substantially come down for the company to survive in the new post–9/11 environment; further, every unionized carrier went through drastic layoffs and wage concessions. So, the question is: How is this process going to be most effectively and fairly done?

At Northwest, where union–management relations were rancorous and bitter, working together with unions was not a realistic option in the short time frame available, and therefore management used unilateral force to wring concessions from labor and the unions reciprocated by resisting management at every step, battling in court and on picket lines and conducting a hate campaign against the executive team. Productivity and customer service fell accordingly. At Delta, the non-union councils knew they did not have an independent power base and so their best hope was not resistance but cooperation in order to gain what they could for employees. Likewise, management knew that Delta's business model depended on above-average customer service and productivity, and they therefore had to preserve a critical element of employee morale and goodwill; hence self-interest led them to not only work with the councils but also give some wins for employees.

Evidence cited in interviews indicates the EIV program at Delta during the Mullin era more than paid for itself through enhanced productivity and preserving a modicum of partnership. However, an EIV program, no matter how effective (and Delta's certainly had shortcomings), cannot make a company profitable if its fundamental business model is noncompetitive or the economic environment has turned unduly hostile. Indeed, at some point these negative fundamentals start to undermine the viability of EIV because it becomes demoralizing for both sides to realize they are frantically bailing a ship that is most likely going to sink anyway.

One sign that the commitment model was not yet dead at Delta or that employees wanted independent representation in place of non-union councils was relative lack of union activity. As noted earlier, the first union election in decades was in early 2000 for ramp workers, and the union got 17.3 percent of the eligible vote. Only one other union (Association of Flight Attendants) was able to muster enough employee support to call for an election during Mullin's tenure and it got 29 percent of the eligible vote.

Mullin was forced out in 2004 and Gerald Grinstein replaced him. Grinstein had been a strong behind-the-scenes supporter of employee involvement since the DBC was formed in 1996. One might have expected, therefore, that the EIV system would expand again when he became CEO. In several respects, the more formal/structured part of the EIV program actually contracted (particularly in bankruptcy); in other less formal ways, Grinstein ramped up EIV.

Delta founder Woolman had spoken of employee goodwill as an asset (earlier quoted). Grinstein was able to cut another $5 billion from Delta's costs, including lower pay, benefits, and vacations, but still emerge with a "renewed love affair" with the employees by calling on and then rebuilding the goodwill asset. The goodwill asset had been severely depleted since the Allen days but had begun so large in the early 1980s—per the *Spirit of* Delta gift—that some still remained in 2004 at the start of bankruptcy. Grinstein observed in 2006 that employees had a "considerable sense of loyalty, a loyalty that has been tested but has been sustained by the lengthy tenure of employees. There's still an incredible sense of history throughout the airline" ("Trust Seeker, *Airline Business*, 8/2006). He also noted, however, that to tap into the remains of this goodwill asset, Delta had to regain the trust and confidence of its workers. It is undoubtedly the case that without employee involvement, this would have been impossible.

Grinstein substantially cleaned house in the executive ranks, money was extremely tight through the bankruptcy period, some of the employee councils needed a shake-up, and employees and managers were embroiled in crisis and firefighting. Hence, the middle part of the Delta EIV system was allowed to contract as several division-level councils were downsized or disbanded. This was reflected in a downsizing of the Delta Board Council from seven to five members. However, in terms of activities and outreach, the top and bottom ends of the EIV program remained fully engaged and even expanded.

At the top end, Grinstein revitalized the role of the Delta Board Council and gave it a renewed strategic direction. He gave the DBC full access to board meetings, a seat on the Finance and Audit committees, and made it a central connecting node between management and employees. Just as four decades earlier, Woolman had made "ceaseless swings" through the route system to stay connected with employees, Grinstein used the DBC as his surrogate. Delta was now spread across four (soon five) continents and many dozen American cities, and it became increasingly difficult for executives in Atlanta and base management and frontline employees in dispersed places such as Rome, Lima, Tokyo, and Albuquerque to effectively coordinate and communicate—particularly in a time of bankruptcy reorganization. DBC members, therefore, shuttled around the system to hold Q&A meetings, shoot down some of the wilder rumors and fears, report on bankruptcy proceedings, give an overview of the company's new strategic direction, and report back to senior management in Atlanta what they heard and saw (but this time with more partnership with base management). Akin to the old personnel meetings, the DBC also served as a listening and feedback group for frontline employees. Better than the old personnel meetings, however, the DBC in certain respects carried more legitimacy and credibility with the front line because it was an employee group outside of management.

The DBC had also from its earliest days served as an internal consultant and employee representative to senior line management and HR leadership on anything affecting the people end of the business. Since a key part of Grinstein's turnaround strategy was to restore trust with the workforce, he insisted that the DBC be given a more consistent and involved voice in decision making so new policies affecting the workforce were not "tossed over the wall" from guys in suits who had never loaded baggage or served a meal. A very sensitive frontline issue, for example was whether the company would use bankruptcy to contract out a significant amount of work. The DBC not only lobbied on behalf of employees to keep jobs in house but also worked with executives to find cost-effective means to do so. Another place the DBC played an important role was in giving more credibility to corporate communications to the workforce. In a climate of low trust, employees often discount or completely ignore messages from top management and search for anticipated hidden agendas and self-serving spin. To help close this gap, Grinstein had the DBC actively review and revise management communiqués before they went out to the workforce and disseminate to employees an independent version via the DBC website, emails, newsletter, and employee meetings. Coming from fellow frontline employees, the corporate messages have more credibility and often are less likely to generate the automatic email "delete" response.

At the bottom level of the EIV structure, dozens of special project teams were used to improve operations, wring out more cost, and improve customer service. Seemingly mundane but cumulatively important places employee teams had input were adoption of self-service ticket kiosks and redesign of flight attendant uniforms. Grinstein also greatly expanded "contact with employee" initiatives. For example, thousands of employees from around the world were flown to Atlanta for town hall–style meetings and dinners with Grinstein and the executive team; likewise, Grinstein and team flew around the system holding dozens of similar events. Grinstein also held monthly employee call-ins, breakfasts, and recognition events. These activities seem small and perhaps inconsequential; however, they collectively represent a huge investment of executive time and in both substance and form helped communicate to the Delta workforce that senior management is "walking the talk" on renewing partnership.

This renewed investment in employee goodwill paid unexpectedly huge dividends in early 2007. In late 2006, US Air launched a hostile takeover of Delta (the much larger company), hoping to get the assets cheap before Delta came out of bankruptcy. By all accounts, US Air's threat to Delta's survival brought the company together as a team in a way not seen in two decades. Employees staged rallies across the country to "Keep Delta My Delta," and the DBC frequently traveled to Washington to lobby Congressmen and testify before regulatory agencies. Against this unexpected wall of opposition, US Air withdrew its bid in early 2007. The Delta COO looked back and said, "The strength of employee voice was absolutely critical. So was the depth of the individual [DBC] committee members. Doug Parker [US Air CEO] didn't understand that" ("Employee Support Saved an Airline," *Financial Times*, 3/28/2007).

A number of insights about EIV emerge from this part of the Delta experience. For example, one concludes that the formal structure of EIV is far less important than management commitment to the process. In particular, people-oriented leadership at the top with trust and credibility at the rank-and-file level is crucial.

Delta's EIV councils and teams were able to creatively help the company through the crisis because they already had a decade of experience and company knowledge. Had they been created in reaction to the crisis, it would have no doubt been too little too late.

The Delta experience also brings to the surface another reality. EIV of a significant nature is not cheap or easy, because it consumes thousands of valuable management and employee hours, requires significant complementary support expenditures, can slow and constrain managerial decision making, requires difficult personal-interaction and problem-solving skills, and inexorably finds new and sometimes expensive ways to spend money on employees when a major goal is to save money.

EIV also has substantial payoffs, however. At Delta during the Grinstein era, the teams and councils contributed to hundreds of millions of dollars of improved operational efficiencies. The larger payoffs, however, were motivating discretionary effort toward organizational goals and (re)building employee goodwill and loyalty. These EIV intangibles come from positive feelings and cannot be purchased on the market or created from a "how-to" manual or "program of the month." In a crisis situation, such as during bankruptcy or the hostile US Air bid, the loyalty and commitment of the Delta workforce probably kept the company from going under; over the longer run, they provide a source of sustained competitive advantage for Delta, albeit also requiring an aligned and competitive business model.

Grinstein left in 2007 and was replaced by Richard Anderson. The structure of EIV at Delta remained largely the same in the Anderson era. In terms of formal organization, EIV cascades downward in three steps:

- Delta Board Council at the apex with five employee-selected members
- Four division-level EIV groups: Flight Attendants (18,000), Airport Customer Service and Cargo (21,000), Technical Operations (8,000), and Reservation Sales and City Ticket Offices (4,000). The first three groups have a two-tier structure with city/base forums (elected members) and systemwide forums (elected members from the city/base forums); the reservation sales group has only city/base forums.
- Dozens of project teams, some cross-divisional and others specific to a worksite

Several of the division-level councils that had become inactive were relaunched. Also, a peer-review dispute-resolution program (formerly found only in the Tech-Ops division) was established in In-Flight. The company also provides support to six systemwide employee diversity/identity groups, such as Asian-Pacific and gay/lesbian. Numerous other EIV activities take place in the company, such as monthly CEO breakfasts with several dozen employees, monthly phone-ins for division-level employees from around the system with their respective vice presidents, and town hall meetings around the system led by division-level executives.

The next section of this chapter describes current EIV events and activities; however, shortly after Anderson took over as CEO, two significant developments with large EIV relevance took place that deserve highlight here. The first is the role of EIV in facilitating the merger between Delta and Northwest Airlines (NWA).

The Delta/NWA integration, according to insiders and news accounts, was remarkably smooth and efficient. Mergers in the airline industry are notoriously difficult because they require integrating two hugely complex systems with different route structures, aircraft, IT systems, cultures, and employment programs while flight operations continue 24/7. Particularly contentious is integrating seniority lists. What made this merger go better was forming twenty-seven new special project teams staffed with volunteers to tackle issues from the most complex to mundane. To create a sense of shared interests and identity, Anderson also insisted that all project teams have equal representation from the two companies, even though by tradition the acquiring company decides the new rules and procedures.

Here are a few examples from the merger to indicate how EIV pays its way. Complex issues facing Delta included choosing city hubs to expand and contract, integrating a Boeing-based fleet (Delta) and Airbus-based fleet (NWA), and integration of 1,200 separate computer systems. Among the mundane issues, Delta served Coke products and NWA served Pepsi, Delta pilots sounded the "take your seats" bell four times but NWA pilots did it twice, and Delta cut limes in ten slices while NWA did sixteen. Without EIV, executives and managers make the decisions even though often unfamiliar with the specific issues; also, the employee grapevine works overtime in spreading false information and stoking fears and worst-case scenarios (e.g., rumors flew that most jobs at the NWA Detroit hub were to be eliminated).

With employee teams, value-creating solutions are worked out at a low level that satisfies both sides and get better employee buy-in. For example, teams decided to serve Coke drinks but Pepsi food products and cut limes in only ten slices since the extra customer satisfaction of first-class passengers was deemed worth the extra $500,000 cost. Likewise, Delta Board Council members regularly visited NWA facilities and, with more credibility than a Delta executive might have, told NWA employees what was fact versus fiction concerning the merger.

EIV was also used to more quickly and effectively integrate Northwest employees into the Delta culture, the formal being adversarial and unionized and the latter partnership and mostly non-union. For this chapter, I interviewed a number of former NWA employees. They sounded similar themes: we have heard about the Delta commitment model but are highly skeptical; Delta management says the right things (e.g., no layoffs because of the merger) but later they will break their promises; without a union we have no one to protect us and stop more give-backs; and employees from the paternalist "aw shucks" South may have bought the Delta family culture, but don't expect northerners with roots in auto factories and sit-down strikes to "drink the Delta Kool-Aid."

Knowing these sentiments, Anderson was very careful that promises were kept: for example, jobs that had been outsourced were brought back in and jobs at the Detroit hub were preserved. Similarly, even though Delta suffered a large loss in 2009 because of fuel costs and low demand, it went ahead with promised pay increases. In another move, thousands of NWA employees were flown to Atlanta for "get acquainted" meetings, and NWA employees were quickly added to division and base forums. Several told me in interviews that they were surprised to see the councils were "real," could achieve positive results faster, and gave genuine protection to people. Two examples came from an interview with members of the Tech-Ops council.

The company wanted to put "winglets" on planes and needed to transfer mechanics from one work area to another; the non-union council worked with the affected employees and in several weeks got buy-in with regard to transfers, scheduling, pay, and so forth, while doing this with a union at NWA, I was told, would probably take a number of months. As a second example, a former NWA mechanic related that an NWA manager after the merger had terminated an outspoken employee, the case was presented to the Tech-Ops peer-review system, and the outcome was the employee was reinstated and the manager let go. He said this was the true test of whether the Delta non-union system had integrity.

The second aspect of EIV that deserves discussion in the early Anderson years is with regard to the union organizing drives that emerged and multiplied around the company. The purpose of the EIV program at Delta is to improve operational efficiency, internal communication, and employees' sense of satisfaction and fair treatment at the company. It is no secret, however, that Delta prefers to operate without unions, and both experience and research suggest that employees who like their company, feel well paid and treated, and have a channel for voice are less likely to want outside representation (Gollan 2006b; Timur, Taras, and Ponak 2012). A former NWA union member said he voted no for the pragmatic reason that so far he is happy with Delta and could not see the union would provide benefits worth its $50 monthly dues. In an indirect sense, therefore, the more successful the Delta EIV system, the less desire employees have for union representation. On the other hand, a flight attendant said she voted yes for the union because it seems Delta, no matter how well intentioned, is caught up with the rest of the airline industry in a destructive race to the bottom on wages and labor conditions that only unions (or reregulation) can stop.

Council and forum members I interviewed all understand that keeping out unions is part of the company's motive in operating the EIV program; nonetheless, they do not see the program or their participation in it as "anti-union." Rather, they look at EIV as a constructive "build a better Delta" project and not a "keep out the flight attendants union" project, and if the former approach reduces interest in unions, then this is a sign that the company and its EIV program are working well.

The executive team and legal department extensively discuss, train, and educate the EIV employee members on the dos and don'ts of the labor law with regard to union activity. They learn that to TIP—threaten, intimidate, promise—is forbidden when talking to employees about unions. Also, there are built-in reasons the EIV groups avoid taking an antiunion position. First, some council/forum representatives are union supporters or former union members and say they would not participate in overt antiunionism. Second, both the company and EIV representatives know that the councils and forums lose credibility as a genuine voice for employees if they take sides with the company on the union issue. Finally, the company does not want the EIV groups to give unions a reason to file an interference charge in a representational election. It would be fatuous to claim, however, that the council and forum members are completely disinterested in the outcome. A common experience is that employees who work in the EIV process develop a greater sense of identification and loyalty with the company, thus tending to make them less likely to side with the unions (Leiserson 1928). Also, they realize a union win may well mean the end of the EIV groups, at least in their current structure.

The "spirit of Delta" has been badly frayed and torn over the last three decades, and the merger with Northwest added 25,000 union members to the Delta ranks. Not surprisingly, therefore, unions representing various airline crafts, including In-Flight, ramp, mechanics, and reservation/gate workers, filed for elections in 2008 through 2011. The largest group took place in late 2010, covered 50,000 workers across Delta, and was the largest union organizing effort since Ford Motor in 1941. The unions lost all the elections, in several cases by a relatively wide margin (e.g., 76 percent to 24 percent in reservations/gate) but with a much closer vote in what both sides regarded as the key contest—the flight attendants (53 percent vs. 47 percent). An interference charge was filed against the EIV councils in the flight attendants election, but the NMB ruled in favor of the company (two of the three current NMB members are former union leaders, so bias in favor of the company is not likely).

CURRENT EIV: ACTIVITIES AND INSIGHTS

I interviewed employees and manages across the different divisions of the company in 2011 and 2012. Here are few examples of what I consider to be meaningful insights about current EIV activities.

First, one has to recognize that the term "employee involvement" does not just mean a one-way "bottom-up" set of activities for frontline employees; it also means an astonishing commitment of time and energy from the CEO and top executives to the process of employee engagement. The DBC members have regular access to Anderson and top executives. The division councils and forums fly representatives to Atlanta for annual or biannual meetings and Anderson regularly meets with them. He also holds town hall meetings around the system, meets with employees flown in from around the system for CEO breakfasts and various employee recognition events, and does phone-in sessions with employees. Although seemingly a small thing, it symbolizes the "Delta family" in action when Anderson was in Minneapolis for meetings and learned an employee's home had burned down. He took his time, as CEO of an 80,000-person company, to drive out to meet the employee and offer the company's sympathy and assistance.

At one step down, here is a sample of the EIV activities done by the vice president for reservation sales and customer care. She holds regular town hall meetings with employees at select bases; flies quarterly to all seventeen call centers in the system and meets with managers and employees; once a month does a one-hour "side-by-side" with a reservations agent at a call center and then meets with the center's leadership team to debrief on problems and procedures needing improvement (e.g., arrangements for unaccompanied children on flights); holds meetings with members of four project teams; hosts twice-a-year meetings in Atlanta with forum members flown in from all parts of the system; holds two call-in sessions per month hosted by the division forum open to all employees with no questions barred and a transcription of the sessions made available on the company's intranet; holds a quarterly recognition luncheon for twenty-five employees from around the system; and has an open email to all division employees and personally responds. She said of her job, "My world revolves around making sure employees are set up for success."

A second feature concerns the way Delta has reengineered its employee compensation system. EIV does not work well if it is not supported by a complementary set of HR practices. Of particular importance is getting the pay system aligned so it promotes and supports EIV. As earlier indicated, Delta had to dramatically bring down its pay structure from "industry leading" to "industry average" in order to survive in the turbulent and fiercely competitive post-deregulation marketplace. At the same time, however, it has created a variety of contingent pay systems that allow employees to get back to industry-leading compensation when the company does well on profitability and various operation and customer satisfaction indices. The company, for example, has a profit-sharing plan that paid out $264 million based on 2011 performance, or an average increase of almost 5 percent to employee pay. It also created a Shared Rewards program through which employees receive a monthly bonus of $50 if the company meets two out of three performance targets and $100 if all three are met. In 2011, this incentive program added nearly $1,000 to employee pay. Finally, Delta has also aligned executive pay with EIV by basing top managers' compensation on the same metrics used for employees; it has also kept base salaries and total compensation of executives well under those of other major airlines.

As indicated at numerous points in this chapter, EIV at Delta requires a very large investment of money, resources, and executive and employee time. Here are three vignettes of how EIV pays for itself taken from my latest round of interviews.

First, base employees in Singapore were given the same standard Delta uniforms as employees in Boston, including a wool overcoat. Temperatures in Singapore, however, are twenty degrees hotter than Boston and no one needs the coat. Without EIV, employees in Singapore might just have shrugged and kept the coat in the closet; alternatively, they might have told local management about this waste of money but local management then shrugs and sits on it or, instead, base management passes it up the line to Atlanta only to see it disappear into the organizational "black hole" at headquarters. Instead, the Singapore employees brought the wool coat matter to the attention of local employee council representatives, who passed it up the line to division representatives who met with the appropriate managers in Atlanta and got the wool coats dropped from standard issue at Singapore and similar bases. Admittedly this is a relatively small savings item but, when multiplied across hundreds and thousands of other examples, adds up in the aggregate to a more profitable airline and higher pay for employees. Parenthetically, one must also consider whether an independent union would have facilitated or inhibited a successful resolution of this matter.

Second, the In-Flight division decided to offer an expanded list of food items for sale on long-haul flights. The service issue was whether to put all the food items on one cart or split them up on two carts. The vice president of In-Flight, having been a flight attendant, had a firm opinion on the matter but presented it to the Employee Involvement Group. The group split on the natter. So a trial run was organized and publicized across the system with one-cart service on one flight and two-cart service on another. The vice president worked one of the flights, with photos later put on the intranet site. The forum representatives voted for the option she opposed; since there were clearly still strong differences of opinion, the group did more brainstorming and came up with a cart solution that pleased both sides. Besides getting the efficient outcome, the 18,000 flight attendants in the system also knew that the choice was made and approved with employee input and thus they could not grouse about "what manager in Atlanta made this brain-dead decision?"

Third, Delta inaugurated new service from Atlanta to Accra, the capital of Ghana in West Africa. Delta employees from ticket sales, ramp service, and In-Flight soon saw the product had a variety of rough spots. The respective forums got involved; however, top management has made it clear in such cases that identifying problems is only one part of their job, and before they go to see senior management, they also need to work up a business plan on solving it. One issue was food, since the standard menu used for flights to Europe was heavy on pasta but West Africans eat mostly rice. Also at issue were cultural things that complicated getting carry-on luggage smoothly on board and stowed. Even the manner of saying "good morning" was off. So the Airport Customer Service (ACS) and In-Flight forums brought 100 employees working the Africa routes together for a discussion group; they then called the head of Delta food service, who came over to the meeting to discuss food options and, at the end, Delta board member Andrew Young came and talked about cultural differences. Here is a fine example of (1) quickly identifying a service problem, (2) mobilizing cross-functional employee groups to investigate the problem and work up an action plan, (3) involve key managers in working out solutions, and (4) get a member of the board of directors involved and feeling ownership with this EIV project and the solution.

The final thing that made a big impression on me was the idea put forward by several vice presidents that Delta is really in the people energy business, and here is where the game is won or lost. Fuel for the planes is the single largest cost component, and labor cost ranks second. It is the labor cost item, however, that has the far greater potential to move the airline. All companies pay a standard wage for the 2,000 hours per year of their employees; the challenge is how much energy—physical, mental, and emotional—the company gets from those 2,000 hours. Some employees are go-getters, others are fence sitters, and others are laggards, but, whatever the case, all have capacity to considerably ramp up their energy commitment to their job and the company. A vice president calls this the "multiplier factor," and leveraging it to a higher level among 80,000 people can make a huge difference in costs, revenues, performance, and customer satisfaction. The only way to activate the multiplier, however, is to get people feeling connected and aligned with the company's game plan, giving them a personal role and financial stake in it, and letting them feel the satisfaction of helping to make the operation better. The role of management and EIV is to arouse this discretionary energy component, get the people the rights skills and resources to effectively use it, and direct them within a broad outline but then let the energy have enough free play to excite people with what they can do and where it can go. Then employees are engaged and, for the same pay, provide a multiple amount of effort and energy for the company's success. As one person put it, "across the company we are continually trying to raise our game."

EIV IMPLICATIONS AND LESSONS

In a 2003 article (Kaufman 2003), I summarized twelve "lessons learned" from my first on-site investigation of the Delta program. I have modestly revised them, mostly for updating purposes, and have added three others that in the interim seem to also merit highlight.

Not for Everyone. All companies have to make a profit, and this requires creating and maintaining some kind of competitive advantage in the marketplace. Likewise, all companies gain when they get more work effort and commitment from their employees. The beginning of wisdom, however, is to realize that there are many alternative ways to achieve a competitive advantage and get employees to work hard, and EIV, particularly of the high-level and advanced form at Delta, is *not* the best (i.e., most profitable) approach to accomplish these ends for many companies. This may be because the costs of EIV outweigh the benefits for certain business models (e.g., competitive advantage from being the low-price leader) or alternative HRM strategies are more cost effective (e.g., using electronic monitoring, assembly lines, and tight discipline to maximize work effort). If any evidence is needed of this proposition, consider that until fifteen years ago, even Delta did not use the EIV strategy. Typically an extensive and formalized EIV program is more likely to be profitable when in-house employee skills and knowledge, discretionary effort and initiative, and employee morale and customer service are important to business success. Also conducive to EIV is when the production process is complex, interdependent, and subject to significant external uncertainty (making coordination through command and control difficult); large size or far-flung operations make communication difficult; the workforce is skilled, educated, and diverse; and the HRM model emphasizes promotion from within, job security, and maintaining internal equity.

Impact the Bottom Line. A high-level EIV program will quickly atrophy unless it demonstrably adds to the bottom line. Although employee involvement has an attractive "feel-good" quality on the front end, the reality is that high-involvement management is time consuming, complicated, and sometimes uncomfortable, and unless it yields a significant ROI (return on investment), all but the most committed management teams will lose interest.

Core Part of the Business. To generate a significant ROI, in turn, the EIV program has to be made a core part of the business and woven into the fabric of the company. It has to demonstrate value added in making the company run leaner, nimbler, and more responsively; it cannot just be an HR/employee relations sideshow or culture piece. The HR function may have an extensive support and liaison role with the councils and forums, but they need to report to and get their marching orders from the top of the executive hierarchy.

Long-Run Focus. A company taking the high-involvement approach has to be in it for the long term, because it requires substantial up-front investment in time, money, and infrastructure, and the payoff in improved organizational performance takes several years to flow in. Companies that seek a quick fix to short-run profitability problems or financial pressures, say by a suddenly announced large-scale layoff or pay freeze, will quickly undermine the success of a high-involvement strategy and destroy the value of its investment in employee goodwill.

Trust and Mutual Gain. The linchpin idea of high involvement is that the employment relation has the potential to be a positive-sum game (mutual-gain outcome) if the employer and employees work together and share the resulting fruits of cooperation. This strategy is difficult to initiate and sustain, however, because each side worries that the other will behave opportunistically and not live up to its promises. For a high-involvement strategy to work, therefore, both sides have to honor in word and deed the principle of mutual gain and must work with each in a spirit of trust, integrity, and commitment. A few poorly communicated or unilateral moves by management on a sensitive issue can threaten years of progress. Therefore, a three-part cardinal principle for managers who are thinking EIV is: (1) you have to steadfastly honor your promises and commitments to the workforce, (2) don't make promises or commitments you most likely can't keep down the road, and (3) if a promise has to be broken, then use EIV on the front end to minimize the damage to goodwill and partnership.

Distributive Items Off the Table. It is difficult to foster and maintain a sense of cooperation, partnership, and esprit de corps when employees are dissatisfied with their pay, benefits, and other parts of the employment package. EIV committees then become a forum for bargaining, griping, and grieving rather than looking for ways to make the company run better. Companies, of course, have cost constraints and cannot give employees everything they want, but to the degree they can take most distributive (economic) issues off the table, say by staying in the top tier of the pay/benefit scale—even if on a contingent performance basis—their EIV programs will perform much more effectively.

Empowerment and Problem Solving. One of the fine arts of successful high-level EIV is keeping the councils and forums energized and focused on organizational excellence. A sure way to sap the energy of the EIV program is to keep most of the control and power in the hands of management. Clear and well-respected boundaries have to be set around the EIV forums and councils, but the wider are the boundaries and the larger the scope for employee responsibility and participation in decision making, the more likely it is that they will stay interested and committed to the process. EIV is not for managers who are risk averse and control oriented, for there are inevitable "sweaty-palm" and "heartburn" episodes and employee choices that appear ill considered. Management can quickly lose interest in the EIV councils if they start to make lots of uneconomic demands, turn into gripe and grievance sessions, or become overly emotional and confrontative, so wise leadership and a consensus-building interpersonal style are also required on the employees' part. Helpful steps include an explicit commitment to mutual gain, a focus on problem solving rather than interest representation, and a mandate that people who raise a problem also take responsibility for searching for a solution. Finding the right mix of management control and council independence is a complex and difficult task.

Management Commitment. Employee involvement will fail without relentless management dedication and commitment to making the process work and a fundamental change in the corporate culture. The CEO must establish a strong commitment to EIV as a core value and way of doing business and then walk the talk. Equally important, people at the executive vice president and vice president levels must also be EIV champions, chosen not only for their support of high involvement but also for their demonstrated ability to practice it. A particularly vulnerable spot in the management chain, however, is at the lower end, such as station managers, call center leaders, or ramp supervisors. These managers often see the least to gain and/or the most to lose from EIV—for example, it threatens to undermine their authority, second-guess their decisions, and make them look bad to their superiors—so they remain noncommitted or resistant. Many supervisors and middle managers can be won over to EIV through strong encouragement from the top, revising performance evaluations to give weight to EIV, and demonstrating that EIV done the right way can benefit them, too. They also get on board if employee representatives are trained to avoid "grenade throwing" and instead work with lower-level managers in a low-key and behind-the-scenes manner. A portion of managers will never abandon command and control methods and have to be replaced.

Early Bumps. There will inevitably be a shakedown period and some early bumps on the road to a high-involvement organization. Both sides will make mistakes. Employees will sometimes be overly aggressive, prone to jump to the top with a problem, and unable to resist going public with confidential information, while management will sometimes act condescending and insincere, make unilateral decisions, punish an outspoken or troublesome employee advocate, and make promises they don't keep. Also, in the first year or two, employee grievances and demands come spilling out but later subside, allowing greater focus on operational and customer service problems.

Training. Successful high-level EIV requires a substantial investment in training and skill building. It is naive to think that frontline employees can suddenly understand balance sheets, have the social graces to interact with executives and board members, or know how to write up a business case. If the EIV program is to be successful, the company has to invest in training programs for the employee members, spanning business, operational, communication, interpersonal, and dispute-resolution skills. Some companies mistakenly think that it is only the employees that need EIV training, but managers also come to the table with skill deficiencies. Many can benefit from training in listening skills, interpersonal relations, and teamwork.

Formation, Selection, Term Limits, and Paid Time. It is difficult to overstate the importance of getting the right people and mix of talents and perspectives on the EIV groups if they are to be really successful. There is no obvious best approach, however. One selection method is elections. Companies like elections because they give the representatives credibility and standing with the front line, while employees like them because the process is more open, democratic, and sensitive to employee preferences. The downsides, however, are several: more politics in the EIV process, elections do not always result in choice of the most effective candidate, and some employees who would be good representatives do not want to go through the running-for-office process. Elections in the 18,000-person In-Flight group, for example, are difficult because the attendants do not have stable work groups so mostly do not know each other even at a particular city base. The other method used at Delta is committee interview and selection. Employees self-apply or are nominated for vacant EIV positions, a small committee of employees (no managers but an HR person for support) interviews candidates, and the committee chooses a winner. This method is more likely to select an effective person for the job but labors under a cloud of suspicion that the choice process is not free and independent. Once selected, the next issue is how many terms a person can serve. Here again are tradeoffs. EIV jobs involve a substantial learning curve, and thus effectiveness suggests multiple term limits; on the other hand, if people serve for six, eight, or ten years, the EIV groups start to look inbred and lacking fresh talent and ideas. A choice also has to be made about the amount of work time people are allowed to devote to EIV and what proportion is paid. At the DBC level, all the positions are full time and members are paid their original salaries; on a division-level forum, the chair and cochair may work full time on EIV, but other members work 10 to 20 hours per month. Whatever they are paid, the EIV members I talked to all claimed with unanimity that the company is typically getting 30 to 50 percent more time and effort (including weekends, travel away from home, 24/7 emails) than what is compensated. [A DBC member described the job as "drinking from a fire hose."] This, of course, is a microcosm of what EIV is meant to accomplish via commitment and enthusiasm. Finally, if EIV is to be meaningful, it has to start at the very front end by giving employees considerable scope and autonomy for setting up the groups' structure, policies, and procedures. At the time of writing, a sixteen-person employee group is chartered to relaunch the In-Flight forum, and they were holding meetings around the system and at an off-site hotel in Atlanta to work up the plan—with one management person in the room as liaison and support.

Staying the Course. A major problem in all longer-term human relationships is keeping the energy, enthusiasm, and passion going. High-level EIV programs are particularly susceptible to loss of momentum and gradual atrophy because one or both sides lose interest and fall back into the command/control and "do my eight hours and go home" comfort zone. Some kind of organizational or external threat to the survival or competitive position of the company and the employees' jobs can thus be very helpful in maintaining everyone's motivation and commitment to the process. Paradoxically, a turbulent business environment on one hand undercuts EIV because employment security and management continuity are more difficult to maintain and yet, on the other, promotes EIV because it throws up more ongoing business problems that keep everybody focused and motivated. Very helpful is periodically hitting the "refresh" button on councils and forums. Structures that once worked get out of alignment, nonproductive activities and expenditures grow and need pruning back, and top management sponsors may get detached or forum members become entitled and out of touch. A problem always needing work is getting the activities and

accomplishments of the councils spread deeper into the workforce in terms
of visibility and recognition.

Power and Influence. Employer-created councils and forums are often
portrayed by critics as manipulated to serve the employer's interests with
little power to promote and protect employees' interests. In this view, ERPs
are a case of "collective begging." Also, just as employers sometimes jigger
the rules of in-house ADR (alternative dispute resolution) systems to favor
the company's interests, the critics see non-union forums and councils as
susceptible to the same tilt. Whether these criticisms apply to other EIV
plans I cannot say; what can be said is they are a considerable caricature
of the situation at Delta. It is true that the councils and forums do not
engage in negotiation or threaten strikes or other punitive actions. But one
has to realize that these tactics are antithetical to the purpose of the EIV
groups and would soon undermine them. The motivating idea is unity of
interest between employer and employees and use of constructive dialogue
and problem solving so the company performs better and all stakeholders
gain. Of course, the idea that "all stakeholders gain" can be empty rhetoric but, if so, the commitment employment model and EIV program soon
collapses. Thus, if the commitment model and EIV program really do have
a profit payoff for the company, then the executives know full well that
they kill the goose that lays the golden egg if they do not share the gains.
Likewise, the councils and forums do not need to bargain for higher wages
and benefits, since in an HPWS situation these are already built in as part
of the strategy. Because the process is more informal, behind the scenes,
and focused on problem solving, it may appear that non-union councils
don't actively push an employee-centered agenda. This is deceiving, however. By their very existence, the forums and councils are always passing on
to management various employees' "wish lists" and educating managers
on the benefits of saying yes and costs of saying no. Further, managers find
saying no to employees difficult and uncomfortable and sometimes cave in
or acquiesce in order not to sour the relationship. Thus, non-union councils
rarely score a big win such as a union does with a new three-year contract
containing specific pay increases, new benefits, and so on. However, in a
quiet and understated "nibbling" process, they continually exert pressure
and influence on the high-priority items of concern to employees with the
tacit threat that failure to at least partially deliver may cost substantial loss
of cooperation and goodwill. In effect, both sides know the employer has
to pay a price for cooperation and commitment and, cumulated over the
months and years, the gains delivered by the non-union councils may compare well to those of their union counterparts. Naturally, there is no gain-
saying the reality that if an employer chooses to abandon its commitment
strategy, then the non-union EIV groups lose their leverage and, indeed, may
be abolished the next day.

Cooperative Employee Relations versus Union Avoidance. The motive
and purpose of high-level EIV programs has to be to foster cooperative,

positive employee relations. Companies that do this successfully will find that employees feel satisfied with their jobs and often express great loyalty and commitment to the company. Hence, an indirect by-product of an EIV program is that many of the conditions that lead employees to seek outside representation are not present. On the other hand, companies that set up a high-level EIV program with forums and councils for the explicit purpose of keeping out unions make a serious mistake, as employees are not fooled for long and quickly grow disillusioned. To date, organized labor in the United States has steadfastly opposed liberalizing the nation's labor law (e.g., NLRA) to give companies more opportunity to create non-union employee councils. However, this policy is arguably short sighted even from a purely self-interested union perspective, for if company managers indeed cannot be trusted to keep their promises— perhaps the number-one union selling point in the recent campaigns at Delta—then the non-union forums and councils will eventually backfire and—as in the 1930s—turn into an inside organizing committee for the unions. This is not speculation but the actual record in Canada. EIV councils and forums are, therefore, a distinctly two-edged sword for any company contemplating them.

The Future of EIV Councils and Forums. It is difficult for me to think that any relatively disinterested observer, after a personal investigation of the EIV program at Delta, would not come away thinking the nation would benefit from having more companies with one. The program is not perfect and not all employees are happy with it; nonetheless, it seems inescapable that without EIV, Delta would not have survived and, further, would not have climbed back from bankruptcy to be not only a profitable company but also the second-largest airline in the world. However, I feel pessimistic that the large-scale EIV program at Delta will any time soon become more than a one-of-a kind example in the United States. A necessary step is reform of the nation's labor law, but political gridlock appears to make any legislative action highly unlikely. Unfortunately, a compromise is possible—drop the company union ban in the NLRA but strengthen the other unfair-labor-practice provisions to ensure employees have a protected right to organize—but the ability of the parties to move toward such a compromise is quite doubtful in the current environment. Even if labor law were no impediment, quite possibly large-scale EIV programs such as at Delta would still remain a relative rarity. My impression is that American companies have gradually been shifting toward a more short-term and finance-driven business model, which is not conducive to EIV either as an up-front HRM cost or long-term sustainable investment. Alternatively stated, EIV has the largest payoff when companies adopt a human capital/goodwill HRM model with some significant ILM features but, unfortunately perhaps, the trend seems to be in the opposite direction of labor commodification and successive dismantling of ILMs.

CONCLUSION

Delta Air Lines probably has the most extensive and advanced employee involvement and voice program in the United States, certainly with regard to representational councils and forums. It is not an employee relations model for everyone and, indeed, one gets the feeling Delta is to some degree iconoclastic not only in the airline industry but in American industry in general. Nonetheless, as a general management principle, it remains the case that numerous companies can gain competitive advantage and a more satisfied and productive workforce with some form of commitment/goodwill HRM strategy. A key ingredient, in turn, is an active and well-functioning EIV program, even if scaled down—perhaps to meet the constraints of American labor law. The EIV route, however, requires considerable investment, a long-term perspective, and dedicated people-oriented management. Whether such an approach remains viable in today's turbulent and short-term economic and political environment is a large and unanswered question, although Delta is trying to show the answer is yes. While the jury is still out on the future, we know from the past—symbolized by the *Spirit of Delta* jetliner in its hangar in Atlanta—that employee commitment can work wonders if effectively tapped. An extensive employee involvement and voice program is not a prerequisite, as the Delta story illustrates, but surely as the days of corporate paternalism fade, it is an ever more necessary component of a high-performance work system. Hopefully this chapter, and the last fifteen years at Delta, provide useful guidance for other companies considering the EIV option.

NOTE

1. Quotations from "Delta Air Lines Heritage Museum: C. E. Woolman" (www.deltamuseum.org).

REFERENCES

Balderston, C. (1935). *Executive Guidance of Industrial Relations*. Philadelphia: University of Pennsylvania Press.
Bamber, G., J. Gittell, T. Kochan, and A. von Nordenflycht. 2009. *Up in the Air: How Airlines Can Improve Performance by Engaging Their Employees*. Ithaca, NY: Cornell University Press.
Basset, W. 1919. *When the Workmen Help You Manage*. New York: Century.
Beer, M. 2009. *High Performance High Commitment Management*. New York: Wiley.
Bernstein, I. 1970. *The Turbulent Years: A History of the American Worker, 1933–1941*. Boston: Houghton-Mifflin.
Cappelli, P., et al. 1997. *Change at Work*. New York: Oxford University Press.
Commons, J. 1919. *Industrial Goodwill*. New York: McGraw Hill.
Cone, C. 2000. "Delta Personnel Board Council." In *Nonunion Employee Representation: History, Contemporary Practice, and Policy*, B. Kaufman and D. Taras (eds.), pp. 469–73. Armonk, NY: M. E. Sharpe.

Davis, S. 1988. *Delta Air Lines: Debunking the Myth*. Atlanta: Peachtree Publishers.

Dulebohn, J., G. Ferris, and J. Stodd. 1995. "The History and Evolution of Human Resource Management." In G. Ferris, S. Rosen, and D. Barnum (eds.), *Handbook of Human Resource Management*, pp. 19–41. Cambridge: Blackwell.

Dundon, T., A. Wilkinson, M. Marchington, and P. Ackers. 2004. "The Meanings and Purpose of Employee Voice." *International Journal of Human Resource Management*, 15(6): 1149–70.

Estreicher, S. 2000. "Nonunion Employee Representation: A Legal/Policy Perspective." In B. Kaufman and D. Taras (eds.), *Nonunion Employee Representation: History, Contemporary Practice, and Policy*, pp. 196–222. Armonk, NY: M. E. Sharpe.

Foulkes, F. 1980. *Personnel Policies in Large Nonunion Companies*. Englewood Cliffs, NJ: Prentice-Hall.

Gittell, J. 2003. *The Southwest Airlines Way*. New York: McGraw Hill.

Gollan, P. 2006a. *Employee Representation in Non-Union Firms*. New York: Sage.

———. 2006b. "Twin Tracks: Employee Representation at Eurotunnel Revisited." *Industrial Relations*, 45(4): 606–49.

Harris, H. 1982. *The Right to Manage: Industrial Relations Practices of American Businesses in the 1940s*. Madison: University of Wisconsin Press.

Hirsch, B., and D. Macpherson. 2000. "Earnings, Rents, and Competition in the Airline Industry." *Journal of Labor Economics*, 18(1): 125–55.

Hogler, R., and G. Grenier. 1992. *Employee Participation and Labor Law in the American Workplace*. Westport, CT: Quorum.

Huselid, M. 1995. "The Impact of Human Resource Management Practices on Turnover, Productivity, and Corporate Financial Performance." *Academy of Management Journal*, 38(3): 635–72.

Jacoby, S. 1997. *Modern Manors: Welfare Capitalism since the New Deal*. Princeton, NJ: Princeton University Press.

———. 2003. "A Century of Human Resource Management." In B. Kaufman, R. Beaumont, and R. Helfgott (eds.), *Industrial Relations to Human Resources and Beyond: The Evolving Process of Employee Relations Management*, pp. 147–71. Armonk, NY: M. E. Sharpe.

Johnson, N. 2002. "Airlines: Can Collective Bargaining Weather the Storm?" In P. Clark, J. Delaney, and A. Frost (eds.), *Collective Bargaining: Current Developments and Future Challenges*, pp. 22–38. Urbana-Champaign, IL: IRRA.

Katz, D. 2011. *Recent Developments in NMB Election Interference Cases and Employee Committees*. Washington, DC: Katz & Rauzman P.C.

Kaufman, B. 1999. "Does the NLRA Constrain Employee Involvement and Participation Programs in Nonunion Companies? A Reassessment." *Yale Law & Policy Review*, 17(2): 729–811.

———. 2000a. "The Case for the Company Union." *Labor History*, 41(3): 321–50.

———. 2001b. "Accomplishments and Shortcomings of Nonunion Employee Representation in the United States." In B. Kaufman and D. Taras (eds.), *Nonunion Employee Representation: History, Contemporary Practice, and Policy*, pp. 21–60. Armonk, NY: M. E. Sharpe.

———. 2003. "High-Level Employee Involvement at Delta Air Lines." *Human Resource Management*, 42(2): 175–90.

———. 2008. *Managing the Human Factor: The Early Years of Human Resource Management in American Industry*. Ithaca, NY: Cornell University Press.

———. 2010. *Hired Hands or Human Resources: Case Studies of Human Resource Management Policies and Practices in Early American Industry*. Ithaca, NY: Cornell University Press.

———. 2012. "Keeping the Commitment Model Up in the Air during Turbulent Times: Employee Involvement at Delta Air Lines." *Industrial Relations*, 52(S1): 343–77.

————, and D. Taras. 2010. "Employee Participation through Nonunion Forms of Employee Representation." In A. Wilkinson, P. Gollan, M. Marchington, and D. Lewin (eds.), *The Oxford Handbook of Participation in Organizations*, pp. 258–85. Oxford: Oxford University Press.

Kochan, T., and P. Osterman. 1994. *The Mutual Gains Enterprise*. Cambridge, MA: Harvard Business School Press.

Lawler, E., S. Albers, and G. Ledford. 2001. *Employee Involvement and Total Quality Management*. San Francisco: Jossey-Bass.

Leiserson, W. 1928. "The Accomplishments and Significance of Employee Representation," *Personnel*, 4(February): 119–35.

LeRoy, M. 2000. "Do Employee Participation Groups Violate Section 8(a)(2) of the National Labor Relations Act? An Empirical Analysis." In *Nonunion Employee Representation: History, Contemporary Practice, and Policy*, B. Kaufman and D. Taras (eds.), pp. 287–306. Armonk, NY: M. E. Sharpe.

Lewis, W., and W. Newton. 1979. *Delta: The History of an Airline*. Athens: University of Georgia Press.

McKelvey, J. 1988. *Cleared for Takeoff: Airline Labor Relations since Deregulation*. Ithaca, NY: ILR Press.

Moriguchi, C. 2005. "Did American Welfare Capitalists Breach Their Implicit Contracts during the Great Depression? Preliminary Findings from Company-Level Data." *Industrial & Labor Relations Review*, 59(1): 51–81.

National Industrial Conference Board. 1922. *Experience with Works Councils in the United States*. New York: NICB.

————. 1933. *Collective Bargaining Through Employee Representation*. New York: NICB.

Nelson, D. 1993. "The Historical Significance of Employee Representation." In B. Kaufman and M. Kleiner (eds.), *Employee Representation: Alternatives and New Directions*, pp. 371–90. Madison, WI: IRRA.

————. 2000. "The AFL and the Challenge of Company Unionism, 1915–1937." In B. Kaufman and D. Taras (eds.), *Nonunion Employee Representation: History, Contemporary Practice, and Policy*, pp. 61–75. Armonk, NY: M. E. Sharpe.

Perlman, S. 1928. *A Theory of the Labor Movement*. New York: Macmillan.

Swiercz, P., and B. Spencer. 1992. "HRM and Sustainable Competitive Advantage: Lessons from Delta Air Lines." *Human Resource Planning*, 15(2): 35–46.

Taras, D. 2003. "Voice in the North American Workplace: From Employee Representation to Employee Involvement." In B. Kaufman, R. Beaumont, and R. Helfott (eds.), *Industrial Relations to Human Resources and Beyond: The Evolving Process of Employee Relations Management*, pp. 293–329. Armonk, NY: M. E. Sharpe.

Timur, A., D. Taras, and A. Ponak. 2012. "Do Pre-Existing Nonunion Representation Plans Matter When Employees Unionize?" *British Journal of Industrial Relations*, 50(2): 214–38.

Walton, R. 1985. "From Control to Commitment in the Workplace." *Harvard University Press*, 63(2): 77–84.

Whitelegg, D. 2005. "From Smiles to Miles: Delta Air Lines Flight Attendants and Southern Hospitality." *Southern Cultures*, 11(4): 7–27.

Wilkinson, A., P. Gollan, M. Marchington, and D. Lewin. 2010. "Conceptualizing Employee Participation in Organizations." In A. Wilkinosn, P. Gollan, M. Marchington, and D. Lewin (eds.), *The Oxford Handbook of Participation in Organizations*, pp. 3–25. Oxford: Oxford University Press.

Zahavi, G. 1988. *Workers, Managers, and Welfare Capitalism: The Shoeworkers and Tanners of Endicott Johnson, 1890–1950*. Chicago: University of Chicago Press.

12 The Intersection of NER and ADR

A Conceptual Analysis and Federal Express Case

David Lewin

INTRODUCTION

The concept of an employee exercising voice in an employment relationship is as old as the concept of a free labor market (Smith 1776). In such a market, individual employees exchange their labor for compensation and other rewards. If dissatisfied with one or another aspect of his/her employment relationship, an employee may voice such dissatisfaction and seek to have it redressed. An employee may also quit a job with his/her present employer and take a presumably more utility-enhancing job elsewhere. Similarly, an employer who is dissatisfied with the performance of an employee may discipline that employee, including ultimately by firing the employee. An employer may also lay off employees—in contemporary parlance, reduce the work force—due to a decline in demand for the company's products or services, substitution of capital and/or technology for labor, organizational restructuring, and other factors.

But of course the employment relationship is not an even-handed relationship. Instead, an employer holds sway—power—over individual employees and can exercise that power in many ways, including by reducing pay and benefits, changing work content and schedules, devising new ways of monitoring employees at work (such as through electronic technology), and firing "troublesome" employees. It is for these and related reasons that employees have sometimes sought to unionize and engage in collective bargaining with employers.

The record of employee unionization in the United States and elsewhere is well known. During the period from the end of World War II through the 1950s, approximately one third of U.S. nonfarm private-sector employees belonged to labor unions and a somewhat larger proportion was represented in collective bargaining. In some nations during this period, employee unionization constituted between 50 and 75 percent of their labor forces. A centerpiece of the collective bargaining agreements negotiated by unions and employers was the grievance procedure through which employees could exercise voice without fear of retribution for having done so. Hence, when it came to employee representation, unionism, collective bargaining, and grievance procedures were the institutional mechanisms by which such representation operated (Kaufman 2005).

During the last half century, however, unionization and collective bargaining declined to the point where, today, less than 7 percent of U.S. private-sector employees belong to and are represented by unions (www. bls.gov 2013). In most other nations, private-sector unionism and collective bargaining also declined, in some instances to roughly the same level as in the United States and in other instances to somewhat higher levels. Many scholars have analyzed this decline and identified various factors that plausibly explain it (e.g., Hirsch 2008); this research will not be reviewed here.

In light of this decline, it might be presumed that there is no longer much of a demand for employee voice in the employment relationship. This presumption is incorrect, however; non-union employers have increasingly adopted policies and practices that provide for one or another type of employee voice, indicating there is a rising demand for such voice among employers or employees or both (Colvin 2003). These voice mechanisms are sometimes referred to as non-union employee representation (NER) and include such examples as employee forums, gain-sharing plans, quality improvement committees, and employee–management advisory committees, which are often considered to be a component of high-involvement work systems that are widely thought to enhance organizational performance (Gollan and Lewin 2013).[1] Other voice mechanisms, which have also been widely adopted by non-union employers, are typically referred to as alternative dispute resolution (ADR) and include such examples as a grievance-like procedure, peer review or consultation, and an ombud. These practices are also sometimes included as a component of high-involvement work systems. From a conceptual perspective, NER and ADR have distinctive components, yet they overlap and may be complementary. This is shown in the Venn diagram of Figure 12.1. Both NER and ADR practices are analyzed in this chapter and are illustrated using FedEx as a case example.

NER AND ADR

What exactly is an NER or ADR system? It is basically a mechanism through which employees can exercise voice about issues or problems they encounter at work. Such voice may be exercised directly by an employee, as occurs when an employee raises an issue in an employee forum, uses a company-provided hotline or website to report a particular issue, or discusses an issue with his/her direct supervisor. Such voice may also be exercised indirectly by an employee through "representation" by someone else, such as an ombud, peer, or human resource staff specialist who in effect acts as an agent for the employee-principal. In exercising direct voice, non-union and unionized employees basically use the same channels. In exercising indirect voice, non-union employees use more varied channels than the highly codified grievance procedure used by unionized employees in which a union official or officials formally represent the employee.

A NER system may stand alone or, alternatively, be part of a larger strategically oriented approach to workforce management. This bundled or package approach is celebrated, indeed advocated, in the contemporary literature, where it is often referred to as high-involvement, high-participation, high-commitment, or high-performance human resource management (HRM). Accompanying NER in this type of HRM system are such practices as employment continuity, selective hiring, team-based work in a decentralized organization, variable pay contingent on organizational performance, substantial training and development, minimal status differentials, and business information sharing with employees (Pfeffer 1998). These practices are aimed at enhancing employee trust in management and commitment to the organization that are, in turn, grounded in the psychological contract between an employee and an employer. From this strategic HRM perspective, employees are assets for which expenditures are in essence a capital—human capital—investment that potentially yields a positive economic return. Substantial empirical evidence produced over the last two decades supports this proposition (e.g., Ichniowski, Shaw, and Prennushi 1997; Huselid 1995; MacDuffie 1995; Ichniowski 1992). More to the point, from this strategic perspective, NER is a proactive approach to workforce management in which employment relationship issues and problems are surfaced—voiced—early on and potentially nipped in the bud. Recent empirical evidence also supports this proposition (Colvin 2013).

Similarly, an ADR system may stand alone or be part of a strategically oriented HRM system. Under this type of system and similar to a NER system, an employee may be able to raise work-related issues and problems directly and informally with his/her immediate supervisor or manager or another supervisor/manager. Such issues and problems may get resolved at this informal stage. If not, however, the employee has to decide whether to exercise indirect voice and invoke the formalities of the ADR system, beginning by putting his/her "grievance" in writing. If this occurs, management proposes terms of settlement that the employee then decides to accept or reject. If accepted, the grievance is considered resolved. If not, the grievance moves to progressively higher steps of the ADR system until it is settled/resolved, just as it does in a unionized context.

Unlike in a unionized context, however, ADR systems vary widely in several respects, including structure, scope of issues, and scope of employee coverage. Regarding structure, some non-union grievance procedures incorporate two steps, others three steps, and still others four steps. Some of these procedures feature peer review of individual employee grievances, usually at the second or third step. Others feature a senior human resource officer or a top management committee to review individual employee grievances and recommend settlement decisions, typically at the third step. A few of these procedures feature a Chief Operating Officer (COO) or even a Chief

Executive Officer (CEO) to review individual employee grievances and make settlement decisions, almost always at the last step of the procedure. Increasingly, however, arbitration is the final step in ADR procedures, just as it is in unionized grievance procedures (Lewin 2008a, 2008b).

Under an ADR procedure, the scope of issues over which non-union employees may file grievances is not determined through a collective bargaining agreement but, instead, by a company's management. Here, too, there is considerable variation. In some instances, the scope may be quite wide and in other instances quite narrow. Further, some ADR procedures are very specific regarding covered issues, while others are very general. In certain instances, non-union employees may have a wider scope of issues over which they can file grievances than unionized employees because the applicable ADR procedures cover most or all terms and conditions of employment contained in a company's employee handbook, whereas unionized dispute resolution procedures apply only to those terms and conditions of employment contained in a collective bargaining agreement. In other instances and compared to unionized employees, non-union employees may have a narrower scope of issues over which they can file grievances.

Another important difference between non-union ADR procedures and unionized grievance procedures concerns the scope of employee coverage. In a unionized grievance procedure, only employees who are represented by the union and are thus part of the bargaining unit may file grievances under the procedure specified in the collective bargaining agreement. Because such bargaining units exclude all supervisors and managers, none of these higher-level employees may exercise voice through the grievance procedure. In a non-union ADR procedure, by contrast, there is no bargaining unit and the procedure may be quite wide in its scope of employee coverage. This means that it may include first-line supervisors, foremen, lower-level managers, mid-level managers, and even senior managers, especially if the procedure is cast as an internal organizational governance mechanism.

When an ADR procedure covers both non-management and management employees, it reflects a unitarist "company as one big team" approach to employee voice and employment conflict resolution. By contrast, a unionized grievance procedure that covers only employees of a specific bargaining unit reflects an institutionalized, pluralist, "we against them" approach to employee voice and employment conflict resolution.[2] In any case, given the decline of unionism and collectively bargained grievance procedures and the growth of non-union ADR procedures (in the United States and elsewhere), it is likely that far more employees are covered by and eligible to use ADR procedures than are covered by unionized grievance procedures or, in other words, exercise voice in the employment relationship (Lewin 2013).

Such coverage and eligibility, however, do not necessarily mean that higher-level non-union employees will actually use ADR procedures. In this regard, empirical studies of non-union ADR find that job/occupational ranking is inversely correlated with grievance filing, meaning that "covered" supervisors and managers are significantly less likely to file grievances—exercise voice—than are non-supervisory and non-management employees. This research also finds that lower- and middle-management employees covered by their organizations' ADR procedures are especially likely to fear retaliation for filing grievances, preferring to remain silent even when they have experienced specific work-related issues and problems (Lewin 2004, 1992; Lewin and Boroff 1996).

This analysis and related empirical findings raise a more fundamental point concerning the concept of private property. In the United States in particular, this concept is dominant. It means that business owners and the management—agents—hired by these owners retain the right to lead and manage the businesses as they see fit, subject only to certain regulations and to contractual arrangements they may reach with employees and others—for example, customers, suppliers, shareholders, and community groups. This is known as the doctrine of management's reserved rights and means that even when a company's employees are unionized and a collective bargaining agreement is in place, employees may not file grievances over any company policy or practice or any term and condition of employment not covered by the collective bargaining agreement (Chamberlain and Kuhn 1965). It also means that grievance arbitration does not apply to these company policies, practices, and non-covered terms and conditions of employment.

The same reasoning applies and even stronger conclusions emerge with respect to non-union ADR procedures. A non-union company's management decides whether to adopt an ADR procedure. If it adopts such a procedure, it then determines the scope of issues over which non-union employees may invoke the procedure as well as the scope of employees who may do so. In both respects, the scope may range from wide to narrow, but also in both respects, employees do not participate—have a voice—in making these determinations. Once again, management's reserved rights are predominant. In light of the continuing experimentation by non-union firms in determining the scope of issues and scope of employees covered by their ADR procedures, such coverage is clearly more elastic—varied—than in unionized firms, where collective bargaining agreements in effect set upper bounds on the scope of issues over which unionized employees can file grievances and the scope of employees who can file grievances.

Under NER, the dominant unit of analysis is a collective, whereas under ADR, the dominant unit of analysis is the individual. To illustrate, under NER, management may consult with employees through forums, quality improvement committees, and joint employee–management advisory committees, relying on their members to identify and articulate workplace issues and problems of concern to them and their colleagues. Under ADR, individual employees file grievances or consult with peers, HR staff specialists, or an ombud in bringing particular issues and problems to the attention of management. In both instances, however, employees exercise voice in the employment relationship. Further, when an NER or ADR system operates as a component of high-involvement HRM or an even broader organization culture system, the dominant unit of analysis is the organization. While this unit of analysis may apply in both non-union and unionized contexts, in practice it appears to be more salient in the former than in the latter.

Although NER and ADR are often separate processes, they may also interact and complement one another, as shown in Figure 12.1. For example, in a company that practices NER, especially as part of high-involvement HRM, employee forums, quality improvement committees, and gain-sharing committees may identify and bring to management's attention conflicts over work flow, work scheduling, or performance-based incentive compensation. Similarly, through their use of ADR procedures, employees may identify and bring to management's attention conflicts over workplace safety, work absences, and supervisory behavior. In both instances, NER and ADR, these processes serve as organizational (or HR) information systems in which employment relationship issues are identified and then presumably diagnosed and resolved. In this sense, employee voice can serve as a positive influence on organizational functioning and performance.[3]

Not all companies maintain both NER and ADR systems. Where only one such system is in place, experience with it may encourage management to adopt the other system. To illustrate, consider a company that maintains an ADR process and that finds that certain recurring issues—for example, reduction in the scope of first-line manager job duties and responsibilities resulting from newly centralized decision making or technological change, employee suspension from work for violating company policies regarding intranet usage, and denial of promotions for employees who work primarily from home—are raised through this process. Each of these issues could be formally addressed through an NER process, especially a process grounded in high-involvement HRM that includes employee–management advisory committees, specialized task forces, and/or employee forums. If a company does not have such an NER process in place, it could decide to adopt one.

Figure 12.1   Venn Diagram NER and ADR Examples and Intersection

A CASE EXAMPLE: FEDERAL EXPRESS (FEDEX)

Federal Express (FedEx) was founded in 1973 by Frederick W. Smith. The company pioneered the concept of overnight package and mail delivery and, for its first fifteen years or so, remained a single-line-of-business company with a classic functional form of organization in which certain staff units, including human resources, assisted line managers in providing overnight package and mail delivery services to customers. FedEx's main claim to fame in this regard, and its early differentiator, was to have sensed and strongly tapped a market for speed in package and mail delivery—that is, overnight delivery. The company also became widely known for its related innovations, including the first wide-scale use of bar coding technology, which together with modern computing capability enabled customers to track their packages and mail at any point in the delivery process. Largely for these reasons, FedEx was able to charge premium prices to customers and to become highly profitable in a relatively short time period. Hence, the company soon became regarded as a leading example of a successful entrepreneurial venture.

From the beginning, Smith and his executive colleagues emphasized employees as a key constituency of the company, as reflected in FedEx's motto, People-Service-Profits. These same executives, however, also sought to avoid employee unionization and were explicit about this objective, yet they also strongly believed in the concepts of employee voice and strong organizational culture. To this end, they established the FedEx Guaranteed Fair Treatment Procedure (GFTP), a three-step process that in some respects closely resembles a unionized grievance procedure (Lewin 2004; Lewin, Dralle, and Thomson 1992) and that remains in place today. The GFTP is a specific example of a non-union ADR system.

At the first step, Management Review, the GFTP requires a "complainant"—an employee—to submit a written complaint to a member of management within seven days of "the occurrence of the eligible issue." A manager, senior manager, and/or managing director then reviews the complaint, meets with the complainant, decides to uphold, modify, or overturn lower management's original action, and communicates this decision in writing to the complainant and to FedEx's HR Department. If the employee accepts this decision, the complaint proceeds no further. If the employee rejects the decision, the complaint proceeds to the second step, Officer Review. At this step, the complainant resubmits his/her written complaint to a vice president or senior vice president of the relevant company division within seven days of the first-step decision. One of these officers reviews the complaint, gathers additional information, and, where necessary, conducts an internal investigation. This officer then decides to uphold, overturn, or modify lower management's original decision and communicates this decision in writing to the complainant and to FedEx's HR Department. If the employee accepts this decision, the complaint proceeds no further. If the employee rejects the decision, the complaint proceeds to the third step, Executive Review. At this step, the complainant again resubmits his/her complaint to the Employee Relations Department, which investigates and prepares the GFTP case file for Appeals Board review. The board reviews all relevant case information and decides to uphold, overturn, or modify senior management's (second-step) decision or take other appropriate action. It then responds in writing to the complainant within three days of making this decision and also communicates the decision to FedEx's HR Department and to the complainant's "chain of command;" this decision is final.

In other respects, the FedEx GFTP does not closely resemble a unionized grievance procedure. This is perhaps most clearly reflected in the scope of employees and scope of issues covered by the procedure. At FedEx, all employees except executives and senior managers are eligible to use the GFTP. This means that non-management employees, supervisors, first-level managers, and mid-level managers, who collectively comprise more than 90 percent of the company's workforce, may file complaints under the GFTP. Further, they may do so over a relatively wide range of issues, including such traditional issues as pay, work schedules, and discipline but also performance appraisals, workflow, technological change, and delivery schedules. Hence, in this company's ADR system, the scope of both employee and issue coverage is considerably greater than that which typically prevails under unionized grievance procedures.

Under the GFTP, which has operated continuously for forty years (i.e., 1973–2013), the "complaint"-filing rate has been about 5 percent, meaning that on average, five written complaints per 100 employees are filed annually. Most of these complaints, roughly 75 percent, are settled at the first step of the GFTP, with about 20 percent settled at the second step and about 5 percent settled at the third step. Delivery drivers, schedulers, office employees, and information technology operatives are far more likely (on a per-capita basis) than supervisors, first-level managers, and mid-level managers to file complaints under the GFTP. The issues most frequently pursued by FedEx employees through the GFTP are discipline, including suspension and termination, workload, pay, performance appraisals, and delivery schedules. Further, the company has won about 60 percent of the complaint cases settled at the first step of the GFTP, about 50 percent at the second step, and about 40 percent at the third step. Thus, while the likelihood that a FedEx employee's complaint proceeds beyond the first step of the GFTP declines markedly at each of the two higher steps, the likelihood of an employee winning his/her complaint case increases notably at the higher steps.

The second main practice used by FedEx to elicit employee voice is Survey-Feedback-Action (SFA). This is FedEx nomenclature for what is basically an employee opinion survey of the type used by many large U.S. companies and that have increasingly become known as employee engagement surveys (Sanborn and Oehler 2013). In this instance, however, FedEx in essence promises employees that their opinions will not only be regularly solicited, they also will be communicated—fed back—to supervisors and managers who will respond to and, where necessary, take corrective action to address issues identified in employee survey responses. In addition, FedEx senior management meets periodically with groups of surveyed employees to discuss various options for responding to the main concerns expressed by these employees and the company's employees more broadly. In these meetings, participating employees are in effect representing their colleagues, though in informal rather than a formal fashion. Analytically, therefore, the SFA is in part an NER mechanism similar in some respects to an employee forum of the type used by other companies.

The SFA is administered twice annually, once to all FedEx employees and secondarily to random samples of FedEx employees. It asks employees to indicate their agreement or disagreement (on a five-point scale) with twenty-nine statements pertaining to such matters as managers' willingness to listen to their concerns and provide them with support and resources, confidence in senior management, pay and benefit fairness, workgroup relationships, and FedEx's relationships with customers. As with the GFTP, the SFA was viewed and adopted by FedEx executives in part as a union-avoidance practice but also as a practice reflecting those executives' belief that employees were a key constituency of a business with a strong organization culture. As with the GFTP, the SFA has operated continuously for forty years and constitutes the second prong of FedEx's two-pronged employee voice system.

This system was fundamentally challenged, however, by FedEx's decision to expand internationally, in particular by its 1988 acquisition of Flying Tigers (FT). Unlike FedEx's fundamental emphasis on speedy delivery of packages, mail, and related items, FT's fundamental emphasis was on the customized, relatively slow delivery of non-standard, odd-lot items. One type of these items, reflected in the company's name, was animals that often had to be shipped over long distances and that required careful handling in order to arrive intact (i.e., alive and in good health) at their destinations. FT was founded by a group of former World War II bush pilots, mostly Australian, who as rugged individualists eschewed such "modern" accouterments as air traffic control systems and controllers, formally demarcated takeoff and landing runways, nighttime landing lights, and elaborate cockpit technology. The company grew rapidly during the third quarter of the twentieth century, and its main asset consisted of landing rights in more than 100 countries, which made it an especially attractive acquisition target for internationally expanding FedEx. This growth together with their independent mindedness motivated FT's pilots to become unionized relatively soon after the company's founding. By the time of its purchase by FedEx, FT's pilots had been unionized for several decades and had regularly negotiated terms and conditions of their employment with the company's management.

This stasis in FT union–management relations was turned on its head by non-union FedEx's acquisition of FT. As the successor employer, FedEx decided to let the FT pilots' contract lapse at the end of its specified date and then refused to recognize the union as the representative of FedEx's pilots. This strategy proved to be relatively short lived, however, because during the first few years (1989–1992) following FedEx's acquisition of FT, a sufficient number of FedEx pilots (including the acquired FT pilots) signed union representation authorization election cards (under U.S. NLRA procedures) to warrant actual elections. The first of those elections resulted in 56 percent of FedEx's pilots voting against and 44 percent voting for union representation. The second election resulted in 54 percent of FedEx's pilots voting against and 46 percent voting for union representation. The third election resulted in a symmetrical switch of the second-year voting results: 54 percent of FedEx's pilots voted for and 46 percent voted against union representation. Hence, four years after it acquired FT, the formerly non-union FedEx became unionized (but only by pilots).

Collective bargaining agreements, including grievance procedures, continue to be negotiated to this day between FedEx management and unionized pilots, who therefore are able to exercise strong collective voice in their employment relationship with the company. For FedEx's non-union employees, the GFTP and SAF also continue in place, providing these employees with a combination of individual and collective voice in their employment relationships with the company. From time to time, FedEx's non-union employees, especially delivery drivers and airplane and vehicle mechanics, have attempted to unionize but to no avail. A main reason for this lack of other-than-pilot unionization is that, during the mid-1990s, FedEx was designated a transportation company rather than a delivery company by the U.S. Congress. Therefore, in so far as employment relations are concerned, the Railway Labor Act (RLA) rather than the National Labor Relations Act (NLRA) covers FedEx. Unlike the NLRA, which permits local unions, the RLA permits only national unionization of a particular employee group. Hence, FedEx non-union employees who desire unionization face a far more difficult task in bringing it about under RLA requirements than they would under NLRA requirements.

This public policy treatment of FedEx did not occur accidentally or incidentally. To the contrary, Fred Smith, FedEx's CEO, and his executive colleagues intensively lobbied the U.S. Congress to switch the company's coverage from the NLRA and the jurisdiction of the National Labor Relations Board (NLRB) to the RLA and the jurisdiction of the Railway Labor Board (RLB). The success of these lobbying efforts is attested to by the fact that the U.S. Congress authorized this "reclassification" only for FedEx rather than for delivery companies as a whole.

In the years immediately following the FT acquisition, FedEx executives and senior managers found that the company's original non-union model and two-pronged employee voice system did not fit well in certain regions and nations. In Europe, for example, FedEx encountered long-standing customs and laws supporting such forms of collective employee voice as unionism, works councils, and codetermination. FedEx could not avoid these institutional arrangements by claiming that it was exempt from them as a U.S.–based company. Outside the United States, therefore, FedEx negotiates collective bargaining agreements with some unionized employees in addition to pilots, discusses operating strategies and practices with members of works councils, including lower-level and mid-level managers, and discusses business strategy with board of director members, some of whom are employees. The latter two examples constituted FedEx's first experience with these employee voice channels or, in other words, NER.

In Asia, FedEx employees were reluctant to use the GFTP. Indeed, in Japan, Indonesia, and China, employee complaint-filing rates under the GFTP were near zero and were only modestly higher in other Asian countries. FedEx supervisors and first-level managers in these countries viewed the three-step GFTP negatively because they believed that they would lose face (i.e., respect) among employees if their immediate supervisors or managers overturned their decisions. Recognizing this concern, FedEx adopted a revised two-step GFTP for use in Asia in which an employee's supervisor or manager and the supervisor or manager's boss jointly served as the first step, and an International Appeals Board (IAB) served as a second, final step. FedEx supervisors and managers in Asia preferred the revised GFTP because their immediate bosses could not by themselves overturn these supervisors' and managers' decisions, thereby mitigating potential loss of face. If a local supervisor's or manager's decision was overturned at the second step of the revised GFTP, it could be attributed to senior management or company policy rather than as a direct reprimand of the local supervisor or manager. More to the point of this chapter, however, because the IAB is a mechanism through which its members in effect represent other senior management colleagues as well as mid-level managers and first-line supervisors, the IAB can be considered a type of NER.

This change in the GFTP did not matter nearly as much to FedEx's Asian employees, however, as it did to FedEx's Asian supervisors and managers. These employees remained reluctant to use the GFTP because by doing so they would cast negative "face" on their own managers, the company, and even themselves. Hence, even after it was revised, this component of FedEx's approach to employee voice did not transport to or fit well in Asia (or in some other, non-Asian countries) due to quite different national culture norms than those that prevailed in the United States. This experience and these dynamics continue to present day.

Regarding the SFA process, it too had only limited international applicability as an employee voice mechanism for reasons both different from and similar to the limited international applicability of the GFTP. In some European countries, such as the UK, France, Germany, and Italy, employee survey response rates were quite low, on the order of 20 to 25 percent compared to 60 to 70 percent in the United States. Several factors contributed to these low response rates. One factor was that, at the time, employee opinion surveys were considerably more common among U.S. companies than among European-based companies. Another factor was that most of FedEx's European employees were formerly FT employees who for the most part resented being acquired and who had not previously been surveyed about their opinions by FT management. Still another factor was that FedEx's European employees were able to exercise voice through their unions, works councils, and board of director representatives.

In Asian countries, by contrast, FedEx employee survey response rates were very high, approaching 100 percent in Japan, 95 percent in Indonesia, and 90 percent elsewhere in Asia. FedEx executives were initially taken aback by these high response rates but later learned that Asian employees tend to regard responding to a company-administered survey as a requirement rather than a voluntary act. Even more surprising to FedEx executives, however, were the actual survey responses. For questions included in this survey, FedEx used a five-point scale, with 1 = strongly disagree and 5 = strongly agree. The neutral point on this scale was three (3), which was labeled "sometimes agree/sometimes disagree." In the United States, Canada, and Europe, FedEx employees' survey responses varied widely and had modest to large standard deviations around the mean scores. In Asian countries, by contrast, the mean scores were always three or very close to three and the standard deviations were close to zero—in Japan the standard deviation was zero!

In attempting to understand these Asian employees' survey responses, FedEx executives learned that something similar to what had occurred with respect to the GFTP also occurred in this instance. They did so by gathering together groups of Asian employees and asking them why they and their colleagues responded in the aforementioned way to the survey. In these meetings, employees explained that they and their colleagues did not want to cast negative "face" on their supervisors/managers, the company, or themselves by strongly agreeing or disagreeing with statements included in the survey. Therefore, they chose the "safe harbor" response, meaning that they circled the number three in responding to most or all statements. This choice, in turn, reflected the dominant national cultural norms of these Asian countries. Consequently, FedEx executives and senior managers realized that Asian employees' survey responses were virtually useless for providing feedback to the supervisors and managers of these employees and for taking corrective action on the basis of those responses. Stated differently, FedEx's use of the SFA process as an employee voice mechanism outside of the United States yielded high "S" response rates, but also yielded data that rendered the "F" and "A" components of this process inoperable. More fundamentally, this realization indicated that while FedEx's traditional two-pronged employee voice system fit the United States reasonably well, it did not do so internationally—and this remains true today. Therefore, FedEx decided to regularize (one might say institutionalize) the postsurvey meetings of Asian employees and, later, did the same with employees in other regions. In these meetings (and similar to the IAB), participating employees are in effect representing their colleagues, which constitutes a type of NER.

FedEx's financial performance deteriorated markedly following its acquisition of FT, which is illustrated by the decline in the company's earnings per share (EPS) from +$3.56 at the time of the FT acquisition to –$1.25 four years later. Although the company's revenue doubled during this period, costs rose about five-fold and operating profit margins therefore turned to losses. This negative experience caused FedEx executives to reconsider the company's business strategy, policies, and operating practices, including those pertaining to employee relations. These executives came to realize that FedEx was operating as a high-control organization that attempted to superimpose the company's U.S.–based policies and practices on its business operations in more than 100 countries and that in many instances the result was misalignment and poor financial performance. Something had to change, and it did.

First, FedEx sold some of its country-based businesses to local companies with which it then contracted to provide delivery and related services to customers. Second, FedEx closed some country-based businesses and consolidated others, which resulted in certain workforce reductions—the first in the company's history. Third, FedEx devolved substantial decision-making and operating responsibility on regional and country general managers. This local autonomy enabled these general managers to adopt policies and practices different from those used by FedEx in the United States. As a result, the hub-and-spoke operating system that FedEx initiated and developed in the United States and that it attempted to replicate abroad was abandoned in favor of "local carting" in certain regions and countries. Also as a result, the GFTP and the SFA were modified in some regions and countries and abandoned in others, especially where employees were able to exercise collective voice through unionization, works councils, and/or codetermination.

Although these were substantial changes, they were undertaken in the context of a business strategy that reaffirmed international expansion as FedEx's way forward (Hastings 1999). The company's executives forecasted increased global demand for speedy delivery of packages and related services of the type provided by FedEx, which implied substantial company growth but only if that demand could be properly met. Further, FedEx's historical competitive advantage in the United States was declining as other companies began to match the universal bar coding, computer-assisted supply chain management, and customer package tracking practices pioneered by FedEx. Some of these competitors, for example, United Parcel Service (UPS), expanded their services beyond delivery to include logistics and transportation, thereby further indicating to FedEx executives that the company had moved from the growth stage to the maturity stage in its U.S. business. This development provided additional impetus to FedEx to emphasize but also revise its international expansion strategy.

With this revised strategy in place, FedEx's financial performance improved considerably during the remainder of the 1990s. By the end of that decade, the company's EPS rose above what it had been just prior to the FT acquisition a decade or so earlier. During this period, regional and country-based FedEx businesses operated in relatively decentralized fashion. Regional and country general managers could add some services, remove others, change service prices, purchase new equipment, and change delivery schedules without having to clear those decisions with FedEx's U.S. headquarters. They could also hire, appraise, promote, demote, transfer, and discipline employees without prenotifying or seeking approval from FedEx "corporate." In some regions and countries, FedEx employees were identifiable by FedEx-labeled uniforms, clothing patches, and delivery vehicles, while in other regions and countries no such identification was apparent or required. This international decentralization of decision making contrasted sharply with FedEx's prior high-centralization, high-control approach to decision making—a change that became even more strongly supported by FedEx executives in light of the company' improved financial performance associated with the change.

This late-twentieth-century experience also set the stage for a new twenty-first-century business acquisition strategy by FedEx. Consider that immediately following its purchase by FedEx, Flying Tigers' (FT's) name ceased to exist, its physical assets, such as aircraft, were repainted with the FedEx logo and colors (i.e., purple, orange, and white), and its human assets—employees—became FedEx employees. As such, the FT purchase was a merger rather than an acquisition. By contrast, during the early twenty-first century, FedEx acquired other companies but treated them as acquisitions rather than as mergers. A leading example is Kinko's, which FedEx purchased in 2002. Kinko's is a retail store chain that provides copying services and office supplies to customers and is a leader in its industry segment. Based largely on its FT experience, FedEx decided to operate Kinko's as a separate, independent business unit. As such, the Kinko's name was retained, the company was headed by a general manager who had profit and loss (P&L) responsibility, and employees remained employees of Kinko's rather than becoming employees of FedEx. For this acquisition, FedEx chose a cobranding strategy, meaning that the company was identified/labeled FedEx-Kinko's, and this strategy remains in place today (though in a slightly modified way). More to the point, Kinko's is now formally considered to be a strategic business unit (SBU) of FedEx.

During the remainder of the 2000s and into the 2010s, this SBU strategy was strengthened, and the SBU structure became FedEx's fundamental organizational arrangement. Today, FedEx maintains seven distinct business units—FedEx Express, FedEx Ground, FedEx Freight, FedEx Kinko's Office and Print Services, FedEx Custom Critical, FedEx Trade Networks, and FedEx Services—and the company as whole has 290,000 employees (Federal Express FedEx Case 2013). Notably, however, despite the decentralization strategy reflected in the existence of these SBUs, the GFTP and the SAF process apply to/cover employees of all of these SBUs. In other words, this two-pronged approach to employee voice continues to be a centralized FedEx policy and practice. All covered employees of the otherwise independent business units are eligible to file complaints under the GFTP and are regularly included in employee opinion surveys and in postsurvey meetings in which participating employees represent both themselves and their non-participating colleagues.

During the first decade of the twenty-first century, 2001 through 2010, the average annual complaint-filing rate among FedEx's U.S. employees and its component SBUs was 3.8 and ranged between 5.1 (2006) and 2.2 (2009). Of these complaints, about 80 percent were settled at the first step of the GFTP, about 17 percent were settled at the second step of the GFTP, and about 3 percent were settled at the third (final) step of the GFTP. The data also indicate that approximately 10 percent of employee complaint filers were repeat filers during this period.[4]

FedEx employee response rates to the SAF survey averaged 72 percent annually during 2001 through 2010, ranging between 63 percent (2008) and 81 percent (2005). About two thirds of these survey respondents expressed high confidence in the fairness of FedEx management, and almost as many, about 64 percent, indicated that they were proud to work for FedEx. Nonetheless, approximately 30 percent of FedEx employees expressed concern about not having enough freedom to do their jobs well, and approximately 35 percent expressed concern about not having enough resources to perform their jobs. With respect to the "F" and "A" components of the SFA process, almost 80 percent of the survey respondents expressed agreement with the survey statement that the "concerns identified by my workgroup during the last year have been satisfactorily addressed." At the other end of the spectrum, so to speak, about 5 percent of FedEx employees expressed strong disagreement with this statement.

Placed in broader context, FedEx's two-pronged employee voice arrangement, that is, the GFTP (a form of ADR) and the SAF process (a form of NER), can be considered components of the company's more fulsome high-involvement HRM practices. As noted earlier, other such practices include employment continuity, substantial training and development, team-based work, variable pay, and business information sharing with employees. For the most part, FedEx engages in these practices: its original no-layoff policy remains in place today (in the United States); it invests heavily in employee training and management development, which are linked to the company's continued practice of promotion from within; most employees are members of workplace, operational, and/or delivery teams; variable pay in the forms of bonuses, profit sharing, and equity participation (mainly through an ESOP) cover virtually all of the company's employees; and detailed business-related information is regularly communicated to employees through the company's intranet, management briefings, and executive video broadcasts. From an organizational behavior (OB) perspective, these HRM practices reflect a combination of high-control and high-commitment organizational characteristics. Yet, with respect to employee voice and participation, this is only part of the story; here's why.

FedEx's unionized pilots are able to exercise collective voice through periodic contract negotiations and FedEx's non-union employees are able to exercise individual and (quasi)collective voice through the GFTP and the SFA process, respectively. The pilot contract negotiations apply worldwide and the GFTP and the SFA process fully apply to the company's U.S. employees and partially to the company's employees in other countries and regions. However, these practices do not apply to others who perform labor services for the company. This is because each FedEx SBU is free to determine whether labor services will be performed by employees or, instead, independent contractors. To illustrate, consider the examples provided by two FedEx SBUs, namely, FedEx Express and FedEx Ground. FedEx Express delivers packages and related items to businesses, and its delivery drivers are employees of this SBU. By contrast, FedEx Ground delivers packages and related items to residences, but its delivery drivers are independent contractors to this SBU. These two sets of delivery drivers perform exactly the same job tasks and services, yet the former (who are non-union) are covered by FedEx's GFTP, SFA process, and other, high-involvement HRM practices, whereas the latter are not.

The concept of an independent contractor is in essence equivalent to that of a vendor, who can presumably choose the customers to which to sell its products and services. But just how independent are FedEx Ground's independent contractors? Consider that such contractors can only provide services to FedEx, deliver only the packages and related items assigned them by FedEx, deliver only to FedEx-specified customers, and drive only the routes specified by FedEx. They must also closely follow the operating rules and procedures specified by FedEx, are supervised and monitored in this respect by terminal managers, regularly have their performance evaluated by terminal managers, and can be disciplined by FedEx, including cancellation of their contracts, for violating FedEx operating rules and procedures. While FedEx independent contractors can protest disciplinary actions taken against them and challenge their performance evaluations, they otherwise are not able to exercise collective or individual voice in their independent contracting relationships with FedEx Ground.[5]

To summarize, FedEx is an example of a well-known, publicly traded, highly successful company that, according to its motto, places employees first among its several constituencies. Regarding employee voice in this company, a multidimensional system is in play featuring the unionization of one key employee group—pilots—and a two-pronged employee voice arrangement covering other employees composed of the GFTP (a type of ADR) and the SFA process (a type of NER). Pilot unionization and collective bargaining operate globally at FedEx, and the GFTP and SFA process can be modified, even abandoned, by regional and country managers. As noted earlier and from an organizational perspective, FedEx is in effect a holding company composed of several SBUs, the general managers of which have considerable autonomy in determining how to run their respective businesses. Two of these SBUs provide delivery services of the type that FedEx pioneered four decades ago. From an employee voice perspective, the striking contrast between these two businesses is that in one of them, delivery driver employees can exercise voice through the aforementioned channels, whereas in the other, delivery driver independent contractors, who provide the same labor services as those provided by employees of the first business, cannot exercise voice through these channels. Hence, this case example shows how employee voice and the processes for eliciting and using such voice can vary markedly within a single organization, not just among organizations.

To place this entire experience within the Venn diagram presented in Figure 12.1, consider the modified, FedEx-specific Venn diagram presented in Figure 12.2. It depicts a relatively large ADR circle and a relatively small NER circle. This is because, as practiced, the FedEx GFTP is a full-blown example of a type of ADR, whereas the SFA is a more modest example of a type of NER. The two circles continue to overlap, however, given the complementarities between the GFTP and the SFA. Also shown in Figure 12.2

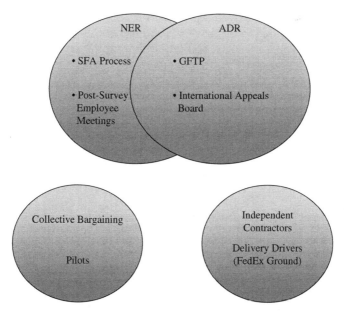

Figure 12.2 FedEx Venn Diagram NER and ADR Examples and Intersection, Collective Bargaining and Independent Contracting

are two separate circles, one depicting unionized FedEx pilots who exercise voice through collective bargaining and the other depicting independent contractor delivery drivers who are for the most part unable to exercise voice in their relationships with FedEx. These circles do not overlap with each other or with the GFTP and SFA circles because there are not complementarities among them.

LEGAL ISSUES IN NER AND ADR

The National Labor Relations Act (NLRA) outlaws company unions and supports the concept of independent employee voice in labor–management relationships—voice that can presumably only be achieved through unionization and collective bargaining. Specifically, section 8(a)(2) of the act states that it is an unfair labor practice (ULP) for an employer "to dominate or interfere with the formation or administration of any labor organization or contribute financial or other support to it." The question then arises as to whether NER and ADR practices of the type featured at FedEx and other non-union or partially unionized companies violate U.S. labor law.

From a historical perspective, contemporary NER and ADR systems and practices are not new. During the 1920s and 1930s, numerous companies adopted employee representation plans (U.S. Bureau of Labor Statistics 1937). While antiunionism motivated some companies in this regard, industrial unionism had not yet emerged in the United States, and many "progressive" companies practiced one or another form of welfare capitalism in which addressing and settling workplace disputes and providing a unity of interest among employees were viewed as serving the objectives of employers and employees alike (Kaufman 2008; Jacoby 1997). Following passage of the NLRA (in 1935) and the rise (during the late 1930s and 1940s) of industrial unionism on a large scale, however, these employee representation plans were declared by the courts to be company unions in violation of the law. Hence, it is no surprise that this type of employee representation faded from the employment relationship scene.

During the 1950s, 1960s, and 1970s, employment dispute resolution research and practice focused largely on unionized companies and employees and on both interest and rights disputes (Lewin 1999; Bemmels and Foley 1996). Interest disputes that featured strikes and/or lockouts came in for particular attention, as did the use of arbitration to settle rights disputes. In 1960, the U.S. Supreme Court rendered a set of decisions, known as the Steelworkers Trilogy, that articulated and codified the doctrine of deferral to arbitration in rights disputes involving unionized companies and employees (Stone 2004). This basically meant that grievance arbitration decisions in unionized contexts were not reviewable by the courts. The trilogy presaged a similar set of decisions rendered a half-century or so later involving grievance arbitration in non-union contexts (Sanchez 2005).

As noted earlier, during the 1980s, 1990s, and 2000s, private-sector unionism and collective bargaining rapidly declined and non-union companies' adoption of NER and ADR rapidly increased (Lewin 2008a; Lipsky, Seeber, and Fincher 2003; McCabe 1988). While an occasional NLRB and court decision found an NER procedure to violate the NLRA,[6] most such decisions did not do so and in fact most non-union NER procedures have rarely been challenged via the National Labor Relations Board (NLRB) or the courts. Recognizing the contemporary progressive approach to employment relations reflected in NER, the 1994 Commission on the Future of Worker Management Relations recommended the legalization of most forms of employee involvement (or HIWS) for employees not covered by collective bargaining agreements with employers (Levine 1997).[7] This recommendation was incorporated into the 1995 Teamwork for Employees and Managers (TEAM) Act passed by the U.S. Congress, but the act was strongly opposed by some large companies and organized labor (which viewed it as a competitor to unionism) and was subsequently vetoed by President Clinton (Logan 2012).[8] Nevertheless, NER procedures, including some that provide for employee selection/election of representatives to advisory boards, consultation committees, and the like, continued to be adopted by companies and now apparently cover a considerably larger proportion of the U.S. workforce than is covered by unionism and collective bargaining. Further and despite section 8(a)(2), the NLRA has not proven to be a bar to these NER arrangements.[9]

Regarding ADR, a series of U.S. Supreme Court decisions rendered during the 1990s and 2000s supported the doctrine of deferral to arbitration in rights disputes involving non-union employees (Colvin, Klaas, and Mahoney 2006; Lipsky, Seeber, and Fincher 2003). It is therefore not surprising that non-union ADR procedures increasingly specify arbitration as the final procedural step. Although some of these court decisions were reached in cases involving alleged employment discrimination (under provisions of the 1964 Civil Rights Act, the 1967 Age Discrimination in Employment Act, and the 1990 Family Medical and Leave Act) or alleged violation of workplace safety and health regulations (under provisions of the 1970 Occupation Safety and Health Act), others were reached in cases involving alleged violation of unfair labor practice provisions of the NLRA (Stallworth 1997). This contemporary deferral to arbitration doctrine has, in turn, motivated certain professional groups to propose new legislation or non-legislative standards governing the use of arbitration in labor and employment cases. Examples include the Model Employment Termination Act (META) proposed by the National Conference of Commissioners of Uniform Laws and the Due Process Protocol for the Arbitration and Mediation of Statutory Workplace Disputes proposed by the Labor and Employment Law Section of the American Bar Association (ABA) and subsequently adopted by the association's delegates (Stallworth 1997).

What may be concluded from this brief historical review is that the NER/
ADR procedures of FedEx don't appear to violate the RLA and that, for
the most part, other non-union and partially unionized companies' NER/
ADR procedures don't appear to violate the NLRA (though they remain
subject to legal challenge).[10] This is especially notable in cases of companies
in which elected employees serve on advisory committees, boards, councils, forums, and other employer-determined employee representation and
voice arrangements. Put differently, it appears that these contemporary non-
union employee representation and voice arrangements will have considerably more staying power than did the employee representation plans of an
earlier, pre–Wagner Act era.

CONCLUSIONS

That NER and ADR have become commonplace among companies in the
United States and abroad is readily evident. This has occurred as employee
unionism and collective bargaining have rapidly declined, implying a causal
relationship between these two developments, but this is unlikely. The demand
for private-sector unionization has declined because employees, especially
newer employees, don't believe that the monetary gains from unionization
(in terms of pay and benefits) will exceed or even equal the costs (in terms of
union dues) of union membership; because unionized companies have substi-
tuted relatively cheaper non-union labor, including offshore labor, and other
factors of production for relatively expensive unionized labor; and because
non-union companies have warded off unionization through "campaigns"
typically assisted by outside counsel and consultants. While some of this
decline may also be attributed to non-union companies' adoption of NER
and ADR systems and practices, the larger story reflected by such adoption
is for the most part one of increasing demand by employers and employees
for voice in the employment relationship—but not unionized voice.

NER has a long tradition in U.S. business and was practiced by some
large companies well before passage of the NLRA. These companies'
founders and the professional managers who succeeded them believed that
employee involvement in decision making enhanced employer–employee
mutual interests and positively contributed to organizational performance.
While many companies' employee representation plans were subsequently
found by the courts to violate NLRA provisions barring company unions,
contemporary experience shows that many business founders and managers
share the same belief in the benefits of employee involvement or, in modern
parlance, high-involvement HRM and a strong organization culture. This
appears to be the main reason these non-union companies have adopted one
or another type of NER, although only some NER systems include or are
accompanied by grievance-like ADR procedures.

When it comes to ADR per se, the story is somewhat different. While
ADR has sometimes been adopted as an antiunionization mechanism, more

recently and spurred by the aforementioned U.S. Supreme Court decisions affirming deferral to arbitration in non-union employment disputes, ADR has mainly been adopted as an antiemployment litigation mechanism (Colvin 2003). Irrespective of the underlying rationale for non-union companies' adoption of ADR, however, these grievance-like procedures constitute a channel through which employees can exercise voice in the employment relationship. Empirical evidence indicates that this voice channel is in fact used and that employees win a nontrivial portion of their grievance claims, especially at higher steps of ADR procedures. Nonetheless, employers hold the upper hand in ADR because they define the scope of issues and the scope of employees included under such procedures, and because they often alone choose ADR arbitrators and pay the costs of arbitration. For these and other reasons, various professional organizations, including the American Bar Association's Labor and Employment Law Section, have enunciated certain principles of ADR aimed providing and ensuring employee due process.

On balance, both NER and ADR stand as institutional arrangements that mitigate pure at-will employment and employment relationships for millions of private-sector employees—far more employees than belong to unions and than are represented in collective bargaining. For this reason alone, NER and ADR are worth celebrating. At the same time, however, non-union employers remain largely free to determine whether to adopt NER and ADR and to determine the type of NER and ADR that is in play. With rare exceptions, employees do not participate—are not "highly involved"—in NER and ADR adoption decisions.

Further and similar to unionized employment relationships, non-union employees who use ADR procedures (including ADR procedures that are components of NER) and the supervisors of these employees tend to experience further deterioration of their employment relationships rather than redress of the workplace issues and problems they surfaced via grievance (or complaint) filing under ADR (Lewin 2008b). Both researchers and practitioners have important stakes in determining whether retaliation explains this outcome and, if it does, how it can be mitigated in order to achieve greater due process in resolving non-union employment relationship conflict (Blancero, DelCampo, and Marron 2010).

LESSONS LEARNED FROM THE FEDEX CASE

From the analysis of the FedEx case presented in this chapter, the following specific and general lessons may be drawn:

- While the GFTP and SFA process are separate and distinct, they are similar in terms of providing voice to employees and information to management that can be used to address workplace issues. Other companies could therefore adopt both processes, with each serving a specific purpose and yet being complementary.

- Both the GFTP and SFA process have stood the test of time for four decades and are more strongly embedded in FedEx than at any other time in the company's history. For other companies, this indicates that a strong initial top management commitment to employee voice arrangements can endure.
- The GFTP and SFA process are accompanied by unionization and collective bargaining between FedEx pilots and the company's management, thereby constituting a three-pronged employee voice system. Other partially unionized companies may be able to replicate this set of voice arrangements.
- Both the GFTP and the SFA process have been modified and in some cases abandoned in certain countries and regions in which FedEx operates, which in turn reflects the strong influence of national/regional norms, customs, and laws on these voice arrangements. For other companies, this implies that fundamental business strategy should be global whereas specific employee voice (and HRM) practices should be adapted to varying international environments.
- Outside the United States, FedEx has accommodated to such employee voice arrangements as unionization (of employees beyond pilots), works councils, and codetermination. The lesson for other companies in this regard is quite similar to that identified immediately above.
- The GFTP and SFA process apply to all domestic employees of FedEx irrespective of the particular SBU in which they are employed. For other companies that feature SBU organization structures, the lesson is that certain employee voice (and HRM) practices can be maintained companywide.
- The GFTP and SFA process do not apply to independent contractors who nonetheless provide labor services, specifically to FedEx Ground. The lesson here for other companies is that providing autonomy to its component business units may result in an other-than-employment arrangement for labor services, which in turn could lead to new alternative voice arrangements for those who provide such services.
- FedEx's employee voice arrangements do not include those that feature the election or selection of employees formally to represent their peers in consultations or joint decision making with management. The lesson here is that this particular approach to employee voice is unlikely to run afoul of legal challenges.

There is of course some danger and certainly some caveats when it comes to generalizing from a particular case—the FedEx case or any other. Nevertheless, the FedEx case provides an important example of NER (i.e., the SFA process), ADR (the GFTP), and unionization operating as a tripronged system of employee voice that seems to have served both the company and its employees well over several decades. The lessons drawn from this case example deserve to be recognized and appreciated by scholars and practitioners alike.

NOTES

1. For a summary and specific examples of NER plans, see Kaufman and Taras (2010: 265–266). The phrase "dual-channel voice" has been used to describe circumstances in which employee unionization coexists with NER procedures in a company. See Campolieti, Gomez, and Gunderson (2013).
2. I am grateful to Bruce Kaufman, coeditor of *Voice and Involvement at Work: Experience with Non-Union Representation*, for suggesting this interpretation of ADR.
3. For a novel approach to the effects of employee voice on organizational performance, see Pohler and Luchak (2013).
4. These data and those presented in the following paragraph were provided to the author on a confidential basis by FedEx executives during interviews conducted in spring 2013.
5. For additional analysis of this independent contracting relationship, see Lewin (2014).
6. See *IBM Corporation*, 341 NLRB No. 148 (2004) and *E.I. Dupont*, 289 NLRB 187 (1988). The NLRB and the courts have flipped-flopped on this issue, as a reading of these and related decisions indicates.
7. However, the commission (popularly known as the Dunlop Commission) did not want NER arrangements to cover terms and conditions of employment.
8. The TEAM Act also reflected the efforts of business leaders and the Republican Party to loosen the provisions of section 8(a)(2) of the NLRA pertaining to company (i.e., employer-dominated) unions.
9. One of the longest-standing NER arrangements is that of Lincoln Electric, a nonunion company that has maintained an employee advisory board for more than a century. See, for example, Koller (2010) and Bartlett and O'Connell (1998). For additional analysis of NLRA limitations on NER arrangements, see Kaufman, Lewin, and Fossum (2000).
10. FedEx's GFTP and SFA process cover almost all of its workforce (top executives being the exception), thereby reflecting the aforementioned "company as one big team" or unitarist approach to employee voice and employment conflict resolution. As such, these ADR– and NER–type practices are unlikely to raise legal issues for FedEx under the RLA or the NLRA.

REFERENCES

Bartlett, C. A., with J. O'Connell. 1998. *Lincoln Electric: Venturing Abroad.* Boston: Harvard Business School Publishing, Case #9–398–095, revised April 22, 22 pp.
Bemmels, B., and J. Foley. 1996. "Grievance Procedure Research: A Review and Theoretical Recommendations." *J. Management,* 22: 359–84.
Blancero, D. M., R. G. DelCampo, and G. F. Marron. 2010. "Just Tell Me! Making Alternative Dispute Resolution Systems Fair." *Industrial and Labor Relations Review,* 49: 524–43.
Campolieti, M., R. Gomez, and M. Gunderson. 2013. "Does Non-Union Employee Representation Act as a Complement or Substitute to Union Voice? Evidence from Canada and the United States." *Industrial Relations,* 52(S1): 378–96.
Chamberlain, N. W., and J. W. Kuhn. 1965. *Collective Bargaining,* 2nd. ed. New York: McGraw-Hill.
Colvin, A. J. S. 2003. "Institutional Pressures, Human Resource Strategies, and the Rise of Nonunion Dispute Resolution Procedures." *Industrial and Labor Relations Review,* 56: 375–92.

———. 2013. "Participation Versus Procedures in Non-Union Dispute Resolution." *Industrial Relations*, 52(S1): 259–83.

Colvin, A. J. S., B. Klaas, and D. Mahoney. 2006. "Research on Alternative Dispute Resolution Procedures." In D. Lewin (ed.), *Contemporary Issues in Employment Relations*, pp. 103–47. Champaign, IL: Labor and Employment Relations Association.

Federal Express FedEx Case. 2013. www.123HelpMe.com/view.asp?id=165018, accessed April 16, 2014.

Gollan, P. J., and D. Lewin. 2013. "Employee Representation in Non-Union Firms: An Overview." *Industrial Relations*, 52(S1): 173–93.

Hastings, D. P. 1999. "Lincoln Electric's Harsh Lessons from International Expansion." *Harvard Business Review*, 77: 3–11.

Hirsch, B. 2008. "Sluggish Institutions in a Dynamic World: Can Unions and Industrial Competition Co-Exist?" *Journal of Labor Research*, 25: 415–55.

Huselid, M. 1995. "The Impact of Human Resource Management Practices on Turnover, Productivity, and Corporate Financial Performance." *Academy of Management Journal*, 38: 635–72.

Ichniowski, C. 1992. "Human Resource Practices and Productive Labor–Management Relations." In D. Lewin, O. S. Mitchell, and P. D. Sherer (eds.), *Research Frontiers in Industrial Relations and Human Resources*, pp. 239–72. Madison, WI: Industrial Relations Research Association.

———, K. Shaw, and G. Prennushi. 1997. "The Effects of Human Resource Management Practices on Productivity: A Study of Steel Finishing Lines." *American Economic Review*, 87: 291–313.

Jacoby, S. M. 1997. *Modern Manors: Welfare Capitalism since the New Deal*. Princeton, NJ: Princeton University Press.

Kaufman, B. E. 2005. "What Do Unions Do?—Evaluation and Commentary." *Journal of Labor Research*, 26: 555–95.

———. 2008. *Managing the Human Factor: The Early Years of Human Resource Management in American Industry*. Ithaca, NY: Cornell University Press.

———, D. Lewin, and J. Fossum. 2000. "Nonunion Employee Involvement and Participation Programs: The Role of Employee Representation and the Impact of the NLRA." In B. E. Kaufman and D. G. Taras (eds.), *Nonunion Employee Representation: History, Contemporary Practice and Policy*, pp. 259–86. New York: Myron D. Sharpe.

———, and D. G. Taras. 2010. "Employee Participation Through Non-Union Forms of Employee Representation." In A. Wilkinson, P. J. Gollan, M. Marchington, and D. Lewin (eds.), *The Oxford Handbook of Participation in Organizations*, pp. 258–85. Oxford, UK: Oxford University Press.

Koller, F. 2010. *Spark: How Old Fashioned Values Drive a Twenty-First Century Corporation: Lessons from Lincoln Electric's Unique Guaranteed Employment Program*. New York: Public Affairs.

Levine, D. 1997. "They Should Solve Their Own Problems: Reinventing Workplace Regulation." In B. E. Kaufman (ed.), *Government Regulation of the Employment Relationship*, pp. 475–97. Madison, WI: Industrial Relations Research Association.

Lewin, D. 1992. "Grievance Procedures in Nonunion Workplaces: An Empirical Analysis of Usage, Dynamics, and Outcomes." *Chicago-Kent Law Review*, 66: 823–44.

———. 1999. "Theoretical and Empirical Research on the Grievance Procedure and Arbitration: A Critical Review." In A. E. Eaton and J. H. Keefe (eds.), *Employment Dispute Resolution and Worker Rights in the Changing Workplace*, pp. 137–86. Champaign, IL: Industrial Relations Research Association.

———. 2004. "Dispute Resolution in Nonunion Organizations: Key Empirical Findings." In S. Estreicher and D. Sherwin (eds.), *Alternative Dispute Resolution in the Employment Arena*, pp. 379–403. New York: Kluwer.

———. 2008a. "Resolving Conflict." In P. Blyton, N. Bacon, J. Fiorito, and E. Heery (eds.), *The Sage Handbook of Industrial Relations*, pp. 447–68. London, UK: Sage.

———. 2008b. "Workplace ADR: What's New and What Matters?" In S. E. Befort and P. Halter (eds.), *Workplace Justice for a Changing Environment: Proceedings of the Sixtieth Annual Meeting, National Academy of Arbitrators*, pp. 23–9. Washington, DC: Bureau of National Affairs.

———. 2013. *The Idea and Practice of Contract in U.S. Employment Relations: Analysis and Policy Implications.* Presidential Address delivered to the Labor and Employment Relations Association (LERA), St. Louis, MO, June 8, 2009.

———. 2014. "Collective Bargaining and Grievance Procedures." In William K. Roche, Paul Teague, and Alex Colvin (eds.), *Oxford Handbook of Conflict Management in Organizations*, pp. 113–31. Oxford, UK: Oxford University Press.

———, and Boroff, K. E. 1996. "The Role of Loyalty in Exit and Voice: A Conceptual and Empirical Analysis." In D. Lewin and B. E. Kaufman (eds.), *Advances in Industrial and Labor Relations*, pp. 69–96. Greenwich, CT: JAI Press.

———, D. Dralle, and C. Thomson. 1992. *Federal Express Inc. (A).* Los Angeles, CA: UCLA Anderson School of Management, 15 pp.

Lipsky, D. B., R. L. Seeber, and R. D. Fincher. 2003. *Emerging Systems for Managing Workplace Conflict.* San Francisco: Jossey-Bass.

Logan, J. 2012. "'All Deals are Off:' The Dunlop Commission and Employer Opposition to Labor Law Reform." In D. Lewin and P. J. Gollan (eds.), *Advances in Industrial and Labor Relations*, pp. 191–220. London: Emerald.

MacDuffie, J. P. 1995. "Human Resource Bundles and Manufacturing Performance: Organizational Logic and Flexible Production Systems in the World Auto Industry." *Industrial and Labor Relations Review*, 48: 197–221.

McCabe, D. 1988. *Corporate Nonunion Complaint Procedures and Systems.* New York: Praeger.

Pfeffer, J. 1998. *The Human Equation: Building Profits by Putting People First.* Boston: Harvard Business School Press.

Pohler, D. M., and Luchak, A. A. 2013. *Are Unions Good or Bad for Organizations? The Moderating Role of Management's Response.* Working Paper, University of Alberta School of Business (conditionally accepted for publication *British Journal of Industrial Relations*).

Sanborn, P., and Oehler, K. 2013. *2013 Trends in Global Employee Engagement.* Chicago: AonHewitt and Aon plc.

Sanchez, V. A. 2005. "A New Look at ADR in New Deal Labor Law Enforcement: The Emergence of a Dispute Processing Continuum Under the Wagner Act." *Ohio State Journal on Dispute Resolution*, 20: 621–82.

Smith, A. 1776. *The Wealth of Nations: An Inquiry into the Nature and Causes of the Wealth of Nations.* London: Strahan and Caddell.

Stallworth, L. E. 1997. "Government Regulation of Workplace Disputes and Alternative Dispute Resolution." In B. E. Kaufman (ed.), *Government Regulation of the Employment Relationship*, pp. 369–401. Madison, WI: Industrial Relations Research Association.

Stone, K. V. W. 2004. *The Steelworkers' Trilogy: The Evolution of Labor Arbitration.* Los Angeles: UCLA School of Law Research Paper No. 04–29, 40 pp.

U.S. Bureau of Labor Statistics. 1937. *Characteristics of Company Unions*, BLS Bulletin 634. Washington, DC: U.S. Government Printing Office. www.bls.gov/news. release/pdf/union2.pdf, accessed January 23, 2013.

13 What Do NLRB Cases Reveal about Non-Union Employee Representation Groups?

A Typology from Post–*Electromation* Cases

Michael H. LeRoy

INTRODUCTION

Since the late 1800s, unions and employers have competed with each other to offer representation groups to employees. In general, these groups have aimed to provide a voice to workers in aspects of their employment. These groups have widely differed, however. Employers have formed some representation groups with progressive aims: to empower individuals to manage their work, to share information about improving a work process, and more broadly, to feel a sense of ownership in the firm. Other groups have extended compensation beyond wages by seeking employee input in designing benefits—for example, a pension plan in the 1920s or child care at work in the 1990s. Other employers have formed groups to mimic a union's functions, believing that a company union is better able than an independent union to voice the interests of employees.

However, some employers have formed employee representation groups without a progressive aim—for example, to frustrate employee support for a union organizing campaign. These groups, composed of representatives handpicked by management for their pliant attitudes, occasionally coincide with termination of employees who support a labor union. The employer establishes the charter of the group and agenda for interactions with employees and monopolizes the power to make group decisions.

Unions, too, form representation groups for employees, either in response to requests from employees or as externally driven organizing drives to raise wages and standards in an area or an industry. Some union groups have cultivated indigenous leadership and employee voice, while others have imposed an outside voice to speak for these workers.

Employers and unions intensely competed to offer representation alternatives to employees in the 1930s. During this time, organized labor succeeded in promoting legislation to significantly limit the use of these representation groups. After enactment of this law, found in Sections 2(5) and 8(a)(2) of the National Labor Relations Act (NLRA), this competition subsided. It was mostly dormant until employers revived non-union employee representation groups in the late 1970s and 1980s. These efforts were partly spurred by Japanese manufacturing transplants that used progressive models of non-union representation and academic research that linked employee productivity and job satisfaction with these groups. Non-union employee representation groups (also called NER groups) remain popular.

NER groups are hard to study, however, because some employers view them as a competitive advantage, while others do not want to expose themselves to complaints under the NLRA. In either case, access is very limited to study these groups. Apart from case studies that offer a rare inside perspective on these groups, there is little information. This chapter addresses that problem by using twenty-three cases decided by the NLRB over the past twenty years that involved a challenge to an NER group. Many of these NLRB cases provide detailed factual information about how the NER group was formed, the group's charter or goals, its method for selecting employees, the topics or subjects of NER group meetings, and how employees and management interacted in formulating policies and decisions. While there are significant drawbacks in this method, it complements studies of a specific company's NER groups by providing a broader scan of the types and forms and the organizational structures and functions of these NER groups.

HISTORICAL PERSPECTIVE

The National Labor Relations Act's (NLRA) broad prohibition against employer-created participation groups has been controversial from its inception in 1935. For some, this law rectifies a serious problem of employer overreaching in the realm of employee selection of a union that provides meaningful voice to workers. To others, it limits and stifles experimentation and innovation in employee representation groups. Before Section 8(a)(2) of the NLRA barred employers from forming and dominating "labor organizations," there were controversies as to whether representation groups should be influenced by employers or left completely to the preferences of workers.

This controversy originated with mass production of goods in the late 1800s, when there was a decline in skilled work performed in smaller organizations. Workers were devalued. By one employer ideology, owners of capital were superior to laborers. The industrialist who introduced open-hearth steel manufacturing, Abram Hewitt, pithily explained, "It is for the master [employer] to do the thinking" (Montgomery 1967). Near the turn of the twentieth century, some employers realized that scientific management of work was just as vital to their success as technological improvements in their factories. They developed bureaucracies "to subdivide, as well as to coordinate, the tasks of administration and production . . . to maximize the efficiency of each operation" (Bendix 1954). The performance of workers was orchestrated in a hierarchy, where management carefully analyzed and coordinated jobs. This marriage of mechanical production to hierarchical management not only created extreme specialization of jobs but also engendered such "standardized procedures . . . that the incumbent has little chance to do [the work] his own way. He has been left with a minimum of decisions about the work itself" (Katz 1954). One woman's experience as a coil winder at a large Westinghouse factory in East Pittsburgh typified this experience: "It was such a monotonous job! Oh, just repetitive! You would do it all automatically. You didn't have to use your head at all. It gave us a lot of time to think about other things" (Schatz 1983).

Some employers resisted, however, the tide of control-management. The Filene Cooperative, founded in 1898 by progressive management, gave workers the right to govern their working conditions, subject to the owners' right to veto (LaDame 1930). Owner Edward Filene believed that

> industrial democracy, under which employees will have an adequate voice in the policies of the industry and an adequate stake in the profits of an industry, is inevitable. . . . because we have given to the masses of employees a political vote with which they can get anything and everything they find themselves unable to get by industrial methods.
>
> (Filene 1925)

By 1901, Filene's association had an arbitration board, consisting of employee representatives, that settled grievances over wages, discharge, and working conditions.

Elton Mayo, another visionary of personnel management, rejected the control-management orthodoxy. In one experiment involving women who made telephone assemblies, he concluded,

> What actually happened was that six individuals became a team and the team gave itself wholeheartedly and spontaneously to cooperation in the experiment. The consequence was that they felt themselves to be participating, freely and without afterthought, and were happy in the knowledge that they were working without coercion from above or limitation below.
>
> (Mayo 1945)

This duality of managerial engagement or control of workers continued into the late 1920s and 1930s. Once the Great Depression became the overriding concern of Congress, lawmakers showed interest in regulating employee representation groups. The National Industrial Recovery Act (NIRA) in 1933 attempted to create a representational role for unions when the law stated a policy "[t]o encourage national industrial recovery, to foster fair competition, and to provide for the construction of certain useful public works."[1] This law depended on employer and union compliance with a set of voluntary work codes. The NIRA law used "fair competition" as a metaphor to foster employee selection of a union to bargain collectively with an employer.

According to Sen. Robert Wagner, the primary architect of the National Labor Relations Act (NLRA), the NIRA was disappointing because employers formed "company unions" to subvert the voluntary principles of the NIRA. In taking this view, he appeared to be unwilling to give credit to progressive forms of company unions that aimed to share managerial power with workers. His focus was on coercive manifestations of company unions. So he used examples that he believed made his point that employers were creating sham unions to avoid collective bargaining. One involved T. H. A. Tiedeman, a leading officer with the Standard Oil Co. of New Jersey. Tiedeman said in *Personnel*, a leading management journal, that his company had sent 2,000 copies of a "how-to" outline for employers to implement a non-union employee representation plan. The guide instructed executives on instituting an internal form of bargaining between elected representatives of employees and management (LeRoy 1996).

Sen. Wagner might have assumed too much: Tiedeman's company operated with a progressive NER plan. Perhaps Tiedeman was promoting an organizational form that met NIRA standards that "dealt with" employees—not by formal bargaining but through give and take between workers and management. Sen. Wagner took a decidedly negative view of this publication. As proof, he offered,

> Yesterday we had a hearing in the automobile industry and it came out very clearly that the company union was formed by sending to each worker a constitution and bylaws telling him, 'This is now your organization.' As the result of that an election was held, and the workers testified that they voted because they knew very well if they did not vote their jobs were gone.
>
> (LeRoy 1996)

This expert lawmaker's view on employee representation groups changed during the heat of intense committee hearings. Prof. Edwin Witte's influence in this legislative process grew. In effect, Witte helped to convince Sen. Wagner to disregard positive examples of company unions.[2] Prof. Witte criticized Sen. Wagner's initial proposal to prohibit company unions. The problem, as he saw it, was that the proposed NLRA defined too narrowly these groups as "labor organizations." Sen. Wagner's original bill defined a "labor organization" as "any organization, labor union, association, corporation, or society of any kind in which employees participate to any degree whatsoever and which exists for the purpose . . . of *dealing with employers concerning grievances of work*" (Leroy 1996, emphasis added). The problem of narrowing "dealing with" to apply only to the adjustment of a grievance was, according to Witte, that all other forms of employer "dealing with" employees—for example, setting a wage rate or a production standard—would legitimate employee representation groups that usurped the true voice of workers. In other words, such a definition would allow collective bargaining to be conducted by an organization other than a freely elected union. Prof. Witte prevailed and convinced Congress to broaden its definition of a "labor organization" to include

> any organization of any kind, or any agency or employee representation committee or plan, in which employees participate and which exists for the purpose, *in whole or in part, of dealing with employers concerning grievances, labor disputes, wages, rates of pay, hours of employment, or conditions of work.*"
>
> (Leroy 1996, emphasis added)

In this very broad definition of employer "dealing with," lawmakers felt they addressed coercive forms of company unions—but they also barred progressive company unions (e.g., the Filene Association).

Several historical studies provide context for this chapter. Looking back at the pivotal New Deal era, Kaufman (1999) observes that

> before the Great Depression commenced in late 1929, even persons sympathetic to the cause of organized labor readily acknowledged that the nonunion representation plans of the welfare capitalist employers of the 1920s were, in general, a positive and praiseworthy innovation in employment practice.
>
> (Kaufman 1999)

In the case of Sen. Wagner, Kaufman argues that he betrayed his own principles of maximizing employee choice of a representation group while also ignoring his own experience that some company unions promoted improved productivity and employee relations on the shop floor. Employers in Kaufman's study widely experimented with worker organizations, setting up shop committees, works councils, employee representation plans, and others. While some NER groups were designed as substitutes for unions, others were "forerunner[s] of today's much-touted 'high-performance workplace' and the employee representation plans of this period were the structure used by employers to promote a 1920s style of employee involvement and participation" (Kaufmann 1999). Kaufman's view is that the NLRA obliterated the 1920s welfare capitalism non-union model, relegating it to a state of prolonged dormancy until the 1970s to 1980s.

Cooper (2011: 845–48) offers more historical evidence showing that lawmakers heard detailed accounts of company unions that could improve internal plant relations but ignored lessons that could be gleaned from these progressive organizations. Cooper explains, for example, that Sen. Wagner's committee heard testimony about the Leeds & Northrup Employees' Association, an organization that went far beyond allowing employees to address workplace conditions and grievances with the employer. The association provided and administered a pension plan, savings plan, unemployment fund, educational plan, and athletic association. In addition, the group occasionally stood up to management by achieving reinstatement of discharged employees and reversing the transfer of workers to other departments. Management did not participate in the consultations of the association, and employees were able to select their own representatives.

Making the testimony more compelling, this information was provided to Congress by an office worker, Edward Fiske. Cooper notes that this ordinary employee suggested that the Wagner Act allow employees to vote on whether they preferred to be represented by an employer-created organization or an outside trade union. Cooper also highlighted the testimony of Henry S. Dennison, owner of a stationery manufacturer. He believed that the law should increase representation choices for workers. In other words, employees should be provided a choice between an employer-created organization and a union. He thought that the legalization of these competing models would ultimately benefit workers. Such an arrangement would drive away "evil" types of company unions by subjecting them to an election involving another representation option. But he also believed that a broad ban on company unions would stifle experimentation and creativity and abolish effective methods for mutual participation in management.

Kohler's historical study (1986) takes a more critical view of non-union Employee Representation Plans (ERPs). Employers felt threatened by the sharp increase in union membership, from 450,000 in 1897 to 5 million by 1920. This growth translated into union challenges to management's absolute control of the workplace. While Kohler acknowledges that some employers offered cooperative and progressive forms of ERPs, he notes that the "development and use of the company union was indigenous and unique to the United States" (Kohler 1986). These groups differed from shop committees and industrial councils in England and Europe, which were coordinated with trade unions. Kohler shows that jointly administered committees were popular in the United States until NIRA was enacted in 1932; but employers quickly abandoned these organizations and instituted company unions to enhance managerial control of employee voice.

By Kohler's account, and in contrast to the Leeds & Northrup Employees' Association that was explained to Sen. Wagner, most company unions amounted to fake forms of employee influence over terms and conditions of work. A common post–NIRA employee committee had elected officers and representatives, employee members, bylaws, and other attributes of independent unions. But management, not labor, usually formed these committees, often in response to a strike for union recognition. Management wrote the group's constitution and bylaws and retained control of these group charters. Most committee actions were subject to managerial approval. Employee eligibility to serve in a representational role was defined by management. Terms were often limited to impede the development of employee expertise and influence. Most representation plans had no provision for general membership meetings. Kohler concludes that "[f]or the majority of company unions then, collective dealings meant discussion, not bargaining an opportunity to make suggestions, not the occasion to participate in the ordering process as an autonomous entity with independent power" (Kohler 1986).

With this background in mind, this chapter examines the extent to which the spectrum of progressive to coercive non-union employee representation (NER) groups has reemerged. Ideally, one would study the full spectrum of NER groups by observing these groups as they operate in workplaces spread across regions, industries, and private and public sectors. But this approach has serious barriers involving cost and organizational access. As an alternative, this chapter uses the legal database in Westlaw's comprehensive collection of NLRB cases from the 1990s through 2012. Even with its serious limitations, this approach has the advantages of offering an inside view of contemporary NER groups through the compulsory evidentiary procedures of the NLRB's unfair labor practice hearings. The fact that Section 8(a)(2) of the NLRA is applicable to non-union workplaces—indeed, its purpose is to regulate NER groups to ensure that company unions do not deprive employees of the opportunity to opt for union representation—means that potentially relevant information is archived in these cases.

SECTION 8(A)(2) OF THE NLRA AND CURRENT FORMS OF EMPLOYEE PARTICIPATION

The NLRA does not outlaw "company unions," but it prohibits an employer from "dealing with" employees. Congress defines a "labor organization" very broadly in Section 2(5) to include

> any organization of any kind, or any agency or employee representation committee or plan, in which employees participate and which exists for the purpose, in whole or in part, of dealing with employers concerning grievances, labor disputes, wages, rates of pay, hours of employment, or conditions of work.

In Section 8(a)(2), the NLRA makes it an unfair labor practice for an employer "to dominate or interfere with the formation or administration of any labor organization or contribute financial or other support to it."

This law was mostly unnoticed from its passage until the late 1980s and early 1990s. In the interim, some employers, such as Polaroid and Thompson Products, heavily emphasized progressive NER groups (Jacoby 1989). Progressive employee participation groups emerged in greater numbers in the 1980s (Adler 1992). Global trade helped to reintroduce team-based employee organizations. In the United States, these groups flourished in Japanese auto transplants (Weiss 1996). By 1992, a survey found that employee involvement teams were widely dispersed across industries, with 35 percent of private-sector firms reporting that they used these workplace groups (Osterman 1994). Research showed that high-performance work systems, including employee participation, self-managed teams, quality circles, and gain-sharing pay plans, were linked to organizational performance (Becker and Gerhart 1996; Huselid 1995; Ichniowski et al. 1996; Kaufman and Miller 2011).

The reemergence of employee participation groups in the 1980s and 1990s coincided with a sharp decline in union fortunes and membership (Chaison and Rose 1991). To a significant degree, the wide spectrum of coercive to progressive NER groups in the 1920 and 1930s reemerged by the early 1990s. To a degree, declining union membership was connected to employer adoption of NER versions of company unions (Harper 1998). James Rundle's study (1998) of 165 NLRB representation elections found that employee involvement programs operated during 32 percent of organizing campaigns. These non-union participation groups were more damaging to union organizing efforts than direct employer confrontation was, according to Rundle.

Just as non-union participation groups were gaining in popularity, an otherwise dull NLRB case thrust itself on the national scene as a legal litmus test for the enforcement of Section 8(a)(2). In *Electromation* (1992), a small manufacturer in Indiana formed five non-union employee teams to discuss wages, bonuses, incentive pay, tardiness and attendance, and sick leave. Unbeknownst to management, a union had started an organizing drive. The company forged ahead, appointing six employees and a management facilitator to various committees and asking for more employees to volunteer. After a short time and no concrete results from these committees, the company disbanded these teams.

The NLRB charged the company with violating Section 8(a)(2). In *Electromation*, the board provided a detailed exposition on the boundary that separates lawful and illicit forms of non-union employee representation groups. An employer is allowed to form, organize, direct, and even control an NER group if its activities relate to efficiency, work process improvement, or product quality.

Employers criticized *Electromation* for its restrictive view of lawful participation groups. They complained that the ruling undercut their efforts to make American industries competitive. For example, a *Wall Street Journal* editorial blasted *Electromation* as a "quality circle buster"; a representative of the National Association of Manufacturers testified that the NLRB essentially said that any time a company works directly with its employees to discuss and address workplace issues without the involvement of a labor union, that company is likely to be in violation of the National Labor Relations Act; and a Republican Congressman, Steve Gunderson, complained that *Electromation* called into question the legality of most employee participation groups (Devaney 1993). The TEAM Act, a bill that simply codified *Electromation*, engendered a wave of complaints that even this limited relaxation of Section 8(a)(2) would undermine the right of employees to form and join unions (LeRoy 1997; *Labor Law Professors* 1995).

In sum, the current reflects that of the late 1920s and early 1930s, when workplaces had a wide spectrum of coercive to progressive NER groups. An important difference between then and now is that Section 8(a)(2) is a law, and this law is enforced by the NLRB to accomplish the congressional intent to eradicate the coercive element of NER groups—that is, employer-created groups that mimic unions while stifling or manipulating employee voice. The cases in the rest of this chapter provide qualitative pictures of current or recent NER groups that fit this reemergent spectrum.

RESEARCH METHODS AND TYPOLOGY

NLRB decisions after *Electromation* (1992) and through 2012 provide cases for this analysis. This study does not examine legal aspects of these board decisions. The database is used to acquire information about characteristics of these groups. As relevant "*Electromation* cases" were identified and read, the following questions were answered:

1. When was the group formed?
2. Why was the group formed?
3. Did a union organizing effort coincide at any point in the group's experience?
4. Who had the idea to form the group: employees or management?
5. What was the structure, size, and composition of the group?
6. How did employees acquire membership in a group? Was membership indefinite or limited?
7. How were ideas or agenda items brought to the group for consideration and possible action?
8. How were group decisions made? In particular, how was decision-making power allocated between employees and management?
9. What issues, subjects, or topics were taken up by the group?
10. What was the scale and scope of a group's activities?
11. What outcomes directly resulted from a group's decisions and activities?

The cases in the sample involved settings in which a union was not in place at the time the participation group was formed or took some action. In each case, there was a complaint that a group violated Section 8(a)(2) of the NLRA. These parameters yielded twenty-three cases from 1993 through 2012. The cases provided a wide range of descriptive information.

The publication of these cases allowed a degree of access not usually provided by private employers. But this sample has serious limitations. Because Section 8(a)(2) cases are litigated infrequently, few cases met the criteria for this study. More generally, it is hard to understand why so few Section 8(a)(2) cases occur. Considering the controversy about the reemergence of NER groups since the 1990s, the small sample is probably not due to infrequent use of these groups. One possible explanation is that where progressive NER groups are in place, a union is not present to make a Section 8(a)(2) complaint to the NLRB, even if such a group is not in compliance with the law. Another problem is that the NLRB has very weak tools to remedy a Section 8(a)(2) violation. In the case of an NLRB election that a union loses, the union might win a rerun election if an NER group runs afoul of this law. The main remedy for a Section 8(a)(2) violation is an order to disestablish the group.

Apart from the small sample, another problem is that some cases provided very detailed information about the NER group, while others focused on just one aspect of the group (e.g., when the group strayed on a one-time basis into the area of discussing wages with an employer). The variable amount and quality of information limited the depth of comparisons across cases. Related to this problem, some groups had a short life and limited purpose, while others had a long history and broad mandate.

The analysis relies on a typology of non-union employee groups that comes from several research streams. The design of the typology in Table 13.1 is guided by three goals. First, the classification system reflects the major employee-group characteristics that appear in recent empirical and theoretical studies. Second, the typology incorporates the main principles in *Electromation*. Thus, the columns under the "degree of employer control" heading mirror the distinction in Section 8(a)(2) between employer domination and permitted forms. The organizational forms in the "scope and purpose" column reflect *Electromation*'s differentiation of "safe harbor" and unlawful activities. Cases are arranged in this typology based on the closest approximation of their structure, activities, and decision-making processes. Third, the table also portrays the range of coercive-progressive NER groups in the sample. Following this typology, Table 13.2 is a roster of the sample.

Table 13.1 Typology of Non-union Employee Representation (NER) Groups

Scope and Purpose	Degree of Employer Control		
	Controlled Exclusively by Management	*Control Shared by Management and Employees*	*Self-Managed Work Teams*
Efficiency, Quality, Process [Quality Circles]	*Simmons* *Aero Detroit* [mixed]		
Work Conditions and Environment [QWL]	*Dillon Stores* *Formosa Plastics Corp.* *Stoody Corp.* *Grouse Mountain*	*EFCO Corp.*	

(Continued)

Table 13.1 (Continued)

Scope and Purpose	Degree of Employer Control		
Compensation [Pay/Gain Sharing]	*CVS Corp.*		
Broad Issues/ Activities			
(Progressive NER Group) [HPWO/HIWP]	*Stabilius*	*Polaroid Corp.* *Crown Cork & Seal*	*Keeler Brass* *Washington County*
(Union Avoidance NER Group) [Mirror of Union Functions]	*Aero Detroit* [mixed] *Webcor* *Addicts Rehab. Center* *Baptist Medical* *Bradford Printing* *Reno Hilton Corp.* *Flying Foods Group* *Laneko Engineering* *Miller Industries* *Vic Koenig Chevrolet*	*Naomi Knitting* *Syracuse University*	

Table 13.2   Cases (Alphabetical Order)

1 Addicts Rehabilitation Center Fund, Inc., 330 NLRB No. 113 (2000)

2 Aero Detroit, Inc., 321 NLRB No. 136 (1996)

3 Baptist Medical Center, 338 NLRB No. 38 (2008)

4 Bradford Printing & Finishing, LLC, 356 NLRB No. 109 (2011)

5 Crown Cork & Seal Co., 334 NLRB No. 92 (2001)

6 CVS Corp., 2001 WL 1631383 (2001)

7 Dillon Stores, 319 NLRB No. 149 (1995)

8 EFCO Corp., 327 NLRB No. 71 (1998)

9 Flying Foods Group, Inc., 345 NLRB No. 10 (2005)

10 Formosa Plastics Corp., 1999 WL 33248326 (1999)

11 Grouse Mountain Associates II, 333 NLRB No. 157 (2001)

12 Keeler Brass Automotive Group, 317 NLRB No. 161 (1995)

13 Laneko Engineering Co., 2004 WL 393228 (2004)

14 Miller Industries & Towing Equipment, Inc., 342 NLRB No. 112 (2004)

15 Naomi Knitting Plant, 328 NLRB No. 180 (1999)

16 Polaroid Corp., 329 NLRB No. 147 (1999)

17 Reno Hilton Resorts Corp., 319 NLRB No. 140 (1995)

Table 13.2   (Continued)

18	Simmons Industries, Inc., 312 NLRB 228 (1996)
19	Stabilius Inc., 355 NLRB No. 161 (2010)
20	Stoody Corp., 320 NLRB No. 1 (1995)
21	Syracuse University, 350 NLRB No. 63 (2007)
22	Vic Koenig Chevrolet, Inc., 321 NLRB 1255 (1996)
23	Washington County Mental Health Services, Inc., 2001 WL 33664213 (2001)

ANALYSIS OF NON-UNION EMPLOYEE REPRESENTATION GROUPS IN NLRB CASES

This discussion begins with types of NER groups that have been studied since the 1980s. These groups, identified by various labels and acronyms, differ by their functions and scale. After a short description of these groups, the discussion turns to NLRB cases that approximate these descriptors. Sometimes the fit between a case and the category is close, especially where an employer used a recognized term such as "quality circle" and implemented an NER group that was true to the label. As the discussion shows, however, some employers invented curious and unique names for their NER groups; and at times, they hybridized several types of employee groups that are found in the research literature. In these situations, NLRB cases were grouped by their most dominant function or structure, even though the employee group was not a perfect fit for the category.

Quality Circles

These employee groups have been used to improve the quality of products or services (Lawler and Mohrman 1985; Ledford et al. 1988). Quality Circles (QCs) are small groups of employees who meet regularly to discuss quality issues (U.S. Department of Labor 1985). Employee participation is often voluntary (Cotton 1993). QCs rely on a supportive management culture and encourage collaboration between rank-and-file workers and managers.

In *Simmons Industries, Inc.* (1996), the company operated total quality management (TQM) committees at its two plants. These TQM groups were intended to promote employee communication, workplace safety, product quality, and efficiency. The plants processed and packaged chicken for KFC. Higher quality standards set by KFC caused Simmons to adopt the TQM concept. This process was considered important in implementing a new type of marinade for a rotisserie product. A separate safety committee operated in conjunction with the TQM program. After the TQM was adopted, a union began to organize the company's two facilities.

The Safety Committees solicited employee input. The program included incentives and gifts. Its purpose was to identify safety risks and develop health and safety programs to mitigate hazards. Plant managers determined rules for selecting employees for these plant-level committees. Participants were volunteer employees from most departments, a plant nurse, and supervisors. Group members asked coworkers for specific concerns about plant safety. Members presented these views to the full committee at monthly meetings. Managers led the meetings in a discussion format.

The rules permitted up to four safety corrections at a time. Consensus was used for reaching decisions. Overall, the committees corrected many safety problems, including slippery floors and catwalks, contaminated air ducts, poor ventilation, exposed or uncovered floor drains, dangerous proximity of employees to mechanical hazards, the failure of some employees to wear protective mesh gloves, poor lighting, the condition and placement of fire extinguishers, dangerous locations for product conveyors, poor protective sleeves for sanitation workers, holes in trailer floors, congested walking and product movement patterns, frayed electrical wire connections, sidewalk and parking lot conditions, equipment shields, improper air temperature, broken entry doors, accumulating food scrap, and worker inattention or horseplay. Problems and corrective actions were prioritized in order of their severity. Upper management either rejected the committee's proposals or acted on them without direct interaction with the committee.

At times, however, the TQM committee took up issues outside the safe harbor of *Electromation*. They considered employee suggestions for an incentive plan and issues such as tardiness, absenteeism, and excessive breaks. After the group reached a consensus on solutions to these concerns, management revised policies for tardiness, unexcused absence from workstations, and bathroom breaks.

Aero Detroit, Inc. (1996) presented an unusually mixed case of a QC program that morphed into an obvious union-avoidance group. An auto parts company won a contract to supply Chrysler with body panels for the Dodge Viper. The company used a new manufacturing process called RTM (resin transfer molding). Aero Detroit originally agreed to supply the automaker daily with fifteen panel sets at a cost of $2,000 apiece. The RTM process worked poorly, however, leading to a much higher cost of production—more than $6,700 per set. The extreme cost was due to a high scrap rate, which forced the company to remake the panels with hand labor. When Chrysler refused to pay for cost overruns, the production process changed. The scrap rate dropped.

Meanwhile, a union began to organize the plant. The plant manager formed and implemented a continuous improvement team (CIT). The group was formed, in part, to forestall the need for a "third party" to speak for employees. The manager asked employees to volunteer to serve on the CIT. A company memo solicited suggestions to improve the business. Eventually, management selected eleven employees for the CIT. The group addressed production costs, safety, product quality, and productivity.

Over time, management asked all employees to complete suggestion forms on topics including working conditions, employee–management relations, and morale. A suggestion box was used to address these issues. The CIT collected and read suggestions. They brainstormed ideas. As they met, they took on wide-ranging issues such as productivity, scrap reduction, quality, cost, safety, attendance, part-time hires, ventilation, employee uniforms, employer contributions to 401(k) plans, personal time off, sick leave, and lockers and exercise equipment. Occasionally, the group voted. When a new idea received majority support, it was forwarded to senior management for a final decision. The CIT was phased out when the organizing campaign grew and employees lost interest in participating.

QWL

Quality of Work Life (QWL) programs focus more broadly on worker satisfaction and quality of life (Kohler 1986). While amorphous, QWLs tend to combine a focus on working conditions and work-life concerns with productivity and product quality. These groups rely on volunteers who serve in a representative capacity (Moe 1993). These workers serve limited terms, as employers strive to broaden the participation of workers (Weiler 1990). This process improves organizational communication—first by providing more direct downward flow of information from managers to shop-floor employees and then by educating managers about the realities that employees confront in their day-to-day work experiences (Bainbridge 1998).

A quality assurance (QA) committee was used in *Grouse Mountain Associates II* (2001). Started by the employer, a resort operator, the QA committee was informal. The QA group had no bylaws, elections, or formal operating procedures. The resort's manager designated dates, times, and locations for all QA meetings, and chaired sessions. He took minutes and distributed these documents to the executive committee and department managers. The resort's director of operations also attended meetings, listened, shared his views, and occasionally took employee suggestions into account when formulating policies with the employer's executive committee. The QA group served as an employee conduit to the executive committee but never bargained with that group. When concerns about guest or employee satisfaction arose, the employer gave employees an opportunity to speak to management. The group occasionally ventured into discussions about wages, hours, and other terms and conditions of employment. On some occasions, however, the QA group dealt with conditions of employment. The hotel's executive committee considered and acted on QA suggestions concerning daycare for the children of employees, employee parking, holiday pay, employee lunches, and employee smoking areas. On at least one occasion, the resort's executive committee used the QA program to determine which holidays would qualify for premium pay.

Dillon Stores (1995) involved an employee QWL group that touched on a comprehensive set of workplace issues for its grocery stores. The employer established the Associates' Committee and developed election procedures for the group. Each store was provided a full-time and part-time

380 Michael H. LeRoy

representative. Elections determined the selection of committee members. Terms were annual. Committee meetings of employees and managers were held quarterly. Employees raised questions or issues and set the agendas. Groups considered new workplace technologies, price tagging, pilferage, customer service, safety, the authority of different types of managers, promotion procedures and criteria, employee dress code, changes to insurance programs, evaluation of store managers, and an employee fitness program. Occasionally, the employee group raised grievances with management. These complaints were granted, denied, or determined by management to be outside the scope of the employee group.

The company in *Formosa Plastics Corp.* (1999) entered into a Sustainable Development Agreement that obligated the company, its employees, and the community to keep the firm operating while protecting the area's environment. A committee called the Technical Review Commission (TRC) solicited input, including from employees, for a sustainable development plan. TRC issued a report that focused on "eco-efficiency," community empowerment, ecology, and meeting basic needs in the employment relationship. Stable employment and worker satisfaction were addressed in this initiative.

During the early phase of implementation, a union began an organizing campaign. The company continued with its sustainable development project by forming project teams. These groups inventoried current policies, determined if procedures met the plan's objectives, and recommended actions or new policies to achieve program goals.

One group, called the Meeting Basic Needs team, dealt exclusively with employment issues. Seven employees and three managers served as volunteers. Its purpose was to establish benchmarks to measure worker satisfaction. The committee met six times over four months to discuss work-related problems. Eventually, the group recommended that an outside party conduct a survey to determine worker satisfaction. The company accepted this recommendation.

An outside firm surveyed 840 hourly and salaried employees. The survey also included a morale section that solicited complaints. Although results of the survey were shared with the Meeting Basic Needs committee, the group took no action. Later, the company distributed results of the survey to managers, supervisors, and hourly employees. Meetings were held among these groups, but no actions or resolutions were solicited or discussed in these meetings.

In *CVS Corp.* (2001), an HR director formed the Compensation Program for its logistics group, which included a warehouse with 900 workers. The concept originated after a union organizing effort failed and another began. The HR director asked volunteers to participate on a compensation task force. Nearly 200 employees came forward. A random selection process across warehouse departments winnowed the group to twelve employees. They met with managers over a two-month period to evaluate and recommend changes to the pay program. Topics included starting wages, job classifications, pay grades, and merit increases. Meetings were informal. Employees were encouraged to talk with coworkers about the meetings and to solicit feedback. These workers were also told their input would be part of a final presentation to management.

The employer in *EFCO Corp.* (1998) started four employee groups, each with its own charter. A Manufacturing Resources Planning program aimed to improve efficiency, quality, and inventory control. It also managed a new just-in-time production system. To aid the new approach, the company sought greater employee involvement. Other committees, started in 1992 and 1993, were meant to educate workers, inform the company's Management Committee, and assist in making policy and benefit decisions.

For example, the Employee Benefits Committee (EBC) started in September 1992, a year before the company learned that a union was organizing its employees. The EBC was intended by management to evaluate existing employee benefit plans and make recommendations to the Management Committee. Committee members were supposed to investigate plans, analyze costs, and solicit ideas and comments from other employees. Twenty employees volunteered to serve on the EBC. The company's chief financial officer selected ten employees and one supervisor to serve on the committee.

The committee considered life insurance, a psychology program, employee-of-the-month awards, sick pay, dental and prescription eye care plans, flextime, jeans day, an employee credit union, savings bond plans, cancer insurance, a cookout and a party for employees, and a Good Friday holiday. It made recommendations to management. The company's senior managers reviewed and accepted committee proposals concerning a health plan, dental plan, and an employee party but rejected other proposals.

Stoody Corp. (1995) involved the employer's formation and administration of a Handbook Committee. When the plant manager announced to employees the formation of this handbook group, he also said its purpose was not to discuss wages, benefits, or working conditions. The committee was to gather information about different areas in the handbook that were inconsistent with current practices or were obsolete or misunderstood by employees. The initial meeting was attended by seven nonsupervisory employees and three supervisors. The discussion drifted, as employees proposed a different method for notification of vacation time. The employees' suggestion was later adopted as a matter of company policy. Apart from this isolated instance, management emphasized that it was not using the committee to negotiate terms and conditions of employment. The committee was disbanded after its first meeting.

HPWO

High- Performance Work Organizations (HPWOs) are broadly gauged. While taking many forms, they provide employees discretion, flexibility, and autonomy in performing their work (Applebaum and Batt 1994). An HPWO may engage in information sharing, worker training, education related to the job, and pay for performance (Applebaum et al. 2000; Lawler 1995, 1998). These organizations can improve quality and productivity (; Ichniowski, Shaw, and Prennushi 1997; Kochan and Osterman 1994; MacDuffie 1995; Osterman 1994, 2000).

In *Stabilius Inc.* (2010) the employer formed department advisory committees while a union organizing campaign was underway. The groups provided employees an opportunity for representation. The committees discussed "issues, solutions and implementation." Committees had a department manager, supervisor, and an hourly employee from each shift. Employees nominated themselves or a coworker. Terms were fixed, and members rotated off to allow other employees an opportunity to participate. HR representatives assisted as facilitators. Group representatives were expected to bring updates to their respective shifts at bimonthly departmental meetings.

The committees were allowed to discuss any topic. These included operations, safety, quality, productivity, training, scheduling, preventive maintenance, overtime, supplies, and staffing. When any issue had plantwide application, facilitators had discretion to convene a special committee to address the matter. Each committee was empowered to enact or implement a decision as long as the action stayed within budget. This broad grant of managerial authority was expressly adopted to avoid bilateral dealing between management and the committee that could lead to a Section 8(a)(2) violation.

Most of the issues involved production, process, and machinery. Working conditions were rarely discussed. Committees implemented solutions to manufacturing issues. They also discussed safety, coverage during vacations, environmental conditions in the workplace, and potholes in the parking lot. Occasionally, discussions occurred over terms and conditions of work such as pay, raises, overtime, and profit sharing.

HIWP

High- Involvement Work Practices (HIWP) is a concept that overlaps with HPWOs (Avgar et al. 2011). HIWPs include self-managed teams, crosstraining, employee participation, and gain sharing (Kaufman and Miller 2011). HIWP practices deemphasize managerial control over the work of employees and rely on employee initiative and problem solving (Black and Lynch 2001).

Polaroid Corp. (1999) was a highly publicized case about the Employee-Owners' Influence Council (EOIC), a company-created group that involved 8,000 employees. Everyone was invited to apply for membership on an EOIC council at the company's major work centers. EOIC terms were staggered over three to five years. After about 150 employees applied, the company conducted interviews and selected thirty.

Following a lengthy first meeting and orientation, the EOIC met for two days every two weeks. The company designated an organizational specialist to facilitate at meetings, but various management officials attended meetings to discuss specific issues. The EOIC met sixty-two times in 1993 through 1994 and discussed medical insurance benefits, distribution of funds from the Employee Stock Ownership Plan, termination policies, FMLA leave, vacation benefits, and transfer policies.

The EOIC process began with employee representatives sharing their thoughts on these subjects. A manager kept a written journal and displayed a summary of ideas on a wall. Once ideas were recorded, another discussion ensued with a manager leading the group. Eventually, a poll of all EOIC members was taken to see if there was a majority sentiment. The manager would determine if there was a sufficient consensus and announce the outcome to the entire EOIC.

For example, the EOIC discussed a change in medical benefits in 1994. One major proposal involved enrollment in an HMO. Managers presented various cost and benefits options, after which a group discussion took place. EOIC members were then presented with twenty-three separate categories of medical benefits and voted on each one. A similar process occurred for the termination policy. Managers wanted to implement a sexual harassment policy that included termination as a possible sanction. This proposal led to a wide-ranging discussion by EOIC members. The organizational specialist running the meeting called the question, and members were individually polled. Most employees favored the proposal, and this became the company's new policy.

The company in *Crown Cork & Seal Co.* (2001) employed about 150 employees at its aluminum can manufacturing plant in Sugar Land, Texas. From its inception, the firm used a Socio-Tech employee management system. Employees were granted substantial authority to operate the plant through their participation on numerous standing and temporary teams, committees, and boards. When the Socio-Tech System was formed, there were no union organizing activities at the plant. The Socio-Tech System revolved around seven committees, all of which made decisions by a process of discussion and consensus. Four production teams had "decide and do" power on issue such as production, quality, training, attendance, safety, maintenance, and discipline. When a committee member could not join in a consensus, he would abstain on the issue. Management members served on these committees but were granted no more authority than other committee members.

The employer in *Washington County Mental Health Services, Inc.* provided treatment and care for people with severe disabilities. In 1994, its executive director proposed an employee empowerment concept to the board. The resulting team, formally titled the Board/Staff Management Committee (BSMC), was formed to take over a variety of management functions from the executive director and other senior-level officers. This concept was embraced before a union organizing drive took place.

Set in an organization with 400 employees, the BSMC had twenty to thirty line staff members, two senior managers, and three members of the board of trustees. Trustees could not vote on matters before the BSMC. An administrative assistant was appointed to serve as a facilitator. She had no vote but moderated meetings, facilitated the BSMC's paper flow, and prepared agendas and minutes.

The BSMC selected work-related issues, solicited necessary information to address these matters, formed committees and subgroups to study an issue, and decided what to do on these various matters. At some point, the BSMC held an all-day retreat to determine future managerial issues. Topics included living wages, facilities and properties, structure of programs, training, health benefits, centralized purchasing, staff accountability, appeals of management determinations regarding agencywide policies, staff morale, and long-range planning.

The company delegated broad management authority and responsibilities to the BSMC. In most instances, the BSMC was authorized to make and implement decisions without review and recommend other decisions to the Board of Trustees. The group often took up companywide policies. More specifically, they discussed and acted on a wide range of managerial issues, including salary levels, bonuses, shift differentials, benefits, holidays, employment policies, working conditions, sick leave, vacation accrual, health insurance for domestic partners, employee sabbaticals, child care benefits, incentive pay plan, supplemental worker's compensation payments, staff recognition, job duties for managers, and hiring of managers.

A BSMC initiative on hiring relatives illustrates the power of the group. A nonmanagerial staff member requested a policy to allow the hiring of relatives of current employees. The group referred the matter to a subcommittee for study. While this took place, the Executive Director who formed the group weighed in with his strong opposition. Nonetheless, the BSMC adopted the proposed hiring policy by an 8–5 vote. The BSMC's policy was presented to the board. The Executive Director presented his views, but the board confirmed the policy over his adamant objections.

In *Keeler Brass Automotive Group* (1995), a manufacturer of auto parts in Michigan formed a Grievance Committee and Complaint Committee to serve as a voice for employees. The group, composed of nine employees, had discretion to call special meetings without management's approval. These workers were paid for time on committee business. After operating for several years, senior management revised the committee to elect employees to two-year terms. The committee's power to call meetings at its discretion was withdrawn. Employees were allowed to sign up, subject to eligibility rules. In a letter for all employees, management announced the approved candidates.

The revised committee discussed and clarified policies in the company's procedure manual. They also considered the grievance of a discharged employee who violated the firm's attendance policy and requested access to this person's employment file. A management representative to the committee suggested that the group allow the former employee to present his case for rehiring. The committee favored reinstatement with a new seniority date. Senior management cited the rules and past practice with similar cases to deny this suggestion. Several months later, the committee took up the case of another terminated employee. In a similar way, the committee recommended reinstatement, but senior management rejected this recommendation. In both cases, the Grievance Committee deliberated without any manager present and was permitted to take testimony from witnesses, including the grievant.

Union Avoidance

While many employers value employee participation and communication, they usually reject the idea that labor unions can play a constructive role in mediating this relationship (Jacoby 1991). Some "high-road employers" avoid unionization by paying wage premiums, offering job security, providing formal dispute resolution, and ensuring a culture of fair dealing; but there are also "low-road employers" who suppress union activity through coercion (Kaufman 1999). Along this high-road–low-road spectrum, some employers create progressive organizations that provide for employee voice, a degree of employee representation, and, occasionally, participation in dispute resolution procedures (Budd 2004; Kaufman and Gottlieb-Taras 2000; Wheeler, Klaas, and Mahony 2004). These progressive groups can be found in high-performance work settings where employee cooperation and engagement are cultivated and adversarial relations are discouraged (Machin and Wood 2005; Taylor and Ramsay 1998).

In sum, the research literature suggests that union-avoidance strategies produce a range from repressive to progressive organizations. The following cases spanned this spectrum, though negative examples occurred more often. Likely, this reflects the nature of the NLRB's complaint system. In other words, progressive groups would be less likely to be referred in a unfair labor practice complaint to the NLRB.

In *Webcor Packaging, Inc.* (1995), the employer established a Plant Council that had a broadly stated purpose of dealing with employees concerning grievances, labor disputes, wages, rates of pay, hours of employment, or conditions of work. The Plant Council made recommendations to management about proposed changes in working conditions. Employees recommended, for example, a revised policy for issuing vacation paychecks. Management considered but rejected the proposal. On the other hand, management approved a proposal by employees to pay for employee safety shoes.

The company established and defined the procedures for the Plant Council. Five hourly employees were elected by coworkers. The council was broadly authorized as a policy-development body, with jurisdiction over plant policies, the employee handbook, a grievance procedure, and hourly compensation and benefits. The company also determined the number of management officials and selected these representatives. The company formed and administered the Plant Council while a union was involved in an organizing campaign. Repeatedly, Webcor emphasized that if the union lost the representation election, the policies of the Plant Council would remain in place. In addition, no changes would be made to company policies without using the Plant Council procedures.

In *Addicts Rehabilitation Center Fund, Inc.* (2000), the employer organized a Pro-Action Committee, an employee group to deal with complaints and grievances, in response to a union organizing campaign. Meeting with the permission of supervisors, a group of employees elected department representatives to participate on the committee. The group took up a series of employee grievances concerning discipline and other terms and conditions of employment. The company determined the size and structure of the group, frequency of meetings, method for investigating grievances, and meeting topics.

In *Baptist Medical Center* (2008), an employer established the Nursing Practice Committee (NPC). Ostensibly, the group was formed to deal with patient care and training issues. However, formation of the group was influenced by a consulting firm retained by the hospital in its efforts to oppose a union's organizing efforts. The first NPC meeting was chaired by a senior manager. Two subcommittees were formed—one for customer services and a second for orientation. The NPC was composed of staff nurses and managers. Nurses were strongly encouraged to attend meetings and were paid for their time. Eventually, management selected nurses to attend meetings. These gatherings had forty or more managers and nurses.

Meetings centered on patient-care issues and employee benefits. Nurses expressed their desire for fewer patients and more time for training. The NPC also discussed employee incentives. Over time, this discussion broadened to tackle the issue of employee retention. Wages and salaries were discussed. The NPC also began to survey area hospitals for wages and benefits before a union complaint was filed with the NLRB.

The employer in *Bradford Printing & Finishing, LLC* (2011) formed a union-avoidance group called the Guiding Coalition on its first day of business. The company shut down a predecessor corporation during a time of declining financial performance and a union organizing campaign. The reconstituted company hired a mix of former employees and new workers. Its president said that a 2008 article in a Harvard Business School publication inspired him to implement the Guiding Coalition. The group aimed to facilitate communication and decision making between management and workers. Every employee and supervisor had a vote. The organization was designed to deal with a broad range of personnel issues, including hours of work, holidays, attendance, and discipline. Meetings were set to occur monthly but ceased after the union that was involved in organizing the predecessor corporation filed an unfair labor practice charge.

The employer in *Reno Hilton Resorts Corp.* (1995) established quality action teams (QATs) during a union organizing campaign. Although the name included the term "quality," these were not quality circles. The broader focus of the organization put it in the union-avoidance category. QATs enabled employees to participate and deal with the company concerning wages, hours, and other terms and conditions of work. Workers made proposals or requests, followed by the employer's acceptance or rejection of these ideas. Topics of meetings included employee pay and overall compensation, hazards in the workplace, employee rotation among jobs, work assignments, staffing levels, starting times, air flow in working areas, job descriptions, paid sick days, and the practice of employees sharing tips with supervisors. The resort's general manager created the QATs, including the number of teams and their structure and size. He also developed meeting agendas. The company paid employees for time at meetings. Managers participated along with employees. The general managers retained all decision-making power within these groups. Any QAT subject of discussion or decision could be cancelled by the general manager at any time.

In *Flying Foods Group, Inc.* (2005), the company withdrew recognition from a union. Eventually, the union was decertified. The company proceeded to establish an employee–management group, called the EAR group, to discuss workplace issues. Management selected employees from each department for the committee after no employees were nominated. EAR was designed to allow employees to discuss a wide range of terms and conditions of employment with management. For example, one set of discussions resulted in a wage increase. In contrast, during earlier talks with the union, the company refused proposals that would grant a pay raise. The EAR group also handled grievances that related to wages, hours, and other terms and conditions of employment.

The employer in *Laneko Engineering Co.* (2004) used a strike to rid itself of union representation. Strikers were encouraged to renounce their union to get their jobs back. With the union no longer in the plant due to the strike, and while the company continued operations, management set up a shop committee and solicited nominations. After no nominations were submitted, management appointed members from work crews. Management determined the committee's responsibilities, including representing workers in grievance or disciplinary matters and creating a guidebook of work rules. Management told workers the shop committee would operate like a union. During one disciplinary proceeding, employees negotiated with management a change to work rules.

In *Miller Industries & Towing Equipment, Inc.* (2004), the employer formed and operated a Continuous Improvement Program (CIP) during a union organizing campaign. The company said the group was formed to foster discussion and gather ideas to improve the business's performance. Management selected employees to participate in the CIP from various departments. Some union supporters were included in the CIP. Employees used the CIP to propose changes to drug testing and the attendance policies. Management acted within two weeks to implement these change. Some insurance issues were also raised during the CIP meetings. Subsequent meetings focused on ways to improve work process and to replace equipment. Topics included installation of Plexiglas on top of forklifts, restroom cleanliness, and the volume of the intercom system in a department.

In the context of a close vote to reject union representation, the employer in *Naomi Knitting Plant* (1999) formed and controlled various employee–management committees. The centerpiece group was called the Design Team, an employee participation committee that was intended to be a conduit for ideas and information generated by brainstorming sessions. When it formed the Design Team, the company told employees that it would be set up to implement policies at the facility. The Design Team was formed during the preelection campaign. A consulting firm suggested the Design Team concept. A facilitator was designated to run the team. Group discussions addressed production, efficiency, quality, and safety. The plant manager served as the facilitator. Nominations were taken for fifteen hourly employees, with five from each shift. At a company-paid luncheon, with the plant manager absent, employees elected two coworkers from each shift to serve a one-year term. Initially, the Design Team met twice a month, but eventually the frequency was reduced to once a month.

Although the Design Team was created to discuss quality and safety issues, it broadened its reach to address policy matters such as job bidding, random drug testing of current employees, an attendance bonus, a no-smoking policy, and an inclement weather policy. Some discussions resulted in policy changes—for example, the job bidding process. The team also made policies for a perfect attendance bonus and smoking ban. A drug-testing program that had mixed support among team members was also started. Pay was also discussed within the team, but no policy was set. Outside the consensus framework of the team, management unilaterally increased premium pay for shift leaders.

While a union was trying to organize parking employees in *Syracuse University* (2007), a manager began to conduct a series of meetings with small employee groups. In meetings, the manager explained why employees should vote against the union. In other meetings, the manager established a Staff Complaint Process(SCP). The SCP was designed to provide employees an opportunity to resolve complaints that involved them and their supervisors. The program was specific and detailed, with provisions for employee advocates, mediators, and an impartial Hearing Panel composed of trained volunteers.

While staff mediators were not advocates, they served in a representational role. The SCP required the complaining employee, not the university, to select the staff mediator at the outset of the dispute-resolution process. The format also allowed a mediator to involve management in an effort to resolve a grievance. Mediators were encouraged to facilitate discussion and brainstorm resolutions.

Each SCP panel was designed to have only one supervisory employee, allowing for majority decision making that included mostly nonsupervisory employees. Two thirds of the volunteers for the SCP staff mediator, staff advocate, and panel positions were nonsupervisory employees. However, the university also paid mediators, advocates, and panelists for their time. The intent of the program was to ensure prompt and impartial resolution of workplace disputes. The SCP was promoted as a reason to vote against the union. The department manager told employees that the SCP would be a method to resolve grievances free of charge and without imposition of union dues.

About the time the employer withdrew recognition from a union in *Vic Koenig Chevrolet, Inc.* (1996), a supervisor appointed an hourly employee to serve as an "intermediary." This person was vaguely designated to work out problems or disagreements with employees. Eventually, the employer advanced this concept to the point of forming a group of four employees that included two union supporters and two opponents. These workers came from the body and mechanical shops. Management referred to this group as the Executive Committee. The group took up the task of recommending an annual pay raise. A manager who participated in the group asked for specific ideas to improve productivity and efficiency.

The committee also discussed costs associated with customer complaints about unsatisfactory repairs. At the time, the company required employees who performed questionable work to absorb some of this cost by reducing their pay. Discussion also included policies for absenteeism and tardiness. After management requested specific ideas to increase revenues and improve the quality of work life, employees made proposals about completion times for jobs and a piecework formula that factored in absenteeism/tardiness and time for shifting one employee's unfinished work to a coworker. The company implemented parts of the plan. Overall, the committee had a limited existence. It lasted four months and met three times.

EVALUATION OF FINDINGS

The non-union employee representation groups in this study were the subject of an NLRB complaint, often involving a union, alleging that an employer violated Section 8(a)(2) of the National Labor Relations Act. Thus, the cases almost assuredly did not reflect the full spectrum of NER groups in the United States. Nonetheless, even in this small and biased sample, a wide variation in NER groups emerged. Several cases portrayed positive examples of NER groups. Polaroid implemented a progressive and deeply embedded employee participation program. This organization was intended to provide a workplace voice for 8,000 employees, with everyone invited to apply for membership on an EOIC council. Each worksite had representation on this companywide council. Much effort was devoted to the process side of the EOIC, with lengthy orientations before any substantive issues were discussed. Forums were facilitated by organizational specialists, a practice that seemed to put employees and managers on a more even footing when they interacted. Great effort went into making meetings open for all ideas, recording those ideas on wall displays, debating the merits and demerits of these thoughts, and trying to come to a consensus view for a policy recommendation. The EOIC format was free of employer coercion, as far as the record disclosed.

The Washington County Mental Health Services case appeared to be the furthest thing from a coercive organization. Employees were placed on the Board/Staff Management Committee (BSMC) with the long-term goal of eliminating the jobs of one or more senior managers. A facilitator was appointed to moderate meetings that involved employees and managers. Broad management authority and responsibilities to the BSMC and members took up a wide range of core employment-relations issues. When the group, in a divided vote, recommended a relaxation of the antinepotism policy and the executive director objected to the proposal, the BSMC's view prevailed.

Other NER groups avoided coercion or manipulation of employee participation, but they accomplished this by narrowing their aims to conform to *Electromation*. In other words, they were neither coercive nor progressive but simply had a task focus that significantly limited employee participation. The safety committees in *Simmons* were narrowly designed to address health and safety programs. This type of NER group, with a singular and intensive focus, was not observable in the 1930s but grew in popularity since the 1980s—perhaps because worker's compensation costs became more of a bottom-line issue for some employers and perhaps, too, because *Electromation* opened the door to this type of worker–manager cooperation.

The sample also included a case, *Aero Detroit*, that mirrored a phenomenon following passage of the NIRA, when some progressive NER groups quickly morphed under the financial pressures of the Depression into a manipulative type of worker organization. Aero Detroit's Quality Circle program was diffused in small work teams and tasked with custom manufacturing of a luxury auto part. But under great financial pressure, the employer radically changed the program to a modern prototype of a coercive company union. This sudden shift appeared to be related in its timing to the acceleration of a union organizing drive.

The sample included other employee groups that manipulated employee voice, for example, *Laneko Engineering* and *Flying Foods Group, Inc.* These employers imposed heavy-handed representation groups in which management strictly controlled employee participation and voice. Similar to company unions in the 1930s, management selected the members of these groups and also controlled the scope of the group's responsibilities. In both cases, the NER group was not formed until the employer actively worked to oust a union from a representational role. This type of direct confrontation with a union seemed to echo Sen. Wagner's concern about company unions.

CONCLUSION

In sum, even with a small sample, this study identified a wide range of progressive and coercive NER groups that emerged in the 1990s and thereafter. The current American workplace offers a diversity of employee participation groups that is comparable to the period leading up to the NLRA. The methodology employed in this study does not begin to answer why a wide array of NER groups, ranging from coercive to progressive, emerged in the current era. Perhaps the plummeting levels of private-sector unionization, combined with ineffective remedies for violations of Section 8(a)(2) violations, recreated the conditions of the early 1900s, when there was no NLRA to regulate non-union NER groups. Current conditions allow for greater employer experimentation with these non-union groups, albeit at the continuing though small risk of NLRB enforcement. This study suggests that employers do not take a uniform approach but instead utilize a wide range of high-road and low-road approaches to employee participation.

NOTES

1. National Industrial Recovery Act, 1933.
2. *Legislative History of the National Labor Relations Act, 1935*, National Labor Relations Board, 1985 (Washington, D.C.), at 271–72. Also see Edwin E. Witte. 1932. *The Government in Labor Disputes*, New York, NY: McGraw-Hill Books, pp. 218–220, taking a pessimistic view of company unions. In footnote 2, however, Witte cites an academic literature of "good accounts of the company union movement," though these accounts did not seem to influence his analysis.

REFERENCES

Adler, Paul S. 1992. "The 'Learning Bureaucracy': New United Motor Manufacturing, Inc." *Research in Organizational Behavior*, 15: 111–94.
Applebaum, Eileen, and Rosemary Batt. 1994. *The New American Workplace: Transforming Work Systems in the United States*. Ithaca, NY: ILR Press.
———, Thomas Bailey, Peter Berg, and Arne L. Kalleberg. 2000. *Manufacturing Advantage: Why High-Performance Work Systems Pay Off*. Ithaca, NY: Cornell University Press.
Avgar, Ariel C., Rebecca Kolins Givan, and Mingwei Liu. 2011. "Patient-Centered but Employee Delivered: Patient Care Innovation, Turnover Intentions, and Organizational Outcomes in Hospitals." *Industrial and Labor Relations Review*, 64: 423–38.
Bainbridge, Stephen M. 1998. "Privately Ordered Participatory Management: An Organizational Failures Analysis." *Delaware Journal of Corporate Law*, 23: 979–1076.
Becker, Brian, and Barry Gerhart. 1996. "The Impact of Human Resource Management on Organizational Performance: Progress and Prospects." *Academy of Management Journal*, 39(4): 779–801.

Bendix, Reinhard. 1954. "Bureaucratization in Industry." In *Industrial Conflict* (Arthur Kornhauser et al., eds.). New York: McGraw-Hill.

Black, Susan, and Lisa Lynch. 2001. "How to Compete; The Impact of Workplace Practices and Information Technology on Productivity." *Review of Economics and Statistics*, 83(3): 434–45.

Budd, John. 2004. *Employment with a Human Face: Balancing Efficiency, Equity, and Voice*. Ithaca, NY: ILR Press.

Chaison, Gary N., and Joseph B. Rose. 1991. "The Macrodeterminants of Union Growth and Decline." In *The State of the Unions* (George Strauss et al., eds.). Madison, WI: Industrial Relations Research Association.

Cooper, Laura J. 2011. "Letting the Puppets Speak: Employee Voice in the Legislative History of the Wagner Act." *Marquette Law Review*, 94: 837–68.

Cotton, John L. 1993. *Employee Involvement: Methods for Improving Performance and Work Attitudes*. Newbury Park, CA: Sage Publications.

Devaney, Dennis. 1993. "Much Ado About Section 8(a)(2): The NLRB and Workplace Cooperation After *Electromation* and *DuPont*." *Stetson Law Review*, 23: 39–52.

Electromation, 309 N.L.R.B. 990 (1992).

Filene, Edward A. 1925. *More Profits from Merchandising*. Chicago: A. W. Shaw Co.

Harper, Michael C. 1998. "The Continuing Relevance of Section 8(a)(2) to the Contemporary Workplace." *Michigan Law Review*, 96: 2322–83.

Huselid, Mark. 1995. "The Impact of Human Resource Management Practices on Turnover, Productivity, and Corporate Financial Performance." *Academy of Management Journal*, 38(3): 635–72.

Ichniowski, Casey, Kathryn Shaw, and Giovanna Prennushi. 1997. "The Effects of Human Resource Management Practices on Productivity: A Study of Steel Finishing Lines." *American Economic Review*, 87(3): 291–313.

———, et al. 1996. "What Works at Work: Overview and Assessment." *Industrial Relations*, 35(3): 299–333.

Jacoby, Sanford M. 1989. "Reckoning with Company Unions: The Case of Thompson Products, 1934–1964." *Industrial and Labor Relations Review*, 43(1): 19–40.

———. 1991. "American Exceptionalism Revisited: The Importance of Management." *Masters to Managers: Historical and Comparative Perspectives on American Employers*. New York: Columbia University Press.

Katz, Daniel. 1954. "Satisfactions and Deprivations in Industrial Life." In *Industrial Conflict* (Arthur Kornhauser et al., eds.). New York: McGraw-Hill.

Kaufman, Bruce. 1999. "Does the NLRA Constrain Employee Involvement and Participation Programs in Nonunion Companies?: A Reassessment." *Yale Law and Policy Review*, 17(2): 729–810.

——— and Daphne Gottlieb-Taras, eds. 2000. *Nonunion Employee Representation: History, Contemporary Practice, and Policy*. Armonk, NY: M. E. Sharpe.

——— and Benjamin Miller. 2011. "The Firm's Choice of HRM Practices: Economics Meets Strategic Human Resource Management." *Industrial and Labor Relations Review*, 64: 526–55.

Kochan, Thomas, and Paul Osterman. 1994. *The Mutual Gains Enterprise*. Cambridge, MA: Harvard Business School Press.

Kohler, Thomas C. 1986. "Models of Worker Participation: The Uncertain Significance of Section 8(a)(2)." *Boston College Law Review*, 27: 499–551.

Labor Law Professors Urge Congress to Reject TEAM Act Before House Panel. 1995. *Daily Labor Report* (BNA). 120, A-10 (June 22).

LaDame, Mary. 1930. *The Filene Store: A Study of Employees' Relation to Management in a Retail Store*. New York: Russell Sage Foundation Press.

Lawler, Edward E., and Susan A. Mohrman. 1985. "Quality Circles After the Fad." *Harvard Business Review* (Jan.–Feb.): 65–71.

———, Susan Albers Mohrman, and Gerald E. Ledford, Jr. 1995. *Creating High Performance Organizations: Practices and Results of Employee Involvement and Total Quality Management in Fortune 1000 Companies.* San Francisco: Jossey-Bass.

———. 1998. *Strategies for High Performance Organizations: The CEO Report: Employee Involvement, TQM, and Reengineering Programs in Fortune 1000 Corporations.* San Francisco: Jossey-Bass.

Ledford, Gerald E. et al. 1988. "The Quality Circle and Its Variations." In *Productivity in Organizations: New Perspectives from Industrial and Organizational Psychology* (John P. Campbell, Richard J. Campbell, et al.). San Francisco: Jossey-Bass.

LeRoy, Michael H. 1996. "Can TEAM Work? Implications of an *Electromation* and *DuPont* Compliance Analysis." *Notre Dame Law Review,* 71: 216–66.

———. 1997. " 'Dealing with' Employee Involvement in Nonunion Workplaces: Empirical Research Implications for the TEAM Act and Electromation." *Notre Dame Law Review,* 72: 31–82.

MacDuffie, John. 1995. "Human Resource Bundles and Manufacturing Performance: Organizational Logic and Flexible Production Systems in the World Auto Industry." *Industrial and Labor Relations Review,* 48(2): 197–221.

Machin, Steve, and Stephen Wood. 2005. "Human Resource Management as a Substitute for Trade Unions in British Workplaces." *Industrial and Labor Relations Review,* 58(2): 201–19.

Mayo, Elton. 1945. *The Social Problems of Industrial Civilization.* Boston: Harvard University.

Moe, Martin T. 1993. "Participatory Workplace Decisionmaking and the NLRA: Section 8(a)(2), *Electromation,* and the Specter of the Company Union." *New York University Law Review,* 68: 1127–86.

Montgomery, David. 1967. *Beyond Equality: Labor and the Radical Republicans, 1862–1872.* New York: Vintage Books.

National Industrial Recovery Act. 1933.

National Labor Relations Act. 1935.

Osterman, Paul. 1994. "How Common Is Workplace Transformation and How Can We Explain Who Adopts It? Evidence From a National Survey." *Industrial and Labor Relations Review,* 47(2): 173–88.

———. 2000. "Work Organization in an Era of Restructuring: Trends in Diffusion and Impacts on Employee Welfare." *Industrial and Labor Relations Review,* 53(2): 179–96.

Rundle, James. 1998. "Winning Hearts and Minds in the Era of Employee Involvement Programs." In *Organizing to Win: New Research on Union Strategies* (Kate Bronfenbrenner et al., eds.). Ithaca, NY: ILR Press.

Schatz, Ronald W. 1983. *The Electrical Workers.* Urbana: University of Illinois Press.

Taylor, Phil, and H. Ramsay. 1998. "Unions, Partnership, and HRM: Sleeping with the Enemy?" *International Journal of Employment Studies,* 6(2): 115–43.

U.S. Department of Labor. 1985. *Quality of Work Life: AT&T and CWA Examine Process After Three Years.* Washington, DC: Government Printing Office.

Weiler, Paul C. 1990. *Governing the Workplace: The Future of Labor and Employment Law.* Cambridge, MA: Harvard University Press.

Weiss, Marley S. 1996. "Innovations in Collective Bargaining: NUMMI—Driven to Excellence." *Hofstra Labor Law Journal,* 13: 433–91.

Wheeler, Hoyt N., Brian S. Klaas, and Douglas M. Mahony. 2004. *Workplace Justice Without Unions.* Kalamazoo, MI: W. E. Upjohn Institute for Employment Research.

Contributors

Alison Barnes is a senior lecturer in the Department of Marketing and Management and Centre for Workforce Futures at Macquarie University, Sydney, Australia.

Richard P. Chaykowski is a professor of policy studies at Queen's University with a joint appointment in the Faculty of Law at Queen's University, Kingston, Canada.

Niall Cullinane is a lecturer in employment relations in the Management School at Queen's University Belfast, Belfast, Northern Ireland.

Jimmy Donaghey is a reader in industrial relations at the University of Warwick, Warwick, United Kingdom.

Tony Dundon is a professor of human resource management and employment relations and head of the management discipline, School of Business and Economics, National University of Ireland Galway, Galway, Ireland.

Paul J. Gollan is a professor of management and associate dean (research) in the Faculty of Business and Economics at Macquarie University, Sydney, Australia.

Stewart Johnstone is a senior lecturer in human resource management at Newcastle University, Newcastle, United Kingdom.

Senia Kalfa is a lecturer in the Department of Marketing and Management at Macquarie University, Sydney, Australia.

Bruce E. Kaufman is a professor of economics at Georgia State University, Atlanta, United States, and a research fellow with the Department of Employment Relations and Human Resources and Centre for Work, Organisation and Wellbeing at Griffith University, Brisbane, Australia.

Michael H. LeRoy is a professor in the School of Labour and Employment Relations, and College of Law, at the University of Illinois, Urbana-Champaign, United States.

David Lewin is the Neil H. Jacoby Professor Emeritus of Management, Human Resources and Organizational Behavior at the UCLA Anderson School of Management, Los Angeles, United States.

Craig MacMillan is a lecturer in the Department of Economics and a member of the Centre for Workforce Futures at Macquarie University, Sydney, Australia.

Sara Slinn is an associate professor of law at Osgoode Hall Law School, York University, Toronto, Canada.

Daphne G. Taras is dean of the Edwards School of Business and a professor of labour relations at the University of Saskatchewan, Saskatoon, Canada.

Adrian Wilkinson is a professor of employment relations and director of the Centre for Work, Organisation and Wellbeing at Griffith University, Brisbane, Australia.

Ying Xu is a research fellow in the Department of Marketing and Management at Macquarie University, Sydney, Australia.

Index